Pronunciation and Phonetics

"*Pronunciation and Phonetics: A Practical Guide for English Language Teachers* is exactly what it claims to be—a treatment of the topic addressed to those who are new to it and who require a grounding in the practical classroom-based aspects of how to teach pronunciation to English learners. The author's use of humor and his engaging, highly accessible writing style make this volume a valuable contribution to the field."
—Donna M. Brinton, Lecturer (Retired), University of California Los Angeles, USA

This engaging, succinct text is an introduction to both phonetics and phonology as applied to the teaching of pronunciation *and* to the teaching of pronunciation to English language learners.

Section 1 selectively covers the main areas of phonetics and phonology, without going into any area in more depth than the average English language teacher requires or that the average English language teacher trainee can handle. It provides the foundation for Section 2, which covers practical issues related to learners and how they learn languages, and what represents good practice in terms of classroom activities for pronunciation—including aspects such as targets, motivation, and priorities. While these elements are involved in all language teaching, the focus is on the way they relate in particular to pronunciation teaching. The chapters end with activities to help the reader understand concepts. Some also can easily be used, with slight adaptation, in the classroom, others are questions to encourage readers to ponder their own language-learning experiences, and for teachers to relate concepts to their classroom experience.

Section 3 provides innovative sample activities which put into practice the theoretical points covered in the first two sections, answers to the various exercises, recommended further reading (both print and non-print), a glossary of technical phonetic terms, and a bibliography of works on pronunciation teaching. The text is accompanied by a Companion Website with audio recordings of model pronunciations and audio material relating to the activities.

Adam Brown is Head (International Business), Senior lecturer and research committee member, Centre for Research in International Education (CRIE), Auckland Institute of Studies, Auckland, New Zealand.

ESL & Applied Linguistics Professional Series

Eli Hinkel, Series Editor

Turner • *Using Statistics in Small-Scale Language Education Research: Focus on Non-Parametric Data*
Lantolf/Poehner • *Sociocultural Theory and the Pedagogical Imperative in L2 Education: Vygotskian Praxis and the Research/Practice Divide*
Brown • *Pronunciation and Phonetics: A Practical Guide for English Language Teachers*
Pu/Pawan • *The Pedagogy and Practice of Western-trained Chinese English Language Teachers: Foreign Education, Chinese Meanings*
Birch • *English Grammar Pedagogy: A Global Perspective*
Liu • *Describing and Explaining Grammar and Vocabulary in ELT: Key Theories and Effective Practices*
deOliviera/Silva, Eds. • *L2 Writing in Secondary Classrooms: Student Experiences, Academic Issues, and Teacher Education*
Andrade/Evans • *Principles and Practices for Response in Second Language Writing: Developing Self-Regulated Learners*
Sayer • *Ambiguities and Tensions in English Language Teaching: Portraits of EFL Teachers as Legitimate Speakers*
Alsagoff/McKay/Hu/Renandya, Eds. • *Principles and Practices of Teaching English as an International Language*
Kumaravadivelu • *Language Teacher Education for A Global Society: A Modular Model for Knowing, Analyzing, Recognizing, Doing, and Seeing*
Vandergrift /Goh • *Teaching and Learning Second Language Listening: Metacognition in Action*
LoCastro • *Pragmatics for Language Educators: A Sociolinguistic Perspective*
Nelson • *Intelligibility in World Englishes: Theory and Practice*
Nation/Macalister, Eds. • *Case Studies in Language Curriculum Design: Concepts and Approaches in Action Around the World*
Johnson/Golumbek, Eds. • *Research on Second Language Teacher Education: A Sociocultural Perspective on Professional Development*
Hinkel, Ed. • *Handbook of Research in Second Language Teaching and Learning, Volume II*
Nassaji /Fotos • *Teaching Grammar in Second Language Classrooms: Integrating Form-Focused Instruction in Communicative Context*
Murray/Christison • *What English Language Teachers Need to Know Volume I: Understanding Learning*
Murray/Christison • *What English Language Teachers Need to Know Volume II: Facilitating Learning*
Wong/Waring • *Conversation Analysis and Second Language Pedagogy: A Guide for ESL/EFL Teachers*
Nunan/Choi, Eds. • *Language and Culture: Reflective Narratives and the Emergence of Identity*
Braine • *Nonnative Speaker English Teachers: Research, Pedagogy, and Professional Growth*
Burns • *Doing Action Research in English Language Teaching: A Guide for Practitioners*
Nation/Macalister • *Language Curriculum Design*
Birch • *The English Language Teacher and Global Civil Society*
Johnson • *Second Language Teacher Education: A Sociocultural Perspective*
Nation • *Teaching ESL/EFL Reading and Writing*

Nation/Newton • *Teaching ESL/EFL Listening and Speaking*
Kachru/Smith • *Cultures, Contexts, and World Englishes*
McKay/Bokhosrt-Heng • *International English in its Sociolinguistic Contexts: Towards a Socially Sensitive EIL Pedagogy*
Christison/Murray, Eds. • *Leadership in English Language Education: Theoretical Foundations and Practical Skills for Changing Times*
McCafferty/Stam, Eds. • *Gesture: Second Language Acquisition and Classroom Research*
Liu • *Idioms: Description, Comprehension, Acquisition, and Pedagogy*
Chapelle/Enright/Jamieson, Eds. • *Building a Validity Argument for the Test of English as a Foreign Language™*
Kondo-Brown/Brown, Eds. • *Teaching Chinese, Japanese, and Korean Heritage Language Students Curriculum Needs, Materials, and Assessments*
Youmans • *Chicano-Anglo Conversations: Truth, Honesty, and Politeness*
Birch • *English L2 Reading: Getting to the Bottom, Second Edition*
Luk/Lin • *Classroom Interactions as Cross-cultural Encounters: Native Speakers in EFL Lessons*
Levy/Stockwell • *CALL Dimensions: Issues and Options in Computer Assisted Language Learning*
Nero, Ed. • *Dialects, Englishes, Creoles, and Education*
Basturkmen • *Ideas and Options in English for Specific Purposes*
Kumaravadivelu • *Understanding Language Teaching: From Method to Postmethod*
McKay • *Researching Second Language Classrooms*
Egbert/Petrie, Eds. • *CALL Research Perspectives*
Canagarajah, Ed. • *Reclaiming the Local in Language Policy and Practice*
Adamson • *Language Minority Students in American Schools: An Education in English*
Fotos/Browne, Eds. • *New Perspectives on CALL for Second Language Classrooms*
Hinkel • *Teaching Academic ESL Writing: Practical Techniques in Vocabulary and Grammar*
Hinkel/Fotos, Eds. • *New Perspectives on Grammar Teaching in Second Language Classrooms*
Hinkel • *Second Language Writers' Text: Linguistic and Rhetorical Features*

Visit **www.routledge.com/education** for additional information on titles in the ESL & Applied Linguistics Professional Series

Pronunciation and Phonetics

A Practical Guide for English Language Teachers

Adam Brown

NEW YORK AND LONDON

Visit the Companion Website for this title at: www.routledge.com/cw/brown

First published 2014
by Routledge
711 Third Avenue, New York, NY 10017

and by Routledge
2 Park Square, Milton Park, Abingdon, Oxon OX14 4RN

Routledge is an imprint of the Taylor & Francis Group, an informa business

Library of Congress Cataloging in Publication Data
Brown, Adam, 1952-
Pronunciation and phonetics : a practical guide for
English language teachers / Adam Brown.
pages cm. — (ESL & Applied Linguistics Professional Series)
Includes bibliographical references and index.
1. English language—Pronunciation—Study and teaching. 2. English language—Study and teaching—Foreign speakers. 3. English language—Pronunciation by foreign speakers. I. Title.
PE1137.B773 2014
421'.5—dc23

2013024091

ISBN: 978-0-415-72275-9 (hbk)
ISBN: 978-0-415-72276-6 (pbk)
ISBN: 978-1-315-85809-8 (ebk)

Typeset in Minion
by RefineCatch Limited, Bungay, Suffolk, UK

Printed and bound in the United States of America by Publishers Graphics, LLC on sustainably sourced paper.

Contents

Symbols for English sounds x
Preface xi

SECTION 1
Phonetics 1

1 Introduction 3

2 Accents of English worldwide 11

3 Airstreams and the vocal cords 15

4 Cardinal vowels 20

5 Vowels 23

6 The vocal organs and consonant classification 30

7 Plosives and nasals 36

8 Fricatives and affricates 45

9 Approximants 50

10 Non-English sounds 58

11 Syllable structure 61

12 Phonemes 69

13 Accent differences 74

14 Phonology 82

15 Weakening and linking 91

16 Assimilation and elision 100

17 Connected speech processes 105

18 Pausing and speed 114

19 Word stress 121

20 Tone groups 132

21 Tones 137

22 Rhythm 145

23 Voice quality 151

SECTION 2
Pronunciation teaching 155

24 Targets 157

25 Integration 166

26 The effectiveness of pronunciation teaching 174

27 Motivation and affect 180

28 Fossilization 186

29 First language influence 191

30 Importance 195

31 Spelling: History 206

32 Spelling: Literacy 212

33 Nonverbal communication 219

34 Listening 227

35 Testing 231

SECTION 3
Sample exercises 239

Sample exercises 241

Answers to exercises 274

Resources 291
Glossary 297
References 301
Index 310

Symbols for English sounds

A list of the sounds of Standard Southern British English (SSBE) and General American (GenAm) accents of English is given below, for easy reference when reading this book. The accents and the sounds are described in greater detail in chapters 5–9. The differences between SSBE and GenAm are discussed in chapter 13. The symbols given below, and used in this book, are those of Wells' (2008) *Longman Pronunciation Dictionary*.

Consonants

p	*pen*	tʃ	*church*	s	*soon*	n	*nice*
b	*back*	dʒ	*judge*	z	*zero*	ŋ	*ring*
t	*tea*	f	*fat*	ʃ	*ship*	l	*light*
d	*day*	v	*view*	ʒ	*pleasure*	r	*right*
k	*key*	θ	*thing*	h	*hot*	j	*yet*
ɡ	*get*	ð	*this*	m	*more*	w	*wet*

Vowels

ɪ	*kit*	ʌ	*strut*	uː	*goose*	eə	*square* (SSBE)*
e	*dress*	ʊ	*foot*	aʊ	*mouth*	ʊə	*cure* (SSBE)*
æ	*trap*	iː	*fleece*	əʊ	*goat* (SSBE)	ɔː	*thought*
ɒ	*lot* (SSBE)	eɪ	*face*	oʊ	*goat* (GenAm)	ɜː	*nurse*†
ɑː	*lot* (GenAm)	ɔɪ	*choice*	ɪə	*near* (SSBE)*	ə	*about*†
ɑː	*father*						

*In GenAm, these words contain a vowel followed by /r/: /nɪr, skwer, kjʊr/.

†GenAm pronunciation of *murder* is transcribed /mɜːrdər/ in this book, although the two vowel plus /r/ sequences may be realized only by r-colored vowels.

Preface

Purpose

The purpose of this book is to equip readers with what they need in order to teach the pronunciation of English. The intended readership is trainee English language teachers, and in-service teachers wanting to increase their expertise in teaching English pronunciation.

The book is divided into three sections. Section 1 deals with phonetics, the study of speech sounds. It also touches on phonology, the way speech sounds pattern. There are many books dealing with the phonetics and phonology of English. However, most of them go into far more detail than the average English language teacher needs, or is prepared to read. The treatment in this book is therefore very selective, covering only those aspects that are important for language teachers. However, just like icebergs, you know that there is more below the surface. Readers who want to delve deeper into the subject can follow up some of the references given.

Section 2 addresses various factors that impinge on the teaching of pronunciation. Language is composed of many interrelated elements. While the focus of this book is pronunciation, it also describes other elements, such as nonverbal communication, which can be exploited by language teachers when teaching pronunciation.

Section 3 contains sample materials that can be used in class. There are of course many books of pronunciation materials, good and bad, interesting and dry. The materials in this section are samples of the kind of exercise that competent teachers can produce themselves for their particular groups of learners.

There are 35 chapters, which may seem incongruous for such a book. However, this has been deliberately done in order to provide short, digestible chapters. This is especially important for the first section, on phonetics, which is necessarily technical in parts, and introduces aspects of speech that readers may be able to command but not be consciously aware of. If you read one chapter per day, you will finish the book in a little over a month.

Like all good pronunciation books, this one is accompanied by audio material. Sound files relating to various parts of the book are housed on the Companion Website: http://www.routledge.com/cw/brown.

Conventions

In this book, standard linguistic conventions are followed:

- Letters of the alphabet and words in spelling are printed in italics, e.g. the letter *a*, *boy*.
- Sounds are printed in square brackets, e.g. [bɔɪ]. Where emphasis is laid on the phonemic status of sounds, slant brackets are used, e.g. /bɔɪ/. The distinction between phonetic and phonemic transcription is explained in chapter 12.
- The meanings of words and expressions are printed in quote marks, e.g. 'male child'.

Acknowledgments

Boggle is a trademark of Hasbro (see www.hasbro.com).

Section 1

Phonetics

1 Introduction

If you can speak, you can do anything.
Sir Winston Churchill (1874–1965), British prime minister

Learning objectives

At the end of this chapter, you will be able to

- define the terms *phonetics*, *phonology*, *pronunciation* and *phonics*
- list the segmental and suprasegmental features of English pronunciation
- draw a hierarchy of functional units of pronunciation.

Introduction

The purpose of this book is to equip readers with what they need in order to teach the pronunciation of English. As pronunciation is one of the skills involved in learning any language, some of this overlaps with what is covered in general courses for English language trainee teachers. However, pronunciation is often poorly covered in such courses.

The coverage in this book is very selective. That is, only those aspects of the technical side of phonetics that have strong implications for English pronunciation teaching are handled. Many other aspects have deliberately been omitted, but can be found in general books on English phonetics (see the Resources section).

First, however, we need to define four terms relating to the whole field: *phonetics, phonology, pronunciation* and *phonics.*

Phonetics

In a sentence, phonetics can be defined as the scientific study of all aspects of the spoken form of language. There are several important terms in this definition:

- ***Scientific***: Phonetics is scientific in the sense that it is objective rather than subjective. That is, phoneticians describe the sounds of languages in an unbiased, dispassionate way. In contrast, many lay people speak in a prejudiced way about the sounds of their language. Very often, this takes the form of preferring aspects of their own pronunciation over those of anyone else's accent, and trying to impose their own thoughts on others. Thus, they tell people how they think a language ought to be pronounced, rather than describing how it actually is pronounced. Such people are prescriptive, while phonetics is a descriptive subject.

- ***Language***: Notice that *language* is used here, rather than *a language*. By language, we mean the human ability to communicate, that underlies all human languages. Although much of phonetics has historically been concerned with English, the study of the sounds of an 'exotic' language spoken by only a few speakers is no less valid.
- ***Spoken form***: Language, the human ability to communicate, may be manifested in different ways (or mediums). By far the most common are the spoken medium and the written medium. Others exist, such as Braille, a tactile medium. Both the spoken and written mediums have a productive and perceptive form. This gives us the categories of writing, reading, speaking and listening, often referred to by language teachers as the four skills (see Table 1.1).

Table 1.1 The four language skills

	Written medium	*Spoken medium*
Production	Writing	Speaking
Perception	Reading	Listening

- ***All aspects***: When we speak to someone, there are three distinguishable phases of the communication process:

  1. The speaker uses his/her vocal organs (lungs, vocal cords, tongue, lips, etc.) to produce sounds. This aspect is known as *articulatory* phonetics.
  2. The sounds are vibrations of air particles (sound waves), that travel from the speaker's mouth to the listener's ear. The technical study of these vibrations is known as *acoustic* phonetics.
  3. The sound waves reach the listener's ear, travel along his/her ear canal and cause the ear drum to vibrate. This movement is transmitted to the brain and ultimately interpreted. This aspect is known as *auditory* phonetics.

While all three aspects belong to the field of phonetics, only the first (articulation) is of real relevance in language teaching.

Phonology

Articulatory phonetics thus describes the way humans use their vocal organs to produce speech sounds. Phonology, on the other hand, describes the way these sounds function in particular languages. For instance, we can describe two sounds as follows:

- For the [pʰ] sound, the two lips come together blocking air from escaping through the mouth. Air does not escape through the nose either. The vocal cords are not vibrating. When the lips are opened again at the end of the sound, there is a burst of air (known as aspiration) before the vocal cords start vibrating for the vowel sound that usually follows.
- The same thing happens for the [p⁼] sound, except that, when the lips are opened, the vocal cords start vibrating immediately for the following sound (usually a vowel). While [p⁼] is not an official symbol of the International Phonetic Association (IPA), it is a useful way of explicitly showing lack of aspiration, and is used by writers such as Wells and Colson (1971).

Notice that there is no mention of any particular language in the above descriptions. We are simply saying that if you make those movements with your vocal organs, we can use that symbol to represent the sound.

Now let us think about the different ways these two sounds are used in actual languages. In some languages such as Arabic, there is no problem, in that neither of these sounds occurs in the language. For example, the English word *Pepsi* borrowed into Arabic is not pronounced with [p] sounds, because they do not occur in Arabic. Instead [b] sounds are substituted: [biːbsiː].

In some languages such as English, the two sounds occur, but never contrast. The [p⁼] sound only occurs after [s], as in *spit*. The [pʰ] sound occurs where it is not preceded by [s], as in *pit*. For this reason, many English speakers may not realize that they have both these distinct sounds. For much the same reason, they are both represented by a *p* letter in spelling.

In some languages such as Thai, the two sounds occur and contrast. For instance, in Thai, [pʰa] means 'cloth,' while [p⁼a] means 'aunt.' For this reason, Thai speakers consider these to be very different sounds. As a result, they are represented by different letters in Thai spelling.

Phonology is thus language-specific, and describes how sounds occur, function and combine in particular languages.

Pronunciation

In language teaching, pronunciation is the term usually given to the process of teaching learners to produce the sounds of a language. Phonetics and phonology, as outlined above, are rather academic subjects that language teachers need to have some knowledge of. Pronunciation teaching, however, is the more practical process of using phonetic and phonological knowledge to identify (potential) problems for learners, and produce sound activities for the classroom and outside, for learners to acquire an acceptable, intelligible accent of the language. It also assumes an understanding of what constitutes good practice in language teaching, factors such as the motivation and attitude of the learners, etc.

Phonics

A confusable fourth term also needs to be explained briefly. Phonics is a method of teaching reading and writing that relies on phonological awareness. That is, learners are trained in dividing spoken words into their constituent syllables, those syllables into their constituent sounds, and then relating these constituent sounds to the letters that represent them in writing. In this way, learners are better equipped for dealing with new words. The relationship between spelling and pronunciation is covered in chapters 31 and 32.

The components of pronunciation

One problem with teaching pronunciation is that the whole concept of pronunciation can be analyzed as being composed of many components, all of which are present at the same time in speech. The average native speaker of a language such as English may feel that they simply open their mouth and produce sounds without thinking too much about the nature of those sounds. However, in general, there is a large difference between knowing a language and knowing about a language. Teachers of English need to know about the language, and, in terms of speech, that includes the various components that make up pronunciation (see Figure 1.1). These are examined in the chapters of this first section of this book.

Suprasegmentals are features that operate over stretches of speech larger than a segment (a consonant or vowel sound). *Voice quality* (see chapter 23) is the overall long-term setting of vocal organs, including the tongue and *vocal cords* (see chapter 3). The term prosody is used in slightly different ways by different writers. Here we take it to include long-term settings and shorter-term variation in *loudness*, as well as *intonation*. Intonation (see chapters 20 and 21) is the use of the pitch of the voice in speech. The metrical analysis of speech concerns *word stress*, the stressing of syllables in multisyllabic words (see chapter 19) and *rhythm*, which has been defined in many different ways (see chapter 22). Temporal features of speech include *speed* and *pausing* (for both, see chapter 18).

The *segmentals* (or segments) are the individual vowel and consonant sound units. These combine one after the other to form syllables, words and utterances. *Consonant* segments can be divided into those that involve vibration of the vocal cords (are *voiced;* see chapter 3) and those that do not (are *voiceless*). Books on pronunciation often divide vowel segments into those that do not involve any change in the position of the lips and tongue in their production (*monophthongs;* see chapter 5) and those that do involve such a change (*diphthongs*). However, it makes more sense to divide vowels by *length*, into (i) long vowels and (ii) short vowels (all of which are monophthongs). This is because long monophthongs and diphthongs (which are also long) tend to behave in similar ways.

Books on pronunciation typically divide features only into suprasegmentals and segmentals. Some writers use the term *pronunciation* to refer only to segmentals (vowel and consonant sounds). However, it is used in this book, and by many other writers, to refer not only to these, but also to suprasegmental features such as voice quality, intonation, stress and rhythm.

There are, moreover, other important features of pronunciation that must be considered, that lie between segment-length consonants and vowels, and utterance-length suprasegmentals. *Syllable structure* (see chapter 11) describes the way the consonant and vowel segments combine to form syllables. The basic division is between any initial consonants (*onset*) on the one hand, and the vowel (*peak*) and any final consonants (*coda*), together giving the *rhyme*, on the other.

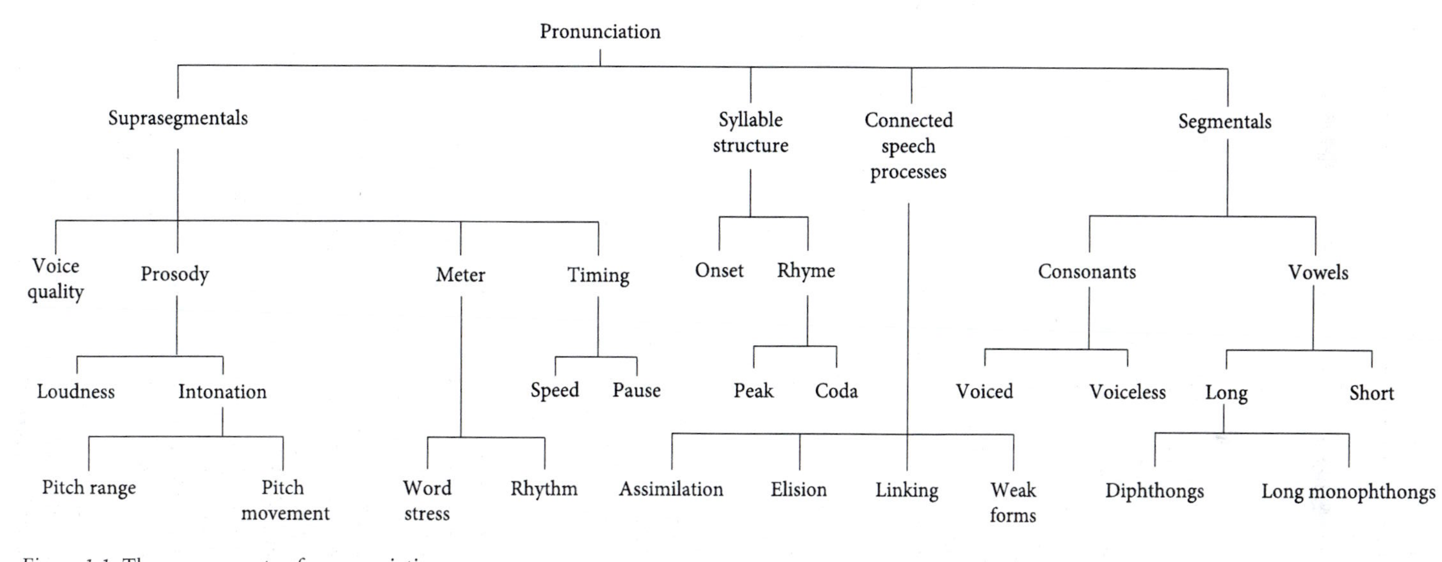

Figure 1.1 The components of pronunciation.

Segments do not occur by themselves. *Connected speech processes* (see chapters 15, 16 and 17) describe the way individual segments are affected (changed, omitted, etc.) as a result of the context of surrounding sounds.

Some readers may be surprised by the left-to-right order of the elements in Figure 1.1. Speakers of a language may be more aware of individual vowel and consonant sounds, because these are what are represented by letters in spelling, and spelling is a more conscious process. Traditionally, English language courses have started with segmentals and concentrated on them, sometimes almost to the exclusion of suprasegmentals. This ordering is followed in this book, too, for the purposes of explanation. It is impossible to explain voice quality without first having described the tongue, lip and vocal cord positions for vowels and consonants. Similarly, syllable structure and connected speech processes depend on a previous understanding of vowel and consonant sounds.

However, since the 1980s, researchers have emphasized that it is the suprasegmentals that cause the major problems of overall intelligibility. While segmentals are of obvious importance too, teachers should not overlook the contribution of suprasegmentals (intonation, stress, etc.) in the intelligibility of learners' speech.

A hierarchy of components

Having briefly introduced the components of pronunciation, we can now show how the functional units of pronunciation can be arranged in a hierarchy (Figure 1.2). The

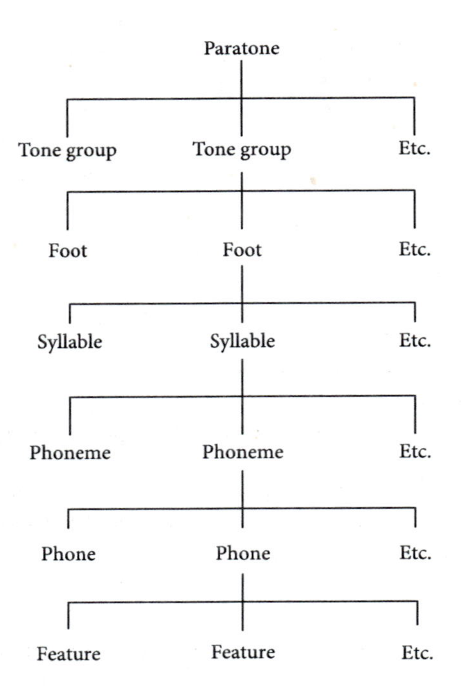

Figure 1.2 A hierarchy of pronunciation features.

smallest unit is the *feature* (see chapter 14). These are aspects of pronunciation such as [± voice], which describes whether the vocal cords are vibrating or not, and [± nasal], which describes whether air escapes through the nose or not. The individual consonant and vowel sounds (*phones*) can be considered to be composed of combinations of these features. Functional consonant and vowel units are called *phonemes* (see chapter 12). *Syllables* (see chapter 11) are composed of one or more consonant and vowel phonemes. In the rhythm of English speech (or at least one account of it: see chapter 22), the *foot* unit is composed of one or more syllables. In the intonation of English (see chapters 20 and 21), pitch contours are said to extend over a stretch of speech known as the *tone group*, which may be considered to be composed of one or more feet. Finally, tone groups may compose what may be likened to a paragraph in written language, sometimes known as a tonal paragraph or *paratone*. The paratone is generally considered to be the largest unit in the analysis of pronunciation phenomena.

Summary

- (Articulatory) phonetics is the study of how speech sounds are produced.
- Phonology is the study of how sounds function in particular languages.
- Pronunciation teaching uses this fundamental knowledge to teach the production of the sounds of another language in an informed way.
- Pronunciation is composed of many features, all of which are present at the same time.
- Suprasegmentals should be not be overlooked in favor of segmentals.
- There is a hierarchical structure to the functional units of pronunciation.

Exercise

Decide whether the following statements relate primarily to phonetics or phonology. In answering this, you might want to ask yourself:

- Are we talking about a particular language?
- Are we talking about how sounds combine?
- Are we talking about how sounds and words are produced?

1. Your vocal cords vibrate when you say the [m] sound.
2. In English, the [v] sound is always spelt with the letter *v*.
3. At the beginning of English words, the [s] sound can be followed by [p, t, k] sounds, but not [b, d, g].
4. You make an [f] sound by putting your lower lip against your upper teeth.
5. At the ends of English words, an [m] sound cannot be followed by a [k] sound.
6. Your lips are spread when you say the vowel in *seek*.
7. The vowel in *seek* is a long vowel.
8. During an [n] sound, air escapes through your nose.
9. English has two different vowels in *seek* and *sick*, while Italian has only one vowel of this type.

Further reading

On the whole process of speaking, see Levelt (1989). For more on the—often very technical—field of acoustic and auditory phonetics, see Kent and Read (2002), Stevens (1998), Pisoni and Remez (Eds, 2004). On the relative communicative importance of segmentals and suprasegmentals, see Pennington and Richards (1986).

2 Accents of English worldwide

> There is no such thing as 'the Queen's English.' The property has gone into the hands of a joint stock company and we own the bulk of the shares!
>
> Mark Twain (1835–1910), US author, *Following the Equator* (1897)

Learning objectives

At the end of this chapter, you will be able to:

- explain the unique place of English as a language of the world
- list problems in the definition of the terms *native speaker* and *official language*
- define English as a native, second and foreign language.

English as a world language

English is a—or, more probably, *the*—major world language nowadays. It is the major world language for science, the internet, commerce, etc. And this has been acknowledged for a long time. For instance, Quirk begins his 1962 book *The Use of English* with an important analogy about the nature of English and other languages. He points out that the question 'Who speaks Swedish?' has a simple answer, both in 1962 and today: it is spoken by the Swedes in Sweden, by about 10% of the population of Finland, by the descendants of Swedish immigrants in places such as Minnesota, USA, and by Swedish migrants to various countries. Since Swedish is mutually intelligible with Danish and Norwegian, speakers of these languages may claim to understand Swedish too. And some others learn Swedish as a foreign language.

In the case of Swedish, the concepts of country, citizenship and language largely coincide: most people who speak Swedish are Swedish and were born in Sweden.

However, the same question asked of English ('Who speaks English?') has a very complex answer that depends on various factors and moot points, including the following:

- ***Proficiency***: How well does a person have to speak English before they can claim to 'speak English'?
- ***Skills***: In English, we use the term 'speak English' to refer to overall proficiency in English—it is not restricted to speaking. There are many speakers of English with

uneven abilities. For instance, they may read and write English much better than they can speak or listen to it. For this and other reasons, the term *users* of English is sometimes preferred to *speakers*.

- ***Measurement***: How can we measure the number of people speaking English? Procedures such as asking people to complete census forms with items such as 'List the languages you can speak' may lead to over-reporting. That is, people may claim to speak a language, but only have a rudimentary knowledge of it. Nobody ever checks how well they speak it.
- ***Status***: A person in the UK, and a person in PRC China, both claiming to speak English, represent two very different types of speaker. The former may speak no language other than English and therefore use it for all communicative functions, while the latter may speak other languages and have learnt English for the purposes of international trade.

The status of English often revolves around the concept of the *native speaker* and English as a *native language*. This is likewise not a simple concept, and may have different definitions such as the following:

- A person's native language is the language they learn first. However, some people may come to be better speakers of other languages because of migration, marriage, etc.
- A person's native language, or mother tongue, is the language they learn from their mother. With the increasing number of inter-racial (and thus inter-language) marriages nowadays, children may not learn the language of their mothers.
- A person's native language is the language they speak to the highest proficiency. However, because of migration and other factors, this may not be the language they learnt first.
- A person's native language is the one they use most often, or for the most functions. Again, this may not be the language they learnt first.

In the case of a person in the UK who speaks no language other than English, all four definition categories will lead to the same conclusion: the person's native language is English. However, for people in more diverse linguistic situations, the categories may not all lead to the same language being called the native language.

A further distinction can be drawn between whether the word *native* refers to people, or to situations and countries. That is, one can say 'John is a native speaker of English' or 'The UK is a native English-speaking country.'

The roles and status of English in countries have traditionally been modeled using a three-way categorization: English as a native, second or foreign language. English is a native language in the UK, from which it originated, and in other countries to which speakers from the UK migrated, such as the USA, Canada, Australia and New Zealand. English is a second language when it has special status and functions in a country, such as in government, law, education and the media. Other languages are widespread in such countries. Countries where English is a second language are often the result of colonization, as in India, Nigeria, Malaysia, Tanzania and the Philippines. Where English is a foreign language, it is typically learnt in school and other educational institutions.

Virtually all the remaining countries of the world (excluding native-language and second-language countries) are foreign-language environments, since English is taught and learnt throughout the world.

A further complicating factor is the existence in many countries of official languages. This confers official recognition on the languages. However, the term *official language* is rather an imprecise one. Official languages:

- may or may not be the languages used in the law
- may or may not be the medium of instruction in schools
- may differ in different regions of a country
- may be the languages of former colonizers, as is often the case with English and French
- may be minority languages
- need not be spoken by everyone in the country.

Many countries have more than one official language, and some countries have no official language.

Crystal (1997) gives the figures of 320–380 million native speakers of English, 150–300 million second-language speakers, and 100–1,000 million foreign-language speakers. These figures are necessarily imprecise, because of the problems of definition outlined above.

In short, English is not a homogeneous monolith. There is a lot of accent variation caused by the fact that it is spoken throughout the world. Like other languages, there is also sociolinguistic variation caused by factors such as the formality of the situation. For this reason, it is not unusual nowadays to hear the term *English languages* (for example, McArthur, 1998) to encompass this variation.

It is impossible, in a book this size, to cover the pronunciation of all the major accents of English. The two major world accents used as the references in this book are a standard US one, and a standard southern British one.

The US accent is known as General American (GenAm), and 'is what is spoken by the majority of Americans, namely those who do not have a noticeable eastern or southern accent' (Wells, 2008, p. xiv).

The British accent used to be referred to as *Received Pronunciation*, a term conceived in the first half of the 20th century by the British phonetician Daniel Jones. However, that term, like *The Queen's English*, is considered out-of-date now, and other labels such as *standard southern British English* (SSBE) and *BBC English* (Jones, 2006) are used. The term SSBE is used in this book.

Other languages

This book is about the pronunciation specifically of English. However, since it is aimed at teachers of English to foreigners who, by definition, come to English classes already speaking other languages fluently, the book also sometimes touches on pronunciation features of other languages. It does this in order to emphasize that English is not a superior or more basic language than others. Consideration of other languages is also needed in order to explain phonetic concepts, some of which do not occur in English. Most importantly, it helps the teacher-reader to understand some of the problems that foreign learners bring with them to the pronunciation classroom as a result of speaking other languages.

Summary

- *The English language* is not a homogeneous concept. The concept is often referred to as *the English languages* nowadays.
- The concept of *the native speaker* is a difficult one to maintain.
- English-speaking countries around the world are often categorized into English as a Native Language (ENL), English as a Second Language (ESL) and English as a Foreign Language (EFL) situations.
- Non-native speakers of English far outnumber native speakers.
- English is not a superior language to learners' native languages.

Exercises

1. Which of the following countries have English as one of their official languages?

The UK	New Zealand	Barbados	Fiji
The USA	India	South Africa	Kenya
Canada	The Philippines	Cameroon	Pakistan

2. Put the following native-speaker Englishes in rank order of their country populations.

Australia	Ireland	South Africa
Canada	New Zealand	The USA
England	Scotland	Wales

Further reading

Crystal (1997) is a short readable introduction to the varieties of English around the world. McArthur (1998, 2002) and Jenkins (2009) also cover the variation in Englishes worldwide, with plenty of examples. Davies (2003) explores the nebulous concept of the native speaker.

3 Airstreams and the vocal cords

Spoken language is merely a series of squeaks.

Alfred North Whitehead (1861–1947),
English mathematician and philosopher

Learning objectives

At the end of this chapter, you will be able to:

- explain the pulmonic egressive airstream
- define the terms *voiced* and *voiceless.*

Airstreams

All English speech sounds are made using air from the lungs. That is, the same apparatus is used in speech as that used for breathing. The lungs take in air (for breathing) and, as the air is expelled, it is obstructed and modified in various ways in order to create different types of sound. Since the air comes from the lungs, the airstream is known as *pulmonic*, and since it travels outwards, it is known as *egressive.*

You may wonder whether other airstreams exist. The answer is that they do, but they are not used for speech sounds in English. For instance, the sound usually represented in spelling by either *tsk-tsk* or *tut-tut* is often used in western cultures to express annoyance or irritation. Similarly, the *gee-up* noise is made to encourage a horse. Neither of these sounds uses a pulmonic egressive airstream. Instead, the movement of air is initiated in the mouth rather than the lungs, and the air rushes inwards rather than outwards. You can prove this by producing these sounds while humming (in effect making a (pulmonic egressive) *ng* sound, as in the word *sing*) at the same time. Technically, the *tut-tut* and *gee-up* sounds are known as velaric ingressive sounds. The important point is that they are not speech sounds in English—they do not combine with other sounds to form words. They are known as *clicks*, and do function as regular speech sounds in some languages in Africa such as Zulu, and Xhosa, whose first sound is the gee-up click sound.

So, all English speech sounds, like almost all speech sounds in languages of the world, are made on a pulmonic egressive airstream. The first organ that the airstream encounters that can obstruct it in some way is the vocal cords.

The vocal cords

The vocal cords are two flaps of skin and muscle located behind the Adam's apple, the point at the front of the throat. Men's Adam's apples stick out further than women's or children's, because their larynxes (the whole voice box containing the vocal cords) are larger. They grow larger at puberty, and are the reason why men's voices are generally lower in pitch than women's and children's.

Notice the spelling of the term *vocal cords*. The second word is *cords*, not *chords*. Many phoneticians use the term vocal *folds*, which is probably a more accurate term for flaps of skin and muscle.

Figure 3.1 shows a diagrammatic representation of the vocal cords and surrounding muscles, as seen from the left (that is, the left of the diagram represents the Adam's apple, the front of the throat).

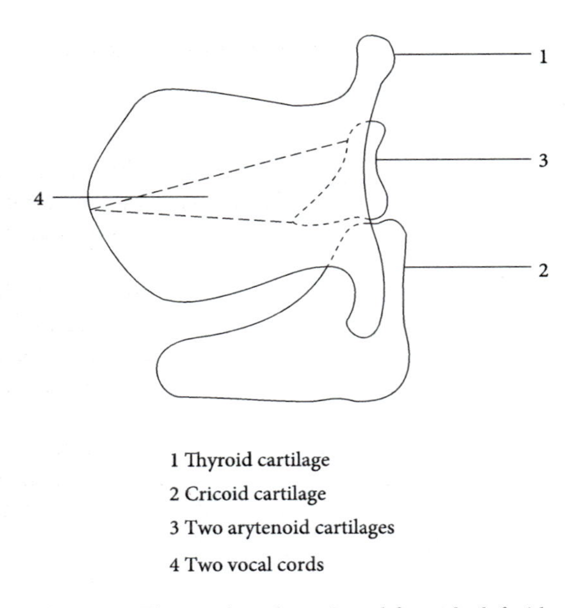

1 Thyroid cartilage
2 Cricoid cartilage
3 Two arytenoid cartilages
4 Two vocal cords

Figure 3.1 The vocal cords as viewed from the left side.

By the action of the muscles surrounding the vocal cords, they can adopt a number of positions. Four will be described here, as they are important for English.

1 Voice

By the action of the muscles that move the small arytenoid cartilages, the two vocal cords may be drawn together. Since they are already together at the front of the throat, this means that the vocal cords completely cover the windpipe and block the airstream from passing through. However, they are held at a light tension, and the airstream forces them apart. Because the air pressure from below is momentarily lost, the vocal cords then snap together again. Then they are blown apart again. And so on. In short, they vibrate.

This vibration occurs at a frequency of about 110–130 times per second (or hertz, Hz) on average for men, and about 200–230 Hz for women. Because women have smaller larynxes, and therefore shorter vocal cords, than men, their cords vibrate at a faster frequency, and sound higher in pitch.

This vibration is known as *voice*, and sounds involving this vibration are known as *voiced*. It is this voicing that gives sounds their carrying power. All vowels and most consonants in English are voiced.

There are various ways of checking if a sound is voiced. Make a loud, strong [z] sound (which is voiced), and:

- put your fingers lightly on your Adam's apple and feel the vibration
- put your fingers in your ears, and hear the booming sound
- put your hand on the top of your head, and feel the vibration (which is essentially your skull vibrating)
- produce a [z] on a rise in pitch; that is, go from a low pitch to a high pitch.

2 Voicelessness

The muscles that move the arytenoid cartilages can pull the vocal cords apart. This, of course, is the normal position when breathing. Since the cords are apart, the air can move freely down to the lungs (when breathing) or up from the lungs (when speaking) without obstruction.

Sounds made with the vocal cords apart like this are called *voiceless*. All English speech sounds can therefore be classified as either voiced (with vocal cord vibration) or voiceless (without). Because the vocal cords are not vibrating, and thus are not regulating the flow of air through them, voiceless sounds may have a greater force of air than voiced ones.

Sixteen English sounds occur in eight pairs of voiced and voiceless equivalents. That is, the only (or main) difference between them is that one has vocal cord vibration, while the other does not. In the following pairs, the first sound is voiced and the second voiceless.

- the [b] sound as in *bill*, and the [p] sound as in *pill*
- the [d] sound as in *door*, and the [t] sound as in *tore*
- the [ɡ] sound as in *game*, and the [k] sound as in *came*
- the [dʒ] sound as in *jeep*, and the [tʃ] sound as in *cheap*
- the [v] sound as in *very*, and the [f] sound as in *ferry*
- the [ð] sound as in *thy*, and the [θ] sound as in *thigh*
- the [z] sound as in *zoo*, and the [s] sound as in *sue*
- the [ʒ] sound in the middle of *confusion*, and the [ʃ] sound in the middle of *Confucian*.

3 The [h] sound

The muscles that move the arytenoid cartilages may bring them almost together, thus leaving a small gap between the vocal cords. In this position, air can escape through the cords, but, because it is a narrow gap, a hissing noise is produced. In chapter 8, we will refer to this hissing noise as *frication*, and to resulting sounds as *fricatives*. The important thing to notice here is that the sound is produced at the vocal cords. The other vocal organs (tongue, lips, etc.) are not involved. Since the vocal cords cannot, at the same time, be vibrating, [h] is considered a voiceless sound.

4 The glottal stop

In category 1 Voice, we said that the vocal cords are drawn together along their length, but at a light tension, so that the airstream can blow them apart and make them vibrate. In this fourth category, the gesture is the same, except that the vocal cords are held at a tension strong enough that the airstream cannot blow the cords apart until the gesture is released. In short, the airstream is blocked from escaping until the vocal cords are drawn apart. In this respect, it is similar to a [p] sound, where the two lips are held together blocking the airstream, until the lips are released. Such a sound is known as a *stop*, and will be handled in more detail in chapter 7. Since it involves the two vocal cords, it is called *glottal* (an adjective referring to the vocal cords).

You can make the gesture involved in a glottal stop by doing the following:

- Hold your breath. The glottal stop traps the air in your lungs.
- Imagine you are a weightlifter going to lift a bar with weights. You are likely to make a glottal stop, so that the air is trapped in your lungs and forms a solid base against which the muscles in your arms and chest can work.
- Cough. The glottal stop allows air pressure to build up below it, which blows away any phlegm when the glottal stop is released.

As a speech sound, the glottal stop is given the symbol [ʔ]. It is found, often replacing [t], in some accents of English, such as Cockney, the urban accent of London, in phrases such as a *li'le bi' of bu'er* for *a little bit of butter*. Since the vocal cords cannot, at the same time, be vibrating, the glottal stop is considered a voiceless sound.

Summary

- All English speech sounds are made on an airstream that uses the lungs (pulmonic) and moves outwards (egressive).
- The vocal cords are two flaps of skin and muscle behind the Adam's apple.
- All English speech sounds can be classified as either voiced (with vocal cord vibration) or voiceless (without).

Exercises

1. Are the following sounds voiced or voiceless?

    - the [m] sound as in *mix*
    - the [uː] sound as in *shoe*
    - the [f] sound as in *five*

- the [r] sound as in *round*
- the [aʊ] sound as in *cow*
- the [h] sound as in *house*
- the [l] sound as in *light*.

2. All the following words contain an *h* letter in the spelling. But does it correspond to an [h] sound in the pronunciation?

behave	*Fulham*	*hotel*
cheetah	*graph*	*hour*
cloth	*H*	*rehearse*
cough	*hate*	*when*
fish	*honest*	*who*

Further reading

For more on non-pulmonic airstreams and the vocal cords, see, for example, Ladefoged and Johnson (2010, chapter 6).

4 Cardinal vowels

> [. . .] Daniel Jones proposed a series of eight cardinal vowels, evenly spaced around the outside of the possible vowel area and designed to act as fixed reference points for phoneticians. In no case is the quality of a cardinal vowel exactly the same as that of an English vowel.
>
> Peter Ladefoged and Keith Johnson, *A Course in Phonetics* (2010)

Learning objectives

At the end of this chapter, you will be able to:

- explain the theory behind the cardinal vowel system
- produce the primary cardinal vowels [i, e, ɛ, a, ɑ, ɔ, o, u].

Vowels and consonants

Most people, on being asked how many vowels there are in English, reply 'Five—*a, e, i, o* and *u* . . . er, and sometimes *y*.' This answer may seem fine if we are talking about spelling. There are 5 (or 5½) vowel letters in the alphabet, and the remaining 21 (or 20½) are consonant letters. The complication about *y* is that it sometimes represents a vowel sound, as in *rhythm*, and sometimes a consonant sound, as at the beginning of *yes*.

However, this is a book about pronunciation. So, the relevant question is 'How many vowel *sounds* are there in English?' As we will see in chapter 31, English spelling is, for various reasons, a poor representation of how words are pronounced. For instance, while the letter *y* clearly represents the sound at the beginning of *yes*, we cannot point to any letter as representing the same sound at the beginning of *unit* or *Europe*.

We therefore need to do two things: firstly, to keep sounds separate from spelling, and secondly, to define what is meant by a vowel sound, as opposed to a consonant sound. We saw in chapter 3 that all English speech sounds are made by expelling air from the lungs through the mouth and/or nose. All English vowel sounds are voiced (that is, the vocal cords are vibrating) and the air escapes through the mouth alone. Vowel sounds are defined as those during which the airstream escapes through the mouth with little or no obstruction. The main organ producing the difference between the different vowel sounds is the tongue which can adopt various positions within the mouth. Since the mouth is a relatively large cavity, and the tongue can adopt any number of positions within it (that is, it is a continuum), the description of vowel sounds is more complex than for consonants.

A reference system for describing the tongue position for any vowel in any accent of any language (that is, any humanly possible vowel sound) was devised by the British phonetician Daniel Jones. They are known as *cardinal vowels.* The system takes the shape of a trapezium (Figure 4.1) and depends on two well-defined anchor points. For the first, Cardinal Vowel 1 [i], the tongue is as high and as front as possible. For the second, Cardinal Vowel 5 [ɑ], the tongue is as low and as back as possible. Since these are extreme vowel sounds on the edge of the trapezium, the tongue is as high/low/front/back as possible, consistent with it still being a vowel sound. That is, for instance, if we raised the tongue in the [i] position, a hissing noise (called frication; see chapters 6 and 8) would start to be caused against the hard palate.

Three other vowels (Cardinal Vowels 2 [e], 3 [ɛ] and 4 [a]) are defined as having the tongue as front as possible, and in equidistant steps from [i] to [ɑ]. Three more (Cardinal Vowels 6 [ɔ], 7 [o] and 8 [u]) are defined as having the tongue as back as possible, and in equidistant steps from [ɑ] to [i].

These eight cardinal vowels are shown in Figure 4.1, where front vowels are on the left, and back vowels on the right. Since these are extreme vowel sounds, they lie on the periphery of the trapezium, which represents the area in which the highest part of the tongue must be in order to produce a vowel sound. Cardinal Vowels 6, 7 and 8 have rounded lips, and the other five are unrounded, because these are the combinations of rounding and tongue position that occur most commonly in languages of the world. The purpose of this trapezium is, after all, as a convenient tool for describing vowel sounds in languages.

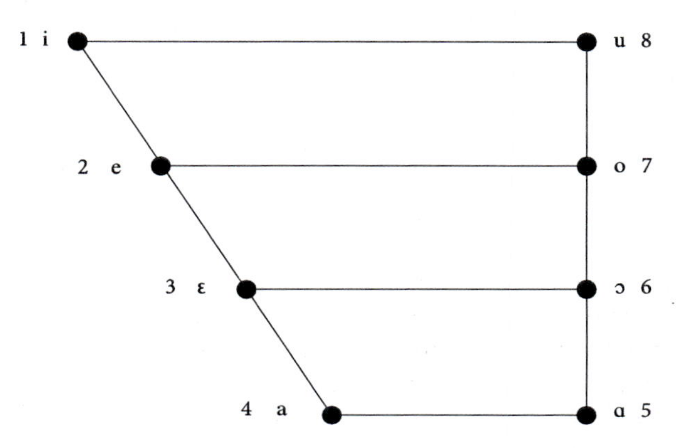

Figure 4.1 Cardinal vowels.

Phoneticians learn the cardinal vowel system largely by repeated listening to the eight cardinal vowel sounds and fixing them in the brain. A vowel sound in any language can then be described by plotting the tongue position on the cardinal vowel trapezium chart, by reference to the eight cardinal vowels. For instance, a vowel may be described as being like Cardinal Vowel 2, but with a somewhat lower and more central tongue position.

Diacritics can be added to the [e] symbol to show this: [ë̞]. The diacritic [̝] is used for higher, [̞] for lower, and [̈] for centralized. Any other phonetician who is well versed in the system will be able to understand the vowel sound being described.

The above is a very brief introduction to the cardinal vowel system, which contains many more sophisticated aspects that we do not need to go into. The purpose of introducing it here is to explain the trapezium which represents the vowel area (that is, the area in which the highest part of the tongue must be in order to produce a vowel sound) and can be used to describe any vowel sound in any accent of any language. This, of course, is exactly what we need to be able to do in the next chapter, where we look at the vowel sounds of the pronunciation of accents of English.

It must be emphasized that, although some of the symbols used for vowel sounds of GenAm and SSBE are the same as, or similar to, symbols for cardinal vowels, they do not necessarily represent exactly the same sound. For example, the symbol for the vowel in *see* is [iː]. However, in SSBE it is not as front and as high as possible (that is, at the top left-hand corner of the diagram). It is rather more central than that. Compare this with the [i] vowels of French, Italian or Spanish, which are typically more peripheral (that is, closer to the corner). We do not have an inexhaustible supply of symbols, and so it is not surprising that all these vowels are transcribed as [i]. However, the precise nature of the vowels has to be interpreted in the context of the language (and the accent of the language) being described.

Summary

- Cardinal vowels, and the trapezium diagram they define, represent the range of humanly possible vowel sounds.
- Cardinal vowels 1 and 5 have precise definitions.
- The trapezium can be used for describing the position of the highest part of the tongue for any vowel sound in any accent of any language.

Exercises

1. Listen to the cardinal vowels spoken by Daniel Jones and Peter Ladefoged at the following website: www.phonetics.ucla.edu/course/chapter9/cardinal/cardinal.html. Imitate them as sounds, trying not be influenced by the sounds of your native language or any other language you may know.
2. Think of any language you know, apart from English. Does it have vowel sounds that are different from those of English? If so, can you tell roughly where in the vowel trapezium they are located (high—low, front—back)? Also, do they have lip rounding?

Further reading

Cardinal vowels are explained in greater detail in the International Phonetic Association (1999), which also contains illustration of how the system can be used for describing the vowel sounds of different languages.

5 Vowels

Playing 'bop' is like playing Scrabble with all the vowels missing.

Duke Ellington (1899–1974), US jazz musician

Learning objectives

At the end of this chapter, you will be able to:

- list the vowel sounds of English
- use phonetic symbols to represent them
- say which vowel sounds occur in which words
- list some of the main spelling correspondences.

Categorization of vowels

In the previous chapter, we saw that vowel sounds can be described in terms of three dimensions:

1. ***Vertical tongue position*** (tongue height): Is the tongue relatively high (that is, close to the roof of the mouth) or low (that is, far from the roof, with the jaw wide open), or somewhere in between?
2. ***Horizontal tongue position:*** Is the tongue relatively far forward in the mouth (so that you can see it easily in a mirror), or at the back, or somewhere in between?

The two dimensions of vertical and horizontal tongue position give us the vowel area trapezium.

3. ***Lip position:*** Are the lips rounded into a circle, or unrounded? This is not shown by the vowel diagram, but can be easily added, for example, by circling the symbols of rounded vowels.

There are two other dimensions that need to be described for English vowel sounds:

4. ***Vowel length:*** Is the vowel pronounced long or short in English?

5. ***Monophthong versus diphthong:*** A monophthong is a vowel sound that does not change during its production. For instance, the [ɑː] vowel as in *spa* starts and ends the same. The tongue and lips do not move during the vowel. In contrast the [ɔɪ] diphthong vowel as in *boy* has different starting and ending sounds. Most obviously, the lips are rounded at the beginning of *boy*, but unrounded at the end. Less obviously, the tongue starts at the back of the mouth and moves towards the front.

We will use these two dimensions to organize the description of the vowel sounds of English into three categories: short monophthongs, long monophthongs, and diphthongs (which are also long). A reference checklist of the vowel symbols for both SSBE and GenAm is given in the Symbols for English Sounds section at the beginning of this book.

Short monophthongs

There are seven short monophthongs in SSBE:

[ɪ] as in *sit*
[e] as in *bet*
[æ] as in *mat*
[ʌ] as in *shut*
[ɒ] as in *plot*
[ʊ] as in *foot*
[ə] as in *about*

Their tongue positions on the vowel chart are given in Figure 5.1.

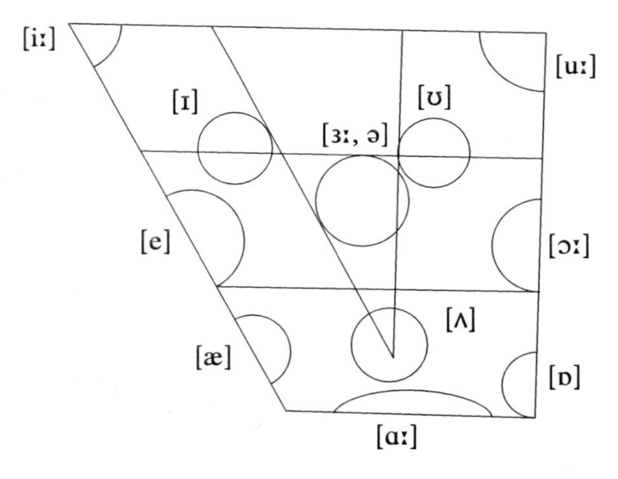

Figure 5.1 Tongue positions for SSBE monophthong vowels.

The main sound-to-spelling correspondences (from Carney, 1994) are given in Table 5.1. Carney's figures relate specifically to SSBE. However, they are unlikely to vary for GenAm, except in those places where there are large differences between GenAm and SSBE sounds, or British and American spelling.

Since the [ə] vowel is intimately connected with the placement of stress in English, it will be covered in chapter 19. It can be represented by a very wide range of spellings.

Table 5.1 Sound-to-spelling correspondences for SSBE short monophthong vowels

Sound	*Spelling*	*% of the time in connected speech*	*Example words*
[ɪ]	*i*	61	*bit*
	y	20	*rhythm*
	e	16	*become*
	a, aCe	2	*spinach, image*
	others	2	
[e]	*e*	84	*ten*
	ea	6	*dead*
	others	9	
[æ]	*a*	100	*bad*
[ʌ]	*u*	63	*mud*
	o	27	*ton*
	ou	8	*touch*
	others	2	
[ɒ]	*o*	92	*not*
	a	6	*wash*
	others	2	
[ʊ]	*oo*	64	*good*
	u	32	*put*
	others	4	

Long monophthongs

There are five long monophthongs in English. Their symbols contain a colon, to indicate length.

[iː] as in *feed*
[ɑː] as in *calm*
[ɔː] as in *board*
[uː] as in *moon*
[ɜː] as in *herb*

Their tongue positions on the vowel chart are also given in Figure 5.1. The main sound-to-spelling correspondences (from Carney, 1994) are given in Table 5.2.

Lip rounding

Four of the long and short SSBE monophthongs are rounded:

[ɔː] as in *board* [ɒ] as in *plot* [ʊ] as in *foot* [uː] as in *moon*

There is a major difference between SSBE and GenAm in the pronunciation of words such as *lot*. In SSBE, this contains the short [ɒ] vowel, while in GenAm it contains the long [ɑː] vowel. It ought also to be pointed out that there is variation within standard US

Table 5.2 Sound-to-spelling correspondences for SSBE long monophthong vowels

Sound	*Spelling*	*% of the time in connected speech*	*Example words*
[iː]	*e, eCe*, final *ee*	38	*be, theme, agree*
	non-final *ee*	26	*deep*
	ea	25	*leaf*
	non-final *ie*	5	*chief*
	i, iCe, final *ie*	2	*motif, police, laddie*
	others	4	
[ɑː]	*ar*	60	*park*
	a	34	*father*
	others	6	
[ɔː]	*a (+ l)*	29	*halt*
	or, ore, ar	25	*cord, core, war*
	au	9	*author*
	aw	9	*jaw*
	our	8	*court*
	ough	6	*ought*
	al ('empty' *l*)	5	*talk*
	others	9	
[uː]	*oo*	39	*moon*
	u, uCe, ue	27	*flu, rule, blue*
	o, oCe, oe	15	*who, move, shoe*
	ew	9	*new*
	ou	7	*group*
	others	3	
[ɜː]	*er(r)*	39	*herb*
	ir(r)	18	*bird*
	or(r)	17	*word*
	ur(r)	15	*turn*
	ear	8	*heard*
	others	3	

accents, especially in the question of which vowels in the low back region occur in words such as *law, lot, cloth* and *thought*. These accent differences are discussed in chapter 13.

Diphthongs

There are eight diphthongs in SSBE, but only five in GenAm. In three of them, the tongue moves towards a high front position, and the second part of the symbol is therefore [ɪ]:

[eɪ] as in *page* [aɪ] as in *five* [ɔɪ] as in *noise*

In two diphthongs, the tongue moves towards a high back position, and the second part of the symbol is therefore [ʊ]:

[aʊ] as in *clown* [əʊ] as in *home*

Wells (2008) uses the symbol [oʊ] to represent the GenAm diphthong in *home*. This represents the fact that the starting point of this diphthong is much further back in GenAm than in SSBE. However, in other respects, SSBE [əʊ] and GenAm [oʊ] are the same.

The final set of three only apply to SSBE. The tongue moves towards a mid-central position, and the second part of the symbol is therefore [ə]:

[ɪə] as in *beard* [eə] as in *cared* [ʊə] as in *pure*

In GenAm, these words have a vowel followed by an [r] consonant: [bɪrd, kerd, pjʊr]. This difference in rhoticity is discussed further in chapter 11.

Three important points should be noted about diphthongs:

- Although the diphthongs are represented by two-part symbols, they represent single sounds (phonemes: see chapter 12).
- Diphthongs are long. That is, they are as long as the long monophthongs. For example, the word *spy* [spaɪ] is as long as the word *spa* [spɑː]. A colon is not needed in the symbol for diphthongs as the two-part symbol implies length.
- Since diphthongs, by definition, involve a movement in tongue position, they cannot be represented by a point on the vowel diagram. Instead, the beginning point (circle) and end point (arrow) are indicated.

The tongue positions of the eight SSBE diphthongs on the vowel chart are given in Figure 5.2.

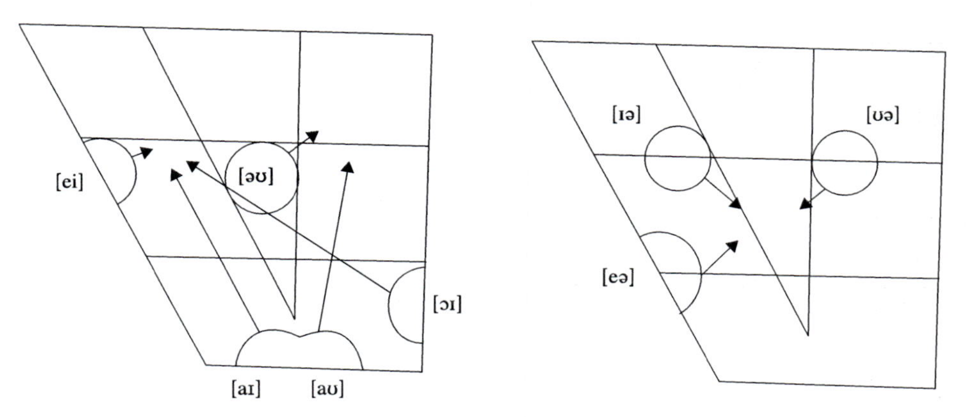

Figure 5.2 Tongue positions and movement for SSBE diphthong vowels.

The main sound-to-spelling correspondences (from Carney, 1994) are given in Table 5.3.

[i] *and* [u]

Two other symbols are often used nowadays by dictionaries. One relates to the underlined sound in words like *easy*, *pretty*, *react* and *glorious*. Many speakers feel this is the

Table 5.3 Sound-to-spelling correspondences for SSBE diphthong vowels

Sound	*Spelling*	*% of the time in connected speech*	*Example words*
[eɪ]	*a, aCe*	65	*labour, lake*
	final *ay*	18	*day*
	ai	12	*rail*
	others	5	
[aɪ]	*i, iCe,* final *ie,* final *y*	80	*bicycle, like, lie, try*
	igh	13	*high*
	non-final *y*	2	*rhyme*
	others	5	
[ɔɪ]	*oi*	61	*boil*
	oy	39	*boy*
[əʊ]	*o, oCe, oe*	75	*go, hope, toe*
	ow	18	*grow*
	oa	4	*coat*
	others	4	
[aʊ]	*ou,* final *ow*	93	*cloud, cow*
	pre-consonantal *ow*	6	*crowd*
	others	1	
[ɪə]	*ear*	28	*dear*
	ea	12	*idea*
	er, ere	12	*hero, mere*
	ia	10	*media*
	eer	4	*deer*
	others	34 *	
[eə]	*ar, are*	59	*librarian, care*
	air	28	*hair*
	ear	10	*wear*
	others	3	
[ʊə]	*u* + /ə/ in suffix	†	*actual, fluent*
	u + /ə/ in stem	†	*cruel*
	oor	†	*poor*
	our	†	*tour*
	ure	†	*sure*

* As Carney (1994, p. 190) says, [ɪə] 'is very divergent' in terms of sound-to-spelling correspondences.

† As Carney (1994, p. 194) notes, many of these words are pronounced with [ɔː] by many speakers. For this reason, he does not give percentages for [ʊə].

same vowel as in *deed* (and therefore can transcribe *easy* [iːziː] with two identical vowels). Others feel it is the vowel of *did* (thus [prɪtɪ] with two identical vowels). Yet others feel that it is neither [iː] nor [ɪ], but something in between. The vowel is always unstressed (as in the above words, and unstressed grammatical words like *we, be*), and therefore harder to identify. Dictionaries often use the symbol [i] for this, and transcribe such words as [iːzi, prɪti, riækt, glɔːriəs].

The same argument applies to the underlined vowel in *sit<u>u</u>ation, ard<u>u</u>ous,* and unstressed grammatical words like *you,* and *to* before vowels. The symbol [u] is used for [uː], [ʊ], or something in between (thus [sɪtʃueɪʃən, ɑː(r)dʒuəs]).

Both [i] and [u] may be considered a compromise solution to an intractable problem in analysis. They are a convenient shorthand, but do not have phonemic status (see chapter 12).

Summary

- Vowel sounds are made without any great obstruction to the airstream.
- All English vowels are voiced and oral.
- English vowels can be divided into long and short vowels.
- Long vowels comprise long monophthongs and diphthongs.
- The production of monophthongs can be described by stating the vertical height of the tongue, its horizontal position and the position of the lips.

Exercises

1. All the following words contain one of the short monophthong vowels [ɪ, e, æ, ʌ, ʊ]. Say the words out loud and decide which vowel they contain.

any	*deaf*	*lump*	*miss*	*skull*	*touch*
blood	*English*	*mash*	*pull*	*stood*	*women*
cat	*friend*	*meringue*	*sank*	*test*	*would*

2. All the following words contain one of the five long monophthong vowels [iː, ɑː, ɔː, uː, ɜː]. Say the words out loud and decide which vowel they contain.

burp	*courtesy*	*feel*	*moon*	*park*	*shirt*
car	*door*	*heart*	*more*	*piece*	*steal*
court	*father*	*June*	*new*	*police*	*term*

3. All the following words contain one of the five diphthong vowels [eɪ, aɪ, ɔɪ, aʊ, əʊ/oʊ]. Say the words out loud and decide which vowel they contain.

boil	*blown*	*fight*	*hate*	*note*	*sigh*
brain	*brown*	*go*	*kite*	*now*	*stay*
break	*choice*	*ground*	*my*	*show*	*toy*

4. Ventriloquists 'throw' their voices, and make it sound as though it comes from their dummy. However, some sounds are particularly difficult for ventriloquists. Can you work out which vowel sounds of English cause particular problems, and why?

Further reading

All the vowels and consonants of English are explained in much greater detail in standard phonetics books such as Cruttenden (2008), Roach (2009) for SSBE; and Avery and Ehrlich (1992), Edwards (2003), Yavaş (2011) for GenAm. Symbols for SSBE are introduced and practiced in Brown (2005).

6 The vocal organs and consonant classification

The tongue of man is a twisty thing. There are plenty of words there of every kind.
Homer (8th century BC), *The Iliad*

Learning objectives

At the end of this chapter, you will be able to:

- name the main parts of the mouth, nose and throat used in pronunciation
- name the places and manners of articulation used in English.

The vocal organs

Before embarking on a description of how consonant sounds are made, we need to examine the vocal organs, that is, the parts of the body that are used in producing speech sounds. Figure 6.1 shows the vocal organs viewed from the side (technically known as a *sagittal section*). As you read the following section, you might like to look in a mirror, feel with your tongue and/or fingers, in order to appreciate the various parts.

The roof of the mouth

The most obvious parts of your vocal organs are your ***lips*** (9). Behind your upper lip are your upper ***teeth*** (8). Put the tip of your tongue on your upper teeth and slowly draw it backwards. Can you feel that there is a ridge before the roof of the mouth rises sharply? This ridge is known as the ***alveolar ridge*** (10). Although the sagittal section view of the mouth shows the lips, teeth and ridge at the front, it should be obvious that all three organs extend round the sides of your mouth in a U shape. This is one of the limitations of a sagittal section view. Put the tip of your tongue on your alveolar ridge and move it from side to side. Can you feel it extending round the sides of your mouth? Does your alveolar ridge have scaly bumps on it? Many people's do.

Behind your alveolar ridge is the large 'vault.' This is your ***hard palate*** (11). Put the tip of your tongue on your hard palate and move it from side to side. Can you feel a ridge running centrally down the middle of the palate? This was created before you were born, as the palate grows in from both sides and meets in the center. For some individuals, the two sides do not meet properly—what is known as a *cleft palate*. A hole is left in the

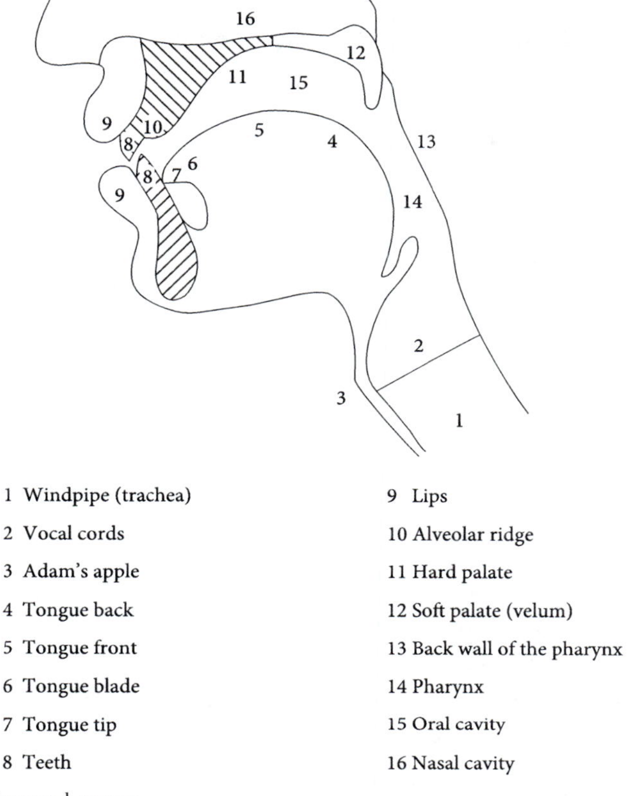

Figure 6.1 The vocal organs.

middle of the palate, and air escapes into the nose, giving the person's speech a nasal quality. Cleft palates can be cured by surgery at an early age.

Use the tip of your finger and feel back from your hard palate. Can you feel where it stops being hard and becomes soft? The hard palate is hard because it has bone above it (part of your skull). The soft palate or ***velum*** (12) is soft because there is no bone. Instead, it contains muscles and can move to block or open the passage to the nose or ***nasal cavity*** (16). This can be easily seen in a mirror. In phonetics, the soft palate is usually referred to as the *velum* and, as a result, the hard palate is often simply called the *palate.* The soft piece of flesh hanging down in the middle of the velum is called the *uvula.*

The floor of the mouth

Behind the ***lower lip*** (9) are your ***lower teeth*** (8). Again, these extend round the sides of the mouth in a U shape. The rest of the floor of the mouth is taken up by the tongue. Unfortunately, as can be seen in a mirror, the tongue has no natural divisions on it, apart from a line down the center for some people. However, for phonetic description, we need to divide the tongue in the front-to-back dimension. This is done by thinking about the part of the roof of the mouth that that part of the tongue lies opposite, and normally articulates with. The ***tip*** of the tongue (7) is the point at the very front. Immediately behind the tip is a part that lies opposite the alveolar ridge, called the ***blade*** (6). For sounds such as [n], either the tip or the blade comes up and touches the alveolar ridge.

Behind the blade is that part of the tongue that lies opposite the hard palate. This is technically known as the ***front*** (5). This may be a misleading term, as it is not the part at the front—that is the tip. The reason why it is called the front is that it is the part used for front vowels (see chapters 4 and 5). For a front vowel such as [iː] as in *see,* this part of the tongue rises towards the hard palate. There is only one English consonant that is produced in this way, and that is the [j] sound as at the beginning of *yes.* It is very like an [iː] vowel; this will be discussed in chapter 9.

Behind the front of the tongue is the ***back*** (4). While this term is more mnemonic (because it is the part at the back of the mouth), it in fact is called the back for the same reason as the front—it is the part used in articulating back vowels such as [uː] as in *zoo,* for which the back of the tongue rises towards the velum. The same gesture is used for consonants such as [k] as in *cat.*

The vocal cords

In chapter 3 we introduced the ***vocal cords*** (2). These are two flaps of skin and muscle located behind the Adam's apple (3), and lying at the top of the windpipe or trachea (1). Their two main positions are open for voiceless sounds, or vibrating for voiced sounds.

The cavities

The cavities from the vocal cords until air escapes from the body are known as the vocal tract. They can be divided into three. The main tract is formed by the throat or ***pharynx*** (14) and mouth or ***oral cavity*** (15). The nose or ***nasal cavity*** (16) can be thought of as a side-chamber to this main tract. It can be connected to it, or separated from it, by the action of the velum (12) against the ***back wall of the pharynx*** (13).

Classification of consonants

Although other features may be used in describing consonant sounds, the three main ones are:

- voiced versus voiceless
- place of articulation
- manner of articulation.

We will consider each of these in turn. Together they give us what are known as *three-term labels.* For instance the [s] sound can be called a *voiceless alveolar* (place) *fricative* (manner).

Voiced versus voiceless

We have already discussed this, in chapter 3. For voiced sounds, the vocal cords are vibrating; for voiceless, they are not.

Place of articulation

The air coming from the lungs can be obstructed at various places in the oral cavity. The following places need to be described for English sounds. In each case (apart from glottal), one articulator moves towards or touches another one. They are known as the active and passive articulators respectively. Passive articulators are on the roof of the mouth, while active ones are below.

- ***Bilabial:*** The lower lip is the active articulator and the upper lip is the passive, as for [p]. (While the upper lip can move somewhat, it moves less than the lower lip, which is attached to the jaw.)
- ***Labio-dental:*** The active articulator is the lower lip, and the passive is the upper teeth, as for [f].
- ***Dental:*** The tongue tip and/or blade is the active articulator, and the upper teeth are the passive, as for [θ] in *thick.* The difference between labio-dental and dental is therefore in the active articulator: the lower lip for labio-dental, and the tongue for dental.
- ***Alveolar:*** The tongue tip and/or blade is again the active articulator, but the passive articulator is the alveolar ridge, just behind the upper teeth, as for [n].
- ***Post-alveolar:*** This category is only needed for the SSBE [r] sound, which involves the tongue tip curling back and lying opposite the back of the alveolar region. The GenAm [r] sound typically curls further back, and can be called retroflex (see chapter 9).
- ***Palato-alveolar:*** A relatively large obstruction is caused by the tongue blade/front (active articulator) and the back of the alveolar region and front of the palatal region (passive), as for [ʃ] in *shoe.*
- ***Palatal:*** The active articulator is the tongue front, and the passive the hard palate, as for [j] in *yes.*
- ***Velar:*** The tongue back is the active articulator, and the velum (soft palate) is the passive, as for [k] in *cat.*
- ***Glottal:*** As we said in chapter 3 for a glottal stop and [h], the articulators are the vocal cords. They both move equally, so we cannot say that one is the active and the other the passive.

Manner of articulation

The final category we need to discuss is the type of obstruction made by the articulators. We can divide them into three broad categories:

- ***Stop:*** A stop involves a complete closure between the articulators, preventing air from escaping from the mouth (until the articulation is released). This is known as *complete closure.*

- ***Fricative:*** One articulator comes towards the other. However, it does not touch (it is not a stop). Instead, it comes so close that, as the air from the lungs escapes, it creates a hissing noise known as frication. This is known as *close approximation.*
- ***Approximant:*** The active articulator comes towards the passive, but without touching it and without causing frication. This is known as *open approximation.*

These three broad divisions can be sub-divided for English sounds.

Stop

- ***Oral stop:*** As for [p] as in *put,* the articulators prevent air from escaping through the mouth. There is also a velic closure between the velum and the back wall of the pharynx, preventing air from escaping through the nose.
- ***Nasal stop:*** As for [m] as in *mat,* the articulators prevent air from escaping through the mouth. But the velum is open, allowing air to escape through the nasal cavity and out through the nostrils.

Approximant

- ***Lateral approximant:*** for the [l] sound, the tongue tip touches the alveolar ridge in the center of the mouth. However, the sides of the tongue are not touching, and this allows the air to escape, without frication, over the sides.
- ***Central approximant:*** for all the other approximants of English (e.g. [r]), and for most approximants in languages of the world, the air escapes over the center of the tongue.

There is one other category (*affricates*) that needs to be described. The [ʃ] sound, as in *shin,* is a simple fricative: the tongue comes towards the palato-alveolar region, causing frication. The [tʃ] sound as in *chin,* however, starts with a complete closure between the tongue and the roof of the mouth. When the tongue is released, it does not come away smartly, but lingers in a fricative stage. It is known as an *affricate.* For this reason, the symbol contains two parts: the first part [t-] signifies the complete closure, and the second part [-ʃ] the fricative release. However, it is one sound unit (phoneme: see chapter 12), not a combination of two; thus, *why cheap* is not the same as *white sheep.*

The above description is a fairly detailed one, showing the relationships between various classes of sounds. In more informal styles, simpler vocabulary is sometimes used:

Oral stops are called ***plosives.***
Nasal stops are called simply ***nasals.***
Lateral approximants are called simply ***laterals.***
Central approximants are called simply ***approximants.***

The consonants of English are described in greater detail in the next three chapters. They vary relatively little between accents of English, far less than vowels do.

Summary

- The various parts of the vocal apparatus need to be named in order to discuss them.
- The only technical terms that are likely to be new or cause confusion are the *alveolar ridge, velum, front* of the tongue, and *pharynx*.
- Consonants are typically classified by using three-term labels: voiced versus voiceless, place of articulation and manner of articulation.

Exercises

1. Ventriloquists 'throw' their voices, and make it sound as though it comes from their dummy. However, some sounds are particularly difficult for ventriloquists. Can you work out which six consonant sounds of English cause particular problems, and why?
2. Which of the following categories of sound involve air escaping during the sound?

    - plosives, e.g. [p] as in *put*
    - nasals, e.g. [m] as in *mat*
    - fricatives, e.g. [s] as in *sit*
    - approximants, e.g. [r] as in *run*
    - vowels, e.g. [ɑː] as in *art*.

Further reading

The physiology of the vocal organs is described in detail in Laver (1994).

7 Plosives and nasals

Old phoneticians never die—they just lose their aspiration.

Graffiti

Learning objectives

At the end of this chapter, you will be able to:

- define the terms *plosive* and *nasal*
- list the main sound-spelling correspondences of these sounds in English
- explain the main variants of plosive and nasal sounds.

Plosives

As we saw in the previous chapter, plosives and nasals are similar in that they both involve a complete closure between the articulators, preventing air from escaping from the mouth. They are both stops. However, plosives (oral stops) also involve a velic closure between the velum and the back wall of the pharynx, preventing air from escaping through the nose. In short, air does not escape until one of the two closures is released. We can show this in Figure 7.1, which traces the movement of the lips through time for a [b] sound, as in *abbey* [æbi]. In this, and all subsequent diagrams in this chapter, time goes from left to right. Such diagrams are called *parametric,* because they plot the state of particular parameters (here, the lips) through time.

If we define the plosive [b] as requiring complete closure, then it extends from the first dotted line to the second (the *hold* phase). Before the first dotted line is the [æ] vowel. And we can see that, in order to form the complete closure, the two lips must come towards each other at the end of this vowel. This is known as the *approach* to the

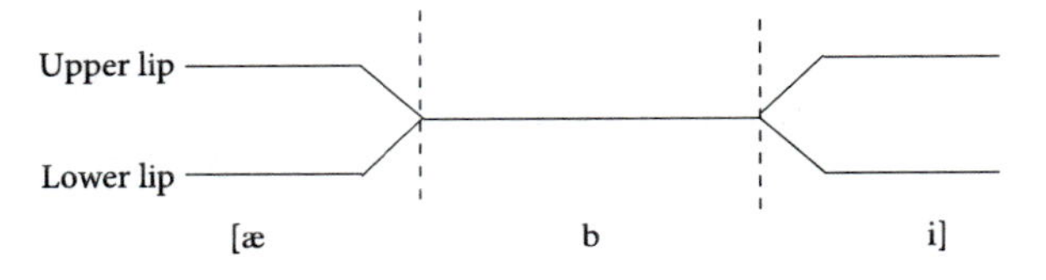

Figure 7.1 Basic movement of articulators for stops.

plosive. Similarly, the parting of the lips at the beginning of the following [i] vowel is known as the *release*.

There are six plosives in English. They divide into three pairs. The pairs are traditionally referred to as voiced and voiceless although, as we shall see, vocal cord vibration is often not the clearest clue to their identity.

The sound [p] is a voiceless bilabial plosive, and [b] is a voiced bilabial plosive. The lips are brought together. The main sound-to-spelling correspondences for plosives (from Carney, 1994) are given in Tables 7.1([p, b]), 7.2 ([t, d]) and 7.3 ([k, g]).

Table 7.1 Sound-to-spelling correspondences for [p, b]

Sound	*Spelling*	*% of the time in connected speech*	*Example words*
[p]	*p*	95	*pan*
	pp	5	*copper*
[b]	*b*	98	*bit*
	others	2	

The sound [t] is a voiceless alveolar plosive, and [d] is a voiced alveolar plosive. The tongue tip and/or blade touches the alveolar ridge.

Table 7.2 Sound-to-spelling correspondences for [t, d]

Sound	*Spelling*	*% of the time in connected speech*	*Example words*
[t]	*t*	96	*ten*
	tt	3	*pattern*
	others	1	
[d]	*d*	98	*dame*
	dd	2	*sudden*

The sound [k] is a voiceless velar plosive, and [g] is a voiced velar plosive. The tongue back touches the velum.

Table 7.3 Sound-to-spelling correspondences for [k, g]

Sound	*Spelling*	*% of the time in connected speech*	*Example words*
[k]	*c*	59	*car*
	k	21	*king*
	ck	6	*back*
	others	14	
[g]	*g*	92	*go*
	gu	3	*guess*
	gg	2	*ragged*
	others	3	

Aspiration

In fact, we have already described aspiration, in chapter 1. Aspiration is the burst of voiceless air that occurs on release of a stressed [p] sound as in *pit.* However, aspiration does not occur where the [p] follows an [s] sound as in *spit.* Nor does the voiced equivalent [b], as in *bit,* have aspiration. Aspiration is thus the difference between the sounds in *pit* (aspirated), and *spit* and *bit* (both unaspirated). It similarly distinguishes *tie* and *cold* (both aspirated) from *sty, die, scold* and *gold* (all unaspirated). This is represented in Figure 7.2 for *pit, spit* and *bit,* where the wavy line represents voicing, and [ʰ] aspiration.

As is clear from the diagrams, voicing is not a major clue here, as [b, d, ɡ] seldom have much voicing. Since plosives, by definition, involve air trapped in the mouth, and since voicing requires air to be forced through the vocal cords making them vibrate, it is difficult to continue to force air through the vocal cords, when it is not travelling anywhere, but building up pressure in the mouth. This is especially true of velar [ɡ], where the closure between the back of the tongue and the velum is not far above the vocal cords.

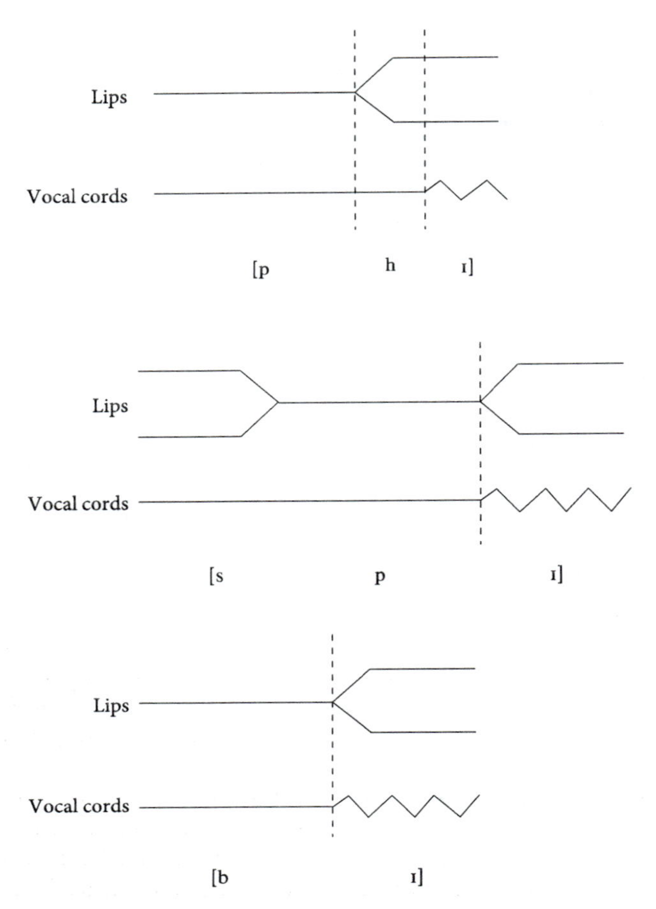

Figure 7.2 Aspiration (*pit, spit, bit*).

Syllable-final plosives

Vowel length

Similarly, voicing is not the major clue between [p, t, k] on the one hand and [b, d, g] on the other, in syllable-final position after a vowel. Compare the words *seed* and *seat.* The first, *seed,* has a long version of the [iː] vowel, while the second, *seat,* has a shorter version. It is the same vowel—it has not become [ɪ]. The pronunciation of the final [d] and [t] consonants is quite similar—neither the voiceless [t] nor the so-called voiced [d] has voicing. Instead, the main clue is the effect the consonant has on the length of the preceding vowel. Since the length of *seed* is similar to that of *see* (which has no final consonant), the effect is that a final voiceless consonant shortens the vowel.

The same is true of the other plosives, for example [b, p] as in *rib, rip,* and [g, k] as in *league, leak.*

We can represent these relationships as in Figure 7.3.

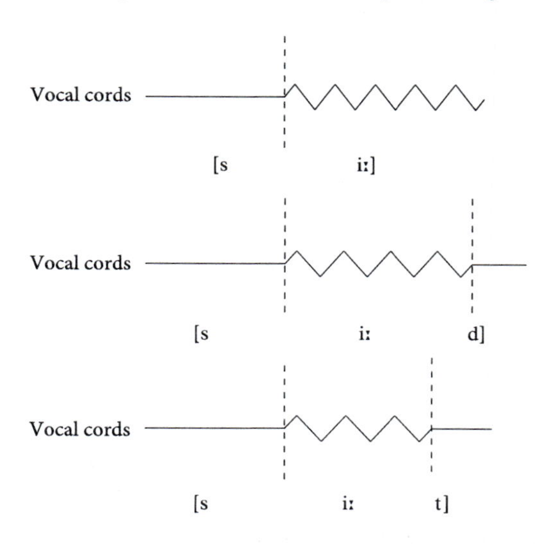

Figure 7.3 The effect of following consonants on vowel length (*see, seed, seat*).

Inaudibly released plosives

English syllable-final plosives, such as the [d] in *seed,* are often difficult to hear, and this may be one reason why foreign learners often drop them. As we have just seen, a voiceless syllable-final plosive has a shortening effect on the preceding vowel, as in *seat.* And this is true even when there is an intervening nasal or [l], as in *bent* versus *bend,* or *kilt* versus *killed.*

The problem often lies, however, not in the approach or hold phases, but in the release. The release is often impossible or difficult to hear. Some writers refer to this as an unreleased plosive. However, this seems an inappropriate term, as, for instance, the tongue does come away (that is, is released) from the alveolar ridge at the end of the [d] in *seed.* It does not remain there forever. A more appropriate term is therefore inaudibly released plosive. The plosive is released but there is insufficient air pressure behind the closure for it to be audible. Inaudibly released plosives are symbolized by a raised circle, e.g. *seed* [siːd°].

Inaudibly released plosives always occur in syllable-final position, in two main cases:

- where they are followed by another consonant, either within the same syllable (e.g. *wrapped* [ræp°t]) or in the following syllable (e.g. *wrap together* [ræp° təgeðə(r)])
- where they are utterance-final, that is, they are followed by nothing, e.g. *That's a wrap!* [ræp°].

Glottal stop

Before leaving the topic of plosives, we should again mention the glottal stop [ʔ]. This was described in chapter 3 as involving a complete closure between the vocal cords. It is found in English accents in four main contexts:

- It may accompany a syllable-final plosive (and perhaps affricate) articulation, where it is followed by another consonant, as in *wrapped* [ræʔpt], *fix* [fɪʔks], *catch* [kæʔtʃ].
- It may replace a syllable-final [t], where it is followed by another consonant, as in *nitwit* [nɪʔwɪt], *eighth* [eɪʔθ], *fat salary* [fæʔ sæləri].
- It may be inserted syllable-finally before a stressed vowel with heavy emphasis, as in *Absolutely!* [ʔæbsəluːtli], *unutterable* [ʌnʔʌtərəbəl].
- It may be used to separate two adjacent vowels, as in *re-enter* [riːʔentə(r)], *extra-ordinary* [ekstrəʔɔːdənəri / ekstrəʔɔːrdəneri] (as in an *extraordinary general meeting*).

Even though the glottal stop is probably becoming more common in native accents, it is still stigmatized to some extent.

> Not only in London Cockney, but also in many rural accents of the south and of East Anglia, and now increasingly in urban accents throughout England, glottaling of /t/ is widespread though overtly stigmatized.
>
> (Wells, 1982, p. 56)

> [In Scottish accents,] sporadic realization of the voiceless plosives /p/, /t/, /k/, when non-initial, with accompanying glottal closure or simply as the glottal stop [ʔ], is now widespread. . . . This, especially when in the intervocalic position, is the most strongly and overtly stigmatized feature of 'gutter Scots.'
>
> (Aitken, 1984, p. 102)

While this stigmatization is an important factor, a more important factor is the risk to intelligibility caused when learners use the glottal stop not only for syllable-final [t], but also for [p] and [k], and perhaps also [tʃ]. Given that many learners do not distinguish voiceless and voiced consonants in syllable-final position, there may be some learners for whom [rɪʔ] represents their pronunciation of *rip, rib, writ, rid, rick, rig, rich* and *ridge*. Two arguments should be presented to such learners. Firstly, use of the glottal stop in these contexts is stigmatized. Secondly, the plosive and affricate sounds of English are represented quite regularly in spelling, as the letters *p, b, t, d, ck, g, (t)ch* and *dge.* Any learner who does not distinguish them in pronunciation may find it difficult to remember their spelling.

Nasals

We saw in the previous chapter that nasals (nasal stops) involve a complete closure between the articulators in the mouth, but there is a velic opening between the velum and the back wall of the pharynx, allowing air to escape through the nose. To show this, say an [m] sound and pinch your nostrils. You will soon stop because the air can no longer escape through the nose.

There are three nasals in English: [m, n, ŋ]. They are all voiced. The [m] sound is bilabial, the [n] sound alveolar, and the [ŋ] sound velar. The main sound-to-spelling correspondences (from Carney, 1994) are given in Table 7.4.

Table 7.4 Sound-to-spelling correspondences for [m, n, ŋ]

Sound	*Spelling*	*% of the time in connected speech*	*Example words*
[m]	*m*	96	*money*
	mm	3	*summer*
	others	1	
[n]	*n*	97	*need*
	nn	1	*tunnel*
	others	2	
[ŋ]	*ng*	75*	*sing*
	n	25*	*sink*

*These figures do not include the common *-ing* inflection.

Nasal approach and release

For a plosive such as [b], two closures are required. Firstly the two lips form a complete closure in the mouth. Secondly, there is a velic closure, preventing air from escaping through the nose. In most cases, such as the word *abbey,* where the [b] is surrounded by vowels, the [b] plosive is formed (approached) by closing the lips. However, where the [b] is preceded by an [m] sound as in the word *amber,* the approach is not by closing the lips, because the lips are already closed for [m]. Instead, the velum, which is open for [m], needs to close for [b]. This is known as *nasal approach* and can be shown by Figure 7.4.

Nasal release is the opposite of this. When a [b] sound is followed by an [m] sound, as in the word *submerge,* the plosive is not released by opening the lips, because they need to remain closed for the [m]. Instead, the velum, which is closed for [b], opens to allow air out through the nose. This is shown by Figure 7.5, which is the mirror image of Figure 7.4.

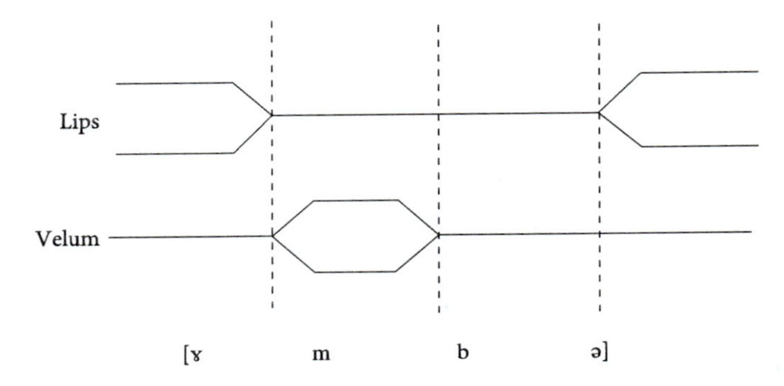

Figure 7.4 Nasal approach (*amber*).

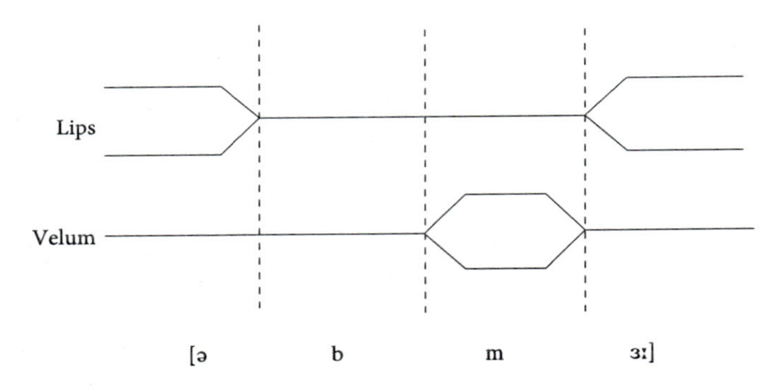

Figure 7.5 Nasal release (*submerge*).

Notice that, in both *amber* and *submerge,* the nasal [m] is at the same place of articulation (bilabial) as the plosive [b]. Two sounds that have the same place of articulation are called *homorganic,* from *homo-* 'same' and *organ.*

Anticipatory nasalization

For nasals, the velum must be open, to allow air to escape through the nose. The timing of the opening of the velum may not coincide precisely with other articulatory events. For example, take the word *ram* [ræm]. For the [æ] vowel, the lips are open, and the velum is closed. For the [m] that follows, the lips are closed, and the velum is open. The changes in position of these two articulators may not coincide. It is common for the velum to open slightly earlier than the closing of the lips. In other words, in the latter part of the vowel, air may escape through both the mouth and nose (see Figure 7.6). This is known as a nasalized vowel, and is symbolized thus: [ræ̃m].

Since English, unlike other languages such as French, does not have distinct nasalized vowels, most English speakers are unaware of this natural process. It is a form of assimilation (see chapter 16).

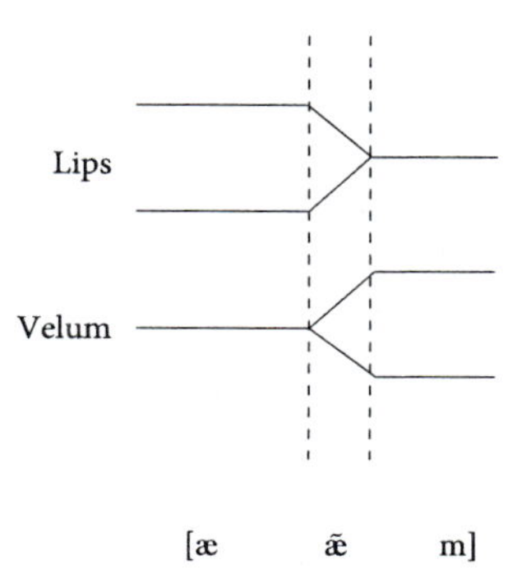

Figure 7.6 Anticipatory nasalization (*ram*).

Summary

- Plosives involve complete closure in the mouth and a velic closure preventing air from escaping through the nose. Air does not escape.
- They are analyzed as having three phases: approach, hold, release.
- There are six plosives in English: [p, b, t, d, k, g].
- Nasals involve complete closure in the mouth, but a velic opening, allowing air to escape through the nose.
- There are three nasals in English: [m, n, ŋ].
- Plosives preceded by homorganic nasals have nasal approach (closing the velum). Those followed by homorganic nasals have nasal release (opening the velum).

Exercises

1. Do the following words start with a plosive or nasal? If so, which one?

build	*done*	*ketchup*	*part*	*quiche*
chaos	*gas*	*khaki*	*physics*	*quick*
chef	*germ*	*knife*	*PM*	*term*
chest	*gnaw*	*MP*	*pneumatic*	*think*
court	*GP*	*NB*	*pterodactyl*	*Thomas*

2. Do the following words end with a plosive or nasal? If so, which one?

bag	*bring*	*herb*	*OK*	*sick*
ballet	*bullet*	*herd*	*panic*	*sponge*
barge	*climb*	*liked*	*ripe*	*start*
blurred	*GP*	*monarch*	*rode*	*wrong*

3. Explain the following mishearings (known as mondegreens and discussed further in chapter 16):

- When I first heard the name of the 1920s jazz musician Bix Beiderbecke, I thought it was Bick Spiderbecke.
- Many people misheard the lyrics of the Jimi Hendrix song *Purple Haze* not as *Excuse me while I kiss the sky* but as *Excuse me while I kiss this guy.*

Further reading

All the vowels and consonants of English are explained in much greater detail in standard phonetics books such as Cruttenden (2008), Roach (2009) for SSBE; and Avery and Ehrlich (1992), Edwards (2003), Yavaş (2011) for GenAm. Symbols for SSBE are introduced and practiced in Brown (2005). For a detailed analysis of stops, fricatives and approximants, see Catford (2001). The dynamic parametric approach to phonetic description is promoted in Nakamura (2005) and Tench (1978).

8 Fricatives and affricates

She sells seashells by the seashore.

Tongue twister, believed to refer to Mary Anning (1799–1847), discoverer of ichthyosaur fossils

Learning objectives

At the end of this chapter, you will be able to:

- explain the terms *fricative* and *affricate*
- illustrate the nine fricative and two affricate sounds of English
- list the main sound-spelling correspondences of these sounds.

Fricatives

We have already discussed fricatives in some depth. For instance, in chapter 3, we described the pronunciation of [h], a voiceless glottal fricative. A small gap is left between the two articulators (the vocal cords for [h]) and, as the air passes through, a hissing noise known as *frication* is produced.

In many phonetics books, this hissing noise is referred to as *friction*, rather than *frication*. However, this seems a misleading term. Friction in physics normally means the resistance when one body is moved in contact with another. It is a kind of rubbing, and as a result often produces heat. The hissing noise of fricatives is nothing like this. The two articulators are not in contact—there is a small gap between them. And no heat is produced.

Fricatives in fact constitute the largest group of consonant sounds in English. There are nine altogether—four pairs of voiced and voiceless equivalents, plus [h]. The [h] sound cannot have a voiced equivalent, because for a glottal fricative a small gap must be left between the two vocal cords. So they cannot be vibrating for voice at the same time.

The four pairs of English fricatives are as follows. The sound [f] is a voiceless labio-dental fricative and [v] is a voiced labio-dental fricative. The lower lip comes towards (the front face of) the upper teeth, causing frication. The main sound-to-spelling correspondences for fricatives (from Carney, 1994) are given in Tables 8.1 ([f, v]), 8.2 ([θ, ð]), 8.3 ([s, z]), 8.4 ([ʃ, ʒ]) and 8.5 ([h]).

Table 8.1 Sound-to-spelling correspondences for [f, v]

Sound	*Spelling*	*% of the time in connected speech*	*Example words*
[f]	*f*	84	*fat*
	ph	11	*phone*
	ff	4	*offer*
	others	1	
[v]	*v*	100	*very*

The sound [θ] is a voiceless dental fricative and [ð] is a voiced dental fricative. The tongue tip and/or blade comes towards (the back face of) the upper teeth, causing frication.

Table 8.2 Sound-to-spelling correspondences for [θ, ð]

Sound	*Spelling*	*% of the time in connected speech*	*Example words*
[θ]	*th*	100	*thigh*
[ð]	*th*	100	*then*

The sound [s] is a voiceless alveolar fricative and [z] is a voiced alveolar fricative. The tongue tip and/or blade comes towards the alveolar ridge, causing frication.

Table 8.3 Sound-to-spelling correspondences for [s, z]

Sound	*Spelling*	*% of the time in connected speech*	*Example words*
[s]	*s, ss*	79	*sit, dress*
	c	15	*cent*
	others	6	
[z]	*s*	93	*rise*
	z, zz	5	*zero, jazz*
	others	2	

The sound [ʃ] is a voiceless palato-alveolar fricative and [ʒ] is a voiced palato-alveolar fricative. A large area of the tongue, comprising parts of the blade and front, comes towards a large area of the roof of the mouth, comprising parts of the alveolar ridge and hard palate, causing frication. For many speakers, there is some lip-rounding for both [ʃ, ʒ].

Table 8.4 Sound-to-spelling correspondences for [ʃ, ʒ]

Sound	*Spelling*	*% of the time in connected speech*	*Example words*
[ʃ]	*sh*	37	*ship*
	ch	1	*chef*
	others	55	Palatalization, eg *dictation, repulsion, logician*
	others	7	
[ʒ]	*s*	91	Palatalization, eg *occasion*
	g	4	*beige*
	others	5	

Palatalization is the process of an original [t, d, k, s, z] coalescing with a following [iː, j(uː)] to give the palato-alveolar sounds [tʃ, dʒ, ʃ, ʒ], eg *combustion, soldier, logician, repulsion, closure.*

The sound-to-spelling correspondences for [h] are given in Table 8.5.

Table 8.5 Sound-to-spelling correspondences for [h]

Sound	*Spelling*	*% of the time in connected speech*	*Example words*
[h]	*h*	99*	*home*
	wh	1*	*whole*

* Estimates (percentages not given by Carney)

Affricates

For the two affricates in English ([tʃ, dʒ]), a large area of the tongue, comprising parts of the blade and front, touches a large area of the roof of the mouth, comprising parts of the alveolar ridge and hard palate. After the initial complete closure, the tongue lowers with a hissing noise (a slow fricative release of the complete closure). Like the fricatives [ʃ, ʒ], they are palato-alveolar and involve lip-rounding for many speakers.

The sound [tʃ] is a voiceless palato-alveolar affricate and [dʒ] is a voiced palato-alveolar affricate (sound-to-spelling correspondences in Table 8.6).

Table 8.6 Sound-to-spelling correspondences for [tʃ, dʒ]

Sound	*Spelling*	*% of the time in connected speech*	*Example words*
[tʃ]	*ch*	65	*chest*
	tch	10	*match*
	others	25	Palatalization, eg *question, ritual*
[dʒ]	*g, ge, dge*	71	*gem, page, badge*
	j	29	*jug*

Summary

- Fricatives involve frication, the hissing noise caused by air escaping through a small gap left between the articulators.
- English has nine fricatives: [h], and the voiced/voiceless pairs [v, f], [ð, θ], [z, s] and [ʒ, ʃ].
- Affricates involve a complete closure followed by a fricative release.
- There are two affricates in English: [dʒ, tʃ].

Exercises

1. The spelling *ch* can represent the affricate [tʃ] in native English words and the fricative [ʃ] in French loanwords (in addition to the plosive [k] in Greek loanwords like *chaos*). Say the following words and decide if they have [tʃ] or [ʃ].

chair	*champagne*	*panache*	*rich*
chalet	*choose*	*quiche*	*such*

2. The dental fricatives [ð, θ] are always represented by *th* in English spelling. However, vice versa, the spelling *th* does not always represent [ð, θ]. In the following list, find those words that contain [ð, θ], and work out the two other possible pronunciations of *th*.

Arthur	*brother*	*lighthouse*	*Thames*	*Thomas*
bath	*carthorse*	*prophethood*	*then*	*those*
breath	*coathanger*	*sweetheart*	*thick*	*thought*
breathe	*Lesotho*	*Thailand*	*this*	*thyme*

3. The dental fricatives [θ, ð] may seem strange to foreigners, because (i) the sounds do not occur in many languages of the world (and therefore probably do not occur in the learners' native language), and (ii) dental fricatives are

often substituted for alveolar fricatives [s, z] when lisping, that is, as a speech defect. Tan's (1989) book *The Teenage Workbook* has a character named Kok Sean, who lapses into lisping. In the following extract, he is discussing Sissy Song, the school heart-throb, with his friend Chung Kai. Read it out loud. Remember that the spelling *th* may represent lisped versions of [s, z] or may be original [θ, ð].

'Hey, man,' Kok Sean nudged Chung Kai. 'Check it out. That'th the famouth Thithy Thong.' Kok Sean's lisp was returning ... he was getting excited. Kok Sean drooled slightly into his bowl of tau suan. He continued. 'She'th a perfect 10, man. Look at that fathe. Ethel Fong would give her life thavingth to wear that fathe. Look at that body. And thothe legth ... Ay, look who'th thitting bethide her—that girl you're alwayth bumping into.'

Kok Sean said, 'Ay, what thay you we move in on them?'

'What?'

Kok Sean was already at Sissy's table.

'Hello, girlth,' Kok Sean gave them his ladykiller smile. 'Do you know, I wath jutht thitting behind you, and I thought to mythelf, thith girl remindth me of thomeone. You mutht be a model. Haven't I theen you in GO magazine?'

Sissy smiled sweetly. She said, 'Oh, so you can read?'

Undeterred, Kok Sean pressed on. 'No, theriouthly, I looked at you and I thaid to mythelf, "That girl ith a perfect 10."'

Sissy smiled even more sweetly, 'I think you're a perfect 10 as well. And that's just your IQ.'

Further reading

All the vowels and consonants of English are explained in much greater detail in standard phonetics books such as Cruttenden (2008), Roach (2009) for SSBE; and Avery and Ehrlich (1992), Edwards (2003), Yavaş (2011) for GenAm. Symbols for SSBE are introduced and practiced in Brown (2005). For a detailed analysis of stops, fricatives and approximants, see Catford (2001).

9 Approximants

Red lorry, yellow lorry.

Tongue twister, and name of a 1980s British rock band

Learning objectives

At the end of this chapter, you will be able to:

- define the terms *approximant* and *lateral*
- list the main sound-spelling correspondences of these sounds in English
- explain the main variants of approximant and lateral sounds.

Introduction

In chapter 6, we defined approximants as sounds where the active articulator comes towards the passive. It does not form complete closure (so it is not a stop), nor does it create frication (so it is not a fricative). Instead, the shape of the vocal tract, especially the tongue, gives the sound a characteristic resonant quality. In this respect, approximants are similar to vowel sounds.

There are four approximants in English: [l, r, w, j]. They are all voiced, as are vowels. The [l] sound is a lateral approximant (often abbreviated to simply *lateral*), while the others are central approximants (often abbreviated to simply *approximants*). However, we will consider them all here, because they often function in similar ways. For instance, in chapter 11, we will see that all four can occur after a plosive at the beginning of words and syllables, e.g. *clip, cry, queen, cute* [klɪp, kraɪ, kwiːn, kjuːt].

The [w] and [j] sounds

If you pronounce very long [w] and [j] sounds, you will find that they sound very like the vowels [uː] and [iː]. In terms of their articulation, they are. However, they do not function like vowels. In English, there are one-syllable words *pet, bet, debt, get, jet, fait, vet, set, met, net* and *let*. They all have the form [*et], and the position shown by the asterisk is filled by [p, b, d, ɡ, dʒ, f, v, s, m, n, l], all of which are indisputably consonants. There are also the words *wet* and *yet*, where the first sounds fill the same position as the previous consonants. This is why, although the [w] and [j] sounds are articulated like vowels, they are classified as consonants. These two sounds are often called *semi-vowels* (but still considered consonants).

The [j] and [w] sounds are both voiced central approximants. In terms of place, the [j] sound is simply palatal. The place for [w] is more complex. It undoubtedly involves lip-rounding, and thus many textbooks use the term *bilabial* for it. However, as we have seen, it also involves the back of the tongue rising towards the velum (as for an [uː] vowel) and can therefore be called velar too. The most precise word for its place is thus the two-part term *labial-velar*, meaning that it involves approximant gestures at both the bilabial and velar places. The main sound-to-spelling correspondences (from Carney, 1994) are given in Table 9.1.

Table 9.1 Sound-to-spelling correspondences for [w, j]

Sound	*Spelling*	*% of the time in connected speech*	*Example words*
[w]	*w*	64	*well*
	qu (= [kw])	27	*quick*
	wh	5	*wheel*
	u	4	*language*
	others	<1	
[j]	*y*	19	*yet*
	as part of [juː]	*	*use*
	reduction of an underlying [iː, ɪ]	*	*behavior*

*Because of problems of assigning letters to the sound [j], Carney does not give full frequency figures.

The [l] and [r] sounds

These two sounds are well known as pronunciation problems for learners from Japan, Korea and other Asian countries. As we will see below, there is a fair amount of variation in the way these two sounds are pronounced in English.

The [r] sound

Of all the consonant and vowel sounds, [r] is generally considered to have the greatest variation among different accents of English. One pervasive difference is the fact that many speakers, including most Americans and GenAm, pronounce [r] in syllable-final position in words like *farmer* (thus [fɑːrmər]), while others, including the SSBE accent, do not (thus [fɑːmə]). However, this relates to the function of [r] in particular positions in syllables, and will be treated in chapter 11 (rhotic versus non-rhotic accents).

What we are interested in here is the way [r] is pronounced, not the way that it functions. The pronunciation of [r] as a voiced post-alveolar central approximant in SSBE entails the tongue tip curling back slightly. However, it does not touch the roof of the mouth, but is held in a position below the back of the alveolar region. This is why the place name is known as *post-alveolar*. In some textbooks, the place of [r] is given as the same as for [ʃ, ʒ, tʃ, dʒ]. However, it is clear that they involve very different tongue shapes and positions. The vocal cords are vibrating. The symbol for explicitly this kind of [r] is [ɹ]. The position of the tongue, as seen from a front-to-back perspective (called a *coronal* section) is shown in Figure 9.1.

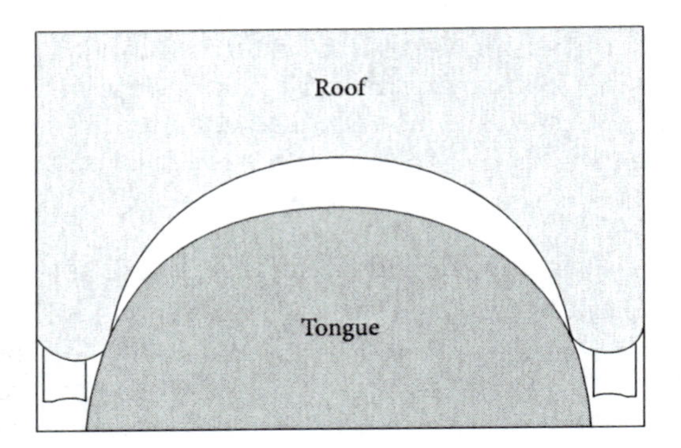

Figure 9.1 Tongue position for [r].

In many American accents, including GenAm, the tongue is curled further back than in SSBE. This is known as a retroflex (rather than post-alveolar) articulation, for which the symbol is [ɻ].

The main sound-to-spelling correspondences (from Carney, 1994) are given in Table 9.2.

Table 9.2 Sound-to-spelling correspondences for [r]

Sound	*Spelling*	*% of the time in connected speech*	*Example words*
	r	94	*real*
[r]	*rr*	4	*carry*
	others	2	

Types of [r]

While the description of [r] as a voiced post-alveolar (SSBE) or retroflex (GenAm) central approximant is accurate, many other pronunciations of [r] are found in accents of English.

A trilled [r] is stereotypically associated with Scottish speakers. The sound is produced by holding the tip of the tongue near the alveolar ridge and at such a muscular tension that the airstream causes it to vibrate aerodynamically against the alveolar ridge. It produces a series of rapid taps, usually only three or four in normal speech. In fact, it is more usual in Scottish, Welsh, South African and Indian speech, not to produce a series of taps, but a single tap in this way (symbol [ɾ]).

In certain northeast England accents, instead of a post-alveolar approximant, a uvular approximant is used. This is produced by raising the back of the tongue towards the uvula, the soft piece of flesh hanging in the middle of the velum, without causing frication. If frication is caused, a uvular fricative is produced. The symbol for both sounds is [ʁ].

In a similar way to the alveolar trill, a uvular trill is produced by holding the back of the tongue close to the uvula, which then vibrates against it as an aerodynamic movement (symbol [ʀ]).

As can be seen, [r] is a sound that has probably the greatest amount of variation in accents of English. The above are the common variants, but the discussion does not exhaust all the possibilities.

The [l] sound

The [l] sound, being a voiced alveolar lateral approximant, is produced by touching the alveolar ridge with the tip of the tongue. However, this contact only occurs in the center of the vocal tract. The sides of the tongue are not touching, allowing air to escape over the sides. Since there are two sides to the tongue, air can escape over both sides at the same time, although it is possible to let air escape over only one side or the other, without any great change in the sound. The vocal cords are vibrating. The position of the tongue, as seen from a front-to-back perspective is shown in Figure 9.2.

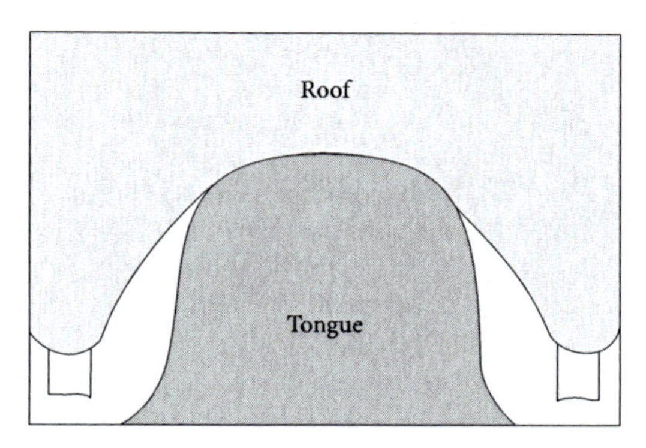

Figure 9.2 Tongue position for [l].

Comparing Figure 9.2 with 9.1, the difference between an [l] and an [r] sound is clear. For [l], the tongue tip touches the roof of the mouth; for [r] it does not.

The main sound-to-spelling correspondences (from Carney, 1994) are given in Table 9.3.

Table 9.3 Sound-to-spelling correspondences for [l]

Sound	*Spelling*	*% of the time in connected speech*	*Example words*
	l	75	*lamp*
[l]	*ll*	18	*follow*
	le	8	*castle*

Clear and dark [l]

The three-term label *voiced alveolar lateral approximant* only tells us what the tip of the tongue is doing. It says nothing about the rest of the tongue. In many accents of English, including SSBE, two positions of the body of the tongue may be distinguished.

In syllable-initial position, as in a word like *lick* [lɪk], the body of the tongue is bunched upwards and forwards towards the hard palate, giving a light or clear quality to the sound. In contrast, in syllable-final position, as in a word like *kill* [kɪl], the body is bunched upwards and backwards towards the velum, giving a dark quality. This variation has nothing to do with surrounding sounds ([ɪ] for both the above words), but with the position in the syllable. The symbols for these types of [l] are [l̥] for clear [l] and [ɫ] for dark [l]. Since the upward and forward bunching of the tongue corresponds to its position for high front vowel [i], and since the upward and backward bunching corresponds to its position for a high back vowel [u], alternative symbols for these sounds are [lⁱ, lᵘ]. The tongue positions are shown in Figure 9.3.

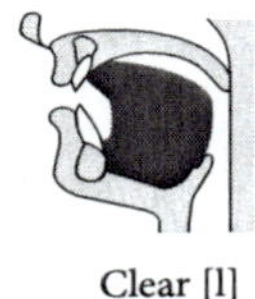

Clear [l]

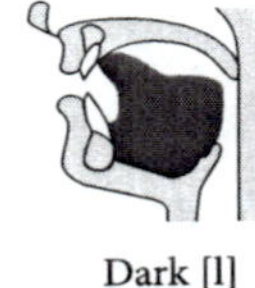

Dark [l]

Figure 9.3 Tongue positions for clear and dark [l].
Source: Wells & Colson, 1971

In GenAm, [l] is generally darker in all positions than SSBE, particularly between vowels, as in *jelly*.

Vocalic and absorbed [l]

We have already noted that approximants share many characteristics with vowel sounds. The only difference between a dark [l] and a high back vowel is that the tip of the tongue touches the alveolar ridge for [l]. In some accents of English, this tongue tip contact is lost, leaving only a high back vowel tongue position, usually symbolized by [ʊ]. Thus, the word *kill* is pronounced as [kɪʊ] instead of [kɪl]. The pronunciation is now totally vowel-like, and is known as vocalic [l]. To complete the picture, it often has lip-rounding, as do high back vowels in English.

This vocalic pronunciation of what would otherwise be a dark [l] is becoming increasingly common in English accents in Britain and the USA (Scobbie and Wrench, 2003).

As a further step, where dark or vocalic [l] follows a rounded back vowel, especially [ɔː], it may be totally absorbed into that vowel. Thus *fault* may be pronounced identically to *fought*: [fɔːt]. Historically, this is precisely what has happened to words like *walk, talk* and *chalk*. Original [l] sounds have been absorbed into the preceding [ɔː] vowels. The *l* letters in the spelling are a vestige of this.

Lateral approach and release

In chapter 7, we discussed nasal approach and release. This is the situation where a plosive is preceded or followed by its homorganic nasal, e.g. [mp, pm]. In order to form or release the [p] plosive, the lips do not need to move because they are also in complete closure for [m]. The change is therefore effected by closing or opening the velum.

A similar situation applies to plosives preceded or followed by the lateral [l]. Since [l] is the only lateral in English, and is alveolar, the plosive must be [t, d]. In short, we are talking about [lt, tl, ld, dl] sequences, as in *alto, atlas, elder* and *sadly*. For the lateral [l], there is closure between the tongue and the alveolar ridge in the center of the mouth, but not at the sides. For the plosives [t, d], there is complete closure both in the center and at the sides. In going from an [l] to a [t, d], the tongue tip is already in the right position against the alveolar ridge—only the sides of the tongue need to be raised and make contact. And vice versa for [t, d] followed by [l], only the sides need to be lowered and lose contact. Figure 9.4 shows the movements of the tip and sides of the tongue for *alto*.

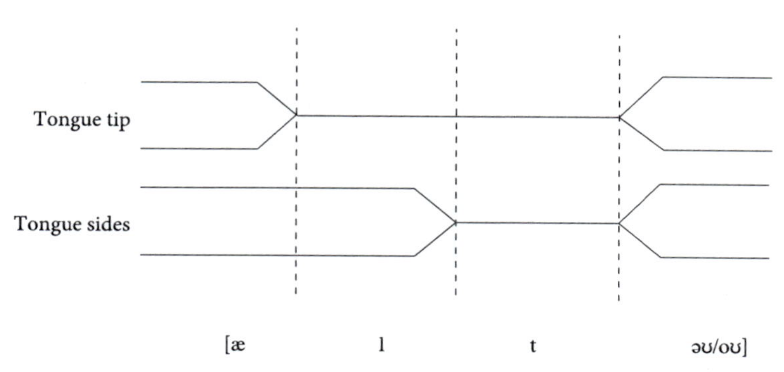

Figure 9.4 Lateral approach (*alto*).

The consonant inventory of English

We have now completed our analysis of consonants, examining the way consonants are classified (chapter 6), and the 24 consonants of English: plosives and nasals (chapter 7), fricatives and affricates (chapter 8) and approximants (this chapter). For easy reference, the consonants of English are typically shown in a table (Figure 9.5), where the columns represent the places of articulation, and the rows the manners of articulation. Voiceless consonants are conventionally shown on the left of any cell in the table, and voiced consonants on the right.

Place Manner	Bilabial	Labio-dental	Dental	Alveolar	Post-alveolar	Palato-alveolar	Palatal	Velar	Glottal
Plosive	p b			t d				k g	
Nasal	m			n				ŋ	
Affricate						tʃ dʒ			
Fricative		f v	θ ð	s z		ʃ ʒ			h
Lateral				l					
Approximant	w				r		j		

Figure 9.5 The consonant chart of English.

Summary

- Approximants do not involve compete closure or frication.
- There are four approximants in English: [l] is a lateral approximant, and the other three [r, w, j] are central approximants.
- While [w, j] are articulated like vowels, they function like consonants. They are often called *semi-vowels*.

Exercises

1. Each of the following words starts with one of the four approximants. Which one?

   Europe *once* *U* *wrinkle*
   ewe *red* *union* *Y*
   like *rhyme* *water* *yes*

2. We have now completed our description of all the 24 consonants of English. Which ones:

   - must involve some movement of the lips?
   - are typically accompanied by lip-rounding?

Further reading

All the vowels and consonants of English are explained in much greater detail in standard phonetics books such as Cruttenden (2008), Roach (2009) for SSBE; and Avery and Ehrlich (1992), Edwards (2003), Yavaş (2011) for GenAm. Symbols for SSBE are introduced and practiced in Brown (2005). For a detailed analysis of stops, fricatives and approximants, see Catford (2001); he calls approximants *resonants*.

10 Non-English sounds

I always feel so ugly when I speak German.

Oscar Wilde (1854–1900), Irish playwright

Learning objectives

At the end of this chapter, you will be able to:

- list some non-English categories of sound
- list some non-English sounds.

Introduction

We have completed our introduction of the consonant and vowel sounds of English. Consonant sounds are typically placed on a consonant chart (see chapter 9). They can also be described by three-term labels, such as *voiceless alveolar fricative* ([s]). Vowels, on the other hand, can be represented diagrammatically by plotting the position of the highest point of the tongue on a trapezium (see chapter 4). They can also be described, somewhat less accurately than consonants, by five-term labels such as *high front unrounded long monophthong* ([iː]). We thus arrive at the consonant and vowel charts to be found in all introductory books on English phonetics.

You may be wondering what other sounds are humanly possible, and what other sounds occur in other languages. For instance, the six rows and nine columns of the English consonant chart (see Figure 9.5) give us 54 pigeonholes. Given that voiceless and voiced consonants (e.g. [s, z]) are conventionally put in the same pigeonhole (voiceless on the left, voiced on the right), this gives us 108 possibilities. Are these the only 108 humanly possible consonant sounds? English has only 24 consonant sounds. Do the other 84 exist, or is there some other reason that they do not? There are various reasons why other sounds do or do not exist.

Non-pulmonic consonants

The consonant chart (see Figure 9.5) only shows the consonants of English. They are all made on a pulmonic egressive airstream, as are almost all consonants in languages of the world. However, other airstreams do exist. In chapter 3, we mentioned the click sounds found in some languages. Such sounds are normally put in a separate chart.

Incompatibility of categories

Some pigeonholes cannot be filled, because the two categories cannot combine. For example, there is no such thing as a glottal nasal. A nasal means that there is a complete closure in the mouth and the air escapes through the nose. However, a complete closure between the vocal cords (the glottal place of articulation) would not allow air to reach the nose.

Extra categories

Other places and manners of articulation are possible. For instance, many Indian languages have an extra place of articulation, not found in English. The tongue is curled back and moves towards/against the back of the alveolar region or front of the palatal region. This is known as *retroflex*. Plosives, nasals and fricatives are all possible at this place of articulation (symbols [ʈ, ɖ, ɳ, ʂ, ʐ]). Consonant charts for these Indian languages would therefore have an extra, retroflex column.

Non-English sounds

While there are a large number of humanly possible sounds, each language 'chooses' which sounds it contains from this inventory. And languages 'choose' differently. Some languages simply have more sounds than others.

Various non-English consonants exist in languages. For example, we have already explained what *voiceless* means (the vocal cords are not vibrating), what *velar* means (the back of the tongue articulates with the velum), and what *fricative* means (a small gap is left between the articulators, causing frication). A voiceless velar fricative (symbol [x]) does not occur in English, but does occur in other languages, including German (e.g. *Bach* [bax] 'stream' and the name of the composer), Scots Gaelic (e.g. *loch* [lɒx] 'lake') and Arabic (e.g. [xair] 'good').

Similarly, we know what *voiced* means (the vocal cords are vibrating), what *palatal* means (the tongue front articulates with the palate), and what *lateral* means (the articulator touches in the center, and air escapes over the sides). A voiced palatal lateral (symbol [ʎ]) occurs in Italian (e.g. *gli* [ʎi] 'the'), Portuguese (e.g. *carvalho* [karvaʎo] 'oak') and Catalan (e.g. *lluna* [ʎunə] 'moon').

English has the affricates [tʃ, dʒ]. Other affricates, such as [ts], occur in languages. Just as English [tʃ, dʒ] are analyzed as single sounds (phonemes), so is [ts] in these languages. They include Italian (e.g. *pizza* [pitsa] 'pizza') and Bantu (e.g. *tsetse* [tsetse] 'tsetse fly').

Just as non-English consonants exist in other languages, so do non-English vowels. The English [iː] vowel is a high front unrounded vowel. If the tongue is kept in the same high front position, but the lips are rounded, the resultant sound has the symbol [y]. It occurs in languages such as French (e.g. *pur* [pyr] 'pure'), German (e.g. *für* [fyr] 'for') and Mandarin (e.g. [y] 'pedantry').

Likewise, [uː] is a high back rounded vowel. If the tongue is kept in the same high back position, but the lips are unrounded, the resultant sound has the symbol [ɯ]. It occurs in languages such as Japanese (e.g. [kɯki] 'air'), Vietnamese (e.g. *tu* [tɯ], 'fourth') and Thai (e.g. [tʃɯ] 'name').

Conclusion

The purpose of this short chapter is to point out that English sounds are precisely that—the sounds of English. Other sounds occur in other languages. And vice versa: some English sounds are not common in other languages. For instance, the voiceless dental fricative [θ] occurs in English (e.g. *think* [θɪŋk]), but not in many other languages. Counterexamples include Greek and classical Arabic.

The relevance of this point is that learners of English bring with them the consonant and vowel sounds of their native language. There may be substantial differences between the phonology of their native language(s) and that of English. Problems in learning English sounds are often attributable to the fact that an English sound does not occur in their native language, and/or that it functions in very different ways. This method of comparing the phonologies of the two languages in order to predict such problems is known as Contrastive Analysis (see chapter 29).

Summary

- Many more sounds (both consonants and vowels) are possible than occur in English.
- Learners' native languages may differ from English in the consonant and vowel sounds they contain.
- This may help in identifying the source of pronunciation problems.

Exercise

If you are a teacher with foreign learners, ask them to pronounce something in their native language, such as a rhyme or their national anthem. Listen and try to identify sounds that are substantially different from English. Then, with the learner as a native informant, try to master those sounds. Learning the 'strange' pronunciation of a foreign language is a good way of putting yourself in your learners' shoes.

Further reading

If the sounds of languages of the world fascinate you, and you are prepared to put in extra work, see Ladefoged and Maddieson (1995). Humanly possible sounds, and their symbols, are introduced in the International Phonetic Association (1999).

11 Syllable structure

Syllables govern the world.

John Selden (1584–1654), English jurist and writer

Learning objectives

At the end of this chapter, you will be able to:

- explain why the syllable is an important unit of speech
- describe the structure of the English syllable
- give some syllable structure rules of English
- show how loanwords are integrated into borrowing languages.

Introduction

It is intuitive to think that the word is the most important unit in language. However, in discussing pronunciation, the syllable is an equally important—if not more important—unit. There are several reasons for this.

- Everyone, regardless of their native language and its writing system, seems to be able to identify how many syllables words contain.
- Some differences between languages can only be stated in terms of the syllable and its structure.
- These differences are likely to lead to difficulties for foreign learners in pronouncing certain English combinations.
- Literacy experts are agreed that an awareness of the syllables in a word, the sounds that make up the syllables, and of phenomena such as alliteration and rhyme, are essential for efficient spellers of English.

The syllables that make up words can be analyzed in terms of three positions. The minimal type of syllable is composed of only a vowel, e.g. *eye* [aɪ]. The vowel is therefore considered a central part of any syllable, and is in peak position (also called *nuclear, syllabic* and *syllable-medial*). Before the vowel, there may be one or more consonants, e.g. *tie* [taɪ], *sty* [staɪ]. This position is known as the onset (also called *syllable-initial*

Table 11.1 Syllable structure of various English words

Word	*Onset*	*Peak*	*Coda*	*Formula*
eye		aɪ		OVO
isle		aɪ	l	OVC
tie	t	aɪ		CVO
tile	t	aɪ	l	CVC
isles		aɪ	lz	OVCC
sty	st	aɪ		CCVO
style	st	aɪ	l	CCVC
tiles	t	aɪ	lz	CVCC
styles	st	aɪ	lz	CCVCC

or *releasing*). After the vowel, there may also be one or more consonants, e.g. *isle* [aɪl], *isles* [aɪlz]. This position is known as the coda (also called *syllable-final* or *arresting*). Table 11.1 shows various possibilities, where C stands for any consonant, V for any vowel, and O for an empty position. Syllables with an empty coda position are called *open* syllables, while *closed* syllables have final consonants.

Where there is more than one consonant in either onset or coda position, this is known as a cluster. So the last five possibilities above contain clusters. The largest cluster in onset position in English has three consonants, as in *string* [strɪŋ]. The largest cluster in the coda has four consonants, as in *sculpts* [skʌlpts]. We can represent this by the formula C_{0-3} V C_{0-4}. This is more complex than for most languages. Syllable structure formulae for other languages are given in Table 11.2.

Table 11.2 Syllable structure of various languages

Maori	C_{0-1} V O	(only V and CV syllables)
Cantonese	C_{0-1} V C_{0-1}	(no clusters)
Spanish	C_{0-2} V C_{0-1}	(initial clusters but no final clusters)
Arabic	C_{0-1} V C_{0-2}	(final clusters but no initial clusters)
Russian	C_{0-4} V C_{0-4}	

Alliteration

Syllables are said to alliterate if they contain identical onsets. Imperfect alliteration involves syllables whose onsets are not quite identical. Alliteration is a common feature of poetry and other genres.

He who laughs last laughs longest.

Hear the loud alarum bells–
Brazen bells!
What a tale of terror, now, their turbulency tells!

Edgar Allen Poe, *The Bells*

Note the [l] of *loud* and *alarum*, the [b] of *brazen bells*, and the [t] of *tale, terror, turbulency* and *tells*.

Rhyme

While alliteration relates to onset position, rhyme relates to the other two (peak and coda). Two syllables rhyme if they have identical peaks and codas (together called rhymes or rimes). Thus, *tile* rhymes with *while* because they both end in [-aɪl]. Multi-syllable words rhyme if everything is identical from the vowel of the stressed syllable onwards, e.g. *computer* and *tutor* rhyme because they have identical [uːtə(r)] from the stressed [uː] vowel. Rhymes are an important part of poetry, song lyrics, rapping, and so on.

> Humpty Dumpty sat on a wall. [wɔːl]
> Humpty Dumpty had a great fall. [fɔːl]
> All the king's horses and all the king's men [men]
> Couldn't put Humpty together again. [əgen]

Syllable structure rules

What follows are some of the major syllable structure rules for English, in the sense of generalizations about what does and does not occur. The technical term for syllable structure is phonotactics.

- The [r] consonant does not occur in the coda in the SSBE accent in words like *murder*. However, many other accents of English, such as GenAm, do allow [r] in the coda. This is a major division in accents of English worldwide between those that allow syllable-final [r] (known as *rhotic* accents) and those that do not (*non-rhotic*). Rhotic accents are in the majority in terms of numbers of speakers, and include most of the USA (including GenAm), most of Canada, Scotland, Ireland, parts of England, and Southland New Zealand. Non-rhotic accents include most of England (including SSBE), Wales, Australia, most of New Zealand, South Africa, and eastern and southern parts of the USA.

  The historical picture is that, in Shakespeare's time, all English speakers were rhotic. It was at this time that the spelling of English became standardized (see chapter 31). As a result, the spelling-sound rule for modern-day rhotic speakers is simple: if there is an *r* letter in the spelling, there is an [r] sound in the pronunciation. However, r-dropping (that is, non-rhoticity) then spread out from southeast England, and to those countries where non-rhotic English speakers migrated (Australia, New Zealand). Syllable-final *r* letters are therefore not pronounced as [r] sounds for these speakers.

  This book uses both SSBE and GenAm as reference accents. As a result, transcriptions may include an [r] in brackets [(r)], meaning that the [r] is pronounced in rhotic GenAm but not in non-rhotic SSBE.
- The velar nasal [ŋ] is never syllable-initial (in the onset) in English. This rule holds for English, but not necessarily other languages. For example, Malay, Thai and Maori all allow syllable-initial [ŋ].

- The [h] consonant is never syllable-final (in the coda) in English. Other languages, such as Arabic and Malay, allow syllable-final [h].
- The [w, j] sounds cannot occur in the coda.
- The [ʒ] sound does not occur at the beginning of words in English, apart from rare French loanwords such as *genre*. Similarly, it does not occur at the end of words, except in French loanwords like *camouflage*. In short, it only occurs in the middle of words, such as *vision*. It is a moot point whether this represents a syllable-initial or syllable-final occurrence (see *Difficulties in syllabification* below).
- In a stressed syllable without a final consonant, the vowel must be a long vowel or diphthong. English long vowels can occur in closed stressed syllables: *seat, calm, pawed, Luke* [siːt, kɑːm, pɔːd, luːk]. They can also occur in open stressed syllables: *see, pa, paw, lieu* [siː, pɑː, pɔː, luː]. Short vowels, on the other hand, only occur in closed stressed syllables: *sit, come, pod, look* [sɪt, kʌm, pɒd, lʊk]. They do not occur in open stressed syllables. Thus there are no words in English such as [sɪ, kʌ, pɒ, lʊ].
- In SSBE, if [ŋ] is a final consonant, then the vowel must be a short vowel: [ɪ] as in *sing*, [æ] as in *hang*, [ʌ] as in *lung*, or [ɒ] as in *strong*. It cannot be a long vowel. Thus [iːŋ, ɜːŋ, uːŋ, eəŋ, aʊŋ] and so on all sound un-English. The only exceptions to this are the result of assimilation (see chapter 16), e.g. *bean curd* [biːnkɜː(r)d] > [biːŋ kɜː(r)d].
- If, in a two-consonant initial cluster, the second consonant is [j], then the vowel is [uː, ʊə] in stressed syllables, for example *pure, few*, [pjʊə, fjuː] (or [ʊ, ə] in unstressed, e.g. *regular* [regjʊlə]). There are very few exceptions to this rule, for instance possible pronunciations of *piano, fjord*.
- Two-consonant initial clusters have two main forms:
  - [s] + a variety of consonants (voiceless plosives, nasals and approximants), e.g. *sky, sneeze* [skaɪ, sniːz].
  - a variety of consonants (plosives and voiceless fricatives) + [l, r, w, j], e.g. *quiz, three, fly* [kwɪz, θriː, flaɪ].
- The possibilities for three-consonant initial clusters are very limited. Their form is [s] + voiceless plosive ([p, t, k]) + [l, r, w, j], e.g. *splash, stripe, squid* [splæʃ, straɪp, skwɪd].
- The third and fourth consonants of three- and four-consonant final clusters are [t, d, s, z, θ]. Very often these represent suffixes (endings for past tense, plural, etc.).

Difficulties in syllabification

There are two main problems in deciding on the division of words into syllables.

Number of syllables

Speakers may differ in their opinions as to the number of syllables particular words have. These differences may arise from the following factors:

- ***Elision of [ə]:*** As we will see in chapter 16, [ə] may be lost in certain environments, e.g. *comfortable* [kʌmfətəbəl] (four syllables) or [kʌmftəbəl] (three).
- ***Morphology:*** The word *evening* is one unit of meaning (*morpheme*) in *good evening*, but is two morphemes (*even* + *ing*) in *evening out numbers.*
- ***Spelling:*** The letter *a* in the spelling may lead speakers to believe there are three syllables in *pedaling*, but only two in *peddling*, even though they both come from verbs pronounced [pedəl].
- ***Long vowels + dark [l]:*** The vocalic nature of the darkness of dark [l] may lead to different opinions, e.g. whether *boil* is one syllable or two.
- ***Triphthongs:*** Differences exist as to the syllabification of SSBE triphthongs, e.g. *fire* [faɪə].

Syllable boundaries

While speakers can usually tell how many syllables a word has, there may be confusion as to where one syllable ends and the next begins, e.g. whether a consonant between two vowels belongs with the first or the second syllable. Various principles have been proposed to handle this. Reasonably uncontroversial ones are the following:

- Syllable boundaries cannot divide the affricates [tʃ, dʒ].
- Syllable divisions cannot create clusters which are otherwise impermissible.
- Syllable boundaries occur at morpheme boundaries e.g. *race-track*.

However, that still leaves a number of more controversial examples, and the following principles (which are incompatible with each other) have been proposed:

- Intervocalic consonants go with the following vowel, wherever possible. This is known as the Maximum Onset Principle.
- Stressed syllables cannot end with a short vowel (that is, they must have a final consonant) and two consonants are split between the two syllables.
- Consonants go with whichever of the two vowels is more strongly stressed (or, if they are equally stressed, with the preceding vowel).

For many purposes, these are problems that do not need to be solved. As Wells (2000, p. xxi), who uses spaces in the *Longman Pronunciation Dictionary* to represent syllable boundaries, says, 'any user of the dictionary who finds it difficult to accept the LPD approach to syllabification can simply ignore the syllable spaces.'

Potential syllables

As stressed above, the syllable structure rules of English are simply generalizations based on the vocabulary of English. However, there are some outstanding problems that can be illustrated by the four syllables SSBE [spɪə, slɪə, sθɪə, sfɪə] or GenAm [spɪr, slɪr, sθɪr, sfɪr]. They can be categorized in terms of whether they are regular (that is, they follow the rules) and/or whether they are occurring (that is, they exist as or in words of English).

- ***Regular and occurring:*** The syllable [spɪə/spɪr] is both regular and occurring—it is the word *spear*. Since the syllable structure rules are generalizations based on the vocabulary of English, it is not surprising that occurring syllables are also regular.
- ***Regular but not occurring:*** The syllable [slɪə/slɪr] is also regular in that it does not break any of the syllable structure rules of English. The cluster [sl] is a permissible initial cluster, as in *sleep*. The [l] consonant can be followed by the [ɪə] vowel (SSBE) or [ɪr] (GenAm), as in *leer*. However, [slɪə/slɪr] happens not to occur as a word of English, or as a syllable in a multi-syllable word. We can call this a *potential* syllable.
- ***Irregular and not occurring:*** The syllable [sθɪə/sθɪr] is not occurring. It is also not regular, because [sθ] is not a permissible initial cluster in English. There are, for example, no words beginning [sθ]. This does not mean to say that English speakers cannot pronounce the [sθ] sequence – it occurs in words like *esthetic*. However, in such words, the [s] belongs to one syllable and the [θ] to the next – they are not a cluster, because clusters belong within the same syllable. In short, the initial cluster [sθ], and therefore the whole syllable [sθɪə, sθɪr], does not sound English. One could not imagine naming a new brand of washing powder [sθɪə/sθɪr], while one might name it [slɪə/slɪr].
- ***Irregular but occurring:*** This combination may seem paradoxical, given that we have said that the syllable structure rules are based on the vocabulary of English. However, syllables and words of this type are usually either of foreign origin, or onomatopoeic in nature. The syllable [sfɪə/sfɪr] is occurring, because it is the word *sphere*. However, it is irregular because:

  - there are no other two-consonant initial clusters in English where the two consonants have the same manner of articulation, i.e. two plosives such as [kt], two nasals such as [mn], etc., with the possible exception of [lj] as in *lurid*.
  - there are no two-consonant initial clusters in English where the second consonant is a fricative.

  The word *sphere* is of Greek origin. Other, rare [sf] words include *sphinx, sphincter, sphagnum*, all of Greek origin.

Integration of loanwords

The word *sphere* stands out as an unusual case, because when it was borrowed into English, its pronunciation (in particular, the [sf] initial cluster) was not changed to conform to English syllable structure rules. The [sf] cluster is permissible in Greek, but not in native English words. Some languages regularly integrate loanwords into their phonological system, while others (and English is a good example of this) do not. This integration may take two forms:

- Where the loanword contains a sound not present in the borrowing language's segmental inventory, the closest sound is usually substituted. For instance, the word *loch*, as in Loch Ness, is from Scottish Gaelic. The final sound is a voiceless velar fricative [x]. Since this is not a native English sound, the voiceless velar plosive [k] is often substituted (much to the annoyance of the Scots).

- Where the loanword contains clusters that are not permissible in the borrowing language, these clusters are broken up, usually by the insertion of vowels. This can be considered a kind of epenthesis (see chapter 17). For example, Japanese allows no clusters—its syllables are mostly CVO. When a word like *screwdriver*, with its [skr] and [dr] clusters, is borrowed into Japanese, it is pronounced [sikorudoraiba]. Note that, because vowels have been added, there are now six syllables in the Japanese pronunciation, compared with just three in the English. Note also that Japanese has no [v] sound, and [b] has been substituted.

An alternative method of dealing with clusters is for a language to simplify them by omitting one or more constituent sound.

Summary

- Syllable structure is an important component of any language's phonology.
- Most people, regardless of their native language, can say how many syllables most words have.
- Syllables are analyzed into three positions: onset (initial consonants, if any), peak (vowels) and coda (final consonants, if any).
- English syllable structure is more complex than that of most other languages.

Exercises

1. In what way, in terms of syllable structure, are the following English words unique? (Each one can be answered by saying 'It's the only word where . . .').

boing!	*fifth*	*sclerosis*	*sphragid*	*view*
depth	*kiln*	*smew*	*thwart*	*warmth*

2. A common pattern for two-consonant initial clusters is for the first consonant to be [s]. If the first consonant is [s], which consonants can be the second? List as many [s] + C clusters as you can, and give an example word for each (in both spelling and transcription), e.g. [sp] *spell* [spel].
3. Analyze the following syllables in terms of being regular and/or occurring in English. If irregular, state which part of the syllable is irregular. If irregular but occurring, explain why.

[stwæm]	[ɔɪŋk]	[fjel]	[tʃɪks]	[ʃliːzd]
[naʊn]	[snɑːm]	[smɑːh]	[sleɪp]	[rɑːʒ]

4. As we have seen, Japanese has no clusters. It only allows [n] in syllable-final position, and has no [l, θ, ð] among other consonants. Vowels and consonants can be long, as shown by a double symbol below. Can you recognize the following English words and expressions, as they are pronounced as loanwords in Japanese? (For the purposes of this task, you can ignore any problems with vowels and geminate consonants.)

[risuku]	[supaamaaketto]
[furasuko]	[buranketto]
[sutoresu]	[rimudʒin]
[hankatʃi]	[saamosutatto]
[erebeetaa]	[oosutoraria]
[aisukuriimu]	[makudonarudo]
[kosumetikku]	[rabu sutoorii]
[koresupondento]	[waiaresu maikurohon]

5. Since the time that Europeans came to New Zealand, many words for new concepts have been borrowed into Maori from English. Maori has the following consonants: [p, t, k, m, n, ŋ, f, h, r, w]. Notice that it does not have a number of consonants found in English: the voiced plosives [b, d, ɡ], any affricates, any of the fricatives except [f, h], the approximants [l, j]. Maori does not allow any clusters or final consonants. Bearing this in mind, can you match up the following English words on the left with their pronunciation as loanwords in Maori on the right? (For the purposes of this task, you can ignore any problems with vowels.)

English word	Pronunciation as a loanword in Maori
beer [bɪə]	[pahi]
sheep [ʃiːp]	[kura]
bus [bʌs]	[parau]
John [dʒɒn]	[pihikete]
plough/plow [plaʊ]	[hipi]
school [skuːl]	[futupoːro]
Bible [baɪbəl]	[pia]
snake [sneɪk]	[arefana]
biscuit [bɪskɪt]	[tounati]
blackberry [blækbəri]	[peːkana]
football [fʊtbɔːl]	[hoːne]
bacon [beɪkən]	[neke]
cricket [krɪkɪt]	[parakipere]
doughnut [dəʊnʌt]	[paipera]
elephant [elɪfənt]	[kirikiti]

Further reading

The topic of syllable structure is well handled by Cruttenden (2008), which contains more detailed treatment of possible combinations. Vaughan-Rees (2010) is a book of classroom activities relying heavily on rhyme and alliteration.

12 Phonemes

> [Daniel] Jones's phoneme concept had the minimum of theory behind it. . . . His phoneme concept was unpretentious and unadventurous. Its purpose was to be of service to applied phonetics, especially the making of transcriptions for language teaching.
>
> David Abercrombie (1983, p. 7)

Learning objectives

At the end of this chapter, you will be able to:

- define the terms *phonetic similarity, complementary distribution* and *minimal pair*
- write phonemes rules for simple allophonic relationships.

An analogy

The topic of this chapter is phonemes, the units of sound. Although the term had been used before him, the concept of the phoneme was popularized by the British phonetician Daniel Jones (1881–1967).

However, since sounds are ephemeral things, many people find it difficult to understand the concept. Let us start therefore with an analogy from spelling, which people are generally much more conscious of.

Look at the following letters: *A* and *a*. Are they the same or different? The answer is that they are different in one respect, but the same in another. They are different in that they are different shapes. Capital *A* is essentially three lines, while lower case *a* is a circle with a line. So, in terms of the physical shapes as marks on paper, they are different. However, they are the same in that there are 26 letters in the Roman alphabet, and both these shapes belong to the first letter.

The full answer is that, while these two shapes belong to the same unit, they occur in different environments. A capital *A* occurs in three main environments: as the first letter in a sentence (e.g. *A dog bit me*), as the first letter in a name (e.g. *Andrew*), and in initials (e.g. *ATM*). Lower case *a* occurs in all other environments. We can represent this as follows, where the arrow means 'is manifested/realized as':

First letter of the alphabet → (i) *A* (a) as the first letter in a sentence
(b) as the first letter in a name
(c) in initials
(ii) *a* elsewhere

The concept of the 'first letter of the alphabet' is therefore a relatively abstract one. It is a unit in the alphabet, we call it [eɪ], but it has different forms.

These are rules that all speakers (writers) of English know, and that children and foreigners learn. Notice that not all languages have a distinction between capital and lower case letters in their spelling systems, e.g. Arabic, Thai.

What happens if someone uses these symbols in the wrong way? For instance, my name is *Adam*. If someone were to spell it *adAm*, it would not be the correct English way of spelling it, but nonetheless it would probably still be recognizable. We would assume that the writer was a child or foreign learner, or someone using the language in an idiosyncratic way for some reason.

However, if someone started spelling my name *Edam*, we would object strongly because my name begins with the first letter of the alphabet, not the fifth. *Edam* happens to be another word with a different meaning ('a kind of cheese'). Changing from one letter of the alphabet to a different one may cause a change from one word to another.

Phonemes

Complementary distribution

In fact, we have already introduced some phoneme rules for English in the preceding chapters. Let us take the example that aspirated [p^h] occurs initially in a stressed syllable, e.g. *pit*, and unaspirated [$p^=$] occurs initially in a stressed syllable after [s], e.g. *spit*. Let us ask the same question: Are [p^h] and [$p^=$] the same or different sounds? The answer is the same answer as for *A* and *a*. The two sounds are different in that we can distinguish them: one has aspiration, the other does not. However, they are the same, in that they are both 'kinds of [p]'. As a result, many speakers of English will not even realize that the two sounds are distinguishably different.

We can represent the rule as follows:

/p/ → (i) [$p^=$] initially in a stressed syllable after [s]
(ii) [p^h] elsewhere

The rule, as stated above, does not exhaust all the possible 'types of /p/', but is sufficient for present purposes.

What happens if someone uses these sounds in the wrong way? If, for example, someone pronounces the word *spit* as [sp^hɪt], listeners will probably understand which word was meant, but will feel that it was being pronounced in an un-English way.

Where sounds such as [$p^=$] and [p^h] occur in environments that do not overlap, this is known as *complementary distribution*. Two sounds are in complementary distribution if one sound only occurs in a particular environment(s) and the other sound never occurs in that environment(s). In other words, the environment for the second sound can usually be expressed as *elsewhere*.

Minimal pairs

You may have noticed a new way of referring to sounds being used. The abstract unit of sound which is manifested by different types of sound is known as a *phoneme*. It is put in slant brackets: /p/. It is in fact a moot point how we should refer to this abstract unit, that is, what symbol to put between the brackets. The symbols used in this book are those used by Wells (2008).

The individual sounds that manifest the phoneme are called *allophones*, and are put in square brackets: [pʰ, p⁼].

If we change from one phoneme to a different one, we change the word. Thus, starting with /k/ gives us /kɪt/ *kit*, which is a different word from *pit* in English. Phonemes are thus important contrastive units because they cause changes in words in the language.

A pair of words like *pit* and *kit* are known as a *minimal pair*. A minimal pair is thus a pair of words with identical pronunciation except that one word has one sound where the other word has a different sound. And this proves that the two sounds belong to different phonemes: we could never write a phoneme rule stating the environments in which the sounds occur because, in a minimal pair, they occur in exactly the same environment.

It is on the basis of minimal pairs that we establish that there are 24 consonant phonemes in GenAm and SSBE, and 16 (GenAm) or 20 (SSBE) vowel phonemes. Other accents of English may have more or fewer phonemes. Other languages may have more or fewer phonemes than English. We have already seen, in chapter 1, that Thai has a contrast between [pʰ] and [p⁼] as in the minimal pair [pʰa] 'cloth' and [p⁼a] 'aunt'. In English, these two sounds belong to the same phoneme. Thai therefore has one more phoneme than English in this respect. English speakers learning Thai will therefore need to pay attention to mastering [p⁼] when it does not follow [s].

Phonetic similarity

However, complementary distribution is not sufficient by itself. Let us illustrate this with an example. In chapter 11, we saw that [h] never occurs syllable-finally (in coda position) in English. Also, [ŋ] never occurs syllable-initially (in onset position). The two sounds are therefore in complementary distribution. Should we then analyze them as belonging to the same phoneme?

The answer is clearly 'no'. No speaker of English thinks of [h] and [ŋ] as being, in any sense, 'the same sound', even though they are, strictly speaking, in complementary distribution. The reason for this is that the two sounds are very different sounds. The [h] sound is a voiceless glottal fricative, while [ŋ] is a voiced velar nasal. They have nothing in common. In contrast, [pʰ] and [p⁼] are both voiceless bilabial plosives. The difference between them is the relatively minor one of aspiration. Phonetic similarity is thus the second criterion needed for deciding that two sounds belong to the same phonemic unit.

The process of deciding whether two sounds belong to the same phoneme or to different phonemes is similar to the story of Superman. Our superhero is in reality Clark Kent, a reporter with *The Daily Planet*. He has a girlfriend called Lois Lane. After going out with Clark for a while, Lois starts to become suspicious, because she notices two things. Firstly, Clark and Superman resemble each other. They are the same height, the same build, etc. There are some differences: Clark wears glasses, while Superman wears his underpants on the outside. But by and large the two men are physically quite similar. Secondly, Lois notices that whenever she is out with Clark, Superman never appears, and when Superman appears, Clark is nowhere to be found. Eventually, Lois comes to the conclusion that Clark and Superman are one and the same person. They resemble each other (phonetic similarity), and they are never found in the same place at the same time (complementary distribution).

Transcription

On the basis of phonetic similarity, complementary distribution and minimal pairs, we arrive at the phonemes of an accent of a language. This is how the phonemes of the SSBE and GenAm accents of English used in this book are established.

We have seen above that the symbols used to refer to these phonemic units are a moot point. In this book, we have used the symbols given in Wells (2008).

Transcriptions can contain only this phonemic information, or they can explicitly include allophonic information, for instance that a plosive in a particular word is aspirated. If a transcription contains only phonemic information, that is, the symbols are chosen from the 24 consonant phonemes and 20 (SSBE) or 16 (GenAm) vowel phonemes, then it is a phonemic transcription and is put within slant brackets / /. If allophonic information is shown, then it is an allophonic transcription, and is put within square brackets [ ]. Cardinal vowels (see chapter 4), being language-independent, must be in square brackets. So far in this book, we have used square brackets. Now we use slant brackets where the phonemic status of the sounds is being emphasized.

The transcriptions given in dictionaries are therefore usually phonemic rather than allophonic (phonetic). Strictly speaking, they ought therefore to be referred to as phonemic symbols, rather than phonetic symbols. One exception to this is Wells (2008), who, because it is a pronunciation dictionary, gives some allophonic detail. For instance, Wells uses the symbol [t̬] for a [t] between a stressed and unstressed vowel, as in a GenAm pronunciation of *atom* [æt̬əm]. This sound is 'the often voiced alveolar tap' (Wells, 2008, p. xviii). If voiced, it is the same as [ɾ], introduced in chapter 9. It is, however, the predictable allophone of the /t/ phoneme in this context.

Summary

- Sounds can be analyzed as belonging to the same phonemic unit if they fulfill the two criteria of phonetic similarity and complementary distribution.
- Phonetic similarity means that the two sounds are articulated in very similar ways, for example, they have the same, or very similar, three-term labels.
- Complementary distribution means that the two sounds never occur in the same environment.
- Words where the two sounds occur in identical environments, that is, the rest of the word is the same, are called minimal pairs. They prove that the two sounds belong to different phonemes.

- It is on the basis of minimal pairs that we state that English has 24 consonant phonemes and 16 (GenAm) or 20 (SSBE) vowel phonemes.

Exercises

1. Find minimal pairs for the following pairs of sounds. This proves that they belong to different phonemes. The sounds can be anywhere in a word, but the rest of the word must comprise the same sounds.

[iː, ɪ]	[n, ŋ]	[æ, aɪ]
[k, g]	[ɔː, əʊ/oʊ]	[f, θ]

2. We have already stated the following patterns, in chapters 7 and 9. Restate them as phoneme rules, using the same pattern as for [pʰ, p⁼] above. This proves that they belong to the same phonemes.

   - Clear [l] ([l̥]) occurs before vowels. Dark [l] ([ɫ]) doesn't.
   - A plosive such as [p] is nasally released ([pᵐ]) before its homorganic nasal ([m]), e.g. *topmost*. It is orally released elsewhere.
   - An alveolar plosive such as [d] is laterally released ([dˡ]) before [l], e. g. *sadly*, but centrally released elsewhere.

Further reading

The classic work on the phoneme is Jones's (1950) *The phoneme: Its nature and use*, and on transcription is Abercrombie (1964). Also see any introductory phonetics book, e.g. Cruttenden (2008), Roach (2009).

13 Accent differences

We have really everything in common with America nowadays, except, of course, language.
Oscar Wilde (1854–1900), Irish playwright

Learning objectives

At the end of this chapter, you will be able to:

- define the four types of accent difference: *phonemic system, allophonic realization, phonotactic distribution* and *lexical distribution*
- explain why accent differences are important
- distinguish Type 1 and Type 2 accents of English.

Introduction

In the previous chapter, we discussed the phonological unit known as the phoneme, and the sounds that are used to manifest phonemes in particular contexts (allophones). This puts us in a position to examine the ways in which vowel and consonant sounds differ between accents of a language. These accents may be geographically or socially defined native-speaker accents, or the accents of foreign learners of the language.

Four types of accent difference

1 Phonemic system

The first type relates to the number of contrasts, and therefore the number of phonemes, in the accents. For instance, most Scots, and many foreign speakers of English, have the same vowel in the words *good* and *food*. This means that pairs of words like *full* and *fool* are pronounced identically as homophones (words that are pronounced the same, but spelt differently; see chapter 32). As a result, such speakers have only one vowel phoneme here. In contrast, most native accents of English distinguish *good* with a short vowel [ɡʊd] from *food* with a long vowel [fuːd]. In this way, *full* and *fool* are minimal pairs, showing that [ʊ] and [uː] belong to two different phonemes. In short, the phonemic systems of the accents are different: Scottish English has only one phonemic vowel unit here, while other accents (including GenAm and SSBE) have two.

Differences of phonemic system have also been called phonological differences.

2 Allophonic realization

The second type of difference does not involve a difference in the number of phonemes in the accents. Instead, corresponding phonemes in each accent are realized allophonically with different articulations. A good example is the pronunciation of the vowels in the word *okay*. In SSBE, GenAm, and many other accents, this is pronounced [əʊkeɪ/oʊkeɪ], with two diphthong vowels. However, Scottish English speakers, and many foreign speakers of English, use (usually long) monophthongs for the two vowels, thus [oːkeː] That is, both accents have the same two phonemic vowel units here: the vowels in *pole* and *pale* contrast with those in *peel, pill, pool, pile*, etc. The difference is merely one of the vowel quality used to manifest the phonemes.

Differences of allophonic realization have also been called phonetic realization differences.

3 Phonotactic distribution

In chapter 11, we discussed rhoticity, that is, the fact that /r/ can occur in coda (syllable-final) position in many accents such as GenAm, but not in other accents such as SSBE. The difference thus relates to the distribution of phonemes in terms of syllable structure (phonotactics), and depends on two factors. Firstly, the difference must be statable in terms of syllable structure. For instance, rhoticity concerns coda position in the syllable. Secondly, the difference must be pervasive for all words in the language. That is, there are no words of English where SSBE has syllable-final /r/. The only exception to this rule are linking and intrusive [r], discussed in chapter 15, which may be considered phenomena of connected speech.

Differences of phonotactic distribution have also been called structural differences.

4 Lexical distribution

It is this all-pervasive nature of differences in phonotactic distribution that distinguishes them from differences in lexical distribution. In this fourth type, the difference applies not to all words, but only to a limited group of words. Sometimes, the group is large, and sometimes it is small—perhaps only a single word. For example, most native accents of English have a distinction between /æ/ as in *Pam* and *Sam* and /ɑː/ as in *palm* and *psalm. Pam/palm* and *Sam/psalm* are minimal pairs, and such accents therefore have two vowel phonemes here. However, in words such as *laugh, path, grass, chance* and *plant*, SSBE uses the /ɑː/ vowel phoneme, while other accents, including most Americans (including GenAm) and northern England speakers, use /æ/. At first glance, it appears that the alternation can be captured by the rule: 'In SSBE, /ɑː/ (not /æ/) occurs (i) before a (nasal and) voiceless fricative, or (ii) before /nt/'. However, SSBE uses /æ/ in words such as *gaffe, psychopath, gas, expanse* and *ant*; that is, they are counterexamples to this rule and show that it does not hold. The alternation applies only to a limited set of words including *laugh, path*, etc. It is a large group of words, but nonetheless finite.

Differences of lexical distribution have also been called lexical-incidental and selectional differences, as well as etymological (because the occurrence of such differences often derives from the historical origins of the particular words).

A brief comparison of GenAm and SSBE

Because the above four categories can be used to describe differences between accents of English, we can now be more precise in describing the differences between GenAm and SSBE. A few examples are sufficient to make the point, but it should be borne in mind that neither accent is totally homogeneous, and further differences could be analyzed.

Consonants

Both accents have 24 consonant phonemes. Any differences are therefore not of phonemic system. The pronunciation in GenAm of an intervocalic /t/ following a stressed syllable as in *phonetics* as a tap [ɾ] is a matter of allophonic realization; in SSBE, this is a voiceless alveolar plosive. Rhoticity, the fact that /r/ can occur in syllable-final coda position, as in *murder*, in GenAm, but not in SSBE, is a difference of phonotactic distribution. Similarly, /j/ can occur in a two-consonant initial cluster after many consonants in SSBE, e.g. *pure, enthusiast, tube, cute, few, huge, music, new*. In GenAm, on the other hand, it does not occur after dentals and alveolars; thus *enthusiast, tube, duke, new* are /ɪnθuːziæst, tuːb, duːk, nuː/. And, contrary to popular belief in the UK, GenAm does pronounce /j/ after /h/; so *Houston* (Texas) is /hjuːstən/ in both SSBE and GenAm.

Vowels

GenAm does not have the same /ɒ/ phoneme of SSBE, as in *lot*. Words which in SSBE have /ɒ/ have /ɑː/ in GenAm, a difference in the number of phonemes, thus phonemic system. GenAm and SSBE have the same vowel phoneme in words like *home*; however, it is pronounced with a central starting point ([əʊ]) in SSBE and a back starting point ([oʊ]) in GenAm, an allophonic realization difference. The occurrence of /æ/ or /ɑː/ in words like *bath, staff, grass*, is a matter of lexical distribution. While this applies to a sizeable group of words, many lexical distribution differences relate to individual words, e.g. *leisure, wrath* (SSBE /leʒə, rɒθ/, GenAm /liːʒər, ræθ/).

The importance of accent differences

We will here discuss five factors related to the importance of accent differences. The first three (impressions of correctness, loss of intelligibility and misspelling) are clearly quite serious for learners and teachers. The other two are trivial by comparison.

Impressions of correctness

As Wells (1982, p. 79) argues, 'Most popular controversies about "right" and "wrong" pronunciation concern issues of lexical distribution.' Thus, for example, teachers are regularly asked by learners whether they should use the /e/ or /iː/ vowel in words such as *economic, amenity, leisure, Kenya, zebra* and *estrogen*. This variation relates only to this small group of isolated words, and is thus one of lexical distribution. In contrast, learners do not typically ask whether they should use diphthongs or monophthongs in words like *okay*, or whether to use rhoticity. However, as we shall see, the isolated differences of lexical distribution are relatively minor compared with the potential problems caused by pervasive differences of the other types.

Loss of intelligibility

Intelligibility, that is the ability for a speaker to be understood by a listener, is clearly an important one in language teaching (see chapter 24). In terms of accent differences, intelligibility often hangs on the concept of predictability. With differences of allophonic realization, predictability is not normally a problem. We can predict the stressed vowels used by SSBE speakers and Scottish speakers in expressions like *okay, payload, stone-mason* and *sailing boat*, because we know that SSBE speakers use [eɪ, əʊ] diphthongs, while Scottish speakers use [eː, oː] monophthongs. That is, we have corresponding phonemes pronounced in slightly different ways. SSBE [eɪ, əʊ] are equivalent to Scottish [eː, oː]. Prediction is possible in both directions.

A slight complication arises when the realization of one phoneme in one accent closely resembles, or may be indistinguishable from, the realization of a different phoneme in another accent. This is shown in the following traditional joke.

> Stoic English (SSBE) soldier: I came here to die.
> Australian soldier: So what, mate? I came here yesterday.

The joke revolves around the pronunciation [daɪ]. In SSBE, the vowel [aɪ] represents the vowel phoneme of *die*, and is in contrast with the vowel phoneme of *day* [deɪ]. For the Australian, the vowel [aɪ] represents the vowel phoneme in *day*, and is in contrast with the vowel phoneme of *die* [dɑɪ]. In order for a listener to assign the pronunciation to a particular phoneme, and thus meaning, it is necessary to be familiar with the accent and know how neighboring vowels are realized.

However, differences of phonemic system are more serious barriers to intelligibility because prediction is not possible in both directions. While we can predict that the SSBE pronunciation [pʊl] corresponds to the Scottish pronunciation [pul], and SSBE [puːl] also corresponds to Scottish [pul], we cannot predict in the other direction, from Scottish to SSBE. Thus, Scottish [luk] may correspond to either SSBE *look* [lʊk] or *Luke* [luːk].

In short, what is more important in the speech of learners is that contrasts are maintained rather than the precise allophonic realization of those contrasting phonemes. That is, matters of allophonic realization are less important than those of phonemic system.

The potential for loss of intelligibility is compounded if learners, in the same way as Scots, do not distinguish what in GenAm and SSBE is /ʊ, uː/, but also do not distinguish other pairs of vowel phonemes, and consonant phonemes. In fact, the consonant phonemes of GenAm and SSBE are, with very little variation, the same in all native accents of English. Any difference of phonemic system caused by the conflation of consonant phoneme pairs may therefore be considered serious. This question is taken up again in chapters 24 and 30.

Differences of phonotactic distribution may be of some limited importance. The rhotic use of /r/ is the only example of phonotactic distribution that is at all common in native English accents. Whether learners adopt a rhotic or non-rhotic pronunciation seems unlikely to affect intelligibility. It may, however, produce stigmatizing reactions from some listeners that are concerned about the conveying of identity (see chapter 24).

A rare instance of intelligibility problems caused by differences in rhoticity occurred when an American colleague, on being offered barley water in a Singapore hospital, wondered why they went to the lengths of importing water from Bali.

The large-scale simplification of consonant clusters found in the speech of some learners may also be considered a feature of phonotactic distribution, and is of importance for intelligibility.

Differences of lexical distribution, by definition, refer to individual words or small groups of words, and therefore cannot be considered serious barriers to intelligibility in everyday speech. This is in contrast to the importance attached to them by the popular view of correctness discussed above.

Misspelling

Spelling is discussed in greater detail in chapters 31 and 32. The relevance of accent differences to spelling is shown by the following example. Many Singaporeans do not distinguish /æ/ from /e/, pronouncing both like [e]. In the spelling system of English, the /e/ vowel is regularly spelt with the letter *e* 84% of the time, with *ea* 6%, and with various other letters and letter combinations 9% (figures from Carney, 1994). The /æ/ vowel is spelt with the letter *a* virtually 100% of the time (there are very very few exceptions like *meringue*). The question then is, 'If a Singaporean does not distinguish /æ/ and /e/, how can they remember which words are spelt with *e* or *ea*, and which ones with *a*?' Other speakers can remember that /e/ words use *e* or *ea*, while /æ/ words use *a*. Singaporeans cannot remember this via the pronunciation, because there is no distinction in their pronunciation. Such Singaporeans have to learn the spellings of all such words by heart, and we would therefore expect them to make mistakes and misspell /e/ words with *a* and, vice versa, /æ/ words with *e*. The following observed examples (from Brown, 2006) show that precisely this occurs.

**frengipani (frangipani)*
**chrysenthemum (chrysanthemum)*
**garlens (garlands)* (assuming this was not schwa)
**extand (extent)*
**expansive (expensive)*

Rhymes

In chapter 11, we saw that words rhyme when they have identical sounds from the vowel of the stressed syllable onwards. Accent differences of phonemic system may mean that words that rhyme in one accent do not rhyme in another. For instance, the following published verse was written by a Singaporean (Ibrahim, 1980). Clearly, he does not distinguish /æ/ and /e/, because *wet* is made to rhyme with *brat*. In other accents, these have two phonemically different vowels.

> When my baby starts to bawl,
> Because his diaper is wet,
> Though he wakes up one and all,
> I've to attend to the brat.

Puns

Similarly, plays-on-words that work in one accent may not work in other accents, as in the following examples.

> Alice couldn't see who was sitting beyond the beetle, but a hoarse voice spoke next.
> 'Change engines—' it said, and there it choked and was obliged to leave off.
> 'It sounds like a horse,' Alice thought to herself.
> (Lewis Carroll, *Through the Looking-Glass, and What Alice Found there*)

> 'When we were little,' the Mock Turtle went on at last, . . . 'we went to school in the sea. The master was an old Turtle—we used to call him Tortoise—'
> 'Why did you call him Tortoise, if he wasn't one?' Alice asked.
> 'We called him Tortoise because he taught us,' said the Mock Turtle angrily: 'really you are very dull!'.
> (Lewis Carroll, *Alice's Adventures in Wonderland*)

Lewis Carroll (real name Charles Dodgson) was born in Cheshire and educated at Rugby School and Oxford University. For him, the words *horse* and *tortoise* are pronounced the same as, but spelled differently than (are homophones of) *hoarse* and *taught us*. However, for many Scottish speakers, *horse* and *hoarse* are not homophones, being [hɔrs] and [hors] respectively. Similarly, for rhotic speakers such as GenAm and Scots, *tortoise* has an [r] sound, whereas *taught us* does not.

One broad characterization of English accents

Pennington (1996), following Giegerich (1992), suggests that accents of English can be divided into two broad categories, labeled Type 1 and Type 2.

The distinguishing characteristics of these two categories are as follows.

- In Type 1 accents, a phonemic distinction is made between [æ, ʌ, ɑː], that is, front/central/back low vowels, whereas in Type 2 accents, there is only one low vowel (a central [a]).

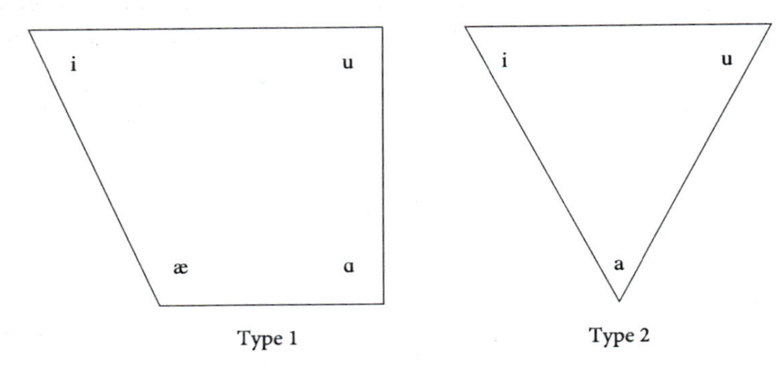

Figure 13.1 Two broad vowel systems for varieties of English.

- As a result of this, Type 1 accents can be represented diagrammatically by a trapezium, while a triangle better captures Type 2 accents.
- In Type 1 accents, long vowels tend to be diphthongal. For instance, in SSBE, [iː] and [uː] are often actually [ɪi] and [ʊu]. However, in Type 2 accents, vowels tend to be monophthongal, regardless of length, and length distinctions are often not maintained.
- Type 1 unstressed vowels often become schwa, whereas in Type 2, reduced vowels such as schwa do not occur, [a] often being used instead.
- Type 1 is exemplified by 'old' English as a Native Language (ENL) varieties such as most British, American, Canadian, Australian and New Zealand varieties. Type 2 is exemplified by the 'new' Second Language (ESL) Englishes, but also by Scottish and Irish English.
- The features of Type 2 'new' English accents may mirror the vowel systems of local languages.
- Type 2 may be used in 'new' English accents because of negative connotations associated with 'old' Type 1 varieties.

Summary

- Accent differences may be described between any accents, whether native accents of English, nonnative accents, or between nonnative and native (such as a teaching model accent).
- There are four types of accent difference: phonemic system, allophonic realization, phonotactic distribution and lexical distribution.
- Differences of phonemic system (where one accent has a distinction that another does not) probably represent the greatest threat to intelligibility.

Exercises

1. Decide whether the following are examples of phonemic system, allophonic realization, phonotactic distribution or lexical distribution.

- a In Liverpool, *fur* and *fair*, and *stir* and *stair* are homophones. In SSBE and GenAm, they are minimal pairs, having [ɜː(r)] and [eə/er] vowels respectively.
- b In SSBE, the [r] sound is a voiced post-alveolar approximant. In Indian speech, this is usually a voiced alveolar tap [ɾ].
- c You say [təmeɪtəʊ] and I say [təmɑːtəʊ].
- d Many New Zealanders pronounce *cheers* and *chairs*, and *fear* and *fair* as homophones. In SSBE and GenAm, they are minimal pairs, having [ɪə, ɪr] and [eə, er] vowels respectively.
- e In SSBE, *stop* is [stɒp]. For many learners, this is [sətɒp].
- f In Cockney, the urban accent of London, *thin* is pronounced [fɪn], the same as *fin*. In other accents, the initial consonants are different.
- g Some English speakers pronounce the words *either* and *neither* with the [aɪ] vowel, while others use the [iː] vowel.
- h In Canada, some speakers pronounce words like *nice, write* and *lifelike* with a [əi] vowel, while other words like *ride, tie, line* and *fire* have [ai]. In SSBE and GenAm, all these words have the same vowel.
- i Most Scots pronounce *ant, have, cam* and *aunt, halve, calm* identically. In SSBE and GenAm, they have different vowels.
- j In words such as *happy*, some speakers use [iː] for the final vowel, while others use [ɪ]. (Ignore the third possibility—that some speakers use something that is neither [iː] nor [ɪ].)

2. Here are two extracts of verse and song. Do they rhyme for all speakers of English?

Why is the milk from a red cow white
If it always eats green grass?
It seems so odd, it can't be right,
It really seems a farce.

(British music-hall song; see Wells, 1982, p. 82)

Me name's Charlie Fook and me spelling's a laugh
I'd rather nick off and sit round in the caugh.
School gives me a pain; I'm no good at study
Can't tell Mr Simms; wouldn't understand, wudy?

(Traditional British rhyme)

Further reading

Wells (1982) is a comprehensive description of English accents around the world, with more in-depth discussion of accent differences.

14 Phonology

Generative phonology can have only minor coincidental effects on something as practical as the teaching of second language pronunciation. On the other hand, articulatory phonetics can be very helpful in yielding useful types of pronunciation exercises [. . .]

Hector Hammerly (1973, p. 489)

Learning objectives

At the end of this chapter, you will be able to:

- clarify the difference between phonetics and phonology
- explain the pronunciation of regular past tense verbs and plural nouns
- list some distinctive features.

Introduction

In chapter 12, we looked at phonemes, the abstract units of sound comprising a number of allophones that occur in particular environments. This was necessary in order (i) to show that it is phonemes that are important because they differentiate words (minimal pairs such as *beat* and *bit*), and (ii) to explain how we arrive at the 40 (GenAm) or 44 (SSBE) phonemes represented in transcriptions found in dictionaries. The analysis of sounds into phonemic units is part of phonology, the study of how sounds function in languages. However, as the initial quote suggests, phonology—as opposed to phonetics—may have limited application in the language classroom. This is especially true of deeper, more abstract forms of phonology, such as the school known as generative phonology.

In this chapter, we will look at two other aspects of phonology that may be considered to have some relevance: morphophonology and distinctive features.

Morphophonology

The term *morphophonology* may seem rather daunting, but the concept is not too difficult to understand. The term is a blend of *morphology* and *phonology*, and refers to the way that morphemes are regularly manifested in pronunciation. Morphemes are the smallest units of meaning. They may be stems that can stand by themselves, such as *table* and *jump*, or may be affixes which occur before the stems (prefixes such as the negating *dis-* of *disagree*) or after the stems (suffixes such as the *-th* of *tenth*, making an ordinal number out of a cardinal number). The word *nonrefundable* is thus analyzable into the morphemes *non-* ('not') + *re-* ('again') + *fund* (stem) + *-able* ('can be . . . -ed').

The affixes *dis-* and *-th* are always pronounced the same. However, as we will see, the pronunciation of some affixes depends on the stem they are attached to. Let us look at the past tense verb suffix *-(e)d*, and the plural noun suffix *-(e)s*.

Past tense verbs

English verbs are regularly made past tense by adding *-(e)d* in the spelling. However, this has three different pronunciations.

Firstly, where the verb stem ends in a voiceless consonant, it is pronounced /t/, e.g. *helped, liked, sniffed, amassed* /helpt, laɪkt, snɪft, əmæst/. If you are unconvinced that the *-(e)d* suffix is pronounced /t/, note that *passed* and *past* are pronounced identically (are homophones) and are common misspellings of each other.

Secondly, where the verb ends in a voiced consonant or a vowel (remembering that all vowels are voiced), it is pronounced /d/, e.g. *rubbed, sagged, loved, praised, tried, agreed* /rʌbd, sægd, lʌvd, preɪzd, traɪd, əgriːd/.

Finally, where the verb ends in /t, d/, the suffix is pronounced /ɪd/, e.g. *hated, landed* /heɪtɪd, lændɪd/. The reason for this is that it would be awkward or impossible to pronounce final /-td, -dd/ without an intervening vowel. Some people call this an example of epenthesis (see chapter 17). Since we are adding a suffix containing a vowel, we are adding an extra syllable: *hate* /heɪt/ is one syllable, whereas *hated* /heɪtɪd/ is two. The nature of the vowel may vary; some accents of English use /əd/.

We can thus write a rule stating the pronunciation of the past tense morpheme:

Past tense → (i) /ɪd/ after /t, d/
(ii) /t/ after other voiceless consonants
(iii) /d/ after other voiced consonants and vowels

While this may appear to resemble the phoneme rules we stated in chapter 12, it is not the same. Instead of phonemes being manifested as allophones, the above rule describes the manifestation of morphemes as phonemes.

Plural nouns

In very similar vein, the regular plural noun suffix is spelt *-(e)s*, but has different pronunciations depending on the stem.

Where the noun stem ends in a voiceless consonant, the suffix is pronounced /s/, e.g. *cats, books, myths, roofs* /kæts, bʊks, mɪθs, ruːfs/.

Where the noun ends in a voiced consonant or vowel, it is pronounced /z/, e.g. *tubs, eggs, gloves, sums, things, walls, days* /tʌbz, egz, glʌvz, sʌmz, θɪŋz, wɔːlz, deɪz/.

Where the noun ends in /s, z, ʃ, ʒ, tʃ, dʒ/, the suffix is pronounced /ɪz/, e.g. *buses, quizzes, bushes, garages, witches, hedges* /bʌsɪz, kwɪzɪz, bʊʃɪz, gærɑːʒɪz, wɪtʃɪz, hedʒɪz/ (*garage* has several possible pronunciations; see Wells, 2000, p. 316 for explanation and a graph). Again, it would be awkward or impossible to pronounce final /-sz, -zz, -ʃz, -ʒz, -tʃz, -dʒz/ without an intervening vowel, which is /ə/ in some accents. As for the past tense rule, we are adding an extra syllable here: *bus* /bʌs/ is one syllable, while *buses* /bʌsɪz/ is two.

The rule stating the pronunciation of the plural morpheme thus resembles the one above for past tense:

Plural → (i) /ɪz/ after /s, z, ʃ, ʒ, tʃ, dʒ/
(ii) /s/ after other voiceless consonants
(iii) /z/ after other voiced consonants and vowels

Discussion

The above two rules are in fact more pervasive than the above description suggests. The past tense rule also applies to the participle used in perfect tenses and in passives (variously referred to as the past participle, *-ed* participle or *-en* participle): *help, I helped, I have helped, I am helped.* Similarly, the plural noun rule (*cat, cats*) also applies to third person singular present tense verbs (*I chat, he chats*), possessives (*Pat, Pat's*), and abbreviations of *is* or *has* (*Pat, Pat's going, Pat's gone*).

In the previous sections, we used the term *regular*. In this context, *regular* means conforming to the rule (think of the word *regulation*). Regular verbs and nouns are thus those that obey the rules given above, that is, form their plurals, past tenses, etc. according to the above rules. However, English also has many irregular verbs (e.g. *I am, I was, I have been*) and nouns (e.g. *child, children*), which do not follow the rules. It is an unfortunate fact of English that many of the commonest verbs and nouns are irregular. Since the past tenses of such verbs and the plurals of such nouns cannot be predicted by applying the above rules, these forms must be contained in dictionaries. The plurals of irregular nouns are usually given in the entry for the noun. The past tense and participle of irregular verbs are either given in the entry for the verb or in an appendix.

Distinctive features

We have already encountered two of the rules describing the following processes:

- The plural of *gem* /dʒem/ is *gems* /dʒemz/. That is, the regular plural of a noun ending in /m/ is pronounced /z/ (see the previous section).
- In a phrase such as *John Major*, the final /n/ of *John* assimilates to an [m] because of the following /m/ of *Major* (/dʒɒm/dʒɑːm meɪdʒə(r)/) (this is discussed in chapter 16).
- In a word like *ram*, the vowel is likely to be at least partially nasalized ([ræ̃m]), because it is followed by /m/ (see chapter 7).

We can see that all three cases involve the sound /m/. However, in none of the three cases is it only the sound /m/; other sounds behave the same way as /m/. In the first case, the plural suffix is pronounced /z/ after any voiced sound (consonant or vowel); thus *ribs, balls, toys* /rɪbz, bɔːlz, tɔɪz/. In the second, the assimilation takes place before any bilabial sound; thus *John Parker, John Brown, John White* dʒɒm/dʒɑːm pɑː(r)kə(r), dʒɒm/dʒɑːm braʊn, dʒɒm/dʒɑːm waɪt. In the third, the nasalization (also a type of assimilation) takes place before any nasal sound; thus *ran, rang* ([rǣn, rǣŋ]).

In short, /m/ is described as a voiced bilabial nasal. But it takes part in the first process by virtue of the fact that it is voiced; the fact that it is also bilabial and nasal is irrelevant here. Similarly, it takes part in the second and third processes because it is bilabial and nasal respectively. In other words, none of these processes are specific to /m/, but apply to other similar sounds.

Phonologists have proposed that sounds should be thought of as being composed of features. One such feature is [± voice]. Along with all other voiced consonants and vowels, /m/ is [+ voice], as opposed to [− voice] meaning voiceless. And it is because of this feature that /m/ participates in the first process above.

There are several reasons why such a view of sounds should be proposed.

1 *Natural classes*

Distinctive features allow us to specify natural classes, that is, groups of sounds that clearly share some basic characteristic. The above example of [± voice] is such a case; [± voice] is a very basic feature characterizing all sounds, because all sounds either have or do not have vocal cord vibration.

2 *Phonological processes*

As we have just seen, phonological rules often depend on distinctive features. It is much simpler to say that the plural suffix is pronounced as /z/ (which is [+ voice]) after any other [+ voice] sound, rather than saying that it occurs after (SSBE) /b, d, g, v, ð, m, n, ŋ, l, iː, ɑː, ɔː, uː, ɜː, ɪ, e, æ, ʌ, ɒ, ʊ, ə, eɪ, aɪ, ɔɪ, aʊ, əʊ, ɪə, eə, ʊə/.

3 *Economy*

One feature that is needed for English is [± lateral]. However, this is only needed in order to distinguish /l/ [+ lateral] from /r/ [− lateral], because they are the same in terms of all other features. When referring to /l/, we therefore only need to describe it as [+ lateral] (and ignore the fact that it is also [+ voice] etc.), because it is the [± lateral] feature that distinguishes it from all other sounds of English.

Phonologists have proposed various sets of distinctive features in order to characterize sounds in different accents of a language, and in different languages, without any overall agreement. Jakobson, Fant and Halle (1952) suggested 14 features, while Chomsky and Halle (1968) proposed around 45. Our job is easier, as we are only dealing with the sounds of SSBE and GenAm. We therefore only need to distinguish between the 44 (SSBE) or 40 (GenAm) phonemic units of these accents.

The [± voice] feature is clearly binary, that is, there is a choice between two values, because the vocal cords are either vibrating or not. However, the other features of /m/ (that it is bilabial and nasal) cannot be handled in a simple binary fashion, as there are nine places of articulation and six manners of articulation for English consonants (see chapters 6 and 9). Yet, with a little flexibility, this can still be managed in a smaller number of features. For instance, English has bilabial plosives (/p, b/), nasal (/m/) and approximant (/w/), but no bilabial fricatives (although these are physiologically possible and occur in other languages). Vice versa, English has labio-dental fricatives (/f, v/), but no labio-dental plosives, nasals or approximants (again, possible and occurring in other languages). So, for English, the two categories of bilabial and labio-dental can be conflated into one category. Similarly, the typical English /r/ is treated here with alveolar sounds, although its articulation is slightly further back at the post-alveolar or retroflex region.

The following set of features would be accepted by most analysts:

- [± voice]: [+ voice] sounds involve vibration of the vocal cords; [– voice] do not.
- [± syllabic]: [+ syllabic] sounds occur in peak position; [– syllabic] sounds occur in the onset or coda.
- [± consonantal]: [+ consonantal] sounds (plosives, affricates, fricatives, nasals, /l/) are produced with contact or frication in the center of the oral tract; [– consonantal] (vowels and semi-vowels) are not. The /r/ consonant is considered [+ consonantal] because it is realized with contact in many accents of English.
- [± sonorant]: [+ sonorant] articulations (vowels, approximants and nasals) involve unimpeded, fricationless and voiced airflow through the mouth or the nose; [– sonorant] sounds, also called obstruents, (stops, fricatives and affricates) involve complete closure or frication.
- [± coronal]: [+ coronal] sounds (dentals, alveolars, post-alveolars, palato-alveolars and palatals) are articulated by raising the tongue blade or front towards the teeth or hard palate; [– coronal] are bilabials, labio-dentals and velars.
- [± anterior]: [+ anterior] sounds (bilabials, labio-dentals, dentals and alveolars) are articulated at or in front of the alveolar ridge; [– anterior] are also called posterior.

Between them, [± coronal] and [± anterior] can account for the places of articulation of English consonants.

- [± labial]: [+ labial] sounds have rounding or constriction at the lips. They are therefore bilabial and labio-dental consonants and rounded vowels.
- [± high]: [+ high] sounds (palatal and velar consonants, semi-vowels and high vowels) are produced by raising the body of the tongue towards the palate.
- [± low]: [+ low] sounds (low vowels) are produced by lowering the body of the tongue away from the palate.

The two features [± high] and [± low] can be used to distinguish three levels of vowel height.

- [± back]: [+ back] sounds (velar consonants, and central and back vowels, and back semi-vowels) are produced with the tongue body relatively retracted.
- [± continuant]: [+ continuant] sounds (vowels, approximants and fricatives) allow the airstream to escape through the mouth; [– continuant] sounds are also called stops, and include plosives and nasals. Affricates are also [– continuant] because of the initial complete closure.

- [± lateral]: the only [+ lateral] sound in English is /l/, which allows air to escape over the sides of the tongue; all other English sounds are [– lateral].
- [± nasal]: [+ nasal] sounds (nasals and nasalized vowels) have a lowered velum, allowing air to escape through the nose.
- [± tense]: [+ tense] vowels are long vowels, produced with greater tension; [– tense] (short) vowels are also called lax.
- [± sibilant]: [+ sibilant] fricatives (/s, z, ʃ, ʒ/) are those with large amounts of acoustic energy at high frequencies.

These distinctive features can then be used to categorize natural classes, as shown in Table 14.1.

Table 14.1 Distinctive feature matrix for English natural classes

	Syllabic	*Consonantal*	*Sonorant*	*Continuant*
Plosives and affricates	–	+	–	–
Nasal stops	–	+	+	–
Fricatives	–	+	–	+
Approximants (/r, l/)	–	+	+	+
Semi-vowels (/w, j/)	–	–	+	+
Vowels	+	–	+	+

Each natural class is now distinguished from every other in terms of the + and – values of the various features; that is, no two classes have the same combinations of + and – values.

The distinctive features used to categorize consonant sounds of English are shown in Table 14.2. All consonants are [– syllabic] (occurring in onset or coda position): that is the definition of a consonant. The [± low] feature does not help to distinguish any consonants, as they by definition involve some kind of obstruction, and therefore the tongue cannot be low. These two features therefore need not appear in this matrix.

This feature matrix captures some of the differences between sounds often confused by learners. The difference between /ʃ/ and /tʃ/ is that /tʃ/ begins with a complete closure (in distinctive feature terms, is not continuant). The /θ/ fricative differs from the /t/ plosive by being prolongable (continuant). The main difference between /r/ and /l/ is that the tongue does not touch the roof of the mouth centrally for /r/ (is not lateral).

The distinctive features used to categorize vowel sounds of SSBE are shown in Table 14.3. The [voice, syllabic, consonantal, sonorant, continuant, lateral, nasal, sibilant] features do not help to distinguish vowels, as all vowels are [+ voice], [+ syllabic], [– consonantal], [+ sonorant], [+ continuant], [– lateral], [– nasal] and [– sibilant].

Differences between similar vowel sounds often confused by learners are captured by these features. The main difference between pairs such as /iː,ɪ/ and /uː, ʊ/ is that /iː, uː/ are long (tense). The /e/ vowel differs from the /æ/ vowel in that /e/ is mid (not low), while /æ/ is low.

Table 14.2 Distinctive feature matrix for English consonants

	voice	*consonantal*	*sonorant*	*coronal*	*anterior*	*labial*	*high*	*back*	*continuant*	*lateral*	*nasal*	*sibilant*
/p/	–	+	–	–	+	+	–	–	–	–	–	–
/b/	+	+	–	–	+	+	–	–	–	–	–	–
/t/	–	+	–	+	+	–	–	–	–	–	–	–
/d/	+	+	–	+	+	–	–	–	–	–	–	–
/k/	–	+	–	–	–	–	+	+	–	–	–	–
/g/	+	+	–	–	–	–	+	+	–	–	–	–
/tʃ/	–	+	–	+	–	–	–	–	–	–	–	+
/dʒ/	+	+	–	+	–	–	–	–	–	–	–	+
/f/	–	+	–	–	+	+	–	–	+	–	–	–
/v/	+	+	–	–	+	+	–	–	+	–	–	–
/θ/	–	+	–	+	+	–	–	–	+	–	–	–
/ð/	+	+	–	+	+	–	–	–	+	–	–	–
/s/	–	+	–	+	+	–	–	–	+	–	–	+
/z/	+	+	–	+	+	–	–	–	+	–	–	+
/ʃ/	–	+	–	+	–	–	–	–	+	–	–	+
/ʒ/	+	+	–	+	–	–	–	–	+	–	–	+
/h/	–	+	–	–	–	–	–	–	+	–	–	–
/m/	+	+	+	–	+	+	–	–	–	–	+	–
/n/	+	+	+	+	+	–	–	–	–	–	+	–
/ŋ/	+	+	+	–	–	–	+	+	–	–	+	–
/l/	+	+	+	+	+	–	–	–	+	+	–	–
/r/	+	+	+	+	+	–	–	–	+	–	–	–
/w/	+	–	+	–	–	+	+	+	+	–	–	–
/j/	+	–	+	+	–	–	+	–	+	–	–	–

Table 14.3 Distinctive feature matrix for SSBE vowels

	labial	*high*	*low*	*back*	*tense*
/iː/	–	+	–	–	+
/ɪ/	–	+	–	–	–
/e/	–	–	–	–	–
/æ/	–	–	+	–	–
/ʌ/	–	–	+	+	–
/ɑː/	–	–	+	+	+
/ɒ/	+	–	+	+	–
/ɔː/	+	–	–	+	+
/ʊ/	+	+	–	+	–
/uː/	+	+	–	+	+
/ɜː/	–	–	–	+	+

Summary

- Morphophonology examines the way morphemes are pronounced.
- While regular past tense verbs are all spelled -*(e)d*, they are not all pronounced the same.
- While regular plural nouns are all spelled -*(e)s*, they are not all pronounced the same.
- Distinctive features allow us to capture the difference between natural classes of sounds, and to describe in a general way processes that affect sounds.
- Since the sounds of English differ from those of other languages, different sets of distinctive features are needed for other languages.

Exercises

1. Name:
    - five nouns that are not regular nouns (i.e. do not form their plural by the rule given in this chapter)
    - five verbs that are not regular verbs (i.e. do not form their past tense and participle by the rule given in this chapter).
2. Are the -*ed* words in the following expressions examples of the regular -*ed* rule described in this chapter? If not, why not?

    a bearded man | *crooked teeth* | *sacred ground*
    a jagged edge | *ragged clothes* | *the naked truth*
    a wretched child | *rugged terrain* | *the wicked witch*

3. Regular plural nouns are pronounced /ɪz/ after /s, z, ʃ, ʒ, tʃ, dʒ/. What do these six sounds have in common, in distinctive feature terms?
4. Regular past tense verbs are pronounced /ɪd/ after /t, d/. Express /t, d/ in distinctive feature terms.

Further reading

There are many introductory books on phonology, including Carr (1993), Katamba (1989), Lass (1984), Odden (2005), However, readers should be aware that while phonology may attempt to capture the systems and processes of the native speaker brain to varying degrees of success, in my opinion it has few strong applications in language teaching.

15 Weakening and linking

A Salt 'N' Battered, Kash n' Karry Food Stores, Love-n-Kisses, Mains 'N' Drains, Memphis Rock 'n' Soul Museum, Pick 'n Pay, Steak n Shake, Wet 'n Wild, Wings N' Things.

Shop signs collected by Cook (2004a)

Learning objectives

At the end of this chapter, you will be able to:

- clarify the distinction between content and function words
- list some of the weak forms of spoken English
- explain various kinds of links between syllables and words
- describe the pronunciation of geminate consonants.

Introduction

In this chapter and the next, we focus on the fact that the sounds of English pronunciation do not occur in isolation. Instead, they occur before and after other sounds in connected speech. Sounds are thus affected in various ways by surrounding sounds. We also need to bear in mind that normal speech is not slow. The faster the speech, the more likely are the processes described in this chapter and the next to occur, because they make normal, fast speech easier. Together, they are therefore often referred to as connected speech processes.

Content and function words

The occurrence of weak forms in connected speech depends on the distinction between lexical content words on the one hand and grammatical function words on the other. The distinction is easy to make in almost all cases, and depends on the following factors:

- Content words are nouns (e.g. *book*), main verbs (*read*), adjectives (*beautiful*) and adverbs (*quickly*). Function words are all the other grammatical categories, such as articles (*a, the*), auxiliary verbs (*be, have, can*), conjunctions (*and, but*), prepositions (*at, to*) and pronouns (*he, them*).

- Content words are the kind of word you might look up in a dictionary. For instance, a teacher might tell a learner to look up the word *blockbuster* in the dictionary. But the teacher would be unlikely to tell the learner to look up a word like *of*.
- Content words can be defined relatively easily, and therefore have short entries in dictionaries. For instance, the entry for *blockbuster* ('a book or film that is very good or successful' *Longman Dictionary of Contemporary English*) is only one line. In contrast, the entry for *of* takes up a page and has 25 subentries. The 'meaning' of *of* depends on its context of use.
- For this reason, content words are also called lexical words, because they have real meaning. Function words are also known as grammatical words, because their meaning depends on their function in sentences.

Content words therefore carry most of the message of an utterance. Producing a meaningful, grammatical sentence in English may be compared with building a wall. You need both bricks and mortar. The bricks are the basic building blocks, the substance. However, you also need the mortar in order to cement the bricks together. Similarly, the content words are the bricks of a sentence, conveying the bulk of the message, while the mortar of the function words is needed to join the content words together into a grammatical sentence, even though they do not contribute much meaning themselves.

Weakening

From the point of view of pronunciation, it makes sense that the content words, being the ones that convey the most information, should be pronounced loudly and clearly (stressed). However, this can only be achieved if the function words are not pronounced loudly and clearly (unstressed). That is, there must be a contrast in order for certain elements to stand out. One way in which many (but not all) function words are shown to be unstressed in connected speech is for them to have weak forms. This process often involves them having the /ə/ vowel (see chapter 19), but other processes such as the loss (elision; see chapter 16) of /h/ may be involved.

Table 15.1 gives a list of the commonest weak forms for function words.

The word *that* has three different uses (or perhaps we should say that there are three different words):

- as a demonstrative, e.g. *I like that T-shirt, What's that?*
- as a relative pronoun, e.g. *The man that I met was my uncle.*
- as a subordinating conjunction, e.g. *He said that he would come to the party.*

The first one is lexical, and is always a strong form with /æ/. The second and third are functional, are therefore usually unstressed, and are pronounced as weak forms with /ə/. Note that they contribute little in terms of meaning and can therefore be omitted in these sentences (*The man I met was my uncle, He said he would come to the party*).

Since function words are usually unstressed in connected speech, the weak form is much commoner than the citation form. And, for instance, good dictionaries give the weak form pronunciation of *of* (/əv/) first, followed by the citation form (/ɒv, ʌv/).

Table 15.1 Weak forms

Word	*Citation form*	*Weak form*	*Example (SSBE transcription)*
Articles			
a	/eɪ/	/ə/	*Take a look* /teɪk ə lʊk/
an	/æn/	/ən/	*Half an hour* /hɑːf ən aʊə/
some	/sʌm/	/səm/	*Have some tea* /hæv səm tiː/
the	/ðiː/	/ðə/	*Mind the gap* /maɪnd ðə gæp/
Auxiliary verbs (including modals)			
am	/æm/	/əm/	*I, Bob, am sorry* /aɪ bɒb əm sɒri/
are	/ɑː(r)/	/ə(r)/	*Exams are hard* /ɪgzæmz ə hɑːd/
been	/biːn/	/bɪn/	*I've been thinking* /aɪv bɪn θɪŋkɪŋ/
do	/duː/	/də/	*Do they know?* /də ðeɪ nəʊ/
does	/dʌz/	/dəz/	*Does John know?* /dəz dʒɒn nəʊ/
can	/kæn/	/kən/	*I can swim* /aɪ kən swɪm/
could	/kʊd/	/kəd/	*Jill could ask* /dʒɪl kəd ɑːsk/
had	/hæd/	/(h)əd/	*Pat had gone* /pæt əd gɒn/
has	/hæz/	/(h)əz/	*Bill has arrived* /bɪl əz əraɪvd/
have	/hæv/	/(h)ə(v)/	*The boys have gone* /ðə bɔɪz əv gɒn/
must	/mʌst/	/məs(t)/	*I must go* /aɪ məs gəʊ/
shall	/ʃæl/	/ʃəl/	*What shall I say?* /wɒt ʃəl aɪ seɪ/
should	/ʃʊd/	/ʃəd/	*They should leave* /ðeɪ ʃəd liːv/
was	/wɒz/	/wəz/	*I was right* /aɪ wəz raɪt/
were	/wɜː/	/wə/	*They were good* /ðeɪ wə gʊd/
will	/wɪl/	/wəl/	*Joe will help* /dʒəʊ wəl help/
would	/wʊd/	/wəd/	*What would do?* /wɒt wəd duː/
Conjunctions			
and	/ænd/	/ən(d)/	*Fish and chips* /fɪʃ ən tʃɪps/
as	/æz/	/əz/	*Twice as much* /twaɪs əz mʌtʃ/
because	/bɪkɒz/	/bɪkəz/	*Die because of thirst* /daɪ bɪkəz əv θɜːst/
but	/bʌt/	/bət/	*Poor but happy* /pʊə bət hæpi/
that	/ðæt/	/ðət/	*So hungry that I fainted* /səʊ hʌŋgri ðət aɪ feɪntɪd/
Prepositions			
at	/æt/	/ət/	*Not at all* /nɒt ət ɔːl/
for	/fɔː(r)/	/fə(r)/	*Looking for work* /lʊkɪŋ fə wɜːk/
from	/frɒm/	/frəm/	*Away from home* /əweɪ frəm həʊm/
of	/ɒv/	/ə(v)/	*Pint of milk* /paɪnt ə mɪlk/
than	/ðæn/	/ðən/	*Holier than thou* /həʊliə ðən ðaʊ/
to	/tuː/	/tə/	*A to Z* /eɪ tə zed/
Pronouns			
he	/hiː/	/(h)ɪ/	*Will he come?* /wɪl ɪ kʌm/
her	/hɜː/	/(h)ə/	*Leave her alone* /liːv ər ələʊn/
hers	/hɜːz/	/(h)əz/	*A friend of hers came* /ə frend əv əz keɪm/
him	/hɪm/	/(h)ɪm/	*Put him down* /pʊt ɪm daʊn/
his	/hɪz/	/(h)ɪz/	*He took his cup* /hiː tʊk ɪz kʌp/
she	/ʃiː/	/ʃɪ/	*Did she say?* /dɪd ʃɪ seɪ/
them	/ðem/	/(ð)əm/	*Tell them now* /tel əm naʊ/
there	/ðeə/	/ðə(r)/	*There are lots* /ðər ə lɒts/

Word	Citation form	Weak form	Example (SSBE transcription)
us	/ʌs/	/əs/	*Make us proud* /meɪk əs praʊd/
we	/wiː/	/wɪ/	*Did we remember?* /dɪd wɪ rɪmembə/
you	/juː/	/jʊ, jə/	*A thank-you card* /ə θæŋk jə kɑːd/
your	/jɔː(r)/	/jə(r)/	*Mind your own business* /maɪnd jər əʊn bɪznɪs/
Miscellaneous weak forms (not necessarily function words)			
just	/dʒʌst/	/dʒəst/	*He just cried* /hiː dʒəst kraɪd/
saint	/seɪnt/	/sənt/	*Saint Joseph* /sənt dʒəʊzɪf/
sir	/sɜː/	/sə(r)/	*Sir Peter* /sə piːtə/
so	/səʊ/	/sə/	*So don't!* /sə dəʊnt/

There are five main environments where strong forms are found:

- As the last word of a sentence, e.g. *What are you looking at?* Some people, rather pedantically, object that you should never finish a sentence with a preposition, but it is extremely common in questions like this.
- Where ellipsis (omission of an easily recoverable word to avoid repetition) has taken place, e.g. A: *Can you swim?* B: *Yes, I can.* The reply is a normal abbreviation of *Yes, I can swim.*
- Where there is some kind of contrast, e.g. A: *I had dinner yesterday with Bradley Cooper.* B: **The** *Bradley Cooper?!* A: *No, you remember my schoolfriend called Bradley Cooper.*
- Where there is some kind of emphasis, e.g. *You must be joking!*
- Where you are quoting the word as a word, e.g. *Some people think that 'but' should never be the first word in a sentence.*

It should be borne in mind, however, that these are the exceptions. Function words are usually unstressed with weak forms.

Linking

In writing we leave spaces between words. This is how a computer's word count works—it counts the spaces and adds one. However, in speech, we do not leave gaps between words. They run smoothly into each other, and this contributes to the flow of connected speech. We can distinguish the following possibilities for the junctures of words (and syllables):

1 Final consonant + initial consonant

The first consonant runs naturally into the second. Thus, in the following examples, the /s/ of *class* and the /r/ of *room* are not separate, regardless of whether they represent two words or one:

Is the classroom big enough?
Has the class room enough to move around?

2 *Final vowel + initial consonant*

This combination does not pose any problems:

An international friendly match
We got into national costume.

3 *Final consonant + initial vowel*

This combination is made easier if the final consonant is linked up to the initial vowel. In this way, the final consonant is not dropped:

A handout
Please hand out these worksheets.

4 *Final vowel + initial vowel*

Four types of link are common in English:

4.1 Linking [j] occurs after /iː, eɪ, aɪ, ɔɪ/.

seeing, see it, playing, play it, flying, fly it, enjoying, enjoy it

4.2 Linking [w] occurs after /uː, əʊ, aʊ/.

gluing, glue it, showing, show it, vowing, vow it

4.3 Linking [r] occurs after /ɑː, ɔː, ɜː, ə, ɪə, eə, ʊə/ in SSBE (GenAm is discussed below).

barring, tore it, preferring, injure it, fearing, tear it, touring

Linking [r] needs further explanation. In the SSBE accent, there is no syllable-final /r/ in words like *four, Singapore* (in chapter 11, we referred to this as a *non-rhotic* accent). However, when the word is followed by anything that begins with a vowel sound, as in *four apples, Singapore Airlines*, an [r] sound is pronounced. This is true whether the next part is a separate word, as in *four apples*, or a suffix, as in *Singapore* > *Singaporean*. Where the next part begins with a consonant sound, there is no [r], e.g. *four pears, Singapore Girl.*

4.4 Intrusive [r] also occurs after /ɑː, ɔː, ɜː, ə, ɪə, eə, ʊə/ in SSBE (GenAm is discussed below).

Ma and Pa, clawing, cordon bleu appetizer, Buddha image, diarrhea again, yeah OK

The difference in SSBE between linking [r] and intrusive [r] is twofold. Firstly, in rhotic accents such as GenAm that do have /r/ in syllable-final position after the vowel, the words in the linking [r] section will always be pronounced with an /r/ (*bar, tore, prefer, injure, fear, tear, tour*), while those words in the intrusive [r] section will never be pronounced with an /r/ (*Ma, claw, bleu, Buddha, diarrhea, yeah*). Secondly, you will probably have noticed that the first set of words all contain an *r* letter in the spelling, while the second set contain no *r*s (see chapter 11).

Two other possibilities exist for these environments. Firstly, zero link means that there is nothing between the first vowel and the second—the first simply runs into the second. This seems unlikely, though, where the two vowels happen to be the same, e.g. *draw orchids, data analysis.* Secondly, a glottal stop (see chapter 3) may be put between the two vowels ([deɪtə ˀ ənæləsɪs]). This is sometimes referred to as a *linking glottal stop*, but its function seems to be to separate rather than to link.

A regular pattern

The processes of linking in SSBE in fact lead to a nice patterning. Linking [j] occurs after four vowels; linking [w] after three; and linking or intrusive [r] after seven. That leaves the six short vowels [ɪ, e, æ, ʌ, ɒ, ʊ] which, as we saw in chapter 11, never occur without a final consonant, that is, could not be followed by another vowel.

Full sounds?

Some phoneticians have pointed out that the [j, w, r] that are present for linking purposes are not identical to the /j, w, r/ that are there in citation form. For instance, *forty years* is not quite identical to *forty ears*, even though both could be transcribed [fɔːtijɪəz, fɔːrtijɪ rz]. Similarly, in Shakespeare's *Julius Caesar*, Mark Anthony is not normally misunderstood to be saying *Friends, Romans, countrymen, lend me your rears*, even though *your ears* and *your rears* could both be transcribed [jɔːrɪəz, jɔːrɪrz]. Segments introduced for linking purposes may therefore have lower status than those already present.

Geminate consonants

We have introduced all the consonants of English (in chapters 7 to 9), and found it useful to use parametric diagrams to explain their articulation. We have just explained how sounds interact by linking when they occur together at syllable and word boundaries. A final note is necessary to explain what happens when the same consonant occurs at the end of one syllable and at the beginning of the next (known as *geminate* consonants). This may happen either at word boundaries (e.g. *good dog*) or in compounds (e.g. *penknife*). In both cases, there is a boundary between two morphemes (units of meaning). We need to consider the consonants by manner of articulation.

Plosives

Let us take the phrase *good dog*. When saying this phrase, it is clear that we do not release the first /d/. Instead, what is pronounced is a single /d/ articulation, that is, a single hold phase, but it is twice the length of a single /d/ sound. This can be shown in Figure 15.1, where the dotted line in the center is notional—it does not represent any change in the articulators.

Nasals

Since nasals are articulated in the oral cavity in exactly the same way as plosives, they follow the same pattern of having a double-length closure. The diagram for a word such

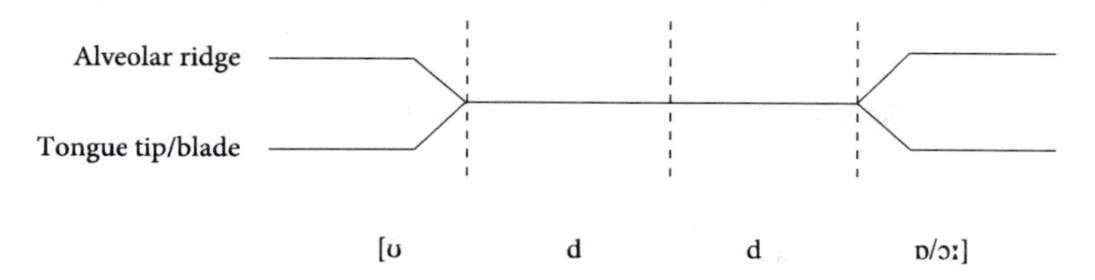

Figure 15.1 Geminate plosives (*good dog*).

as *penknife* /pennaɪf/ therefore looks identical to that for the phrase *good dog*. The difference is that, while the velum is closed throughout the phrase *good dog*, it is open for the /nn/ of *penknife*. Again, the central dotted line is notional (Figure 15.2).

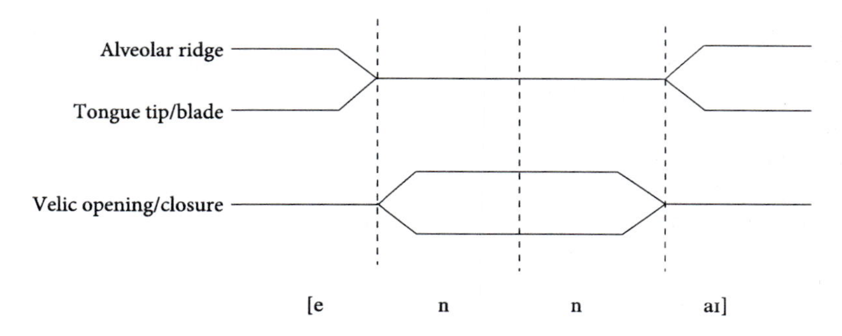

Figure 15.2 Geminate nasals (*penknife*).

Affricates

Affricates are composed of two distinct parts—a complete closure followed by a fricative release. Where they are geminate, as in *orange juice* /ɒ/ɔːrɪndʒ dʒuːs/, the first affricate is typically released and then the second is formed. In short, we have two full affricate sounds.

Fricatives

Fricatives, on the other hand, do not have distinct beginnings and endings. They can therefore be prolonged as geminate consonants. In a word such as *misspell* /mɪsspel/, there is one double-length [s] articulation.

Approximants

As for fricatives, air escapes during approximants. They can therefore be prolonged when geminate. Thus the phrase *real life* has one double-length [l] articulation.

Kaye (2005) gives measurements for the nasals in *unaimed* versus *unnamed*. They show that speakers have longer [n] articulations in *unnamed*. However, his data involves minimal pairs in direct competition (*named* versus *unnamed*), where any difference would be emphasized. There is also wide variation in the amount of lengthening shown by Kaye's subjects. Kaye claims that he does not have gemination in his (Los Angeles) accent, and that a word like *roommate* is pronounced [ruːmeɪt] (and thus presumably a homophone of *room 8*). He quotes data from Delattre (1968) that shows geminate consonants are only 1.3 to 1.0 longer than non-geminate (1.0 implying that they are not longer at all).

It should also be noted that gemination is not normally present in examples such as *immature, illogical, irrational* and *innate* (thus /ɪmətʃʊə/tʊr, ɪlɒ/ɑːdʒɪkəl, ɪræʃənəl, ɪneɪt/). Regardless of the spelling, the first three words can all be considered to have the same /ɪ/ negative prefix. The prefix in the fourth word is also pronounced /ɪ/, but is a different prefix on grounds of meaning.

Summary

- In connected speech, lexical content words (nouns, verbs, adjectives and adverbs) are usually stressed, while grammatical function words are unstressed.
- Many grammatical function words have weak forms, often containing /ə/.
- Speakers do not leave gaps (silences, pauses) between words in normal connected speech.
- Linking [j, w] and (in SSBE) linking/intrusive [r] are ways of making speech sound fluent.
- Geminate consonants do not typically involve two articulations.

Exercises

1. Here is the first paragraph of this chapter. However, all the grammatical function words have been left out. Can you supply them?

   ______ this chapter ______ ______ next, ______ focus ______ ______ fact ______ ______ sounds ______ English pronunciation ______ not occur ______ isolation. Instead, ______ occur before ______ after other sounds ______ connected speech. Sounds ______ thus affected ______ various ways ______ surrounding sounds. ______ also need ______ bear ______ mind ______ normal speech ______ not slow. ______ faster ______ speech, ______ more likely ______ ______ processes described ______ this chapter ______ ______ next ______ occur, ______ ______ make normal, fast speech easier. Together, ______ ______ therefore often referred ______ ______ connected speech processes.

   (Although *before* and *after* are prepositions, they would be stressed here because they are in contrast.)

2. We noted in this chapter that geminate consonants such as the /nn/ in *unnamed* are longer than single consonants such as the /n/ in *unaimed*. Spelling is often a misleading factor here. Note, for instance that *runny* and *unnamed* both have two *n* letters in the spelling, although *runny* has a single /n/ sound, and *unnamed* a

geminate /nn/. The reason for this is that a double consonant letter in English usually signals a preceding short vowel. Compare the short vowel in *runny* /rʌni/ with the long vowel in *puny* /pjuːni/.

Can you supply an example word for each of the following single or geminate sounds? Since the geminate sounds occur between two vowels (intervocalically), try to supply an intervocalic single consonant example too, as in the first two given answers. You will find that some geminates are not possible. Why not?

1	/n/ *penny* /peni/	13	/s/
2	/nn/ *penknife* /pennaɪf/	14	/ss/
3	/l/	15	/z/
4	/ll/	16	/zz/
5	/d/	17	/ʃ/
6	/dd/	18	/ʃʃ/
7	/m/	19	/ŋ/
8	/mm/	20	/ŋŋ/
9	/v/	21	/h/
10	/vv/	22	/hh/
11	/θ/	23	/ʒ/
12	/θθ/	24	/ʒʒ/

Further reading

Introductory phonetics books such as Cruttenden (2008), Roach (2009) for SSBE; and Avery and Ehrlich (1992), Edwards (2003), Yavaş (2011) for GenAm contain greater descriptions of all connected speech processes. Vaughan-Rees (2010) is a book of classroom activities relying heavily on connected speech processes.

16 Assimilation and elision

> Placing an onClick handler in *imput* fields fixes a bug where *input* objects inside tables are reflected more than once.
>
> Ryserson University Canada webpage (emphasis added)

Learning objectives

At the end of this chapter, you will be able to:

- provide examples of de-alveolar regressive assimilation of place
- list the four main types of elision
- explain coalescent assimilation.

Assimilation

In the previous chapter, we examined weak forms and linking as connected speech processes. In this chapter, we study two more such features: assimilation and elision. Assimilation is the process whereby one sound changes in order to become similar to a neighboring sound. Since words are joined together without a break by linking, it is irrelevant whether the two parts belong to the same or different words. We can classify assimilation in terms of two categorizations.

1 Assimilation of voice, place and manner

The question here is what feature of the sound changes.

Assimilation of voice

Assimilation of voice occurs when one sound changes from voiced to voiceless, or vice versa, because of a surrounding sound. For instance, the words *have, supposed* and *used* all end in voiced sounds when pronounced in isolation: /hæv, səpəʊ/oʊzd, ju:zd/. However, when they are followed by the word *to*, which begins with voiceless /t/, their final consonants are often made voiceless: /hæf tə, səpəʊ/oʊst tə, ju:st tə/.

Assimilation of place

When an alveolar stop (plosive or nasal) is followed by a consonant that is not alveolar, the first consonant often changes its place of articulation to that of the second sound. For instance, the /t/ of *Batman* is followed by a bilabial /m/. It is common for the voiceless alveolar plosive /t/ to change to a voiceless bilabial plosive /p/ because the following sound is bilabial; thus /bæpmæn/.

Assimilation of manner

Here, one sound changes its manner in order to be similar to that of a surrounding sound. For example, the first word of the phrase *good night* contains a final /d/, and the second word begins with an /n/. The first sound may change from a voiced alveolar plosive /d/ to a voiced alveolar nasal /n/; thus /gʊn naɪt/.

2 *Progressive and Regressive Assimilation*

The question here is whether the first sound affects the second, or vice versa.

Progressive assimilation

Here, the first sound influences the second. For example, the plural of regular nouns in English is formed by adding *-s* or *-es* to the singular form, e.g. *cats, dogs.* However, in terms of sound, the ending has two possible pronunciations. Where the singular noun ends in a voiceless consonant such as the /t/ of *cat*, the ending is voiceless /s/ (/kæts/). Where the final consonant is voiced, such as the /g/ of *dog*, the ending is voiced /z/. In other words, the ending shares the same voicing as the final consonant of the stem. The voicing state of the final consonant perseveres through the ending; progressive assimilation is also known as *perseverative.* (In chapter 14, we saw that there is a third possibility for the pronunciation of the–*(e)s* ending.)

Regressive assimilation

The opposite is where the second sound affects the first. For instance, the opposites of the adjectives *polite, definite* and *correct* are *impolite, indefinite* and *incorrect* (/ɪmpəlaɪt, ɪndefənət, ɪŋkərekt/). We can analyze the prefix as being the same in each case: it has the vowel /ɪ/ followed by a nasal which has the same place of articulation as the following consonant. In other words, the form of the nasal anticipates the place of articulation of the following consonant; regressive assimilation is also known as *anticipatory.* Some people analyze the negatives *irregular* and *illiterate* in the same way. While this may seem to make sense from the point of view of spelling, it does not from the pronunciation perspective. *Irregular* normally has only one /r/ sound, and *illiterate* only one /l/ sound.

By far the commonest type of assimilation is where an alveolar stop (plosive or nasal) changes its place of articulation to that of a following consonant. This is known as *de-alveolar regressive assimilation of place.* Table 16.1 gives the various possibilities. In

Table 16.1 De-alveolar regressive assimilation of place

	followed by		
	a bilabial	*an alveolar*	*a velar*
final /t/	*eight boys* /eɪp bɔɪz/	*eight days* /eɪt deɪz/	*eight guys* /eɪk gaɪz/
final /d/	*bad boy* /bæb bɔɪ/	*bad day* /bæd deɪ/	*bad guy* /bæg gaɪ/
final /n/	*one boy* /wʌm bɔɪ/	*one day* /wʌn deɪ/	*one guy* /wʌŋ gaɪ/

the central column (followed by an alveolar), no assimilation of place is possible, as both the final and initial consonants are alveolar.

A further common kind of assimilation happens where a final /s, z/ occurs before either palato-alveolar /ʃ/ or palatal /j/. In this case, the alveolar /s, z/ changes into palato-alveolar /ʃ, ʒ/ respectively.

spaceship /speɪsʃɪp/ > /speɪʃʃɪp/

as yet /əz jet/ > /əʒ jet/

Intervocalic /t/

We noted above that assimilation may involve voice (/hæv tə > hæf tə/). A common example of this in accents of English (and particularly American accents such as GenAm) is where a /t/ consonant occurs between two vowels, follows a stressed syllable and begins an unstressed syllable, as in *phonetics* /fə'netɪks/. Vowels are voiced, whereas /t/ is voiceless. Assimilation causes /t/ to become voiced, thus /d/. If the articulation is very short, it is known as a tap, for which the symbol is /ɾ/ (thus, /fə'neɾɪks/). This was mentioned in chapter 12.

Elision

In the previous section, we looked at assimilation, the process whereby sounds change because of their environment. In this section, we look at the loss of sounds, technically known as *elision*. There are four main cases where this occurs in English:

- When syllable-final /t/ follows a voiceless consonant (often /s/) and precedes any consonant, e.g. *next week* /nekst wiːk/ > /neks wiːk/.
- When syllable-final /d/ follows a voiced consonant (it cannot follow a voiceless one) and precedes any consonant, e.g. *handstand* /hændstænd/ > /hænstænd/.
- When /ə/ (which is always unstressed) is between consonants in a non-word-final syllable, e.g. *national* /næʃənəl/ > /næʃnəl/. Since a vowel is being lost, a syllable is

also being lost; the/næʃənəl/ pronunciation has three syllables, while /næʃnəl/ has only two. Elision of /ə/ is particularly common in SSBE where strings of /ə/ and /r/ occur, e.g. *literary* /lɪtərəri/ (four syllables) > /lɪtrəri/ (three) > /lɪtri/ (two). In GenAm, this elision does not occur: /lɪtəreri/.

- When /h/ begins an unstressed syllable, e.g. *Take him* /teɪk hɪm/ > /teɪk ɪm/.

There are several other elisions affecting particular words and phrases.

- The /v/ of *of, have* is often elided when they are unstressed (that is, the verb *have* is functioning as an auxiliary), for example, *loads of money* /ləʊdz/loʊdz əv mʌni/ > /ləʊdz/loʊdz ə mʌni/, *should have done* /ʃʊd əv dʌn/ > /ʃʊd ə dʌn/.
- The /t/ of *to*, and the /t/ of *want, don't*, are elided in the following common phrases: *want to* /wɒnt tə/ > *wanna* /wɒnə, wɑːnə/, *going to* /gəʊɪŋ/goʊɪŋ tə/ > *gonna* /gənə/, *don't know* /dəʊ/oʊnt nəʊ/oʊ/ > *dunno* /dənəʊ, dənoʊ/.
- We have already seen how syllable-final /t, d/ may be elided in certain circumstances. English allows relatively large syllable-final clusters, because of endings such as /-θ/ (e.g. *ten* > *tenth*) and /-s/ (e.g. *Mike* > *Mike's*). It is not surprising that awkward clusters are simplified by the omission of one or more of the constituent consonants. An example well-known in phonetics circles is the phrase *George the Sixth's throne*, where the final cluster /-ksθs/ is regularly simplified to just /ks/, especially as it is followed by the similarly awkward /θr -/ of *throne*.

Contractions

The elisions we have just outlined need to be distinguished from contractions such as *I'm*. Although it may seem that both processes involve the deletion of sounds, there are some crucial differences:

- Contractions involve the conflation of two words, e.g. *should not* > *shouldn't, he will* > *he'll*. In contrast, elision may take place within words and even within syllables, as in the elision of /d/ in *handful, sounds*.
- Contractions are often monosyllabic, e.g. *we are* (two syllables) > *we're* (one). Even contractions like *didn't* may be pronounced monosyllabically.
- The pronunciation of the contraction is often rather different from that of the full form, e.g. *shall not* /ʃæl nɒt/ > *shan't* /ʃɑːnt, ʃænt/, *will not* /wɪl nɒt/ > *won't* /wəʊnt, woʊnt/, *do not* /duː nɒt/ > *don't* /dəʊnt, doʊnt/. In contrast, it is usually easy to explain the omitted elements in elision.
- The pronunciation of the contraction is represented in spelling, as in dialogue in novels and plays. Thus, *they've, she's, I'll* are all clearly contractions. However, *handful, sounds* are spelt the same, whether the /d/ is elided or not.

Coalescent assimilation

The process of coalescent assimilation is a combination of assimilation and elision. It is like elision in that there are fewer segments after than before. It is like assimilation in that the resulting sound resembles both the original sounds. In a previous section, we saw that alveolar /s, z/ become palato-alveolar /ʃ, ʒ/ before palatal /j/, e.g. *this year* /ðɪs jɪə/jɪr/ > /ðɪʃ jɪə/jɪr/. The /j/ may be elided, giving the pronunciation /ðɪʃɪə, ðɪʃɪr/.

The rule is, in fact, that /s, z, t, d/ followed by /j/ become /ʃ, ʒ, tʃ, dʒ/ respectively. This is especially common where auxiliary verbs are followed by *you* in questions, e.g. *would you, did you* /wʊdʒuː, dɪdʒuː/. Also, *do you* often becomes /dʒə/ by the eliding of the unstressed vowel of *do*, and coalescent assimilation.

Summary

- Assimilation is the process whereby one sound changes in order to become similar to a neighboring sound.
- Assimilation may affect voice, place or manner; and may be progressive (where the first sound affects the second) or regressive (where the second affects the first).
- The commonest form of assimilation is de-alveolar regressive assimilation of place.
- Elision is the process of omitting certain sounds in certain environments. It is different from assimilation, which involves change, not omission.
- Elision in English typically affects syllable-final /t, d/, unstressed /h/, and /ə/.

Exercises

1. What kinds of assimilation are possible in the following words and phrases?

art gallery	*goodbye*	*John Major*	*salad cream*
broad beans	*Great Britain*	*Mrs Young*	*tennis shoes*
Citizen Kane	*headmaster*	*please yourself*	*tenpin bowling*
disused	*input*	*SUV*	*United Kingdom*

2. What elision is possible in the following words and phrases?

backhand	*handshake*	*loved ones*	*temperature*
family	*left luggage*	*penthouse*	*West Side Story*

Further reading

Introductory phonetics books such as Cruttenden (2008), Roach (2009) for SSBE; and Avery and Ehrlich (1992), Edwards (2003), Yavaş (2011) for GenAm contain greater descriptions of all connected speech processes. Vaughan-Rees (2010) is a book of classroom activities relying heavily on connected speech processes.

17 Connected speech processes

> Speaking English is like tongue-twist for me. I can speak each word perfect, but then you have to string them together like, 'Blah, blah, blah.' That's when I get crazy.
>
> Jackie Chan (b. 1954), Hong Kong actor

Learning objectives

At the end of this chapter, you will be able to:

- give examples of connected speech processes occurring together
- justify why connected speech processes are not instances of sloppy speech
- define the terms *epenthesis* and *mondegreen.*

Connected speech processes occurring together

We have looked at the four processes of weak forms, linking, assimilation and elision one by one. However, they can of course occur together at the same time, as in the following three examples.

- *handbag*: This is a compound of *hand* + *bag*. Note the /ndb/ sequence in the middle. This is the type of environment where /d/ is elided, giving /nb/. Now, an alveolar nasal before a bilabial is likely to assimilate to a bilabial nasal /m/. The resulting pronunciation /hæmbæg/ thus starts the same way as *hamburger*, which always has /mb/.
- *all present and correct*: Note the /ndk/ sequence in the middle. Again, the /d/ is elided, giving /nk/. Alveolar /n/ now assimilates to /ŋ/ before the velar /k/, giving /əŋ kərekt/.
- *the rise in crime rate*: I misheard this expression as *the rising crime rate*. The /n/ of *in* has become velar because of the following velar /k/. Linking then makes this identical to *rising*.

Slovenly speech?

Readers sometimes object that processes like assimilation and elision are symptoms of slovenly speech, that they never speak that way and doubt that these processes exist. Five arguments may be brought forward to refute this claim.

1 Natural processes

It must be emphasized that the connected speech processes of weak forms, linking, assimilation and elision are natural processes. That is, they can be easily explained as leading to sequences of sounds that are less awkward to pronounce. For instance, it is natural to pronounce the /n/ in the phrase *in part* as an /m/. Instead of the tongue being used as the active articulator for /n/ and the lips for /m/, there is now only one gesture for both /mp/, using just the lips. The resulting pronunciation is identical to *impart.*

2 Common features

I personally find it almost impossible to pronounce the phrase *George the Sixth's throne,* even in a slow deliberate style, without simplifying the /ksθsθr/ sequence by eliding some consonants. It is not difficult to find similar examples of connected speech processes, even in the speech of those persons who protest most vehemently that they do not have them.

3 Historical evidence

Perhaps the strongest evidence for connected speech processes in ordinary speech is the fact that the standard modern pronunciation of many words is the result of processes having taken place over the centuries. Four examples are enough to make the point:

- *division*: All nouns ending in *-ion* were originally pronounced /iən/. The /i/ became weakened to /j/. If, as in the case of *division*, this followed a /z/, this became /ʒ/ by coalescent assimilation, giving us modern /dɪvɪʒən/.
- *handkerchief*: This was originally a compound of *hand* + *kerchief* 'a cloth to hold in your hand.' Note the /ndk/ sequence in the middle. The /d/ was in a suitable environment to be elided. Then, the alveolar /n/ preceding a velar /k/ was changed to velar /ŋ/ by assimilation, giving us the modern pronunciation /hæŋkə(r)tʃɪf/. This is thus an identical example to *all present and correct*. Note that the first two syllables of the modern pronunciation of *handkerchief* are the same as for the verb *hanker after*, which is always /hæŋkə(r)/.
- *shepherd*: This was originally a compound of *sheep* + *herd* 'a person who looks after sheep' (compare *goatherd*). The /h/ at the beginning of the second, unstressed syllable was lost, as in the modern pronunciation /ʃepə(r)d/.
- *orchard*: This was originally a compound of *hort* + *yard* 'a yard that is a garden,' *hort* being an old word still existing in the compound *horticulture*. The initial /h/ was elided, and the /tj/ sequence in the middle became /tʃ/ by coalescent assimilation, giving us the modern pronunciation /ɔː(r)tʃə(r)d/.

4 Spelling

As in the case of *orchard*, the spelling is sometimes changed in order to reflect changes in pronunciation. There is no *h* letter at the beginning of *orchard* because an /h/ sound is no longer pronounced. The coalescent assimilation in the middle of the word is reflected in the *ch* spelling. Similarly, the surname *Sheppard* is a respelling of the word *shepherd*, without any representation of the original /h/.

The results of connected speech processes are sometimes reflected in informal spellings. A famous example is the 1982 headline *Gotcha!* in the British *Sun* newspaper, referring to the British navy's sinking of the Argentinean cruiser *General Belgrano* in the Falklands War. This is an informal version of *got you*. Firstly, the vowel of unstressed *you* is written as *a* to represent /ə/. Secondly, the coalescent assimilation in the middle of the phrase is reflected in the *tch* spelling.

Another example is the common spellings *rock 'n' roll, fish 'n' chips*, reflecting the elision of /d/ and use of /ə/ in *and* (see the examples at the beginning of chapter 15).

The word *input* is quite regularly (mis?)spelled as *imput*, reflecting the assimilation of /n/ to /m/ before /p/ (see the quotation at the beginning of this chapter). This is an especially common word in computer circles, and the spelling *imput* leads to problems, as programs have to include lines allowing the computer to recognize both spellings.

In chapter 9, we saw that the /w/ sound is both bilabial and velar (*labial-velar*). In terms of assimilation, the bilabial feature seems to exert greater influence, and thus preceding alveolars become bilabial rather than velar. This can be seen in the word *sandwich*. By elision, the /d/ is lost. The alveolar /n/ then becomes /m/ by assimilation to the following /w/. This is reflected in the informal spelling *samwidge*. (Note that the final sound is /dʒ/ rather than /tʃ/.)

The results of connected speech processes are sometimes reflected in the spellings of children. A common example is the misspelling *I should of done it*. Two processes have affected the grammatically correct word *have*: (i) since the auxiliary verb is unstressed, the vowel is weakened to /ə/ rather than /æ/, and (ii) the initial /h/ has been elided. The resulting pronunciation /əv/ is identical to the normal pronunciation of the preposition *of*.

5 *Ambiguity*

Connected speech processes occur despite the fact that occasionally they may lead to ambiguous pronunciations. For instance, the pronunciation (in GenAm transcription) /aɪ bɔːroʊd ə bʊk/ may represent *I borrowed a book* (where *a* is always pronounced as /ə/) or *I borrowed her book* (where the /h/ of /hə/ has been elided in unstressed position). Similarly, where final /t, d/ represent past tense endings, they are often elided when the following word begins with a consonant. Thus, the past tense *I liked John* is pronounced the same as the present tense *I like John*, if the /t/ of *liked* is elided. The intended meaning will usually be clear from the context, though.

However, such ambiguities are rare. Even if you try to come up with examples, the results sound contrived (in GenAm transcription below):

- /wiː niːd ðə fæks tədeɪ/: *We need the fax/facts today.*
- /kʌm ɪn ən sɪp baɪ ðə faɪr/: *Come in and sip/sit by the fire.*
- /həv juː hɜːrd əbaʊt ðə faɪnz/: *Have you heard about the fines/finds?*
- /juː niːd səm hɑːp mənʊr/: *You need some hop/hot manure.*
- /faɪnd miː ə raɪp per/: *Find me a ripe pear/right pair.*

There is a suburb of Birmingham (UK) called *Sutton Coldfield*. Many people think that this is *Coalfield—coalfield* is a common word in English and it is pronounced identically to *Coldfield* if the /d/ is elided. In fact, the origin of the name *Sutton Coldfield* is thought to be the practice of burning charcoal in Sutton Park, so the modern *d* in the spelling may have been inserted as a result of historical epenthesis (see the next section). Vice versa, some people think that *coleslaw* is *coldslaw*—it is always served cold as part of a salad, and the *cole* element is not known. If it were *coldslaw*, the /d/ would be regularly elided. In fact, *cole* is an old word meaning 'cabbage'—it is the origin of the modern word *kale*, and the first part of the respelled *cauliflower*.

Nobody would object that /ɔːtʃəd, ɔːrtʃərd/ is a slovenly pronunciation for what should be /hɔːtjəd, hɔːrtjərd/, or that the spelling *orchard* is somehow wrong. However, this is the same sort of objection that certain people make to the results of connected speech processes that are common in everyday speech.

Epenthesis

While elision means the deleting in connected speech of sounds that would be present in a careful pronunciation, epenthesis means the opposite—the insertion of sounds in connected speech, such as the insertion of a /p/ in *hamster* /hæmpstə/ (often misspelled *hampster* as a result). The sound that is inserted:

- is a plosive
- follows a nasal
- is homorganic with the nasal
- precedes an oral sound
- has the same voicing as the following sound.

In order to understand this, we need to look at a word like *hamster* from a parametric viewpoint, examining the coordination of three parameters: (i) the velum, which is open for the nasal /m/, but closed for the oral /s/, (ii) the lips, which are closed for /m/, but open for /s/, and (iii) the vocal cords, which are vibrating for /m/, but not vibrating for /s/ (see Figure 17.1).

The changes have to be coordinated in time, and if, as usually happens, they are not quite coordinated exactly, a epenthetic /p/ will result. The same is true in the following pronunciations: a /p/ in *warmth* /wɔː(r)mpθ/, a /t/ in *chance* /tʃɑːnts, tʃænts/ (thus the same as *chants*), a /k/ in *youngster* /jʌŋkstə(r)/, a /k/ in *length* /leŋkθ/.

Historically, the same process has happened with place-names like *Hamstead* (which may be alternatively spelled *Hampstead*) and surnames like *Thomson* (which may be alternatively spelled *Thompson*).

Historically, it has happened with the following words, none of which originally had a /b, d/, which was inserted later by epenthesis: *crumble* (that is, originally /krʌməl/), *cucumber, dwindle, ember, fumble, gamble, glimpse, humble, mumble, nimble, shambles, slumber, spindle, thimble, thunder.*

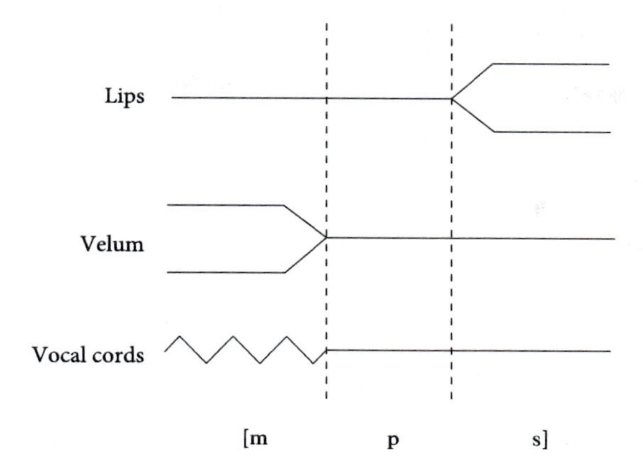

Figure 17.1 Epenthesis (*hamster*).

Mondegreens

A mondegreen is the mishearing of a phrase, often as the result of the occurrence of connected speech processes, but also involving individual consonant and vowel segments, and other features. The word *mondegreen* itself comes from such a mishearing of a line from 'The Bonnie Earl O' Murray,' a ballad from *Reliques of Ancient English Poetry* collected by Thomas Percy (1765).

> Ye Highlands and ye Lowlands,
> Oh, where hae ye been?
> They hae slain the Earl O' Murray
> And Lady Mondegreen.

The last line actually reads *And laid him on the green.* Note that this mishearing involves the elision of unstressed /h/, the hearing of /ð/ as /d/, and linking.

Such mondegreens were common with early computerized speech recognition systems. It is said that the sentence *It's hard to recognize speech* was recognized as *It's hard to wreck a nice beach.*

In fact, we have already quoted two mondegreens, in chapter 7: *Bick Spiderbecke* and *Excuse me while I kiss this guy.* There are many other, famous ones, often from popular song and hymn lyrics (some perhaps invented). Often mondegreens are a strategy for trying to understand unusual place-names or foreign elements. The mondegreen examples below are preceded by an asterisk, with the correct version given in brackets.

> *Are you going to starve an old friend? (Are you going to Scarborough Fair?)
> from *Scarborough Fair* by Simon and Garfunkel

*Sunday monkey won't play piano song (Sont des mots qui vont très bien ensemble; French for 'Are words that go together very well')

from *Michelle* by The Beatles

They are also indicative of features of pronunciation, such as the voicing of intervocalic [t] noted earlier in chapter 16.

*The girl with colitis goes by (The girl with kaleidoscope eyes)

from *Lucy in the Sky With Diamonds* by The Beatles

Mondegreens often involve the wrong assumed placement of word divisions, caused by the process of linking.

*Hope the city voted for you (Hopelessly devoted to you)

from *Hopelessly Devoted to You* from the musical *Grease*

A popular song from the 1940s relied totally on the above features of intervocalic voiced [t], linking and word division.

Mairzy doats, and dozy doats, and liddle lamzy divey.
A kiddley divey too, wouldn't you?
(Mares eat oats, and does eat oats, and little lambs eat ivy.
A kid'll eat ivy too, wouldn't you?)

from *Mairzy Doats* by Milton Drake, Al Hoffman and Jerry Livingston

Summary

- All the connected speech processes (weakening, linking, assimilation and elision) are natural processes common in everyday speech, and can occur together.
- Epenthesis is the insertion of plosives in certain circumstances.
- Mondegreens are mishearings, often because of connected speech processes.

Exercises

1. Explain the following informal spellings, expressions, jokes, etc., all of which depend on connected speech processes.

   - *spose*
   - *triffic*
   - *a cuppa*
   - *a wannabe*
   - *a whatchamacallit*
   - *Godzone* (a common name for New Zealand)
   - Pokemon–gotta catch'em all.
   - Q: Why should you not take a shower in a Pokemon's house?
     A: Because he might Pikachu.

- Q: What do you call a short-sighted dinosaur?
  A: A Juthinkesaurus.
- Q: How can I find out more about Dracula?
  A: Join his fang club.
- Q: How does the man in the moon have his hair cut?
  A: Eclipse it.
- That's all you monks think of – sects, sects, sects!
- If you've seen one shopping center, you've seen a mall.

2. What kinds of connected speech processes (weakening, linking, assimilation and elision) are possible in the following words and phrases?

bat and ball	*king and queen*	*Tottenham*
concertgoer	*last year*	*vegetable*
every second counts	*sandcastle*	*Westminster*
factory	*Soviet Union*	*windpower*

3. What kinds of assimilation and elision are possible in the following names of Major League Baseball (MLB), National Basketball Association (NBA), National Football League (NFL) and National Hockey League (NHL) teams?

Arizona Diamondbacks	Detroit Pistons
Boston Bruins	Green Bay Packers
Charlotte Bobcats	New England Patriots
Cleveland Browns	Oakland Raiders
Cleveland Cavaliers	Washington Capitals

4. Explain why the following common abbreviations are in fact rather misleading, from the pronunciation perspective.

- Car 4 sale
- House 2 let

5. The following passage is from J K Rowling's (1999) *Harry Potter and the Prisoner of Azkaban* (pp. 153–4). Hagrid, the gamekeeper at Hogwarts, Harry's school, is telling some professors the story of how Lord Voldemort (You-Know-Who) killed Harry's parents, with the help of Sirius Black. Note instances of elision, weak forms, and linking represented in the spelling. (The forms *somethin', goin', givin'* and *nothin'* do not represent connected speech processes. They represent the pronunciation of /n/ instead of /ŋ/.)

> 'How was I ter know he wasn' upset abou' Lily an' James? It was You-Know-Who he cared abou'! An' then he says, "Give Harry ter me, Hagrid, I'm his god-father, I'll look after him–" Ha! But I'd had me orders from Dumbledore, an' I told Black no, Dumbledore said Harry was ter go ter his aunt an' uncle's. Black argued, but in the end he gave in. Told me ter take his motorbike ter get Harry there. "I won't need it any more," he says.
>
> 'I shoulda known there was somethin' fishy goin' on then. He loved that motorbike, what was he was givin' it ter me for? Why wouldn' he need it any more? Fact was, it was too easy ter trace. Dumbledore knew he'd bin the Potters'

Secret-Keeper. Black knew he was goin' ter have ter run fer it that night, knew it was a matter o' hours before the Ministry was after him.

'But what if I'd given Harry to him, eh? I bet he'd've pitched him off the bike halfway out ter sea. His bes' friend's son! But when a wizard goes over ter the dark side, there's nothin' and no one that matters to 'em any more . . .'.

6. a Explain how the following mishearings (mondegreens) came about.

Popular songs

*I sometimes wish I'd never been boiled in oil (I sometimes wish I'd never been born at all)
*Beelzebub has a devil for a sideboard (Beelzebub has a devil put aside for me)
from **Bohemian Rap City* (*Bohemian Rhapsody*) by Queen

*Warm smell of policemen rising up through the air (Warm smell of colitas rising up through the air)
*What a nice surprise when you're out of ice (What a nice surprise bring your alibis)
from *Hotel California* by The Eagles

*Don't chew on me, baby (Don't you want me, baby?)
from *Don't You Want Me* by The Human League

*Like a drifter I was born to wear cologne
(Like a drifter I was born to walk alone)
from *Here I Go Again* by Whitesnake

Christian hymns and prayers

*Round John Virgin (Round yon virgin mother and child)
from *Silent Night*

*Gladly the cross-eyed bear (Gladly the cross I'd bear)
from the hymn *Keep Thou My Way*

*Blessed art thou, a monk swimming (Blessed art thou amongst women)
from *Hail Mary*

b Explain, in terms of distinctive features (chapter 14), the following misheard song lyrics.

*But I get no offers
Just a come-on from the horse on Seventh Avenue
(Just a come-on from the whores on Seventh Avenue)
from *The Boxer* by Simon and Garfunkel

*I had a dream, there were clowns in my coffee
(I had a dream, there were clouds in my coffee)
from *You're so Vain* by Carly Simon

*Reagan rots in the hot sun (Breaking rocks in the hot sun)
from *I Fought The Law* by The Clash

Further reading

Introductory phonetics books such as Cruttenden (2008), Roach (2009) for SSBE; and Avery and Ehrlich (1992), Edwards (2003), Yavaş (2011) for GenAm contain greater description of all connected speech processes. Vaughan-Rees (2010) is a book of classroom activities relying heavily on connected speech processes. Mondegreens can be found in several websites, and in Edwards (1995). Smith (2003) analyses mondegreens from learners.

18 Pausing and speed

> The most precious things in speech are pauses.
>
> Sir Ralph Richardson (1902–1983), British actor

Learning objectives

At the end of this chapter, you will be able to:

- list reasons why pausing is important in speech
- explain problems in the measurement of speaking speed
- control speaking more slowly, as a teacher.

Introduction

This chapter deals with two aspects of speech that are seldom mentioned in books on phonetics and pronunciation teaching—pausing and speed. However, they are aspects that are omnipresent in speech, and speakers are consciously aware of them. They often lead to comments such as 'English speakers speak so fast!' and may be one of the major factors separating native speakers from foreign learners. Moreover, they can be exploited by astute language teachers.

Pausing

Mark Twain is quoted as saying 'The right word may be effective, but no word was ever as effective as a rightly timed pause.' This may seem incongruous, as speech is normally interpreted as meaning the making of meaningful sounds, while pauses are exactly the opposite—silence, the lack of sound.

Pauses are important in speech for several reasons. First, on a basic level, they allow the speaker to take breath. Speakers cannot realistically continue speaking without a pause for more than about five seconds. Pauses are therefore important in that they allow the speaker to replenish the pulmonic egressive airstream that is essential for English speech. However, it is clear that the location of pauses is not random, but can be exploited for effect.

Second, pauses are used to show what belongs together grammatically. Pauses therefore typically occur at the boundaries of stretches of speech corresponding to phrases (for instance, between a long subject noun phrase and the predicate), clauses, sentences and paragraphs.

Third, since punctuation is used in written English to show the same thing (what belongs together grammatically), pauses usually coincide with punctuation in a written text. Or, to put it the other way round, speakers reading out a written text should pay attention to the punctuation used in the text, and pause accordingly. In most cases, the following rule of thumb can be used: Use a long pause for a paragraph break, a medium pause for a period (full stop), and a short pause for a comma. That is, a long pause corresponds to a paragraph break, where there is a change of topic or of speaker in dialogue; a medium pause to a sentence break, i.e. a period (full stop) or equivalent punctuation mark (question mark, exclamation mark, etc.), separating grammatically complete stretches; and a short break to a comma, demarcating stretches that belong together grammatically in clauses or phrases, but do not finish the sentence.

There are two views regarding the function of punctuation. The rhetorical tradition 'sees the role of punctuation to be assisting readers in re-creating oral renditions of texts, either by reading the text aloud or memorizing it. . . . [The grammatical tradition] views punctuation as a set of conventions for marking grammatical relationships in stand-alone written documents' (Baron, 2000, p. 170). Since we are dealing with pronunciation here, the rhetorical tradition is the more relevant, although the practical differences between the two traditions are not large. The rhetorical tradition, of using punctuation to distinguish three different lengths of pause, dates back to Aristophanes of Byzantium (3rd century BCE).

Such well-placed pauses will help the listener to understand speech, whether rehearsed or spontaneous. In *A Passage to India* (1924), E. M. Forster wrote 'A pause in the wrong place, an intonation misunderstood, and a whole conversation went awry.' Or, as Franken (2003, p. 351) points out, there is a world of difference between *George W Bush is the President who, in God's name, will protect our children* and *George W Bush is the President. Who, in God's name, will protect our children?!*

Fourth, when reading a dialogue out loud, it is important to leave long pauses at paragraph breaks that involve a change of speaker. Take the following short dialogue.

> 'Where have you been?' asked her mother angrily.
>
> 'And why did you not bother to phone us to let us know where you were?' added her father.

A long pause is needed at the paragraph break after *angrily*. Such a long pause to indicate a change of speaker is especially important in English, because phrases such as *asked her mother angrily*, and *added her father* tend to occur after the direct speech, not before it. That is, English tends to favor *'Where have you been?' asked her mother angrily* rather than *her mother asked angrily, 'Where have you been?.'* A pause is therefore needed after *angrily* and before *'And why . . .'* in order to show that the speaker of *'And why . . .'* is her father, and that this is not a continuation of what her mother said.

Fifth, a pause can often be employed after an item in order to add emphasis and importance to that item. This is especially so if the item is also emphasized by nonverbal means (such as gestures and facial expressions), intonation, stress, etc. Thus, there is less emphasis in *Money is the root of all evil*, as opposed to *Money . . . is the root of all evil*.

Finally, by concentrating on pausing, speakers are able to control their breathing and avoid speeding up to unacceptable rates. This is especially useful for presenters who may be nervous.

Speed

The measurement of speaking speed

Speed (often referred to, in connection with speech, as tempo or rate) is a simple concept to understand, but a surprisingly difficult one to measure. Just as in other fields, it refers to the number of units per unit of time. Thus, a car's speedometer measures the number of kilometers/miles per hour, and the speed of typists is measured in words per minute.

When we come to measure speaking speed, the unit of time is not a problem—it can be seconds or minutes. However, deciding on the units to be counted during that time is less simple.

The typist's measure of words per minute (or per second) could be used. However, this would not be reliable, because it would depend on the length of the particular words being spoken. Thus, for instance, a *very hard task* /veri hɑː(r)d tɑːsk/tæsk/ and an *extremely difficult exercise* /ɪkstriːmli dɪfɪkʊlt eksə(r)saɪz/ have the same meaning, and thus could both be chosen for the same utterance. However, although both phrases contain three words, the first has only four syllables and 11 sounds, while the second has nine syllables and 24 sounds. We would therefore expect the second to take much longer to say than the first.

We might therefore think that counting syllables rather than words would give a more reliable measurement. If we are solely talking about English, this may be acceptable. However, when we consider other languages, for example in order to compare speeds in different languages, this measure becomes problematic, because of differences in syllable structure possibilities. We have already seen in chapter 11 that English has a relatively complex syllable structure, allowing both syllable-initial and -final consonant clusters. Japanese, on the other hand, has no clusters, and all syllables are of the V, CV or CV/n/ pattern. As Roach (1998, p. 152) points out, an English sentence like *Smith's strength crunched twelve strong trucks* /smɪθs streŋθ krʌntʃt twelv strɒŋ trʌks/ (SSBE transcription) would take much longer to say than a Japanese sentence like /wataʃiwa jomu/ ('I read'). Both sentences contain six syllables. However, the English sentence contains many clusters and a total of 32 sounds, whereas the Japanese sentence, with CV syllables, only contains 12 sounds.

It would therefore seem that the most reliable measure of speaking speed is sounds per second.

Our problems do not end there. We still need to consider two other factors: pauses and variability. As we have emphasized in the first part of this chapter, pauses are an important part of speech, and can be exploited by speakers and teachers. The question is whether we should calculate speaking speed by considering whole utterances inclusive of pauses, or only those stretches of speech between the pauses, when the speaker is actually uttering sounds. These are sometimes referred to as *speaking rate* and *articulation rate* respectively (Laver, 1994). However, the difference between the two measures is not large.

Second, it is clear that different speaking styles typically entail different speaking speeds. Fonagy and Magdics (1960) measured different styles and found rates ranging from 9.4 sounds per second for poetry reading to 13.83 for sports commentary in English. Similarly, Yuan, Liberman and Cieri (2006) report that males tend to speak slightly faster than females, older people have slower speech, and people tend to speak more slowly when talking with strangers or discussing certain topics, perhaps as a sign of politeness or formality. Not surprisingly, non-native speakers have slower speaking rates than native speakers. There is also personal variation, that is, some people are simply typically faster speakers than others.

In conclusion, the above discussion of measuring speaking speed shows that there are many problems associated with the exercise. Nevertheless, people have clear ideas about whether certain speakers, certain styles and certain languages are spoken faster than others. It may often be difficult to provide unexceptionable data to support these claims, though.

Speaking speed and learning English

It is a common complaint from foreign learners that English speakers (including some teachers) speak too fast, as in the title of Renandya and Farrell's (2010) article 'Teacher, the tape is too fast!' They therefore find it difficult to understand the speech, or indeed to segment the stream of speech into its constituent words.

One major reason for this is the connected speech processes discussed in the previous three chapters. Features such as assimilation and elision may produce a very reduced utterance from what learners expect from the written form, or from how they themselves would pronounce it. As Rogerson and Gilbert (1990, p. 31) state, '[Connected speech] helps explain why written English is so different from spoken English.' Linking is a natural feature of native pronunciation, but does not help learners to segment stretches of speech into words.

So, is English really spoken at a faster average speed than other languages? Arnfield, Roach, Setter, Greasley and Horton (1995) found a range of 3.3 to 5.9 syllables per second for English, while Goldman-Eisler (1968) found a range of 4.4 to 5.9. This compares with the figures in Table 18.1 (in syllables per second) for various languages.

Table 18.1 Average speaking speed for various languages

Language	*Gósy (1991)*	*Dankovicova (1994)*
French	4.7–6.8	5.2–5.7
German	–	5.55–5.7
Spanish	4.6–7.0	–
Arabic	4.6–7.0	–
Italian	5.3–8.9	6.4
Dutch	5.5–9.3	6.1

Roach (1998, p. 153) concludes that 'it seems that, on the evidence available at present, there is no real difference between different languages in terms of sounds per second in normal speaking styles.'

Does speaking more slowly help learners? A slower reading speed is a feature of the US radio station Voice of America's Special English, in which it has broadcast programs worldwide since 1959. Special English has three characteristics:

- a restricted vocabulary of 1,500 words
- simplified grammar, using short, simple sentences in the active voice and avoiding idioms
- a slower reading speed, about two-thirds that of normal speech.

The original goal of Special English was to communicate by radio in clear and simple English with people whose native language was not English (Voice of America, n.d.). Its role has since expanded to include learning American English, and learning about American life, world news and developments in science. Although Special English was not originally devised as a teaching tool, it is being used as one by many people around the world. Transcripts of what is being said are available on the Voice of America (VOA) website. It is therefore a useful listening exercise, but may be expected to have benefit for pronunciation too. As a Brazilian listener says, 'I really appreciate the Special English program. It was very helpful, especially to increase my awful pronunciation. I usually listen to the same news many times, then I try to write what I am listening and then I compare on VOA's page if I did it right.'

It seems then that it is worthwhile for teachers to make a conscious effort not to speak too fast in class. However, it is important that, if teachers slow down, the features of connected speech that are characteristic of native speech at faster speeds (weak forms, elision, etc.) should not disappear. Nor should teachers begin to place stress on more words in the utterance than would be natural.

It is worth knowing that it is possible to slow down speech (or any other soundfile) in Windows Media Player, without altering the frequencies (as would have been the case with a tape recorder). To do this, click the arrow below the 'Now Playing' tab, point to 'Enhancements,' and then click 'Play Speed Settings.' You can slow down the payback to various speeds (or indeed speed it up).

However, an alternative point of view relates to the ability of the human brain to process speech. Sentences spoken at two-thirds normal speed are inevitably 50% longer. Such sentences may put a strain on the listener's working memory and make them more difficult for the listener to process. If a slower speaking speed is used by teachers, then perhaps shorter sentences should also be used, to avoid this burden on the listener's memory. VOA Special English does this, using an average of about 13 words per sentence. The ideal is for learners to graduate from shorter utterances at deliberately slower speeds to longer utterances at normal conversational speed as soon as possible. In this way, learners can process longer sentences, and learn to utter sentences themselves at more normal speeds.

Finally, it is perhaps more obvious that when giving a presentation, speakers should not speak too fast. This is especially true if the audience are not native speakers of English, if the topic is technical, and if the audience is large (in which case loudness should be increased, but speed should be decreased).

Summary

- Pauses are important to show what belongs together both grammatically and in terms of topic.
- By concentrating on pauses, speakers can avoid speaking too fast.
- It is not easy to measure speaking speed.
- English is not spoken more slowly or faster than other languages, but may seem to be, because of connected speech processes.
- Teachers of learners at lower levels may try to speak more slowly, but without unnaturally eliminating connected speech processes.

Exercises

1. a The following pairs of sentences contain the same words in the same order. However, the punctuation is a clear clue to the two different meanings of the sentences. Explain how, in terms of pauses, the different meanings would be expressed in speech.

   Shirley said, 'The teacher is stupid.'
   'Shirley,' said the teacher, 'is stupid.'

   What would you like? Cheese sandwich, apple pie, a drink?
   What would you like? Cheese, sandwich, apple, pie, a drink?

   b Similarly, explain the occurrence of pauses in the following equations.

   $4 + 6 \div 2 = 5$
   $4 + 6 \div 2 = 7$

2. The following joke has often appeared on many internet websites, and is the basis of the title of Truss's (2003) book on punctuation. Read the joke and, bearing pauses in mind, explain the double meaning in the final line.

   A panda walks into a café and sits down at a table. The waiter comes up to him and asks, 'What can I get you, sir?'
   'Just a bambooburger.'
   The waiter brings the panda his meal, and the panda eats it in silence. When he finishes it, the panda gets up to leave.
   'Sir! You haven't paid your bill,' the waiter shouts after him.
   The panda pulls a revolver from his pocket, and guns the waiter down.
   The café manager, horrified at seeing his waiter lying in a pool of blood on the floor, exclaims 'My God! What have you done?'
   'Hey! Back off, man,' replies the panda. 'I'm a panda. Look it up in the dictionary.' And the panda walks out of the café.
   The manager, perplexed, takes out a dictionary, and looks up the word *panda*.
   '***Panda*** (noun): Black-and-white bear-like mammal found in China. Eats shoots and leaves.'

3. The following passage is from Douglas Adams' (1979) *The Hitchhiker's Guide to the Galaxy*. In it, Deep Thought, the second greatest computer in the Universe of Space and Time has spent seven and a half million years calculating the answer to the Great Question of Life, the Universe and Everything. The passage has been printed here without any punctuation. However, it should be thought of as a script to be read aloud, as a teacher might to a class, or a parent to a child, rather than as a written passage to be punctuated. Where do you think the speaker should pause? Should it be a long, medium or short pause?

    Good morning said Deep Thought at last er good morning O Deep Thought said Loonqwall nervously do you have er that is an answer for you interrupted Deep Thought majestically yes I have the two men shivered with expectancy their waiting had not been in vain there really is one breathed Phouchg there really is one confirmed Deep Thought to Everything to the great Question of Life the Universe and Everything yes both of the men had been trained for this moment their lives had been a preparation for it they had been selected at birth as those who would witness the answer but even so they found themselves gasping and squirming like excited children and you're ready to give it to us urged Loonqwall I am now now said Deep Thought they both licked their dry lips though I don't think added Deep Thought that you're going to like it doesn't matter said Phouchg we must know it now now inquired Deep Thought yes now alright said the computer and settled into silence again the two men fidgeted the tension was unbearable you're really not going to like it observed Deep Thought tell us alright said Deep Thought the answer to the Great Question yes of Life the Universe and Everything said Deep Thought yes is said Deep Thought and paused yes is yes forty-two said Deep Thought with infinite majesty and calm

4. a Read the 'Eats shoots and leaves' passage in 2 above, and note how long it takes you (probably about 50 seconds).

   b Now try reading the same passage, but one third faster, i.e. taking about 34 seconds. Notice how you will probably introduce more connected speech processes (elision, linking, etc.).

   c Finally, read the passage one third more slowly, i.e. taking about 66 seconds. Try not to eliminate the connected speech processes.

Further reading

Roach (1998) summarizes the problems of measuring speaking speed, and suggests reasons why some languages are thought to be faster than others. Baron (2000, chapter 6 'Commas and canaries') describes the historical development and use of English punctuation. For an interesting piece of research about the different placement of pauses around the word *that* by Turkish and English speakers, see Bada (2006).

19 Word stress

How dare you speak to me like that! I'll have you know I am a very impotent man.

Perhaps apocryphal utterance by
a foreign speaker

Learning objectives

At the end of this chapter, you will be able to:

- list ways in which stressed syllables differ from unstressed syllables
- mark stress in different ways
- explain the importance of the schwa vowel in English
- identify *stress-attracting, -preserving* and *-shifting* suffixes
- define *compound stress* and *stress shift.*

Introduction

As we saw in chapter 11, words are made up of syllables. They may contain one syllable (e.g. *school, class*), two syllables (e.g. *teacher, student, exam, today*), three syllables (e.g. *register, monitor, assignment, computer, absentee*), four syllables (e.g. *exercises*), five syllables (*vocabulary*), and so on. Where there is only one syllable in nouns like these, then that one must be stressed. Where there is more than one syllable, English tends to give stress to only one of them.

The main stress in the above words can therefore be represented as follows, by rewriting them using capital letters for the stressed syllable:

TEACHer, STUdent, eXAM, toDAY
REgister, MOnitor, asSIGNment, comPUter, absenTEE
EXercises
voCABulary

There are various ways (or combinations of ways) in which classroom teachers could represent the stressed syllable graphically:

Capital letters:	TEACHer, toDAY
Underlining:	teacher, today
Bold type:	**teach**er, to**day**
Circle the stressed syllable:	teacher, today
Mark over stressed vowel:	téacher, todáy
Circles for stressed and unstressed syllables:	Oo, oO

In most modern English dictionaries, a tick is placed above the line (superscript) at the beginning of the stressed syllable in the transcription:

/ˈtiːtʃə(r), təˈdeɪ/

The placement of the stress on a particular syllable within the word is part of the overall phonological shape of the word. As was shown by the anecdote at the beginning of the chapter, listeners use the stress pattern to recognize the words being said. The word *important* (imPORTant) is thus very different from *impotent* (IMpotent). Indeed, there are some words of English where the only difference in the pronunciation is the placement of stress, for example *insight* (INsight) versus *incite* (inCITE), *an import* (IMport) versus *to import* (imPORT).

The nature of stress

So far, we have mentioned the occurrence of stress, but have not defined exactly what stress is. This is a more complex question than it might appear. It is related to four factors:

- Stressed syllables are usually louder than unstressed ones.
- Stressed syllables are usually longer than they would be if they were unstressed.
- Stressed syllables are usually pronounced on a different pitch (usually a higher one) than surrounding syllables (see chapter 20 for the definition of pitch).
- Stressed syllables are never weak syllables, but have a full quality. Weak syllables are those that contain [ə] or [i, u]. The vowel [ɪ] is also very common in unstressed syllables (but may also occur in stressed syllables).

Stress is a complex mixture of these factors. Pitch and length have the greatest effect.

It is also worth pointing out that stress is a physical phenomenon. It is therefore not surprising that other bodily actions, such as gestures and facial expressions, typically coincide with stressed syllables (see chapter 33).

The schwa vowel

In chapter 5 on vowels, we did not discuss the vowel known as schwa (/ʃwɑː/). This is the indistinct, neutral vowel at the beginning of *about* or the end of *cheetah*. Its symbol is /ə/. However, this vowel is a very important and special vowel in English, for three reasons:

1 It only occurs in unstressed syllables

The stress falls on the second syllable in *about*, and on the first syllable in *cheetah*. One way in which the other syllables are shown to be unstressed is by containing the schwa vowel. The first syllable in *cheetah* stands out as stressed precisely because it contrasts with the unstressed final syllable. If the final syllable is not unstressed, then the first syllable does not sound stressed by comparison.

2 It is the commonest vowel in connected spoken english

The schwa vowel accounts for about a quarter of all vowels, and a tenth of all phonemes (consonants and vowels) in connected speech (see Table 30.3). It is thus by far the commonest vowel sound. The second commonest vowel is /ɪ/, because (i) it can occur in both stressed and unstressed syllables, and (ii) like schwa, it is also quite common in unstressed syllables.

3 It has no regular spelling

The schwa vowel has no sound-spelling correspondence. Indeed, it may be represented by any of the vowel letters, or almost any combination of letters. In the following examples, the schwa vowel would be followed by /r/ in GenAm but not SSBE.

> *begg<u>a</u>r, teach<u>e</u>r, Yorksh<u>i</u>re, doct<u>o</u>r, murm<u>u</u>r, mart<u>y</u>r*

For this reason, many people, even proficient adult speakers of English, find it difficult to remember the spelling of the unstressed parts of certain words. For example, is it *calendar* or *calender, definite* or *definate, dependance* or *dependence, grammar* or *grammer, indestructable* or *indestructible, memento* or *momento, miniscule* or *minuscule, occurrance* or *occurrence, separate* or *seperate*?

The (un)predictability of English stress

In some languages of the world, the placement of stress within the word is predictable. In Czech, the first syllable is usually stressed. In French, it is usually the last syllable. In Polish, it is the second-to-last (penultimate) syllable. However, stress placement in English is not as simple as this.

Writers often debate whether stress placement in English is or is not predictable. For our present purposes of describing English for pronunciation teachers, the question is rather whether English stress placement is predictable enough to give us rules that are usable in the classroom. A related question is whether rules that can be devised represent regularities that native-speaker teachers and proficient foreign teachers are consciously aware of.

The approach that is adopted here is that, while English stress placement is not totally predictable, there are some regularities that are usable in the classroom. However, teachers should not go overboard with long lists of stress placement rules. For instance, Roach (2009, p. 76) states that in order to decide on stress placement, it is necessary to make use of some or all of the following information:

(i) Whether the word is morphologically simple, or whether it is complex as a result either of containing one or more affixes (that is, prefixes and suffixes) or of being a compound word.
(ii) What the grammatical category of the word is (noun, verb, adjective, etc.).
(iii) How many syllables the word has.
(iv) What the phonological structure of those syllables is.

He then gives three pages of rules with examples, but most of these rules have exceptions. This strikes me as fine from the point of view of an introductory book on English phonetics (which is what Roach (2009) is), but as too complex for English language teaching purposes.

As an example of the complexity of stress placement rules, let us consider the rule that the suffix *-able* does not change the stress placement. That is, if we add *-able* to *allow* /ə'laʊ/, where the stress is on the second syllable, we produce *allowable* /ə'laʊəbəl/, where the stress is still on the second syllable. There are various problems with this. Not all the problems are phonological, and many of them relate to the fact that the words come originally from Latin.

- The pronunciation and spelling of the stem may change slightly. Thus *despise* gives us *despicable, explain explicable, apply applicable, defend defensible, divide divisible,* and *correct incorrigible.* This may lead some speakers and learners not to see the connection between, for instance, *despise* and *despicable.*
- The suffix can be spelt *-ible* (e.g. *admissible*) and *-uble* (e.g. *soluble*), as well as the (five times) more regular *-able.* It is not usually possible to predict which vowel letter will occur (compare *dispensable* with *sensible*). Indeed, some words can be spelt both ways, e.g. the *Cambridge Advanced Learner's Dictionary* gives both *collectable* and *collectible.* Some writers have produced complex rules depending on the historical origins of words; however, that is of little benefit to foreign learners.
- The meaning of the suffix is not straightforward. The regular meaning is that *-able* is added to a verb to mean 'that can be [verb]*-ed.*' That is, it has a passive feel to it: for example, *doable* means 'that can be done.'
- However, *-able* can also be added to stems that are not verbs, e.g. *charitable, fashionable, impressionable, knowledgeable, marriageable, peaceable, pleasurable, saleable, seasonable, sizeable.*

  Perhaps as a result of this, there is a second meaning, namely 'worth, deserving, easy to be [verb]*-ed.*' Thus, *remarkable* means 'worth mentioning,' *notable* means 'deserving attention,' and *likeable* means 'easy to like.'
- Some words seem to contain this morpheme, but cannot be analyzed this way, because what is left as a stem is meaningless. For instance, *culpable, pliable, portable, legible, tangible* and *risible* mean 'that can be blamed, bent, carried, read, touched, laughed at,' but the forms *culp-, pli-, port-, leg-, tang-* and *ris-* have no real meaning by themselves. Similarly, *insuperable, intractable, invulnerable* and *invincible* mean

'that cannot be overcome, controlled, hurt, conquered,' but *super-*, *tract-*, *vulner-* and *vinc-* have no real meaning. All these elements have Latin origins.

- Some examples, far from having a passive feel to them, instead have an active feel. Thus, *changeable, fallible, perishable, presentable* and *sociable* mean 'able/suitable to change, fail, perish, present oneself, act socially.'
- Most importantly for teaching purposes, there are exceptions to the stress placement rules. That is, there are examples where adding *-able* does change the stress. For instance, *admire* has stress on the second syllable while *admirable* is stressed on the first. Similarly, *repair* (second), *repairable* (second) but *irreparable* (first syllable of the stem), *prefer* (second) and *preferable* (first), *neglect* (second) and *negligible* (first).
- Changes to make words conform to the rule seem to be in progress. For instance, *compare* has stress on the second syllable. However, the stress in the adjective *comparable*, or often the negative *incomparable*, is preferred on the first syllable (*com*) by older speakers, but on the second (*par*) by younger speakers in both British and American English (see Wells, 2000, p. 386 for a graph). Similarly, *prefer* has second-syllable stress. Wells gives stress for the adjective *preferable* on the first syllable (*pre*), but also cites possible stress placement on the second syllable (*fer*), with a warning symbol that it is 'considered incorrect,' but perhaps used more commonly by younger speakers. *Admirable* may also be heard with second-syllable stress (*mir*). Indeed, Wells (2000, 2008) includes several graphs containing the results of research into preferred stress placement for words such as *applicable, demonstrable, hospitable, irrefutable, justifiable, lamentable, transferable*, showing that younger speakers prefer the suffix to be stress-preserving, although in some cases, the split is almost equal: *formidable* (46% first-syllable stress, 54% second-syllable stress in British English).

Teachers generally prefer rules that are easy to state and have no, or very few, exceptions. Unfortunately, there are very few stress rules that are like this. As a result, some writers and teachers resort to the 100% foolproof rule: look the word up in a good dictionary. Since stress is generally not predictable in English, dictionaries must show the stress placement as part of the phonemic transcription. This simply means looking for the superscript tick.

Nevertheless, the rest of this chapter presents some rules that are not too difficult to state, and thus not too difficult for learners to understand and remember, and are fairly pervasive, that is, they have relatively few exceptions. Often the rules can be quickly deduced by analogy. For instance, by considering words such as *absentee, addressee, amputee, appointee, consignee, deportee, detainee, employee, evacuee, internee, interviewee* and *nominee*, both teachers and learners should be able to establish that English words ending in the suffix *-ee* have stress on the suffix. This can be easily tested by extending the rule to new examples. Thus, while the words *mentor* and *tutor* can be found in dictionaries, the words *mentee* and *tutee* cannot. However, if they existed (and some people do use them as nonce forms), they must be stressed on the last syllable.

Stress and suffixes

The effect, in terms of stress placement, of adding suffixes to stems is usually described in three categories.

1 Stress-attracting suffixes

When stress-attracting suffixes are added to stems, the suffix itself receives the stress, regardless of where the stress originally fell. The *-ee* examples just quoted are thus stress-attracting. Table 19.1 gives some common examples (adj = adjective).

Table 19.1 Stress-attracting suffixes

Suffix	*Usual stem*	*Resulting word class*	*Usual meaning*	*Examples*
-ee	verb	noun	someone who is [verb]-ed	*employee, interviewee*
-eer	noun	noun	someone involved with the noun	*engineer, mountaineer*
-ese	noun	adj	nationality	*Japanese, Taiwanese*
-ette	noun	noun	small	*diskette, kitchenette*
-esque	noun	adj	like a [noun]	*picturesque, statuesque*
-ography	noun	noun	the study of [noun]	*oceanography, typography*

2 Stress-preserving suffixes

Stress-preserving suffixes do not alter the placement of stress. That is, whichever syllable in the stem was stressed is still the stressed syllable after the suffix has been added. The *-able* suffix we discussed earlier is thus an example of this category. So are all the eight inflectional suffixes of English: *she catch<u>es</u>, he want<u>ed</u>, swimm<u>ing</u>, tak<u>en</u>, bigg<u>er</u>, tall<u>est</u>, hors<u>es</u>, Alice<u>'s</u>.* Table 19.2 gives some common examples.

Prefixes, that is affixes that come before the stem, are usually stress-preserving in English, e.g. *do, redo; agree, disagree.*

3 Stress-fixing suffixes

The final category of suffix is those that are not attracting or preserving, that is, the stress falls within the stem, not on the suffix, but the addition of the suffix does change the stress placement within the stem. Such suffixes are often called stress-shifting. However, while this tells us that the stress shifts within the stem, it does not allow us to predict where in the stem it falls. Often, the stress placement can be stated by counting syllables backwards from the end of the word. For this reason, the term *stress-fixing* is preferred. For example, we can state that the suffix *-eous* causes the stress to fall on the syllable preceding this suffix (the second-to-last, or penultimate, in the word), regardless of

Table 19.2 Stress-preserving suffixes

Suffix	*Usual stem*	*Resulting word class*	*Meaning*	*Examples*
-able	verb	adj	that can be [verb]-ed	*adjustable, maneuverable*
-age	noun or verb	noun	various	*leverage, percentage*
-al	noun	adj	to do with [noun]	*central, seasonal*
-al	verb	noun	the act of [verb]ing	*refusal, removal*
-en	adj	verb	to make more [adj]	*loosen, sweeten*
-er	verb	noun	some who [verb]s	*teacher, writer*
-ful	noun	adj	full of [noun]	*beautiful, wonderful*
-hood	noun	noun	the state of being [noun]	*childhood, motherhood*
-ify	noun or adj	verb	to increase the quality	*beautify, simplify*
-ise, -ize	adj	verb	to make [adj]	*finalize, modernize*
-ish	noun	adj	like a [noun]	*childish, foolish*
-ish	adj	adj	to some degree	*greenish, oldish*
-ism	noun or adj	noun	social, political or religious belief or behavior	*extremism, sexism*
-ive	verb	adj	being able to [verb]	*descriptive, imaginative*
-like	noun	adj	in the manner of [noun]	*businesslike, workmanlike*
-less	noun	adj	without [noun]	*powerless, meaningless*
-ly	adj	adverb	in a [adj] manner	*quickly, sadly*
-ly	noun	adj	like a [noun]	*brotherly, friendly*
-ment	verb	noun	the process of [verb]ing	*achievement, management*
-ness	adj	noun	the quality of being [adj]	*kindness, nervousness*
-ous	noun	adj	related to [noun]	*adventurous, disastrous*
-y	noun	adj	with [noun]	*cloudy, lucky*

where it originally fell, e.g. *couRAGeous, erRONeous, GASeous, miscelLANeous, outRAGeous.* Table 19.3 gives some common examples.

Stress in (some) words of more than one grammatical class

There is a group of words that undergoes a change in stress placement depending on whether the word is being used as a noun or adjective on the one hand, or a verb on the other. Take, for example, the word *present*. This can be a noun (*a birthday present*), an adjective (*your present address*) or a verb (*presented with medals*). In the first two uses, the stress is on the first syllable: PREsent. However, in the last, it is on the second: preSENT. This is shown in the pronunciation, not only by the stressed syllables having

Table 19.3 Stress-fixing suffixes

Suffix	*Usual stem*	*Resulting word class*	*Meaning*	*Stressed syllable*	*Examples*
-eous	noun	adj	with [noun]	2nd-to-last	*courageous, erroneous*
-ial	noun	adj	related to [noun]	2nd-to-last	*industrial, presidential*
-ic	noun	adj	related to [noun]	2nd-to-last	*athletic, diplomatic*
-ical	noun	adj	related to [noun]	3rd-to-last	*alphabetical, mechanical*
-sion, -ssion, -tion	verb	noun	the act of [verb]-ing	2nd-to-last	*compulsion, progression, restoration, repetition*
-ious	noun	adj	with [noun]	2nd-to-last	*conscientious, harmonious*
-ity	adj	noun	the state of being [adj]	2nd-to-last	*brutality, inaccessibility*

full vowels (both /e/ in this case), but also by the unstressed syllables having weak vowels (/ə/ and /ɪ/): /ˈprezənt, prɪˈzent/.

This alternation between first-syllable stress for the noun or adjective, and second-syllable stress for the verb is shown in the following words: *abstract, compress, concert, conduct, conflict, consort, contract, contrast, convert, convict, defect, desert, digest, discharge, escort, export, extract, frequent, implant, import, incline, increase, insert, insult, object, perfect, permit, present, proceeds, produce, progress, project, protest, rebel, record, refund, refuse, reject, retard, segment, subject, survey, suspect, torment, transfer, transport.*

It must be emphasized that this alternation does not apply to *all* words that can be used as nouns/adjectives and verbs. There is a very productive word-formation process called conversion, whereby words of one original grammatical class are used in a different grammatical class, without changing their form. For instance, the word *carpet* is originally a noun (*a carpet*). However, it is nowadays very commonly used as a verb too: *We carpeted the living room.* Whether it is used as a noun or a verb, the stress still falls on the first syllable: /ˈkɑː(r)pɪt/. The lack of stress movement is true of many other words, e.g. *copy, alarm, control.*

Compound stress

Compounding is another very common word-formation process. A new word, usually a noun, is produced by combining two previously existing words. Thus, for example, *white* + *board* gives us *whiteboard, lesson* + *plan* produces *lesson plan*, and *reading* + *list* creates *reading list.*

Readers may be wondering why *lesson plan* and *reading list* are considered compound words, when they are usually spelled as two words. In fact, spelling is not a reliable criterion here, as compounds may be spelled as one word, two words, or one word hyphenated. For instance, the make-up that women put on their eyelids is spelled as *eyeshadow* in the *Oxford Advanced Learner's Dictionary*, but as '*eye shadow*, also *eye-shadow*' by the *Cobuild Advanced Learner's Dictionary*. For that matter, would you spell the title of this chapter *wordstress, word-stress* or *word stress*?

In terms of stress, the important point about compounds is that the stress falls on (the stressed syllable of) the first element. Thus, the above compounds are WHITEboard, LESSon plan and READing list. This may seem counterintuitive to foreign learners, because a whiteboard is a kind of board, and thus *board* seems the more important element. Nevertheless, native speakers regularly place stress on the first element.

Three common structures for compound nouns are:

- Noun + noun, e.g. *classroom, bookshop, tennis player*
- Adj + noun, e.g. *shortbread, hardware*
- Gerund (verb + *ing*) + noun, e.g. *dining room, swimming pool.*

Compounds like this can be contrasted with simple noun phrases made up of nouns with premodifying adjectives or nouns.

> The teacher wrote the answer on the whiteboard.
> Jack used a white board to hold the mirror in place.

The first sentence above contains the compound, which is thus pronounced WHITEboard. The second, however, is not a compound; it is a simple noun phrase composed of the head noun *board*, with the premodifying adjective *white*. It is literally a board that is white. The stress thus falls on the head noun: white BOARD.

Vaughan-Rees (2010) gives the following simple description of the main differences in meaning between compounds and noun phrases:

Compounds are often:

- X is a special type of Y, e.g. the *White House* is a particular house that is white
- X is for Y, e.g. a *bookshop* is a shop for books
- an X [verb]-*er* of Y, e.g. a *meat packer* is someone who packs meat.

Noun phrases are often:

- X is made of Y, e.g. a *meat pie* is a pie made of meat
- X is Y, e.g. an *Australian teacher* is a teacher who is Australian.

Stress shift

The final aspect of word stress we will consider here occurs when words are in phrases. For instance, we have already said that words ending in *-ese*, such as *Japanese*, have stress on the suffix (japanESE). This is true when the word is said by itself, or at the end of an utterance, as in the first two sentences below.

> *JapanESE*
> *He speaks JapanESE.*

However, when the word is followed by a noun in a noun phrase, the stress shifts from the final syllable to the first, as in the following sentences.

a JAPanese teacher
the JAPanese ambassador

English does this because it seems to avoid, where possible, having two stressed syllables next to each other or in close proximity. The stress shifts in the above two examples, so that it is further from the stressed syllables of *TEACHer* and *amBASSador*.

Summary

- Word stress is an important aspect of English pronunciation, as listeners use it to recognize words.
- As Dalton and Seidlhofer (1994; see chapter 30) point out, it is important for teaching purposes, as it combines teachability with communicative importance.
- Stress is marked in transcriptions, as in dictionaries, by a superscript tick at the beginning of the stressed syllable.
- Stress cannot exist without unstress. The schwa vowel is important for signaling unstress.
- Many stress rules are complex, and they often have exceptions.
- The foolproof method of finding out the stress pattern of unfamiliar words is to look them up in a dictionary.

Exercises

1. Which is the stressed syllable in the following English Premier League football team names? Which is the odd-one-out?

Arsenal	Chelsea	Liverpool	Southampton	Swansea
Cardiff	Everton	Norwich	Sunderland	Tottenham

2. Which is the stressed syllable in the following English names?

Denise	Helen	Raymond
Douglas	Jonathan	Sandra
Elizabeth	Melissa	Yvonne

   Now transcribe them, bearing in mind that the unstressed syllables are likely to contain schwa or /ɪ/.

3. Decide whether the underlined stretches of the following sentences (in SSBE transcription) are compounds or not, and mark the stress. The sentences are given in transcription, so that you cannot tell from the spelling—as one or two words, or hyphenated—whether they are compounds.

   a /dʒɑn lɪvz ɪn ə waɪt haʊs/
   b /ðə prezɪdənt lɪvz ɪn ðə waɪt haʊs/

   c /mɪstə ʃmɪt kʌmz frəm dʒɜːməni ənd ɪz ən ɪŋglɪʃ tiːtʃə/
   d /mɪstə smɪθ ɪz ən ɪŋglɪʃ tiːtʃə hɪz sʌbdʒɪkt ɪz mæθs/

e /ʃiː wəz weərɪŋ ə kɒtən dres/
f /ðeɪ wɜːk ɪn ə kɒtən fæktri/

g /mɑːk ɪz sʌtʃ ə sləʊ kəʊtʃ/
h /wiː trævəld ɪn sʌtʃ ə sləʊ kəʊtʃ/

i /dəʊnt dʒʌmp ɒn ə muːvɪŋ bʌs/
j /ə muːvɪŋ væn tʊk ɔːl aʊə fɜːnɪtʃə/

k /aɪ bɔːt maɪ sʌn ə tɔɪ ʃɒp/
l /aɪ went intʊ ə tɔɪ ʃɒp/

Further reading

The classic work on English word stress, analyzing the subject in depth, is Fudge (1984).

20 Tone groups

> If the child could paint the picture, these [intonation and rhythm] would be the wave on which the other components ride up and down; but the linguist is older and stronger, and has his way—he calls them suprasegmentals, and makes the wave ride on top of the ship.
>
> Dwight Bolinger (1907–1992), *Forms of English* (1961)

Learning objectives

At the end of this chapter, you will be able to:

- define the terms *intonation* and *tone group*
- segment stretches of speech into tone groups
- identify the tonic within the tone group
- explain the importance of the placement of tone group boundaries and tonics.

Definition of intonation

In this chapter and the next, we deal with the topic of intonation. Like many other terms in phonetics, it is one that is also often used imprecisely in everyday language.

In phonetics, intonation can be defined as how we use the way the pitch of our voices goes up and down in order to convey meaning. This definition then leads on to two other questions. First, how do we analyze the pitch movement of our voices? Second, what kinds of meaning are conveyed by intonation?

In terms of the first question, about the analysis of pitch movement, we will need to define three basic concepts in intonation:

- The *tone group* is the stretch of speech over which a pitch contour extends.
- The *tonic* is the syllable/word that is the intonational focus of the tone group.
- The *tone* is the direction of the pitch movement on the tonic.

We will discuss the first two of these concepts in this chapter, and tone in the next. The relationship of intonational features to meaning will be discussed at various points in both chapters.

Tone groups

The pitch of the voice is the note on which sounds are said. This pitch depends on the frequency of vibration of the vocal cords. If the vocal cords are vibrating relatively fast, this gives a high pitch. If they are vibrating slowly, the pitch is low. Try saying a vowel such as [ɑː] or a consonant such as [z] on a high note, and then on a low note. Then say them going from a low note to a high one, that is, rising pitch. Then, from a high to a low, that is, falling pitch.

It may have occurred to you that, since pitch depends on vocal cord vibration (that is, voicing), and since some consonants such as [s] are voiceless, that is, do not involve vocal cord vibration, they cannot be used for this demonstration. The voiceless consonants do not have pitch in this sense. You cannot, for instance, pronounce [s] on a rising or falling pitch. However, we have already seen that the majority of English consonants, and all vowels, are voiced. The intermittent breaks in pitch in connected speech for voiceless consonants do not disrupt listeners' perception of overall pitch patterns.

The tone group (also known, by different writers, as tone unit, intonation unit, breath group and sense group) can be defined as the stretch of speech over which a pitch contour extends. In fact, we have already talked about tone group-sized stretches of speech, in chapter 18, as tone group boundaries are very often associated with pauses. We argued in chapter 18 that pauses often coincide with punctuation in a written version of the language. Since punctuation is normally used to delineate stretches of language that are grammatically complete (phrases, clauses, sentences and paragraphs), tone group boundaries usually correspond to grammatically complete stretches. It is therefore a good idea, whenever learners have to read a passage aloud, for them to mark it up in terms of pauses, as we did in the *Hitchhiker's Guide to the Galaxy* exercise in chapter 18. This not only helps learners to remember to pause and to avoid reading too fast, thus making the passage easier for the listener to understand. It will also help with the learner's intonation patterns.

Let us take some examples, and see the importance of tone groups (the number of tone groups in an utterance, and the location of boundaries). As in the exercise in chapter 18, the sentences contain the same words in the same order but, because of grammatical differences reflected in the location of punctuation in writing, and tone group boundaries and pauses in pronunciation, they have different meanings.

1 *My car which is 12 years old keeps breaking down.*
2 *My car, which is 12 years old, keeps breaking down.*

In the situation in the first sentence, I have more than one car. The car that keeps breaking down is the one that is 12 years old—the other cars run well. In the situation in the second sentence, I have only one car. Thus, when I say the phrase *my car*, it refers to only one possible car. The information that it is 12 years old is thus extra added information, and sounds like an aside. It could just as easily be put in dashes or brackets. Grammarians refer to constructions as in 1 as restrictive or defining relative clauses, and in 2 as nonrestrictive or nondefining. There have to be tone group boundaries at the commas in sentence 2, whereas sentence 1 is likely to have only one break, after *old*, separating the grammatical subject from the predicate. Sentence 1 cannot have a break after *car*.

3 *I don't like Susan, because she's cute.*
4 *I don't like Susan because she's cute . . .*

The difference in meaning here depends on what the negative element (the *-n't* of *don't*) relates to. In the first sentence, it negates the verb *like*. The first sentence thus means the same as *I dislike/hate Susan, because she's cute* (and I don't like cuteness). However, in the second, the negative element actually relates to the second clause *because she's cute*. It thus means the same as *I like Susan, not because she's cute . . .* (but because she's rich). This case depends on the tendency in English for *not* to migrate to the main verb regardless of what it actually negates. Thus, we normally say *I don't think that's right* rather than *I think that's not right*. Sentence 3 will thus have two tone groups, the boundary coinciding with the comma, while sentence 4 has only one.

5 *The children the doorman admitted were a nuisance.*
6 *The children, the doorman admitted, were a nuisance.*

Sentence 5 contains a restrictive relative clause, like sentence 1. It means 'Only those children that the doorman allowed to enter were a nuisance.' Sentence 6, however, does not contain a nonrestrictive relative clause. Instead, the verb *admit* has a different meaning ('concede, acknowledge, grant'). It can move to different places in the sentence: *The doorman admitted that the children were a nuisance; The children were a nuisance, the doorman admitted.* Sentence 5 will have two tone groups, the boundary coming after *admitted*, and separating the subject from the predicate. Sentence 6, however, will contain three tone groups, the breaks coinciding with the commas.

Intonation is typically marked in the following way. Sentences are written, not in italics, and with features like numbers spelt out in full. The capitals used in spelling are not used because, as we shall see in the next section, capitalization is used for another feature. Other punctuation, such as commas and full stops, are not used. Tone group boundaries are typically marked by putting a large vertical stroke. Thus, sentence 2 above, which contains three tone groups, is marked as follows.

| my car | which is twelve years old | keeps breaking down |

Tonics

Within the tone group, and within sentences generally, it is the lexical content words that receive stress. This was presented in chapter 15 as a natural process, because it is the content words that convey the bulk of the meaning in a sentence. Vice versa, grammatical function words do not convey so much meaning, and are thus usually unstressed, often by using schwa.

Within the tone group, the tonic word is the one that carries the greatest pitch movement. In a neutral pronunciation, this is the last lexical word (*car* (noun), *old* (adjective) and *down* (adverb) in the above example). Where the tonic word contains more than one syllable, it is the stressed syllable that carries the tonic movement. The tonic syllable/word is also known as the nucleus, or nuclear syllable/word.

In intonational terms, stressed (prominent) syllables are marked by capitalization, and the tonic syllable is underlined. Sentence 2 is thus as follows.

| my <u>CAR</u> | which is TWELVE YEARS <u>OLD</u> | KEEPS BREAKing <u>DOWN</u> |

Contrastive and correcting stress

It can be seen that intonation, in the strict sense of pitch movement, and stress are closely related here. Tonics such as *down* will be marked not only by having the greatest pitch movement (probably a fall from high to low), but also by being pronounced with greater stress than other lexical items in the tone group.

One influential property of English, often described as a feature of stress although it is properly one more generally of intonation, is contrastive stress. This means that elements that are being contrasted in a sentence will be tonics, regardless of whether they are lexical items, or other considerations. For instance, in the sentence *I said he was my boss, not my worker,* the words *boss* and *worker* are clearly in contrast, and will therefore be tonics. Perhaps even more surprisingly, in the sentence *I said he was my employer, not my employee,* the elements that are in contrast are the words *employer* and *employee,* which themselves contrast only in the *-er* and *-ee* endings. These endings will therefore be tonics, even though the *-er* of *employer* is not normally even the stressed syllable within that word.

The concept of correcting stress can be thought of as a subset of contrastive stress. This occurs where one speaker corrects what another has said.

7 A: *I'll offer you $5,500 for the car.*
  B: *I won't take less than $6,500.*
8 A: *I'll offer you $6,200 for the car.*
  B: *I won't take less than $6,500.*

In sentence 7, the contrast is between *$5,500* and *$6,500,* which is why speaker B will place the tonic on the contrasting element, which is the word 6. However, in sentence 8, the contrast is between *$6,200* and *$6,500,* and speaker B will place the tonic on the contrasting word 5.

Intonation, including the placement of tonics, thus relates to the context of utterance, and what has been said before.

9 A: *Who is it here who hates strawberries?*
  B: *I hate strawberries.*
10 A: *Would you like some strawberries?*
  B: *I hate strawberries.*
11 A: *Was it strawberries or raspberries you hate?*
  B: *I hate strawberries.*

Although what B says in each case is the same words, the sentences are pronounced differently because of the context given by the preceding questions. In sentence 9, the tonic will be on *I,* because it is the answer to the question *who.* In 10, the tonic is *hate,* which contrasts with *like* in the question. In 11, the tonic is *strawberries*, because B is choosing between two alternatives.

In short, we cannot say that a particular sentence will be pronounced in a fixed way. It depends very much on the context and on the subtleties of meaning that the speaker wants to convey. For this reason, I have used words such as *normally* and *probably* in the above description—other pronunciations in terms of intonation are possible.

Summary

- The *tone group* is the stretch of speech over which a pitch contour extends. Tone groups are often separated by pauses.
- The *tonic* is the syllable/word that is the intonational focus of the tone group. In a neutral pronunciation, this occurs on the last lexical word.
- Both tone groups and tonics help the listener to understand the grammatical and semantic meaning of the utterance.

Exercise

Explain (i) the difference in meaning, and (ii) the difference in pronunciation (tone group boundary placement) between the following pairs of sentences.

If you understand the instructions clearly, there's no problem.
If you understand the instructions, clearly there's no problem.

The boy and the girl in jeans were late.
The boy, and the girl in jeans were late.

Further reading

While there are many books on English intonation, most of them cover the subject in too much detail for teachers. The most accessible in this respect are Tench (1996) and Wells (2007). Taylor (1993) approaches the topic from the teacher's point of view. Levis (2001) discusses tonic placement in pronunciation teaching, with sample exercises.

21 Tones

> One often contradicts an opinion when what is uncongenial is really the tone in which it was conveyed.
>
> Friedrich Nietzsche (1844–1900), German philosopher, *Human, All Too Human* (1878)

Learning objectives

At the end of this chapter, you will be able to:

- define the term *tone*
- illustrate the fall, rise, fall-rise, rise-fall and level tones
- list some of the meanings associated with these tones
- explain the four types of meaning associated with intonation: attitudinal, grammatical, accentual, discoursal.

Tones

In the previous chapter, we introduced two elements of intonation. Firstly, the tone group is the stretch of speech over which a pitch contour extends. Secondly, the tonic word, containing as its stressed syllable the tonic syllable, is the intonational focus of the tone group, often the last lexical word. In this chapter, we describe the nature of the pitch on the tonic syllable, known as the tone.

Analyses of the nature of tones began as quite complex descriptions. For instance, O'Connor and Arnold's (1961) account described eight different tones, and ten commonly occurring combinations of pitch features (tone groups). These had picturesque names such as the switchback, the long jump, the jackknife and the terrace, intended as mnemonics but ultimately difficult to remember, and describing patterns that were too sophisticated for learners to distinguish. Halliday (1970) distinguished seven tones. The most recent large-scale analysis of (British) English intonation, that of Brazil (see Brazil, 1997; Brazil, Coulthard and Johns, 1980) has as its basis a two-way distinction, admittedly with subdivisions. This may be taken as an admission that, while English intonation is quite complex in many areas, complex descriptions may be unhelpful for foreign learners.

The following sections describe five tones: the fall, the rise, the fall-rise, the rise-fall, and the level tone. Some writers have defined the tonic syllable as being the one on which the maximum pitch movement within the tone group occurs. This is fine for most tones except, of course, the level tone. By definition this does not have movement up or down. This is why we have defined the tonic here as having the intonational focus by virtue of being the most important word in the tone group in terms of meaning.

In each of the following subsections, we will describe the main functions of the tones. However, it must be emphasized that tones do not stand in a simple one-to-one relationship with meaning. While the functions described below are probably the most common, and the most useful for learners, other tones and other meanings are often possible.

Fall

A falling tone, marked here by the symbol \ before the tonic syllable, represents a movement from a higher pitch to a lower one. It is probably the commonest tone in English.

The main meaning of the fall tone is finality, completion or definiteness. It is therefore found very often in statements.

| JOHN'S a million \ NAIRE |

Since it conveys completion, a fall is usually found on the last item in a closed list. Thus a fall on *Luxembourg* shows that the following list has only these three items. (The tones of the other tone groups are discussed below.)

| The BENelux COUNtries | are BELgium | the NETHerlands | and \ LUXembourg |

Rise

A rising tone, marked here by the symbol / before the tonic syllable, represents a movement from a lower pitch to a higher one.

A rise may be thought of as the opposite of a fall. That is, a rise conveys lack of finality, completion or definiteness. It is therefore used for nonfinal items in a closed list.

| The / BENelux COUNtries | are / BELgium | the / NETHerlands | and \ LUXembourg |

Since it conveys incompleteness, it may also be used for the final item in an open list. Thus, while Benelux comprises only three countries, Europe comprises many more.

| / EUrope | comprises / BELgium | the / NETHerlands | / LUXembourg |

In writing, this would often be conveyed by the ellipsis punctuation '. . .' : *Europe comprises Belgium, the Netherlands, Luxembourg . . .*

The difference between a *wh-* question and a yes-no question is often signaled by the difference between a fall and a rise. *Wh-* questions are those that contain one of the seven *wh-* words (*who, which, what, when, where, how, why*). They are usually pronounced on a falling tone.

| HOW WELL can you \ SWIM |

Yes-no questions, on the other hand, do not involve one of the *wh-* words, and are usually pronounced on rising tones.

| can you / SWIM |

The difference between a fall and a rise is also typically used for tag questions with different implications. Tag questions are the short questions put at the end of statements in order to make questions. If they are pronounced with a fall, their function is to confirm something that the speaker is already confident is true.

| you DON'T KNOW the \ ANswer | \ DO you |

Alternatively, the speaker may be asking a genuine question, because he/she does not know the answer. In this case, the tag question is pronounced with a rise.

| you DON'T KNOW the \ ANswer | / DO you |

Finally, a rise is always used in echo questions, where the speaker repeats (the bulk of) what the other person has said, in order to show surprise.

A: | JOHN'S a million \ NAIRE |
B: | JOHN'S a million / NAIRE |

Fall-rise

The fall-rise tone, marked here by the symbol ∨ before the tonic syllable, is similar in function to the rise, namely lack of finality, completion or definiteness.

| The ∨ BENelux COUNtries | are ∨ BELgium | the ∨ NETHerlands | and \ LUXembourg |

Indeed, in Brazil's analysis of British English intonation, the fall-rise is given as the common tone in such circumstances, the plain rise being a subset of the fall-rise. While it may be the more common in British English, a fall-rise often strikes foreign learners as strange. The important point, then, is perhaps that they both end in rises, that is, high pitches rather than low ones.

One function of the fall-rise tone, that is not usually possible with the plain rise, is to convey uncertainty, reservation or hesitation.

| the HOUSE was ∨ NICE | but VEry ex \ PENsive |

It may also convey tentativeness, politeness or deference.

| WHAT are you ∨ DOing toNIGHT |

Rise-fall

The rise-fall tone, marked here by the symbol ∧ before the tonic syllable, is by far the rarest of the tones considered here. It is said to convey either being overawed or impressed, or being suggestive.

A: | he WON the NObel \ PRIZE |
B: | ∧ REALly |

A: | WHAT are you ∨ DOing toNIGHT |
B: | ∧ NOthing |

Level

The level tone, marked here by the symbol ¯ before the tonic syllable, is a mid pitch with little upward or downward movement. Although there is no movement, it is still considered the tonic, because it usually occurs on the last lexical word, may be followed by a pause, and carries the greatest stress. It is often used to show that what the speaker is saying is routine and uninteresting. It is, for instance, used when the teacher calls the register in class and, similarly, when the learners reply.

Teacher: | ¯ ADams |
Learner: | ¯ PRESent |
Teacher: | ¯ BLACKburn |
Learner: | ¯ HERE |
Teacher: | ¯ BROWN |
Learner: | ¯ YES |

It is also often used when asking a series of routine questions, as in the following medical examination.

Doctor: | have you EVer SUFfered from tubercu ¯ LOsis |
Applicant: | ¯ NO |
Doctor: | leu ¯ KEmia |
Applicant: | ¯ NO |
Doctor: | ¯ WHOOPing COUGH |
Applicant: | ¯ NO |

The tail

Many people find it difficult to tell whether the pitch is going up or down. Indeed, many learners that I have taught have consistently given me the wrong answer—they heard a rise when it was a fall, and a fall when it was a rise. Often this is because they are paying too much attention to the wrong part of the tone group. It is not because they are 'tone deaf': everyone can produce the intonation of their native language perfectly, even if not consciously.

Let is take the utterance *I'm not angry*, said in contradiction.

A: | WHY are you so \ ANGry |
B: | I'm \ NOT angry |

The tonic in the response is on *not*, because that conveys the contradiction. The other elements in the utterance (*I* and *angry*) have already been mentioned. A diagrammatic representation of the intonation of the utterance is thus as follows, with the horizontal lines representing the habitual highest and lowest pitch.

| I'm \ NOT angry |

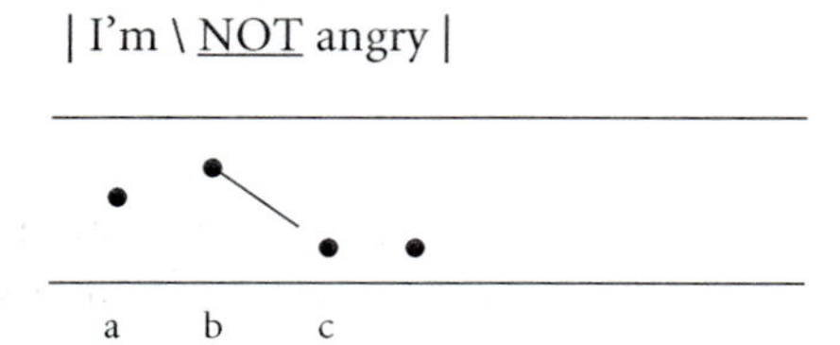

Learners often concentrate on what precedes the tonic. By comparing the mid pitch of preceding syllables (in this case, *I'm*) with the high pitch of the tonic (*not*) (that is, position a with b), they conclude that it must be a rise. Instead, what they should be concentrating on is what follows the tonic (that is, comparing position b with c), because any pitch movement started in the tonic is continued in what follows (known as the tail). The tonic *not* is at a high pitch, while *angry* is at a low pitch, showing that the pitch has fallen. The pitch rose from *I'm* to *not* in order to make room for this fall.

Let us continue the conversation.

A: | WHY are you so \ ANGry |
B: | I'm \ NOT angry |
A: | you're / NOT angry |

A's echo question can be represented as follows.

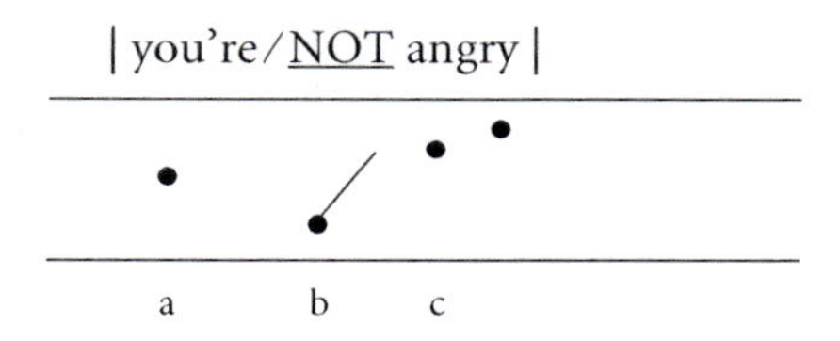

Again, by wrongly comparing the mid pitch of *you're* (a) with the low pitch of *not* (b), learners conclude that it is a fall. Instead, by comparing the low pitch of the tonic *not* (b) with the high pitch of *angry* (c), it is seen to be a rise. The pitch fell from *you're* to *not* in order to make room for the rise.

Key

We have seen how intonation works within utterances and sentences. We have also seen that the intonation chosen for one sentence depends on preceding sentences from the same speaker or the interlocutor. A final element of intonation to be covered here stretches even further, to the same extent as what in writing we would call a paragraph.

Paragraphs in writing signal a change in topic. As we saw in chapter 18, paragraphs are usually also signaled by long pauses. They may also be signaled in the intonation. The beginnings of paragraphs are usually said more upbeat, using higher pitches in the overall range. This has been referred to as high key. Vice versa, at the ends of paragraphs, pitches tend be in the lower part of the range (low key). Paragraphs may also be signaled in pronunciation by a slight increase in speed and loudness at the beginning, and a decrease in both dimensions at the end. These paragraph-style stretches of speech have sometimes, from the intonational point of view, been called *paratones*.

The nature of intonation

In this chapter, we have described the major tones, and the major meanings that are typically associated with those tones. However, we have not tackled the essential nature of intonation, by examining what kind of meaning is conveyed. It is convenient to look at this question from four perspectives.

Attitudinal

When we say that a fall-rise conveys uncertainty, or that a rise-fall conveys being over-awed, the meaning can be described as attitudinal. That is, the speaker uses the tone in order to convey their feeling at the time.

Grammatical

When we say that a *wh*- question is usually pronounced on a fall, while a yes-no question is usually on a rise, the tone can be described as fulfilling a grammatical function.

Accentual

The placement of the tonic syllable within the tone group is of importance, as it shows the focus of the information. As we have seen, the tonic is on the last lexical word in a neutral pronunciation. However, it can easily move to a different position, depending on the desired emphasis. Thus, the second utterance below is more emphatic than the first.

| it's VEry \ QUIET |
| it's \ VEry QUIET |

Discoursal

Intonation can also help to show an utterance's place within a discourse, that is, a connected spoken passage, or a conversation with several turns. We have already seen examples of this. The placement of the tonic in the following answers depends on the question being asked.

A: | can ANYone here / SWIM |
B: | ∨ I can SWIM |

A: | HOW come you NEVER LEARNT to \ SWIM |
B: | i \ CAN swim |

A: | can you ∨ SNORKel |
B: | i can ∨ SWIM |

We can also show that a particular tone group is of relatively low importance by subordinating it. This is the equivalent of making it an aside by putting it in brackets in writing. It is achieved in pronunciation by using low key, low loudness but increased speed, as in the middle tone group below.

| the ∨ ANSwer | as you'd ex ∨ PECT | was \ NO |

Brazil's discourse intonation analysis of English is based on a two-way distinction between proclaiming tone (a fall, used for information that has not been mentioned before) and referring tone (a fall-rise, for information that is shared, or common ground). Claims have been made that all intonation is discourse intonation, in that all pitch movement can be explained in terms of the co-text (what is said before and after the utterance) and the context (the speakers and the physical situation of utterance). However, this does not necessarily mean that a discourse analysis is the most useful one for language teaching purposes.

Summary

- The main tones of English can be analyzed as the fall, rise, fall-rise, rise-fall, and level tone.
- Tones do not stand in a one-to-one relationship with meaning. Many utterances can be said with more than one tone, sometimes with very little difference in meaning.
- The meaning conveyed by intonation can be analyzed into attitudinal, grammatical, accentual and discoursal types.

Exercises

1. Decide which tone you would use on the reply *no* in each of the following examples.

   A: That's not the right answer.
   B: (Disbelieving) No?

   A: Is Istanbul the capital of Turkey?
   B: (Factually) No.

   A: Is that the right answer?
   B: No, but you're warm.

   A: Have you ever been convicted of a crime?
   B: No.
   A: Have you ever been refused a visa?
   B: No.

   A: You'll drive me home, won't you?
   B: (Indignantly) No.

2. Here is the word-for-word transcript of part of a radio news broadcast.

   a Read through it and mark where you think the newsreader's script had new paragraphs.
   b Now read the passage aloud, paying attention to the use of key and other features at paragraph breaks.

To end the news, here are the main points again. The prime minister has set off on an official visit to Pakistan. Before he left, he said that he would be covering many topics with his counterpart, Mr Rahman. In particular, he hoped to bring the controversy over the recent cricket tour to a satisfactory conclusion. He now continues to India, the next stop on his South Asian tour. Official statistics just released show a sharp increase in the number of deaths on the road over the recent Christmas period. As a result, the traffic police state they are carrying out an investigation into the causes of the rise, and will be stepping up breathalyzer testing over the coming Easter holiday. In the latest round of league matches, West Ham edged out Newcastle 2–1, to ease their relegation worries. Fellow relegation-battlers Stoke drew 1–1 with Aston Villa, and are now three points behind West Ham. The two teams meet in a bottom-of-the-table six-pointer on Saturday. The Scottish film Edinburgh Tales has been nominated for four Oscars, including Best Picture, and Best Actor for George McQueen. The winners will be announced at the ceremony on Tuesday evening. And that's the end of the news.

Further reading

Tench (1996) and Wells (2007) may also be read for this chapter. Wong (1987) contains many practical exercises in intonation and rhythm. Brazil's discoursal analysis of intonation is to be found in Brazil (1997) and Brazil, Coulthard and Johns (1980). Cauldwell and Hewings (1996) and Ranalli (2002) argue that it is important for pronunciation teaching. A coursebook based on the discourse intonation model is Bradford (1988). The tones found in questions are examined by Levis (1999) and Thompson (1995).

22 Rhythm

A speech is poetry: cadence, rhythm, imagery, sweep! A speech reminds us that words, like children, have the power to make dance the dullest beanbag of a heart.

Peggy Noonan (b. 1950), US author and presidential speechwriter

Learning objectives

At the end of this chapter, you will be able to:

- describe the main distinguishing features of the three accounts of English rhythm.

Introduction

Most readers, especially those who are not native speakers of English, or those native speakers who have an intimate knowledge of another language, will probably have little problem with the statement that the rhythm of English speech is different from that of other languages. It may therefore surprise them that there is no universally accepted analysis of English speech rhythm, nor indeed of what speech rhythm means. In this chapter, three different ways of analyzing English speech rhythm will be discussed.

Abercrombie's theory of stress- and syllable-timing

The traditional analysis of English speech rhythm, and one which is held by many people and often quoted, is that of Abercrombie (1967). It has a physiological basis. In chapter 3, we noted that all English speech sounds, and almost all speech sounds in languages of the world, are made on a pulmonic egressive airstream, that is, the lungs push air outwards. However, the expulsion of air by the muscles surrounding the lungs is not steady, but rather is pulsed. Each of these chest pulses constitutes a syllable. Some of the chest pulses are reinforced, giving stressed syllables. A two-way distinction in speech rhythm is proposed, depending on the regularity of pulses. In syllable-timed languages, it is the chest pulses (syllables) that occur at roughly equal intervals of time (isochronously). In stress-timed languages, it is the reinforced pulses (stressed syllables) that are isochronous.

Abercrombie used the sentence *This is the house that Jack built* to illustrate stress-timing in English. In a normal pronunciation, the words *This, house, Jack* and *built,*

This	is	the	house	that	Jack	built
ˈðɪs	ɪz	ðə	ˈhaʊs	ðət	ˈdʒæk	ˈbɪlt

Figure 22.1 Rhythmic feet.

being lexical content words (see chapter 15), are stressed (shown by the superscript tick in Figure 22.1). The sentence can be divided into four feet, each foot representing the interval from one stressed syllable up to, but not including, the following one. The feet are shown in Figure 22.1 with vertical lines, but these are being used in a different way from the vertical lines representing tone group boundaries in chapter 20.

The first foot contains three syllables: a stressed syllable (*this*) and two unstressed (*is*, *the*). However, the third and fourth feet each contain only the one stressed syllable (*Jack*, *built*). In order to maintain the isochrony of the stressed syllables, the unstressed ones are shortened to varying degrees. This is informally known as the concertina effect.

Abercrombie (1967, p. 97) maintains that 'as far as is known, every language in the world is spoken with one kind of rhythm or with the other.' Traditionally quoted examples of syllable-timed languages are French, Spanish, Portuguese, Telugu (southeast India) and Yoruba (Nigeria), while English, Russian and Arabic are quoted as stress-timed.

Many people have taken Abercrombie's dichotomy and applied it to other varieties of English (West Indian, West African, Indian, Filipino, Singaporean and Hawaiian English, as well as learners' varieties), claiming that they are syllable-timed rather than stress-timed. However, there is any equally large number of people who do not believe in Abercrombie's analysis, for the following reasons:

- The physiological basis of the chest pulse theory has been disproved instrumentally.
- English rhythm has been shown instrumentally to be only very roughly isochronous, even in read prose.
- Traditionally quoted examples of languages with one kind of rhythm or the other have not stood up well to instrumental investigation.
- Abercrombie himself claimed that there was reason to believe that languages, and different accents of the same language, had historically made the transition from one type of timing to the other. He gave Provençal French (stress-timed) and standard Parisian French (syllable-timed) as an example. If such possibilities exist, then we would expect to find languages and varieties in transition, that are neither syllable-timed nor stress-timed, but somewhere in the middle.
- Writers have claimed that syllable- and stress-timing should not be thought of as a dichotomy (syllable-timed versus stress-timed), but as a scale (more syllable-timed versus more stress-timed). Dauer (1983) proposes a change in terminology, suggesting that languages are more or less stress-based.
- Some writers have suggested that syllable-/stress-timing is more of a perceptual phenomenon related to the way the brain perceives and interprets physical

information, rather than a physical articulatory one open to instrumental measurement.

- O'Connor (1973, pp. 239–240) asserts that 'there is no reason why there should be any rhythmical basis at all in the sense of some feature recurring at regular time intervals.'
- Many of Abercrombie's examples are taken from poetry. However, writers have objected that the rhythm of poetry is different from the rhythm of everyday speech, especially spontaneous speech. The whole premise of traditional poetry is that it is based on a very regular beat system. English language teachers who try to impose such a regular rhythm on speech usually end up sounding like metronomes.

While most commentators have been happy to acknowledge that languages differ in their rhythm, and that rhythm depends on the temporal regularity of features, there is less agreement about exactly what features these are. Factors claimed to influence rhythmic patterning include (i) the complexity of syllable structure (for instance, whether a language allows consonant clusters), (ii) the presence or absence of vowel reduction to /ə/, (iii) the stress patterning of a language and (iv) the presence or absence of a distinction between long and short vowels in a language.

The pairwise variability index

One problem in deciding whether the rhythm of English displays stress-timing, in which stressed syllables occur regularly, is that it is often difficult to identify which syllables in an utterance are stressed, especially in spontaneous everyday speech.

A solution has been proposed that looks at the problem from another perspective. If a language or utterance is syllable-timed, then the syllables should all be of roughly equal length. This is regardless of stress, and there is no need to specify (perhaps problematically) which syllables are the stressed ones. Deterding (2001) and Low, Grabe and Nolan (2000) carried out such measurements for SSBE (traditionally labeled stress-timed) and Singapore English (traditionally called syllable-timed). Deterding measured the variation in length between one syllable and the following one. Low et al. measured the length of just the vowels in those syllables. This measure, known as the pairwise variability index (PVI), therefore gives us an indication of the concertina effect, which should be greatest for stress-timed languages. In both studies, the measure for Singapore English was found to be smaller than that for SSBE, where syllable lengths varied more greatly. This is taken as an indication that Singapore English is more syllable-timed than SSBE.

Several variations of the PVI method of calculation have been tried, in order to see which best captured the rhythmic differences between languages. One modification has been to normalize for speaking rate across each successive pair of vowels (known as the normalized PVI or nPVI). Another (the raw PVI or rPVI) excludes pauses and periods of silence from consideration. Both measures can be applied to either the length of vowels (vocalic, that is, the period from the start of one vowel to the end of the same vowel) and consonants (intervocalic, that is, the period from the end of one vowel to the start of the next). Grabe and Low (2002) applied the PVI to various languages (see Figure 22.2), showing that this was one way in which the different rhythms of languages could be captured.

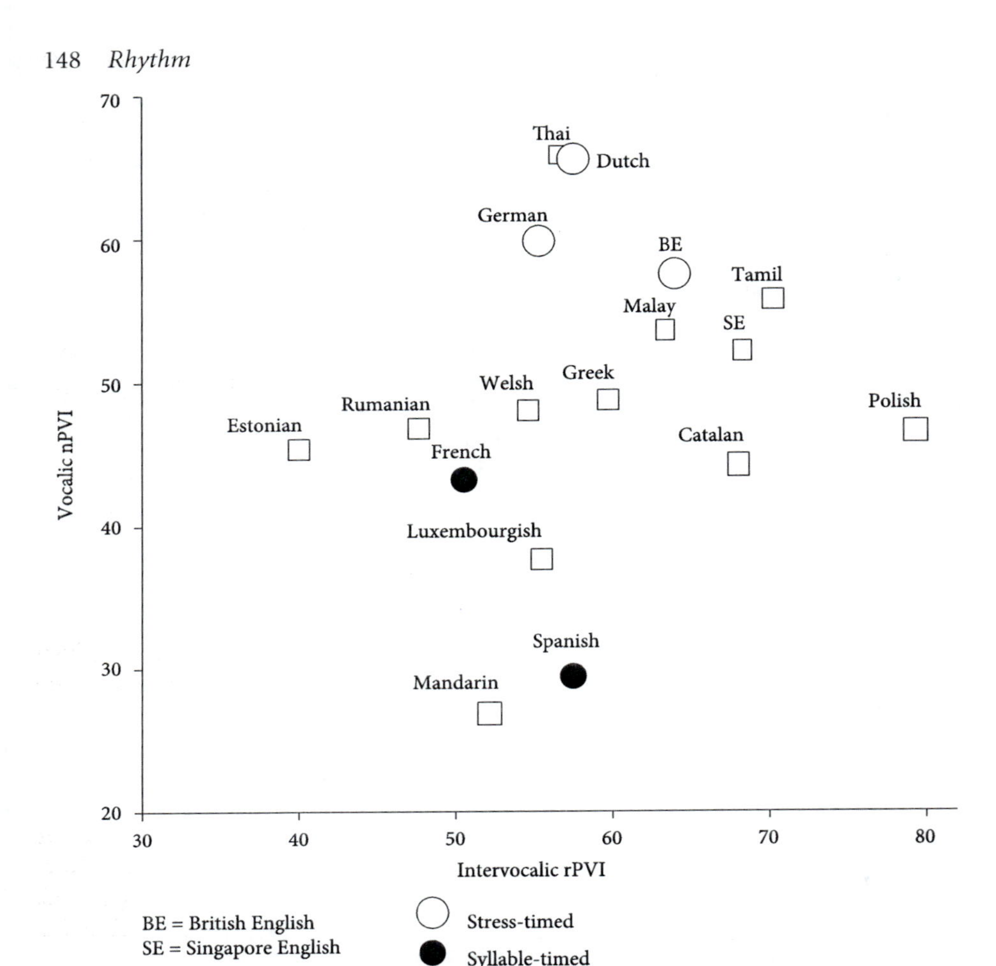

Figure 22.2 PVI profiles for data from 18 languages.

Source: Grabe & Low, 2004

Bolinger's theory of syllable length

A different account of speech rhythm has been proposed by Bolinger (1981). In this theory, rhythm is seen not as a function of syllables and stresses, but of syllable type.

Syllables may be of two types: long (L) syllables contain full (F) vowels, while short (S) syllables contain reduced (R) vowels. Reduced vowels comprise not only schwa [ə], but also [ɨ] as in *sillịness*, and [ɵ] as in *solọist*. These are the symbols Bolinger uses, and may be thought of as similar to [i, u], as discussed in chapter 5.

Abercrombie's illustrative sentence may therefore be represented as shown in Figure 22.3.

A rule then states that a long syllable becomes extra long (LL) when it is followed by another long syllable or a pause (such as at the end of the sentence). This then gives us

This	is	the	house	that	Jack	built	orthography
ðɪs	ɪz	ðə	haʊs	ðət	dʒæk	bɪlt	transcription
F	R	R	F	R	F	F	vowel type
L	S	S	L	S	L	L	syllable type

Figure 22.3 Long and short vowels.

the following final pronunciation, and explains why *Jack* and *built* are each longer than *this* and *house*, even though they all contain full vowels and are stressed (Figure 22.4).

This	is	the	house	that	Jack	built	orthography
L	S	S	L	S	LL	LL	syllable type

Figure 22.4 Extra long vowels.

Faber (1986) suggests that, instead of calling *Jack* and *built* extra long, we might, from the opposite point of view, say that *this* and *house* are shortened, because they are followed by reduced-vowel syllables.

Conclusion

It can be seen that there is relatively little agreement, not only over how rhythm can be measured, but also over what rhythm is. Abercrombie's theory claims that it is a function of the length of syllables and the occurrence of stresses. Deterding and Low et al. only measure vowel or syllable length, ignoring stress. For Bolinger, rhythm is a function of vowel and syllable type, while stress is irrelevant.

It seems clear that rhythm is an important, large-scale feature of languages, and one quite evident way in which languages differ. Since it is difficult to explain or measure rhythm, the solution for the teacher may simply be to expose their learners to plenty of natural occurrences of the language being learnt, in the hope that the learners will subconsciously acquire an appreciation of the rhythm of the language.

It is also clear that certain forms of English, such as poetry, song lyrics and very emphatic speech, have a more regular stress than other forms. They may therefore be used with learners whose native language has a very different rhythmic basis, and who may therefore have trouble with English rhythm.

Summary

- Some languages clearly have different rhythms from others.
- This informal observation does not mean that it is easy to define rhythm or measure it.
- Exposure to the language is an important aspect of learning the rhythm of English.

Exercises

1. Sing your country's national anthem. Now say the words of the anthem in a normal speaking voice. What differences are there?
2. Songs, poetry and raps of course have regular rhythm. Find a simple poem or rap. Read it out loud and note the concertina effect, that is, how the words between the stresses are pronounced indistinctly (often with schwa) and shortened in order to maintain the rhythm.

Further reading

Marks (1999) questions the validity of stress-timing within an English language teaching (ELT) perspective. Vaughan-Rees (2010) contains many fun activities based on rhythm; many of these exercises, however, relate to poetry of various types, and may thus depend on more regular rhythm than normal speech.

23 Voice quality

> Act modestly in the way you walk, and lower your voice. Indeed, the harshest of sounds is the voice of the ass.
>
> The Qur'an (chapter 31, verse 19)

Learning objectives

At the end of this chapter, you will be able to:

- give a technical definition of the term *voice quality*
- list some of the ways in which voice qualities differ.

Definition

The term *voice quality*, like the more everyday expression *tone of voice*, is often used by English language teachers and writers. However, in phonetics, it has a fairly precise definition, unknown to many teachers and writers, who therefore wrongly include many other features (such as rhythm or speed) under the umbrella term *voice quality*. The major work in this area of phonetics has been carried out by Laver (1980, 1994), who has come to use the term *articulatory settings* instead. He defines an articulatory setting as 'any tendency for the vocal apparatus to maintain a given configuration or featural state over two or more segments in close proximity in the stream of speech' (1994, p. 153). Two aspects of this definition should be understood. First, voice quality refers to states or positions of parts of the vocal apparatus. It should also perhaps be pointed out that voice quality does not refer to *voice* in the sense of vibration of the vocal cords, although the state of the vocal cords is one of the possible components of voice quality. Second, these states or positions are long-term effects.

Voice quality features may be caused by various factors.

- They may simply be ***idiosyncratic*** features, that is, characteristic of individual speakers. We may know speakers who habitually have nasalized voices (with more than usual air escaping through the nose), or harsh voices (caused by a particular setting of the vocal cords).
- They may be used on particular occasions in order to convey particular ***attitudes***. For instance, we can all smile while speaking (that is, pronounce all segments with

spread lips) in order to appear friendly. When conveying a secret, we normally use a whispery voice, caused by a particular setting of the vocal cords.

- Finally, different voice qualities are characteristic of different ***languages***, and different accents of languages. For example, Honikman (1964) describes a difference between English and French in long-term lip position as neutral and moderately active for English, but rounded and vigorously active in spreading and rounding for French. Similarly, in some accents of Arabic and the Liverpool accent of English, all sounds tend to be slightly further back in the mouth. This can be analyzed as an overall tendency for the tongue to be drawn back towards the velum or uvula (known as velarization or uvularization).

Voice quality features

What follows is a brief checklist of common voice quality features. A much more detailed discussion of features in this underanalyzed area of phonetics can be found in Laver (1980, 1994).

- ***Lips:*** In the front-to-back dimension, the lips may be protruded. In the side-to-side dimension, they may be rounded or spread.
- ***Jaw:*** The jaw may be held in a relatively close position with little movement (that is, with the two sets of teeth close to each other), or may be opened widely for susceptible segments.
- ***Tongue tip:*** The tongue tip may be very active, being used for alveolar segments, as in Italian and Indian languages. Alternatively, it may be the tongue blade that is used.
- ***Tongue body:*** The tongue body may be raised or lowered, advanced or retracted, giving rise to settings such as palatalized voice (with the tongue staying relatively close to the hard palate) or velarized voice (with the tongue staying relatively close to the soft palate). It may also be retroflex, with the tip curled back, as in some languages of India.
- ***Velic coupling:*** The velum, which regulates the flow of air into the nose, may be held relatively open (nasalized voice) or closed (denasal voice).
- ***Vocal cords:*** The vocal cords may be held in various states. Harsh voice involves increased muscular tension in the vocal cords. In breathy voice, the vocal cords vibrate but with a greater than normal escape of air. Falsetto voice allows the vocal cords to vibrate at a higher than normal pitch. Creaky voice sounds like a stick being rattled against railings, and usually occurs at lower pitches. Finally, whispery voice uses a fricative articulation rather than normal vibration. Various combinations of these vocal cord states are possible.
- ***Tension:*** Overall tension in the vocal apparatus above the vocal cords may be higher than normal (tense) or lower (lax).
- ***Pitch and loudness:*** The means, ranges and variability in these two dimensions may vary as a feature of voice quality.

Voice quality and pronunciation teaching

Jenner (1987) summarizes the settings of English as 'loose, inactive lips, concave tongue with active tip, neutral larynx position and relative relaxation throughout. In simple terms this means that one has to be relatively lazy to speak English well. This requires, paradoxically, great mental if not physical effort.' Jenner assumes that the learner is aiming at acquiring a native-like pronunciation of English, and that factors such as identity are not important (see chapter 24). He is also presumably describing British English, as Esling and Wong (1983) give a different array of settings for US English: spread lips, open jaw, palatalized tongue body position, retroflex articulation, nasal voice, lowered larynx and creaky voice.

While there may be some disagreement over the precise nature of the voice quality of English, most teachers will be aware of overall voice quality features that distinguish their learners. Such teachers may be able to imitate the features without being able to describe precisely how they are caused physiologically.

Cultural factors may play a part in some learners' reluctance or aversion to acquiring a native-like voice quality. For instance, we have already seen that French is characterized by more vigorous lip movement, including protrusion, than English. In English-speaking cultures, lip protrusion is common, but for purposes such as conveying condescension. English speakers learning French may therefore find it strange that their teacher is encouraging them to sound condescending in order to sound authentically French.

The field of voice quality is one that has not been well researched. However, this does not mean that it is unimportant for pronunciation teaching. If learners can acquire an appreciation of what English voice quality is like, then this may help them to acquire many of the individual segments of English more accurately, since the voice quality is, as it were, the underlying common core of all the segments.

The above discussion argues for the importance of the teacher familiarizing learners with the voice quality of English by exposing learners to natural samples of the language, by recordings, films, songs, etc.

Summary

- *Voice quality* refers to long-term positions and states of the various vocal organs: lips, jaw, tongue, velum, vocal cords, as well as tension, pitch and loudness.
- Voice quality may characterize individuals, and may be used to convey attitudes, but may also be characteristic of different languages and different accents of languages.
- Since voice quality underlies all the segments of a language, teachers may improve segmental pronunciation by first concentrating on voice quality.

Exercises

1. Name someone you know who habitually uses:

    - nasal voice
    - harsh voice

- whispery voice
- a large pitch range
- protruded lips
- a close jaw.

2. Think of any language, other than English, that you know well. Can you describe the typical settings of speakers of that language? Think of lip and jaw settings, tongue position, nasality, vocal cord settings, tension and pitch settings.

Further reading

The seminal treatment of voice quality is Laver (1980; also see 1994). It is, however, a very detailed treatment. A case study using voice quality is described by Kerr (2000).

Section 2

Pronunciation teaching

24 Targets

> I ascribe a basic importance to the phenomenon of language. . . . To speak means to be in a position to use a certain syntax, to grasp the morphology of this or that language, but it means above all to assume a culture, to support the weight of a civilization.
>
> Frantz Fanon (1925–1961), Martiniquan psychiatrist, philosopher, political activist, *Black Skin, White Masks* (1952)

Learning objectives

At the end of this chapter, you will be able to:

- distinguish the considerations of intelligibility, image and identity
- list the pros and cons of the three types of target: major world accents, model speakers, and the Lingua Franca Core.

Introduction

The topic of this chapter is targets, that is, the pronunciation that the learner is aiming to acquire. Unless some thought is given to this, it is impossible for the learner or the teacher to determine whether they have been successful.

One problem in discussing this topic is the glut of terms used inconsistently and sometimes interchangeably, including *target, aim, model, norm* and *standard* (Brown, 1989). More worrying, perhaps, is that there may be substantial differences between what learners are being taught, and what they are achieving in the classroom. As a result, there may be one pronunciation variety implicitly contained in pronunciation textbooks, recorded materials, etc.; a different variety represented by the teacher's own accent, especially if the teacher is a nonnative speaker; and finally the learners' achieved performance, which may lie somewhere between a major world model variety, an educated local variety (the teacher's accent) and a pronunciation with limited, local intelligibility (see p. 158).

The three Is of language targets

The types of consideration that determine the targets that language learners are aiming for can be divided into three broad categories (although, as we shall see below, two of them are probably related).

Intelligibility

The first such consideration is intelligibility. Intelligibility is a basic factor of all language teaching, and is therefore appreciated by language teachers and learners. If you cannot be understood when speaking a language, then you do not 'speak that language.' This does not mean, however, that it is an easy concept to define. It is clearly a scalar continuum (more easily versus less easily intelligible) rather than a binary one (intelligible versus non-intelligible).

The distinction has been drawn between intra-national intelligibility, where speakers are intelligible only to speakers from their own or similar communities, and international intelligibility, where their pronunciation is more intelligible in worldwide terms. More intra-national pronunciations are referred to by Gimson (Cruttenden, 2001, p. 299) as having *restricted intelligibility*, where 'phonetic and phonological interference from the indigenous languages may erect a formidable barrier.'

The term *comfortable intelligibility* has been used by many writers, but was first coined by Abercrombie (1956, p. 37), who defined it as 'a pronunciation which can be understood with little or no conscious effort on the part of the listener.' Such pronunciations may possess some local features from the speaker's native language(s) but not those that would impede wider international intelligibility. Comfortable intelligibility may be achieved by paying attention to features contained in Jenkins' (2000) Lingua Franca Core (LFC) (discussed in greater detail on p. 162).

The difference in the standpoints of Jenkins and Gimson may be explained by their time of writing. Jenkins' LFC was devised on the basis that the majority of conversations in English around the world nowadays take place between nonnative speakers, without involving a native speaker from the UK, USA, Australia, etc.

> In EIL [English as an International Language], we are concerned above all with safeguarding intelligibility among speakers for whom English is nobody's L1. The interests of 'native speakers' are secondary to the enterprise.
>
> (Jenkins, 2000, p. 147)

On the other hand, Gimson, who died in 1985, was writing at a time when the success of pronunciation was judged against a native speaker/listener. He proposed a category of *minimum general intelligibility* (Cruttenden, 2001, p. 298) 'which is capable of conveying a message efficiently *from a native English listener's standpoint*' (italics added). Apart from this, Gimson's category of minimum general intelligibility seems to correspond by and large with comfortable intelligibility.

Gimson proposes another category: *high acceptability*, 'defined as a level of attainment in production which, *for the native listener*, is as readily intelligible as that of a native RP speaker and which is not immediately recognizable as foreign' (Cruttenden, 1994, p. 276, italics added). It is noteworthy that this is proposed as a category of intelligibility rather than of acceptability, that is, of being understood rather than of being accepted as prestigious or appropriate, or avoiding stigmatization. No evidence is given by Gimson that native accents are more intelligible in global terms than nonnative ones. Indeed, native-like accents may be highly unacceptable, and thought of as putting on airs, to nonnative listeners in local contexts. It is significant that the phrase *for the native listener* is omitted from the next edition of the work (Cruttenden, 2001, p. 302). Discussion of intelligibility and acceptability always begs the question 'intelligible and acceptable to whom?'

Intelligibility is of especial importance for certain groups of learners of English for Specific Purposes (ESP). In jobs where communication often takes place via electronic channels such as the telephone, public address systems, radio, walkie-talkies and the internet, intelligibility is paramount because of the distortion possible in these channels. Speakers with jobs such as call centre staff, secretaries, hotel staff, airline pilots and flight attendants therefore all need to be very easily understood by a wide range of listeners.

For many individual learners, a minimal level of comfortable intelligibility may be all they are aiming for.

Image

There may be other learners for whom a minimal level of comfortable intelligibility is not enough. Instead, they would like to be perceived as good confident English speakers. This may be a personal attitude on the part of the speaker towards pronunciation, language learning and education in general. However, it may also relate to job prospects. Frontline professions such as hotel receptionists, bank tellers and flight attendants are usually required to convey the impression of polished English speakers, because poor language skills (including pronunciation) reflect poorly on the professional image of the company they work for. Such companies are therefore usually prepared to invest a sizeable portion of the staff training budget towards this.

Identity

The way that you speak says a lot about the person you are. This may be idiosyncratic, that is, characteristic of you alone. However, it also relates to your country of origin and native language(s). Speakers from a certain country may be proud of their nationality and be happy to speak English with a recognizable accent from that country and language. Such learners may be resistant to acquiring a native-like accent of English, feeling that this would be tantamount to changing their personality and identity.

A continuum of targets

The three factors (intelligibility, image and identity) can be synthesized into two related continua of pronunciations ranging from more international pronunciation at the one end to more local pronunciation at the other. One is that of intelligibility, which we have discussed above.

The two other dimensions (image and identity) can be considered as occurring on the same continuum. Whether native speakers or learners, we choose our pronunciation (and other aspects of a language) in order to identify ourselves on a personal or group basis. Le Page and Tabouret-Keller (1985, p. 14) point out that linguistic behavior is 'a series of acts of identity in which people reveal both their personal identity and their search for social roles.'

The factors of image and identity pull in different directions. Image involves trying to convey an impression of being a prestigious speaker of English, by using a pronunciation that is recognized internationally. Identity involves using a pronunciation that lets your compatriots know that you share solidarity with them. This is the distinction between international and intra-national intelligibility.

Figure 24.1 attempts to capture the relationships between these factors.

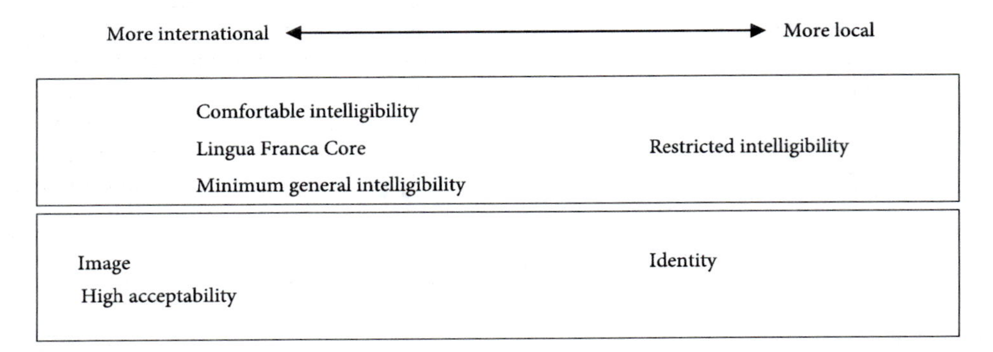

Figure 24.1 Diagrammatic summary of pronunciation targets and the factors of intelligibility, image and identity.

In short, as teachers, we cannot assume that all learners are aiming for the same target. If, after investigation, we find that our learners do all want to acquire the same kind of pronunciation target, this makes it easier for us to conduct classes, because we know what we are aiming for. However, many classes involve learners with different kinds of target, and the task is more difficult.

A plethora of terms

Several terms are used in the literature for the process of teaching pronunciation to foreign learners. These terms are widely used in the context of teaching English (including pronunciation) to migrants to English-speaking countries. The terms are especially popular in the USA, but many of them carry unnecessarily negative overtones.

The term *accent elimination* seems meaningless, because an accent cannot be eliminated. An accent cannot be unlearned, in such a way that the speaker can no longer pronounce that way.

The term *accent neutralization* implies that the accent being learned is neutral. However, no accent is neutral, in that each accent conveys information about the speaker. For native speakers, this may be geographical and social information. For foreign speakers, this information relates not only to their foreign origin, but also to their strength of identity, the context in which they learned the language, etc.

Accent reduction implies that the speaker's accent is influenced by the transfer of features from the speaker's native language(s) (see chapter 29). This may, however, have positive benefits of conveying identity for certain speakers and in certain contexts.

The terms *accent change* and *modification* are based on the premise that each speaker has only one accent. However, all speakers of all languages command a repertoire of different ways of pronouncing their languages, depending on the addressee, formality, spontaneity, etc. of the situation.

The term *accent addition* seems the most appropriate one. It does not imply that any accent of English already possessed by the learner can be eliminated. Instead, what we are trying to do as pronunciation teachers is to add another accent that is more standard and less influenced by the learner's native language(s). In this way, we are increasing the repertoire of accents of English the speaker has mastered, so that they can choose the most appropriate pronunciation for the situation. They will thus choose a more standard and more international pronunciation in appropriate contexts, such as migrating to a country, being interviewed for a job and operating a call centre. A less standard and more local pronunciation can be used in appropriate contexts, such as conversing with speakers with similar origins, in informal settings. In a nutshell, we are empowering learners by increasing their range of available choices in the horizontal dimension of Figure 24.1.

Three categories of target for teaching

In this section, we examine three approaches that have been proposed for specifying targets for teaching.

Major world accents

If a major world accent is chosen as the model for imitation, the choice is normally among the native-speaker accents of the UK, USA, Canada, Australia and New Zealand. This procedure has advantages, but also important disadvantages. Among the advantages are that these accents are well documented, and materials are readily available that use the accent as their reference accent.

However, a major disadvantage is that it ignores learners' attitudes towards the model accents. If learners have no intention of using an accent outside the classroom, then there seems to be little point in teaching the accent inside the classroom. Native-speaker accents are relevant models in the case of migrants to native-speaking countries. However, for the majority of learners who are not learning English for this purpose, it may not be relevant.

Indeed, it may be counter productive, in that there may be downright hostility to the accents. British Received Pronunciation (RP) was the obvious choice for a pronunciation model in British ELT circles half a century ago. However, its prestige has declined drastically within Britain, and few learners would nowadays say that they wanted to acquire it as their accent of English. For this reason, we have used the term Standard Southern British English (SSBE) here.

A more 'downmarket' form of RP (between RP and Cockney, the popular urban accent of London) has been described in the last three decades. Known as Estuary English, it has been claimed that it may supersede RP as a pronunciation model for teaching purposes within British ELT circles (see Wells, n.d.).

General American is so widely spread in the USA that it is the obvious model for teaching in American ELT circles. However, just like SSBE, this is not to say that it is a homogeneous accent without some variation.

Model speakers

An alternative procedure is to stop thinking of pronunciation models as accents—as disembodied systems of vowels, consonants, stress, intonation, etc. Instead, we must remember that accents are generally not homogeneous monoliths, but are the common denominators of people who share geographical and social characteristics, but also exhibit personal variation. That is, no two people speak in *exactly* the same way. Accents are spoken by real people, and learners may decide to model their pronunciation on particular individuals. Obvious candidates for such model speakers include teachers. They may also be people who are role models for the learners in other ways, such as native-speaker friends, broadcasters, and TV and film characters and personalities.

The clear disadvantage of such an approach is that no materials are available for the pronunciation of individual film stars, etc. Also, a class of learners would presumably have many such model speakers. However, the model is precisely defined as the pronunciation of a particular film star, and motivating learners to accept the model would not be a problem.

Jenkins' Lingua Franca Core

A third approach to specifying pronunciation models is proposed by Jenkins (2000). Her work is based on the following premises, some of which are radically different from those held in the past. Opinion is divided over the validity of these premises.

- Intelligibility is the main criterion.
- Native speakers (NS) of English are far outnumbered by nonnative speakers (NNS) nowadays. Attention should therefore be focused on those features that disrupt intelligibility for NNS–NNS interaction, since these interactions are far more common than NNS–NS or NS–NS.
- As a result of the first two points, the concerns of NS are irrelevant.
- There is no need to have a reference accent.
- Those features that disrupt intelligibility for NNS–NNS interaction should be determined on the basis of observed data.

Jenkins carried out several experiments using communicative information exchange tasks, and noted those occasions where communication broke down. Around two-thirds of these breakdowns in intelligibility were attributable to features of pronunciation. As a result, she identified several pronunciation features that need to be pronounced accurately. No special attention need be paid to all other pronunciation features (within reasonable bounds). The critical pronunciation features (which she calls the Lingua Franca Core) include the following.

Consonants

All 24 consonant sounds of (major accents of) English need to be mastered, with the following provisos:

- Rhotic use of /r/ (ie pronouncing /r/ in coda position, as in *forward*) is encouraged, the /r/ being pronounced as a retroflex approximant [ɻ] (with the tongue curled back) rather than other varieties of /r/.
- In intervocalic position, as in *phonetics*, /t/ should be pronounced as an alveolar plosive [t], rather than the tap [ɾ] typical of American accents including GenAm.
- Most substitutions of /θ, ð/ (e.g. as [t, d, s, z, f, v]) and of (what in accents such as SSBE is) dark /l/ ([ɫ]) are permissible. This includes vocalic /l/ (that is, pronouncing *kill* as [kɪʊ]).
- Close approximations to core consonant sounds are generally permissible, but certain approximations are not permissible, where there is a risk that they will be heard as a different consonant sound from that intended.
- Initial voiceless plosives /p, t, k/ should be aspirated.
- The voiceless/voiced differential effect on preceding vowel length should be maintained. That is, the vowels in *cart, bus, etch* are shorter than in *card, buzz, edge*, because of the effect of the final consonants.
- Initial consonant clusters are not simplified.
- Medial and final clusters are simplified only according to NS rules of elision.

Vowels

- Vowel length contrasts are maintained (e.g. /ɑː/ is longer than /ʌ/).
- Regional qualities associated with the speaker's first language are permissible if they are consistent. However, /ɜː/ needs to be preserved.

Stress

- Nuclear stress (tonic syllable) production and placement is important.
- The division of the speech stream into tone groups must be accurate.

Not all writers agree that this is the best approach to pronunciation models. However, it is an approach that has been around for decades.

> I believe that pronunciation teaching should have, not a goal which must of necessity be normally an unrealized ideal [a 'perfect' native-like accent], but a *limited* purpose which will be completely fulfilled: the attainment of intelligibility. The learner, instead of being taken systematically through each English vowel and each consonant, and later, if there is time, through the complexities of intonation and rhythm, would have presented to him certain carefully chosen features on which to concentrate, the rest of his pronunciation being left to no more than a general supervision.
>
> (Abercrombie, 1956, p. 37)

Conclusion

The development of thought about English pronunciation models over the decades has resulted from changes in the social status of native-speaker accents of English, and attitudes towards what it is appropriate to teach nonnative speakers. This can be traced in the various editions of Gimson's *Pronunciation of English*. In those quoted above, the original criterion was intelligibility to a native speaker. Then, the same criteria relating to intelligibility were maintained, but without the reference to the native speaker. In the latest edition (Cruttenden, 2008), this whole approach has been abandoned in favor of two alternative targets. The first, known as Amalgam English, is 'for those learning English as an additional (often official) language' (p. xiii) and is 'based on an amalgam of native-speaker Englishes, together with some local features arising from a local L1' (p. 317). The second, International English, is for those 'who use it as a lingua franca on a more international basis and need a minimum standard for occasional communication' (p. 317).

Pronunciation targets for English learners are still a matter of debate among writers. Cruttenden summarizes, 'This area is a particularly hot subject at the moment and the alternative models I have suggested will remain speculative and controversial both as models and in their details' (2008, p. xiii).

Summary

- It is self-evident that, if you do not know what you are trying to achieve, you cannot tell if you have succeeded.
- Pronunciation targets are heavily influenced by intelligibility, image and identity.
- Jenkins' Lingua Franca Core is a research-based attempt to state those pronunciation features that are most important for intelligibility in NNS–NNS interactions.

Exercises

1. Who has the same pronunciation of English as you?
2. Think back to any language(s) that you have learned. What level of pronunciation proficiency were you hoping to achieve? A smattering, if poorly pronounced, to make a holiday more pleasant and interesting? Good command of a restricted vocabulary, to avoid getting ripped off in shops? A high level, to impress the lecturers at an educational institution?
3. If a foreigner told you that you had a good pronunciation of their language, how would you feel? Satisfied that many years of hard work had paid off? Skeptical that they were only being polite? Worried that you were losing your original identity? Doubtful that, at your age, you could ever achieve the excellent pronunciation the foreigner claimed you had?
4. Discuss whether you agree with the following quotations.

> To correct an Englishman's pronunciation is to imply that he is not quite a gentleman.
>
> George Bernard Shaw (1856–1950),
> Irish playwright

> If writers wrote as carelessly as some people talk, then adhasdh asdglaseuyt [bn[pasdlgkhasdfasdf.
>
> Lemony Snicket, pen name of novelist
> Daniel Handler (b. 1970), American children's writer

> It's a damn shame we have this immediate ticking off in the mind about how people sound. On the other hand, how many people really want to be operated upon by a surgeon who talks broad Cockney?
>
> Eileen Atkins (b. 1934),
> British stage and screen actress

5. For each of the following situations, describe what the speaker is aiming for, in terms of pronunciation.

> After using four different languages on an album, it's tough to decide which one I'm gonna actually learn to speak. I always study the lyric, make sure I know what I'm singing, and try to get the pronunciation as perfect as possible.
> Josh Groban (b. 1981) American singer, who has recorded songs in Spanish, Italian, French, Portuguese, etc.

> I worked on my voice for *Sweet Dreams*, but only to match my speaking voice to Patsy's actual singing voice. That was my way into that character.
> Jessica Lange (b. 1949), who played US country music singer
> Patsy Cline in the 1985 film *Sweet Dreams*

> Mr Zhang from China is emigrating to Canada, and is taking English lessons before he leaves China.

> Mr Patel, a Gujarati speaker in Ahmedabad, is talking in English on the phone with his business partner, Mr Mohanan, a Malayalam speaker in Kerala.

> Mr Schmidt, a pilot with Lufthansa, is coming in to land at Leonardo da Vinci Airport Rome.

Further reading

Exercises designed to make learners reflect on the language targets they are aiming for, are contained in Ellis and Sinclair (1989). The Lingua Franca Core is contained in Jenkins (2000). The principles underlying the Lingua Franca Core are debated by Keys and Walker (2002). Walker (2010) discusses English as a Lingua Franca (ELF) and how to teach it.

25 Integration

Drill: a device used for boring.

ELT saying

Learning objectives

At the end of this chapter, you will be able to:

- describe some of the approaches and methods used in English language teaching
- list features of good pronunciation teaching
- integrate pronunciation into English classes.

Introduction

This chapter is a brief introduction to language teaching and the various approaches and methods that have been proposed for English. In particular, we will look at whether these various approaches and methods have any specific focus on speaking (including pronunciation) and listening, rather than reading and writing. Only those approaches and methods that contain elements important to pronunciation teaching will be covered, rather than trying to provide a comprehensive overview by including approaches and methods that ignore or say little about pronunciation.

A brief history of English language teaching

While languages have been taught for many centuries, we begin this history of English language teaching with three methods practiced from the middle of the 19th century until the middle of the 20th.

Traditional methods

1 The reform movement

The Grammar-Translation method, influential from the mid 19th to mid 20th century, approached the language through a detailed study of its grammar rules, which were then applied to the translation of sentences and (often literary) texts. The focus was on reading and writing. As a reaction to the Grammar-Translation method, the field of linguistics, including phonetics, flourished in the late 19th century. The International Phonetic Association (IPA) was established in 1886, emphasizing, among other things, the importance of speech in language teaching by using phonetic training, and conversations and dialogues. Learners were presented with the spoken form of a language before seeing it in writing.

2 The natural/direct method

At the same time, interest grew in teaching foreign languages according to the same principles underlying a child's acquisition of a first language. Speaking, including pronunciation, was emphasized, and the teacher encouraged learners to use the foreign language rather than relying on translation. As in the Reform Movement, grammar was taught inductively, deriving rules from examples presented orally. Such principles still underlie the teaching in Berlitz schools.

3 Audiolingualism

In the mid 20th century, the principles of structural linguistics were applied to language teaching, at a time when the importance of learning foreign languages was stressed in the USA because of the Cold War. The approach was based on a behaviorist psychological model of learning, involving the establishment of language habits in the learner, by using stimulus and response exercises. Audiolingualism classes thus comprised dialogues, drills and practice, again focusing on the spoken form of the language.

Alternative approaches and methods in the 1970s and 1980s

The 1970s and 1980s saw a number of alternative approaches and methods to those outlined so far. Six will be outlined here. Although still practiced by some individual teachers and institutions, they are not generally widespread nowadays.

1 Total physical response

Total Physical Response required the performance of physical actions in response to commands and questions from the teacher (e.g. *Brush your teeth, Where is the towel?*).

2 The silent way

The Silent Way resembled Audiolingualism, in that it entailed accurate repetition of sentences leading to freer production. However, the teacher took a more indirect role, allowing the learner to create and test their own hypotheses about the language, often in the form of problem-solving. Teaching concentrated on speaking and listening, and was often supported by the use of colored Cuisenaire rods and colorful Fidel charts.

3 Humanistic methods

'Humanistic techniques engage the whole person, including the emotions and feelings (the affective realm) as well as linguistic knowledge and behavioral skills' (Richards and Rodgers, 2001, p. 90). Humanistic methods thus focus on psychological factors such as the emotions of the learners and the classroom environment, rather than proposing a theory of language. Community Language Learning used a counseling metaphor. Learners sat in a circle, and one gave a message in their first language (L1) to the knower (teacher). The teacher whispered the translation of the message in the foreign language (L2) to that learner. The learner repeated the L2 message to another learner, and was tape-recorded. After each learner had a turn, the tape was replayed. In Suggestopedia, a conducive environment was produced by way of the décor of the classroom and the use of music, said to help intonation and rhythm.

4 Whole language

This approach, proposed in the 1980s, emphasized that language should be taught as a whole. It also stressed creative language, and thus concentrated on reading and writing, including literature. It rejected the basis of phonics, that spelling can be taught by relating letters and sounds.

5 Multiple intelligences

This approach was a response to traditional intelligence tests, that rely on only logic and language. It proposed that there are eight intelligences that different individuals have strengths or weaknesses in. Linguistic intelligence is clearly the most important for language learning. However, others can be relevant: musical intelligence (having a good ear for music, which may help with mimicry, intonation, rhythm, etc.), bodily intelligence (for body language), and interpersonal intelligence (being able to relate well to other people). The other intelligences were logical, spatial, intrapersonal and naturalist.

6 Competency-based language teaching

This approach related to the situation of refugees and other migrants to countries such as the USA and Australia. The focus was on what the learners should be able to do at the end of a course, especially in terms of the language skills involved in particular jobs.

Current approaches

The following five approaches may be considered current approaches to language teaching.

1 Communicative language teaching

This approach began as a reaction to previous approaches that emphasized the mastery of grammatical structures and vocabulary lists. This led to many learners knowing a lot about the language, but being unable to communicate in it in real situations. The Communicative Approach sees language as a means for communication, and that one learns the language by using it. Syllabuses in the Communicative Approach embrace functional, notional, situational and task-based elements of previous methods. The primary focus is on fluency and function, rather than accuracy and form. Tasks involve authentic and meaningful communication in realistic settings.

2 The natural approach

In this approach, the learning of a foreign language is taken to conform to the principles underlying naturalistic language learning in children. Vocabulary is emphasized rather than grammar. Grammatical structures are taken to be acquired in a predictable order. In order for learners to progress, input (material learners are exposed to) is required that is at a level above the current level of the learners (known as I + 1). Learners hear before they are required to speak or write. Consciously learned systems can only monitor what the learner produces.

3 Cooperative language learning

Group work and pair work are essential components of this approach. Interaction between learners is thus important, and learners are held responsible for their own learning.

4 Content-based instruction

Rather than concentrating on the linguistic (grammatical, vocabulary, etc.) features of a language, this approach is organized around the content that the learners are studying. It is thus claimed to be relevant in immersion programs and for immigrants. While this creates great motivation, it may be necessary for language teachers to work alongside content teachers.

5 Task-based language learning

Tasks, such as giving directions or making a phone call, have been a feature of many previous approaches. Task-based language learning proposes that tasks should be the primary source of language input.

The post-methods era

The above description of some of the major approaches and methods used in language teaching over the last century has been necessarily brief. This is, after all, a book on the teaching of pronunciation rather than language teaching in general. For a more detailed description of language teaching approaches and methods, see Richards and Rodgers (2001).

Richards and Rodgers (2001) contains a final chapter entitled 'The post-methods era'. Approaches, being philosophies of language and language teaching, tend not to specify precisely how these principles should be carried out in the classroom. As a result, approaches are usually longer-lived than methods, which are specific instructional designs based on more specific claims. However, precisely because of their specificity as to what should happen in the classroom, methods are more popular than approaches with teachers, especially new teachers still finding their way.

Richards and Rodgers describe the heyday of methods as lasting up till the late 1980s. We are now in a post-methods era, in which each teacher may develop their own eclectic approach to teaching, drawing on aspects of previous approaches and methods.

Features of good pronunciation teaching

What follows is a list of features common to many of the approaches and methods outlined previously. Most present-day teachers would ascribe to these as important elements in pronunciation teaching.

Orientation of the syllabus: Early approaches put grammar squarely at the center of the language syllabus. Grammar rules were the basis of the syllabus, with vocabulary learning being necessary in order to flesh out those rules. No systematic treatment was given to speaking or listening skills. In the Lexical Approach, popular since the 1980s, vocabulary has been placed at the center of the syllabus. Language is said to be grammaticalized lexis rather than lexicalized grammar. But as for many previous approaches, the Lexical Approach has little to say about pronunciation. In contrast, some approaches emphasize the primacy of the spoken form of language over the written. Learners are thus given speaking and listening tasks before reading and writing are introduced.

Communicativeness: The communicative revolution, begun in the 1970s, emphasized that learners learn a language by using it to communicate. That is, the focus is on the functions that language can convey rather than the forms of grammar, etc. Learners should therefore be engaged in interesting tasks that represent meaningful communication with authentic materials. These may involve realistic problem-solving exercises, often carried out in pairs or groups. Teaching can thus be learner-centered, rather than teacher-driven. Translation should be avoided as much as possible.

Affective factors: While earlier approaches and methods emphasized the analysis of language patterns and the creation of materials, modern humanistic approaches have focused more on the fact that learners are individuals with human feelings. A classroom atmosphere is desirable that is conducive for language learning in a non-threatening way, where learners are not inhibited to make potentially embarrassing mistakes. The reduction of stress for learners, cooperation rather than competition between learners, and a pleasant classroom environment, by the use of features such as décor and background music, are features of such approaches.

Learner responsibility: Several approaches have emphasized that there are three elements to the whole learning situation. First, there is the teacher and the materials. These are clearly the responsibility of the teacher. Second, the focus in the classroom should be on learning rather than teaching. The responsibility for learning lies as much with the learner as with the teacher. Admittedly, the learners will probably not learn much with a poor teacher and/or poor materials. But neither will they learn if they are not in the mood to. Learner training should therefore be included, to emphasize the importance of language learning, to convince the learners that much of the responsibility is theirs, and to inculcate effective strategies. Third, the teaching and learning are not complete if the skills are not put into practice outside the classroom (see the next point, and chapter 26).

Transfer of skills: Although learning a language in the classroom is important, it is of little value if the learning is not transferred to real life outside the classroom. Many learners nowadays learn English for instrumental reasons such as doing business, getting a job and study. This transfer of skills is clearly important for migrants. The classroom use of simulation tasks in quasi-realistic settings, perhaps with the use of physical objects, pictures, etc., should be encouraged.

Use of literature: As a source of materials, and as the creative use of the language, literature should not be overlooked in the teaching of the whole language.

Mention ought also to be made of two other techniques, often used in pronunciation teaching but potentially quite ineffective:

Drills: Drills were a central feature of audiolingualism. However, they relate to a behaviorist view of language learning that is not widely held nowadays. Nevertheless, drills are a useful quick way of focusing learners' attention on a particular point. But they cannot be considered interesting, authentic or motivating in themselves. They should therefore be used sparingly.

Tongue twisters: Some teachers and textbooks use tongue twisters. Tongue twisters often rely on awkward sequences of sounds, such as plosives (e.g. *a cricket critic*), fricatives (e.g. *She sells seashells by the seashore*) and approximants (e.g. *red lorry, yellow lorry*). Tongue twisters, by definition, are difficult to say—even proficient native speakers find them hard. It therefore seems counterproductive to use them with foreign learners. They are likely to frustrate and disappoint learners rather than motivate them.

Integrating pronunciation into lessons

Finally in this chapter, we come to the question of how pronunciation can be integrated into English language lessons. The most large-scale approach would be to devote whole lessons to pronunciation features, in the same way that lessons are sometimes devoted to points of grammar, particular sets of vocabulary items, etc. However, even the most dedicated of learners would probably find it tiring to concentrate for 30, 45 or 60 minutes solely on particular pronunciation items.

Instead, teachers often include pronunciation slots of, say, 5, 10 or 15 minutes, in longer lessons. While this alleviates the burden for the learners, the teacher is then faced with the question of what pronunciation features to cover, and in what order. In this respect, pronunciation is quite different from grammar or vocabulary. We are familiar with syllabuses that progressively introduce grammatical items, such as the present simple and progressive tenses, the past simple and progressive, the present perfect, the past perfect, etc. in that order. They can be covered in that order because we feel that there is some kind of natural progression here from tenses that are easy to learn and useful, to others that are less easy and rarer. Similarly, particularly in the Lexical Approach, a syllabus can be organized around vocabulary, starting with basic, useful, everyday vocabulary before progressing to rarer items or vocabulary that is only useful in academic situations. However, pronunciation does not have such an obvious sense of progression. We cannot, for example, decide to conduct a lesson without using the /θ, ð/ sounds, because we feel they are difficult for our learners. As soon as the teacher opens his or her mouth in class, the learners are exposed to every feature of pronunciation, which is not the case for grammar or vocabulary.

Writers have produced materials claiming to introduce and practice pronunciation in an integrated way. This could easily be done by linking pronunciation to grammatical features. For instance, the pronunciation of the past tense ending and the fact that what is written as *-ed* has three different possible pronunciations (see chapter 14) can be covered when the past tense is introduced, for example in narrative writing. The pronunciation of the dental fricative /θ/ can be covered when ordinal numbers (*fourth, fifth, sixth,* etc.) are introduced. Similarly, pronunciation can be linked to vocabulary. Celce-Murcia (1987) points out that the situation of a restaurant is an opportunity to cover the /iː/ and /ɪ/ vowels, as in words such as *veal, beef, peas, beans, cheese, ice cream* and *tea* for /iː/, and *chicken, fish, liver, spinach, mint, milk* and *mineral water* for /ɪ/.

Finally, pronunciation can be handled in an incidental way. That is, pronunciation problems are dealt with as-and-when they occur. Following the adage 'If it isn't broken, don't try to fix it,' a learner's pronunciation can be ignored provided there are no features that stick out like a sore thumb or interfere with intelligibility. This is essentially the principle underlying Jenkins' Lingua Franca Core (see chapter 24).

Any of the four above methods, or any combination of them, can be used for teaching pronunciation. The worst possible solution is to sweep pronunciation under the carpet and not deal with it at all. However, that seems to be what happens in many teachers' lessons. Such teachers would not think of teaching a lesson ignoring grammar or vocabulary problems. As we will see in chapter 30, pronunciation is equally important—if not more so—to most learners.

Summary

- Many different, but often overlapping, approaches and methods to language teaching have been proposed, sometimes as reactions to previous approaches.
- Generally accepted current theory is that pronunciation teaching should:
    - be communicative
    - be learner-centered
    - respect the learners' affective states
    - entail learner training
    - use authentic materials
    - ensure the transfer of skills outside the classroom
    - involve aspects of literature.

Exercises

1. Think back to any language(s) that you have learned. What type of methodology did the teacher use?

2. If you are a teacher, think of any language course(s) you are teaching. What methodology does it use? Do the materials assume a particular approach or method?
3. What similarities are there between learning your native language and learning a foreign language? What differences are there? (Answers are given in chapters 28 and 29.)

Further reading

Further details of the approaches and methods outlined in this chapter, along with several others that are of little relevance to pronunciation teaching, are given by English Raven (n.d.), Larsen-Freeman and Anderson (2011), and Richards and Rodgers (2001).

26 The effectiveness of pronunciation teaching

Knowledge is not what is memorized. Knowledge is what benefits.
Imam al-Shafi'i (150–204), Arabic jurist

Learning objectives

At the end of this chapter, you will be able to:

- list some factors affecting success in pronunciation learning.

The determinants of pronunciation success

We begin this chapter with a look at an often-quoted piece of seminal research into the effectiveness of pronunciation teaching (Purcell and Suter, 1980). The pronunciation accuracy of 61 nonnative speakers of English was rated by 14 judges. The speakers, whose native languages were Arabic, Japanese, Persian and Thai, were immigrants to the USA. The speakers were also asked to provide personal details, and to rate themselves according to various other criteria that had been proposed by writers as important variables. Which of these factors do you think had an influence on their pronunciation accuracy?

- their sex
- their first language
- the number of languages they can converse in
- their social prestige motivation
- their integrative orientation
- their cultural allegiance
- their aptitude for oral mimicry
- the age at which they were first able to converse meaningfully in English
- the age at which they first lived in an English-speaking country
- the number of years they had lived in an English-speaking country and/or the number of months they had lived with a native speaker
- the percentage of conversation at work or school carried on in English with native speakers of English
- the percentage of conversation at home carried on in English with native speakers of English

- the number of years they had received formal classroom training in English
- the number of months of intensive formal classroom training in English
- the number of weeks of formal classroom training focused specifically on English pronunciation
- the strength of their concern for pronunciation accuracy.

The results of Purcell and Suter's analysis are statistically sound, as they represent a statistical re-examination of Suter's (1976) previous work. Purcell and Suter's results show that only four of the above variables are significant. Once these four are taken into account, the other factors made no contribution to any statistical correlation. Those four factors were the following:

> First language: The Persian and Arabic speakers had better overall pronunciation than the Japanese or Thais.
> Aptitude for oral mimicry: Respondents who reported that they thought they were good mimics had better overall pronunciation than those who did not.
> Length of time in an English-speaking country and/or living with a native speaker: The longer respondents had this exposure to the language, the better their pronunciation.
> Strength of concern for pronunciation accuracy: Those respondents who reported that they felt they were very concerned about their pronunciation had better pronunciation than those who did not.

Purcell and Suter (1980, p. 285) describe a theoretically superior pronouncer:

> We might call her Nazila (or him Mohammed, since sex is not a meaningful predictor). She is Persian. She arrived in the United States nine years ago and has remained here ever since. Two years after her arrival she married Fred, an American, and continues to share a home with him. Although she is a good mimic, Nazila continues to worry about what remains of her 'foreign accent.'

Two rather ominous conclusions can be drawn. Firstly, none of the factors relating to formal classroom training were found to be of any statistical significance. However, this finding has been questioned by others, who argue that it is not the amount of training but its quality that is important. Nevertheless, Purcell and Suter's findings may make us aware of the limitations of formal training as against other forms of exposure to the language and its pronunciation.

Secondly, the four factors found to be significant are ones over which the teacher has little control. Speakers from languages that, in a language family tree, are related to English, such as German and Dutch, as well as speakers from languages that, in terms of their consonant and vowel sounds, syllable structure, etc., are similar to English, may be at a natural advantage over others.

Teachers have no control over how long a learner has lived in an English-speaking country and/or with a native speaker.

While many feel that having 'a good ear' is an innate phenomenon that cannot be taught, teachers can nonetheless carry out some exercises in producing unfamiliar sounds, so that learners are happy or willing to try out new sounds that depart from those of their native language (see chapter 29). However, such exercises require some phonetic training on the part of the teacher.

Strength of concern for pronunciation accuracy may result from motivation and attitudes formed before the pronunciation course. Even so, this is probably the one factor among the four significant ones that teachers can influence in some way. Tasks can be carried out to inculcate the attitude that pronunciation is important for most speakers of a language, that poor pronunciation can lead to loss of intelligibility, embarrassment, even offence, and that a change in pronunciation is both desirable and possible (see chapter 28).

Short- and long-term improvement

Research carried out in the mid 1990s by Yule, Macdonald and Powers also raised important concerns about the effectiveness of pronunciation teaching. In any teaching situation, there are three distinguishable elements:

> The teaching: That is, the materials that the teacher prepares, and the way that they are delivered in class. It is clearly the teacher's responsibility to ensure that this aspect of the teaching situation is carried out professionally.
>
> The learning: To some extent this depends on the teacher, in that, if the teacher and/or the materials are poor, then the learners are unlikely to learn. However, the learners are also unlikely to learn if they are not in the appropriate frame of mind to learn, because of factors such as not seeing the point in learning English, boredom or tiredness. Increasingly, the learner is being seen as having greater responsibility for successful learning.
>
> Putting it into practice: Any teaching is unsuccessful if the learners forget it as soon as the class is finished, or have no intention of using newly learnt skills outside the classroom. Tongue in cheek, this situation has been referred to by the acronym TEFLON: Teaching English as a Foreign Language, but it doesn't stick. While the teacher may emphasize the importance of this aspect, it is primarily the responsibility of the learners, because the teacher does not see the learners outside the classroom or after the course has finished.

Yule and Macdonald (1995) remind us that it is the last of these three elements that is the true measure of success of pronunciation teaching. In their research, they obtained perceptual judgments of the pronunciation of 23 learners from the People's Republic of China at three points: first (T1) at the beginning of the course of instruction, second (T2), at the end of the 15-week course, and third (T3), two days after the end of the instruction (Figure 26.1).

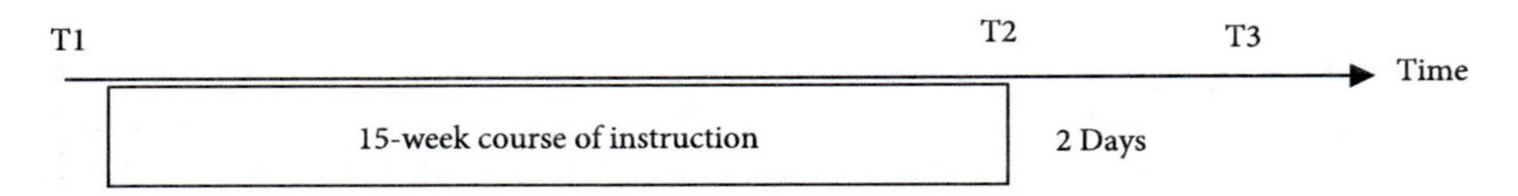

Figure 26.1 Three measurement points for pronunciation improvement.

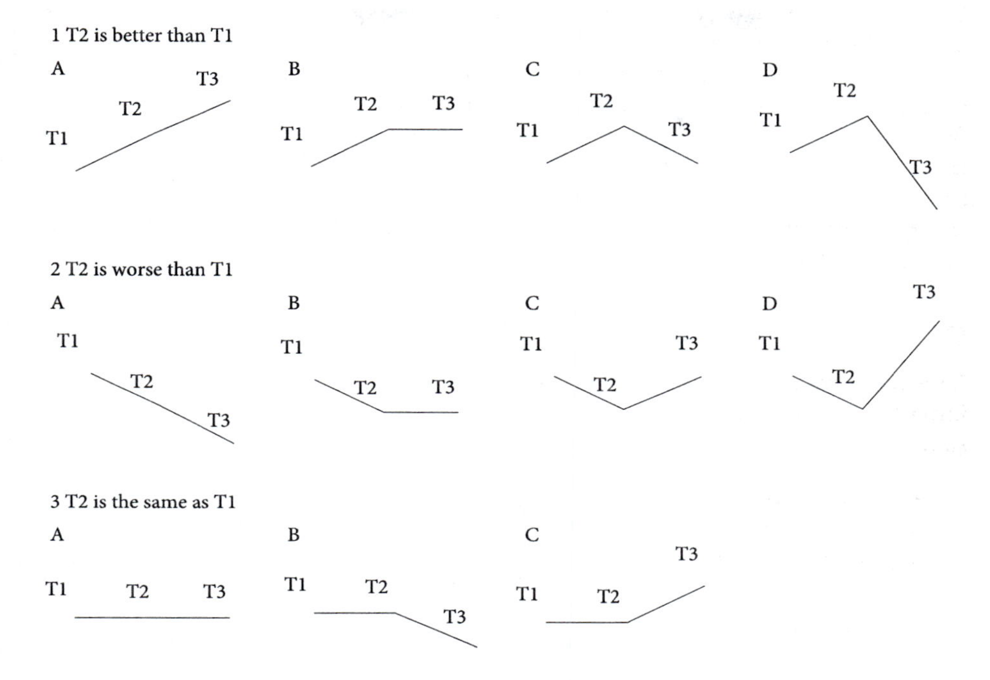

Figure 26.2 Eleven possible outcomes for pronunciation improvement.

They identified eleven possible outcomes, depending on performance at T2 relative to T1, and at T3 relative to T2 and/or T1 (Figure 26.2). For example, outcome 2D means that the learner showed deterioration at the end of the course (T2) compared with the start of the course (T1), but subsequently (T3) the pronunciation became even better than when the course started.

Four types of instruction were used on different groups of learners:

- teacher-directed drill
- language laboratory work, without a teacher
- a teacher asking for clarification of key words
- silent revision without a teacher, that is, no instruction.

In fact, while the language laboratory condition gave the best overall improvement, the results are generally inconclusive. However, three general conclusions can be drawn. First, we should not overlook the importance of individual differences.

> It is apparent that no single intervention was beneficial to all the learners who experienced it. Moreover, the wide range of different individual reactions should serve as a reminder that the individual learner may represent a more powerful variable than does the instructional setting in the acquisition of pronunciation.
>
> (Macdonald, Yule and Powers, 1994, pp. 95–6)

Second, they note that their results may lend some support to the findings of writers such as Pennington and Richards (1986) and Purcell and Suter (1980) that pronunciation teaching may not lead to acquisition in a one-to-one fashion.

Third, any effects of pronunciation teaching may not be immediately apparent, because of a restructuring (McLaughlin, 1990) of the phonological system within the learner.

> Moreover, the changes in direction observed in many cases across the three points in time should also make us cautious about jumping to premature decisions about the effectiveness (or not) of our instructional procedures. Indications of immediate improvement can disappear after a few days and signs of immediate deterioration can, in the same time span, be noticeably reversed.
>
> (Yule and Macdonald, 1995, p. 438)

Overview

Saito (2012) summarizes the findings of 15 pronunciation teaching studies with pre- and post-test design. Only nine of these relate to English pronunciation; however, the findings of the others are not irrelevant. The studies differed in terms of whether they emphasized segmentals or suprasegmentals; whether the focus on form included communicative practice; and whether measurements were made of controlled or spontaneous production. It is therefore difficult sometimes to compare results. He criticizes the Macdonald et al. work for the brevity of the instruction (less than 30 minutes).

Nevertheless, his conclusion is that 'instruction is effective not only for improving specific segmental and suprasegmental aspects of L2 sounds . . . but also for enhancing listeners' overall judgment of comprehensibility' (Saito, 2012, p. 849). Also, that 'teachers should carefully select target features' (p. 850), that is, only work on those features that are known to be problems for the particular group of learners, and where improvement can be expected for the class time devoted to it.

Summary

- While it is tempting to believe that improvement in pronunciation must result from instruction, this is not necessarily the case.
- Factors outside the teacher's control may play major roles in pronunciation improvement.
- The measure of success in pronunciation teaching lies in long-term improvement, outside the classroom and after the course has finished.

Exercises

1. How could you increase learners' aptitude for oral mimicry, and strength of concern for pronunciation accuracy?
2. If you are a teacher, interview your learners with the best pronunciation (and general proficiency). Can they tell you the reasons why their pronunciation is better than other learners'? Of the factors they mention, are any under the control of the teacher?

Further reading

The original sources of the research summarized in this chapter may be profitably consulted: Macdonald, Yule and Powers (1994), Purcell and Suter (1980), Saito (2012) and Yule and Macdonald (1995). Munro and Derwing (2011) give an overview of research into the effectiveness of pronunciation instruction.

27 Motivation and affect

> Nothing great was ever achieved without enthusiasm.
>
> Ralph Waldo Emerson (1803–1882), American essayist and poet

Learning objectives

At the end of this chapter, you will be able to:

- define intrinsic, extrinsic, instrumental and integrative motivation
- increase learners' motivation.

The importance of motivation

Motivation has long been acknowledged as an important factor in successful language learning. Motivation is considered an important factor for children learning their native language. They want to participate in, and gain identity in their immediate family unit and the wider language community, and an important part of this is being able to communicate in those social units through language.

Motivation is no less important a factor in learning a second language. This may be especially important for pronunciation, where the potential for acceptance, and conversely embarrassment, is great.

A socio-educational model

The most influential work on motivation has been carried out by Lambert and Gardner (see Gardner, 1982; Gardner and Lambert, 1972). They investigated the contribution of motivation, among other factors, to successful language learning. Their socio-educational model deals specifically with second language acquisition in a structured foreign language classroom setting. The model explores the relationship between four factors: the social and cultural milieu; individual learner differences; the setting in which learning takes place; and linguistic outcomes. Among the second factor, individual differences, are the variables of intelligence, language aptitude, situational anxiety, and motivation.

Motivation is considered to be composed of three elements:

- ***Effort*** is the drive of the learner, and the amount of time spent studying the language.
- ***Desire*** is a measure of how much the learner wants to become proficient in the language.
- ***Affect*** is the feelings of the learner towards language study.

Affect

Bloom (1956) proposes a taxonomy of educational objectives (commonly known as Bloom's taxonomy). It divides objectives into three domains: affective, psychomotor (physical skills) and cognitive (knowledge and comprehension). Each domain contains different levels of learning, the higher levels being more complex and closer to mastery of the material.

There are five levels in Bloom's affective domain, in ascending order:

- ***Receiving:*** the learner pays attention passively.
- ***Responding:*** the learner actively participates by not only attending but also reacting.
- ***Valuing:*** the learner ascribes some value to the topic, and skills and information learned.
- ***Organizing:*** the learner can relate, compare and elaborate on what is learned.
- ***Characterizing:*** because of values and beliefs, a learner's behavior becomes a characteristic.

Affect is an important feature of the language learning approach known as the Natural Approach (see chapter 25). This emphasizes the fact that the process of learning another language is not only complex, but also precarious. Whenever learners try to speak another language, they run the risk of not succeeding, and thus being liable to embarrassment, ridicule and loss of face. This seems especially important for pronunciation.

Krashen (1981, 1982) proposes that learners have an affective filter. If they feel uncomfortable in a learning situation, their affective filter will be high, they are less likely to participate and consequently will learn less well.

There are several factors that contribute to the level of comfort in a learning situation: emotion (for instance, the learner feels upset), physical state (such as illness), attitude (for example, having no love for the language), needs (e.g. seeing no reason to be studying the language) and motivation (see below). For immigrants to an English-speaking country, factors include disorientation in a new culture, different ways of communicating and aspects of the new learning environment (for instance, single sex versus mixed classes).

Motivation in language learning is often divided into two dichotomies: intrinsic and extrinsic motivation, and instrumental and integrative motivation.

Intrinsic motivation

Learners may also be motivated because they find what goes on in class interesting. That is, the enthusiasm and likeability of the teacher, and the engaging nature of the materials and activities used in the class may be motivation enough. In such cases, the learners' attitudes towards the language, its culture and its usefulness may be irrelevant.

Extrinsic motivation

In contrast, external motivation is generated by factors such as culture, a class system, parental pressure, passing examinations and financial reward.

Instrumental motivation

The main distinction in Gardner and Lambert's work is between instrumental and integrative motivation. Instrumental motivation is essentially utilitarian in nature. That is, the learner is learning the language for some fairly specific purpose that brings practical rewards. Such purposes may include:

- to pass an examination
- to meet the requirements for entry to, or graduation from, an educational institution
- to apply for a job, or a better job
- to study at a foreign university
- to be able to read material in technical subjects such as science and medicine
- to be able to undertake translation work
- to do international business
- to cope when transferred overseas for work.

Utilitarian purposes such as the above mean that it is easier for the teacher to specify exactly what the learners need, and to tailor courses and materials accordingly. However, once the purpose has disappeared, for instance because the person has passed the relevant examination, then the motivation may also disappear and along with it the benefit of precisely specified objectives.

Integrative motivation

Integrative motivation, on the other hand, is driven by the desire of the learner to associate themselves with the culture of the speakers of that language; that is, to become a quasi-native speaker and be accepted into the community of native speakers. This motivation may be driven by an admiration for or interest in the history, music, art, sport, literature, and other aspects of the culture and lifestyle of the speakers of the language. In short, the learner becomes more or less bilingual and bicultural.

In early work, the importance of integrative motivation was stressed (but see the results of Purcell and Suter in chapter 26). That is, language learning was thought to be more successful where the learner had integrative motivation. Integrative motivation is still thought to be important, but the contribution of instrumental motivation is also stressed nowadays. This may be as a result of the large numbers of people learning English for utilitarian purposes, such as international business, and the passing of examinations.

Resultative motivation

While motivation is usually thought to be the cause of successful language learning, it may also be the result of it. That is, learners who start to be successful in learning a language may, as a result, become more motivated to find out about the culture and learn to speak the language better. For instance, English-speaking Canadians who learn French may come to appreciate French culture. However, learners may also become less motivated. It has been reported that, on learning English, Spanish-speaking Mexican women in California may find themselves in situations where they are discriminated against, thus lowering their admiration of Americans and American culture.

Both instrumental and integrative motivation may be present in any learner. That is, it is not a two-way choice between instrumental or integrative. For example, migrants to countries such as the UK, USA and Australia need to have instrumental motivation in the first place, in order to understand immigration procedures, find a job, find accommodation, do the shopping, etc. In the longer term, however, they are likely to acquire integrative motivation as they work with native speaker colleagues, interact with neighbors, travel to different parts of the country, are concerned with their children's education, etc.

Motivation may also change over time, depending on the situation and the person's needs. For instance, a change of teacher may result in a change in a learner's intrinsic motivation.

Increasing learners' motivation

While we may argue about the precise nature of motivation, writers are agreed with the commonsensical assertion that motivated learners make better learners. We therefore need to explore ways of increasing the motivation of learners.

Among the plethora of acronyms in English language teaching (ELT!) is the whimsical one TENOR: Teaching English for No Obvious Reason. It is a sad fact about English teaching at school level in many countries that the learners have no clear reasons for learning English. While some may realize that English is an important world language, they may not have any easily specifiable purpose for studying it in the short term, other than that they have to as part of the curriculum and in order to pass the examination at the end of the course. They may have little access to native speakers, and have few occasions to use their English outside the classroom. In such cases, it is worthwhile for the teacher to spend time finding out about the learners' attitudes towards English, and their personal goals. It may be necessary to reinforce the importance of English nowadays, and to explore ways in which a command of English could be of use to individual learners in future life. Even female learners who perhaps do not expect to join the workforce, but get married and raise children, may be motivated if they can see the connection between English and personal goals such as overseas travel and reading publications (novels, magazines, the internet) in English.

Since writers have always stressed the importance of integrative motivation for language learners, teachers should search for ways of increasing this in their teaching. Activities aimed at increasing integrative motivation include:

- Encouraging learners to correspond with penpals in English-speaking countries.
- Teaming up with a sister school or university in an English-speaking country. This would be particularly convenient if the learners in the English-speaking country are

learning the language of the English learners. Then learners from both sides can exchange short articles written in their foreign languages, about aspects of their life and culture.
- Arranging exchange programs with foreign learners, or overseas homestays.
- Relating study of the language to study of the culture. Courses, or parts of courses, could be organized around aspects of English-speaking cultures that appeal to the learners, such as the English Premier League, American rap music, Australian short story writers, Scottish school/campus life, the New Zealand electoral system, or the Canadian landscape and weather.

Activities aimed at increasing intrinsic motivation, that is motivation because of the interest value of classroom activities, include:

- Making sure that learners understand the purpose of classroom activities. This is especially important in cultures where teaching methods common in the West, such as pair and group work, have not been part of the teaching culture.
- Making sure that learners understand instructions. Learners from countries where instructions in English classrooms are given in the native language, may as a result be unfamiliar with common English classroom expressions.

Finally, methods of lowering learners' affective filters include:

- Encouragement by taking an interest in each learner and their individual worries and interests.
- Active listening on the part of the teacher.
- Involving the learner as a full member of the class.

Summary

- Forms of motivation can be divided into intrinsic (generated by inherent interest) and extrinsic (driven by external factors), and instrumental (for some utilitarian purpose) and integrative (driven by a desire to integrate with the society and culture of the language).
- It is debatable whether instrumental or integrative motivation leads to greater success in language learning. But both are preferable to a lack of motivation.
- To lower the learner's affective filter, a conducive, non-threatening classroom environment is desirable.

Exercises

1. Think of foreign languages you have learned. What was your prime motivation in learning them?
2. If you are a teacher, think of your most motivated learner, and your least motivated. What are the factors accounting for their levels of motivation?

Further reading

The topic of motivation in language learning is reviewed by Crookes and Schmidt (1991), Dörnyei (Ed. 2003) and Spolsky (2000). There are many articles and webpages with tips for increasing student motivation. Molan Network Project (2010), (Motivation for Languages) funded by the European Commission, contains many European case studies.

28 Fossilization

I . . . think the pronunciation of a foreign tongue could be better taught than by demanding from the pupil those internal acrobatics that are generally impossible and always useless. This is the sort of instruction one receives. 'Press your tonsils against the underside of your larynx. Then with the convex part of the septum curved upwards so as to almost but not quite touch the uvula, try with the tip of your tongue to reach your thyroid. Take a deep breath and compress your glottis. Now, without opening your lips, say "Garoo".' And when you have done it they are not satisfied.

Jerome K. Jerome (1859–1927), *Three men on the Bummel* (1900) (In case it is not obvious, the instructions are gibberish from the phonetic point of view.)

Learning objectives

At the end of this chapter, you will be able to:

- define fossilization
- list ways of helping fossilized learners.

The critical period hypothesis

Lenneberg (1964) claimed that there was a critical period for learning one's native language: if a language is not learned before the age of approximately 12 years, it is impossible to learn one in a full sense. Evidence for such claims comes from extraordinary cases of children being subjected to terrible abuse and isolation by their parents, or being raised by animals. This theory was never fully supported, its opponents pointing out that the children in such cases had far from normal childhoods, lacking in exposure to the language, social interaction and nurturing adults.

The theory has often been broadened from first language acquisition to second language acquisition: if a learner does not start to learn a foreign language before the age of about 12, it is impossible to learn one in a full sense. Again, there have been many detractors, quoting examples of adults who learn foreign languages well.

There are clearly many differences between the experiences of learning a first language and learning a second one. Young children learning their first language are in the simultaneous process of discovering their own identity, of establishing relationships with other people, of learning to express themselves, and generally of making sense of the world around them. As we noted in chapter 27, the process of learning a second language is affected by the purpose for learning, and the motivation of the learner. Learners of a second language in school may or may not see the point of it and have motivation, whereas the children of immigrants to an English-speaking country will probably have high motivation. Other factors that may have greater influence than simple age in the learning of a second language include anxiety, the educational setting (teacher, materials, etc.), and the amount of time the learner commits to the process.

The returns (in terms of the improvement of ability as against the amount of time invested) are greater for older learners. That is, older learners make faster learners because they have a better understanding of the categories of their native language, greater cognitive maturity and better developed learning strategies.

It has been suggested that any critical age for the learning of a second language may be related to the aspect of language being investigated, and that grammar and vocabulary may be learned at a later age than pronunciation. This is caused by the different plasticity of the brain and organs for the physiological nature of pronunciation.

Reviewing the literature on the critical period hypothesis for second language learning, Bialystok and Hakuta (1994) conclude that 'on average, there is a continuous decline in ability [to learn] with age.'

Innocence and sophistication

The relative merits of learning to pronounce a second language at a younger age, and the different ways in which foreign pronunciation is learned, have been commented on by Strevens (1974). He distinguishes two principles.

- ***The innocence principle:*** Most learners will learn to produce most sound features of a foreign language with reasonable accuracy by mimicry alone, given the opportunity; this ability tends to decrease with age.
- ***The sophistication principle:*** Older learners can derive more benefit than younger learners from formal, specialized, intellectualized teaching methods; the more sophisticated the learner, the more sophisticated the instruction that can be used, and the higher the standard of achievement per hour of instruction he will typically reach.

In short, the majority of pronunciation features of a second language can be learned by imitation by learners of any age. This is, after all, how we learn the pronunciation of our native language(s). For learning the pronunciation of a second language, it depends, however, on the learner's aptitude for mimicry, the plasticity of their brain, and their willingness to temporarily abandon the pronunciation habits of their native language.

It is perhaps also worth pointing out that much successful pronunciation teaching can be carried out without resorting to technical terminology in the classroom. In the first section of this book, you have already learned technical vocabulary such as *voiced, labio-dental, plosive, diphthong* and *coda*, which you probably had never heard before, and certainly could not define. As the quotation from Jerome K. Jerome at the beginning of this chapter shows (although this is literature, not observed feedback), there are many learners who are hostile to the use of terminology (sophistication) in learning foreign pronunciation. Such terminology would surely be even more counterproductive for young learners. If teachers need to draw learners' attention to such concepts, it is usually possible to explain the concept in more everyday terms. *Voiced* means 'the vocal cords are vibrating: you can feel this in the throat.' *Labio-dental* means 'the bottom lip with the upper teeth.' *Plosive* means 'the air is stopped from coming out through the mouth and nose.' A *diphthong* vowel 'begins and ends with different sounds.' *Coda* is 'the position after the vowel.'

Teaching fossilized learners

Acton (1984) describes a methodology for teaching fossilized learners on a 12-week course. His learners were 'foreign professionals who have at least a bachelor's degree and who have been in the United States or another English-speaking country for an average of five years or more' (p. 72). Since many of them had been passed over for promotion at work, because of their poor pronunciation and communication skills, motivation was not generally a problem.

Acton's approach is based on four assumptions:

- ***The context of learning and change:*** The most important learning and change must go on outside the class.
- ***Learner resources:*** Many of the activities are aimed at getting participants to find ways of using in spontaneous speech what they are capable of doing in formal pronunciation exercises.
- ***Responsibility for change:*** The responsibility for success in the course is placed on the learners.
- ***Intelligibility:*** Although the focus of the course is ostensibly on pronunciation, it is actually on overall communicative effectiveness and intelligibility.

His method has seven features, some of which have already been discussed in this book:

1 ***Conversational control:*** Learners must be taught to stay relaxed and confident in at least one kind of conversation, namely, the type of informal dialogue where they do not feel threatened and where they can assume some degree of control over the topic development. Acton's learners worked in threes: speaker, attender and observer.
2 ***Monitoring strategies:*** Fossilized learners generally find it necessary to do some type of conscious monitoring in order to be able ultimately to effect change in everyday conversation. However, this monitoring is only carried out in the latter part of the course, after it has been decided what features need to be monitored, and how. Also, in post hoc monitoring, learners are taught to scan their speech after the event, suppressing the urge to consciously monitor sounds and structures as they speak them.
3 ***Nonverbal correlates:*** The correlation between nonverbal features and speech are discussed in chapter 33. Nonverbal features are emphasized in Acton's approach, by strategies such as tracking and mirroring.
4 ***Dictionary use:*** The correlation between pronunciation and spelling is also emphasized. By developing skills in use of the dictionary, especially by familiarity with phonemic symbols and the transcriptions used, learners will at least know what

sounds the language has, and which sounds occur in which words, even if they cannot pronounce them all accurately.

Modern dictionaries have accompanying CD-ROMs or online support. There are two main benefits to this. Firstly, words are found much more quickly by clicking on a computer screen rather than by flicking through the pages of a printed dictionary. However, this must be pitted against the length of time it takes to turn on the computer and load the CD-ROM or access the internet. CD-ROMs and the internet are therefore faster only if several words are being looked up at the same time. Secondly, dictionary CD-ROMs and online support webpages contain soundfiles with model pronunciations of the words. Learners can thus hear what the word sounds like and imitate it (the innocence mimicry approach).

5 ***Oral reading:*** Acton's learners prepared and recorded various versions of an oral reading of a 200–300 word passage. The benefits of such recordings are discussed in chapters 34 (on listening) and 35 (on testing). The importance of learners marking up passages to be read aloud is discussed in chapter 18 (on pauses).
6 ***Informant use:*** Since the most important learning goes on outside the class without the presence of the teacher, it is important that the learners should make use of native speaker informants. These are often workmates, who may help learners with problematic on-the-job terms. However, the informant scheme also attempts to redefine the social relationships at work.
7 ***Integration:*** The integration phase entails using, in on-the-job conversation, what learners have learned and corrected in classroom exercises and oral readings. At the end of the course, detailed recommendations are provided to each learner for further study.

Acton notes that, because of the demands of the course, there is usually a dropout rate of 25%. A further 25% do not complete enough of the work to demonstrate significant, lasting change. It is difficult to quantify the progress made by the remaining 50%. However, reports by workmates indicate improvement in the learners' speech. The learners themselves are enthusiastic about the program, and intend to continue to use the techniques after the course.

Summary

- There is disagreement over whether the concept of a critical period, originally proposed for first language acquisition, can be extended to second language acquisition.
- If so, it may be around 12 years of age, although this does not mean that it is impossible to master a second language after that age.
- Fossilized learners represent a special category, but one that is quite common in matters of migration.

Exercises

1. Which languages do you speak? Rank them in order of your pronunciation accuracy. Do you feel that you speak a particular language best because you started to learn it at a younger age? If not, what other factors were involved?

2. Do you feel that you personally respond better to an innocence (mimicry) or sophistication (formal teaching) approach to learning pronunciation?

Further reading

Acton (1984) is the classic work on pronunciation fossilization. Strategies for dealing with adult learners are also given by Graham (1994).

29 First language influence

> '*Alex & Emma*' is an amalgam of clichés about writers and burlesque stereotypes of foreigners. The French say 'zees' and 'zat' for 'this' and 'that,' the Germans bark out their courtesies like SS officers and beefy Cuban thugs talk like Charo puppets, as in 'You pay us back or I'll keel joo.' So much for literary aspirations.
>
> Internet (Newsday.com) review of 2003 film *Alex & Emma*

Learning objectives

At the end of this chapter, you will be able to:

- carry out a contrastive analysis of your learners' pronunciation.

First and second language learning

Learning a second language differs from the process of learning a first language, although some writers have sought to draw parallels between the two. In terms of phonology, babies learning their first language (native language, mother tongue) pass through various stages. At an early age, they experiment to see what noises they can make using their vocal organs. These noises may correspond to speech sounds, but may also be other non-speech noises such as laughter and blowing raspberries. Later, they come to understand the differences between speech and non-speech sounds, and experiment with speech sounds. These may or may not correspond to the speech sounds of their first language. Then, children gradually work out, by listening to speakers around them, which sounds are needed for the first language, and which are not. Certain sounds are acquired earlier than others. For instance, the plosives /p, t/ are acquired earlier than the velar plosive /k/. The plosives as a class are acquired earlier than fricatives, especially /θ ʃ/, and affricates.

The process of learning a second language is different in crucial ways. Second language learners have already learned their first language. They have therefore already internalized the set of sounds used in their first language, but these sounds will not correspond exactly to those of the second language.

Second language learners are usually much older than first language learners. We normally start to learn our first language at the age of one or two years, and have mastered its phonology by the time we start school. However, unless we grow up in bilingual circumstances, we typically start to learn second languages in secondary school, in our teens. Some second language learners are much older than this, leading to the problem of fossilization (see chapter 28).

Second language learners of, say, English may have already learned another language as a second language. In other words, they have already gone through the process of learning a foreign language, and may be well aware of the problems and strategies associated with this.

Contrastive analysis

The fact that second language learners have already learned their first language, and have internalized its sounds, led to the hypothesis known as contrastive analysis. There are strong and weak forms of this hypothesis.

The strong form

The strong form of the hypothesis (Lado, 1957) claimed that, by analyzing the phonological systems of the first and a second language, and by comparing them, one could predict the problems that learners from that first language would encounter in learning that second language. That is, the phonological features that are the same in the two languages would not pose any learning problem, while features that differed would be difficult. The same argument was made for grammar, vocabulary and other aspects of language. With this approach, which formed one of the bases of the audiolingual method (see chapter 25), it was claimed that curriculum design would be more efficient and effective.

While this approach was popular in the 1960s and 1970s, there were various problems with it. First, it assumed that there was a set of universal phonological features within a comprehensive linguistic theory. Second, it required extensive phonological descriptions of the two languages. Third, it assumed that, if one entered these descriptions as the input to a theory of contrastive linguistics, then the differences (that is, problems) would be generated quasi-automatically. None of these claims was realistic or practicable. They have been described as a pseudo-procedure (Abercrombie, 1965, Wardhaugh, 1974), that is, a procedure that the analyst claims would give the expected result, but which has never actually been carried out for reasons of impracticability, time, etc.

Most importantly, it was found in the 1970s that there were certain features of learners' speech that could not be accounted for by contrastive analysis. Many errors predicted by contrastive analysis did not occur in the speech of learners. Vice versa, some errors were regularly made by learners regardless of their first language. Thus they were not due to interference (also, more euphemistically, known as negative transfer or crosslingual influence) and not predictable by contrastive analysis.

The weak form

It thus became clear that the problems of learners could not be reliably predicted by contrastive analysis. Instead, some observed errors could be explained retrospectively by comparing the two languages. This post hoc analysis is the weak form of contrastive analysis, and led to the field of enquiry known as error analysis.

Common errors

Nevertheless, in the field of pronunciation teaching, it is clear that many features of learners' speech can be predicted or explained by reference to features of their first language. Books of common errors have been published as a result, aimed at helping teachers with learners from particular linguistic backgrounds. Perhaps the most commonly used one is Swan and Smith (2001), which lists the common errors in pronunciation, grammar, vocabulary, discourse structure, spelling, punctuation and handwriting for 22 languages or language groups. Other books on pronunciation teaching have listed purely phonological features.

Table 29.1 gives a comparison of the pronunciation features mentioned by two books (Kenworthy, 1987; Swan and Smith, 2001). For illustration, we will use learners whose

Table 29.1 Common errors in the English speech of Arabic native speakers

	Swan & Smith	*Kenworthy*
Confusion between /ɪ, e/	✓	✓
Confusion between /e, æ, ʌ/		✓
Confusion between /ɒ, ɔː/	✓	
Shortening of /eɪ, əʊ/, and thus confusion with /e, ɒ/	✓	✓
Confusion between /g, dʒ/	✓	
Confusion between /dʒ, ʒ, tʃ/		✓
Pronunciation of /r/ as a tap or trill	✓	✓
Confusion between /p, b/	✓	✓
Confusion between /f, v/	✓	
Confusion between /k, g/	✓	
Pronunciation of /θ, ð/ as /t, d/	✓	
Pronunciation of /θ, ð/ as /s, z/		✓
Use of clear /l/ in all contexts		✓
Pronunciation of /ŋ/ as /n, ŋg, ŋk/	✓	✓
Use of glottal stop before initial vowels, thus lack of linking	✓	✓
Pronunciation of all initial clusters with epenthetic vowels	✓	✓
Pronunciation of final clusters with simplification and/or epenthetic vowels	✓	✓
Lack of omission of consonants, given the spelling	✓	
Avoidance of coalescent assimilation	✓	
More energetic articulation	✓	✓
More stressed syllables	✓	✓
Fewer weak forms	✓	✓
Problems with unpredictable word stress placement	✓	✓
Lack of use of contrastive stress		✓
Stressing the last syllable in a word ending -VCC or V:C		✓
Use of steady pitch with jumps from one syllable to another		✓
Overuse of rising tone for questions, suggestions and offers	✓	
Overuse of low fall at the ends of sentences	✓	✓

Sources of data: Swan & Smith, 2001, Kenworthy, 1987

first language is Arabic, which is spoken as a first language with some variation throughout the middle east and north Africa, and as a major language in the former Soviet republics, and a few other countries in Africa. In brief, Arabic has eight vowels (that is, far fewer contrasts than the 20 (SSBE) or 16 (GenAm) vowels of English) and 32 consonants (that is, rather more than the 24 of English). Greater importance is attached to consonants than vowels in Arabic, and elision and weak forms are avoided. The /θ, ð/ sounds, while occurring in classical, literary, Qur'anic Arabic, are replaced by the closest occurring sounds in many modern accents. Arabic has no initial clusters, and only two-consonant final clusters.

The popularity of books such as Kenworthy (1987) and Swan and Smith (2001) shows that guidelines on common errors teachers can expect from learners of particular nationalities and first languages are found useful, especially perhaps by teachers with minimal pronunciation training.

Summary

- Contrastive analysis is based on the principle that the pronunciation problems of learners of English can be predicted by analyzing the phonological systems of English and their first language.
- There are, however, many problems with the strong form of this hypothesis.
- Inventories of common errors made by speakers of particular first languages are, nevertheless, helpful to teachers.

Exercises

1. Which sounds of foreign languages you know give you the most trouble? Can they all be explained by contrastive analysis, in terms of interference from your native language?
2. Look at the chapter in Swan and Smith (2001) that deals with learners from a native language you have some experience of. That is, you know that language to some extent, and you know the problems speakers of that language have with English. Can the common errors listed be explained by contrastive analysis, in terms of interference from the native language? (You could consider errors of grammar, vocabulary, etc., as well as pronunciation.)

Further reading

James (1980) describes the claims of contrastive analysis. Avery and Ehrlich (1992), Kenworthy (1987), Swan and Smith (2001) and Yates and Zielinski (2009) contain lists of common pronunciation errors of learners from various languages.

30 Importance

Not everything that can be counted counts, and not everything that counts can be counted.
Attributed to Albert Einstein (1879–1955),
German-born US physicist

Learning objectives

At the end of this chapter, you will be able to:

- state which pronunciation features are considered important by experts
- explain the concept of functional load.

Introduction

Pronunciation has been described as the Cinderella of the ELT world. That is, it is an aspect of language teaching that is often neglected. The purpose of this chapter is to examine how the concept of importance relates to pronunciation, and pronunciation teaching. In particular, we will look at four questions:

- whether pronunciation is considered important by learners of English
- why teachers often treat pronunciation as if it were not important
- which of the features that make up pronunciation are more important than others
- which consonant and vowel contrasts are more important than others.

Importance of pronunciation to learners

Researched writing (e.g. Willing, 1988), as well as informal comments by learners, clearly show that pronunciation is a priority for most learners. For instance, Shaw (1981) conducted a questionnaire survey among final year bachelor degree students (ages 20.4 to 22.1 years) in Asian countries: 170 in Singapore, 342 in India and 313 in Thailand. Among many other questions, the students were asked to rank the four skills (reading, writing, speaking and listening) in order of their own command of the skills. Each nationality group rated speaking as their worst skill: 47% of the Singaporeans, 59% of the Indians and 62% of the Thais. The groups were then asked to name the skill that they wanted to be their best skill of the four. Overwhelmingly, they chose speaking: 71% of the Singaporeans, 71% of the Indians and 88% of the Thais. As Shaw (1981, p. 116) concludes, 'if these statistics are a true reflection of reality, there is a great difference between what the students want and what they are getting from their English classes.'

While speaking skills subsume aspects other than pronunciation, such as oral fluency and confidence, other questions in Shaw's study show that pronunciation is a significant factor here.

Reluctance of teachers to teach pronunciation

Many English language teachers treat pronunciation as if it were not important, by sweeping it under the carpet. Common remarks from teachers are that they are not good at teaching pronunciation, they do not like teaching it, they do not teach it often, and, as a result, the pronunciation work they do carry out is probably not enough to meet the learners' needs.

Macdonald (2002) carried out an in-depth interview study with eight such reluctant teachers in Australia. His results indicate that teachers do not teach pronunciation—or enough pronunciation—for the following reasons.

First, the curriculum that the teachers have to follow may not have a pronunciation requirement. Alternatively, since there are so many other areas to teach, pronunciation is often left to be taught through these other areas. Instead, pronunciation should be a central and integrated part of the curriculum, rather than an add-on. Materials that confer such a position on pronunciation are rare, the *Headway Pronunciation* series (Bowler, Cunningham, Moor and Parminter, 1999) being an often-quoted counterexample.

Second, there was no systematic way of assessing learners' pronunciation, or at least of monitoring learner progress. Again, pronunciation was seen as an add-on, and attention was paid to it only when intelligibility became an issue. If the teacher could understand the learner easily enough, pronunciation was largely ignored.

Third, the question of identity may cause pronunciation to be an embarrassment on the part of both the learner and the teacher. Speech is a central element of one's identity. In view of this, learners may harbor resistance towards being asked to change their pronunciation, and any attempts to do so may cause embarrassment or discomfort. As a result, many teachers may have ethical objections to trying to effect such a change, and therefore be reluctant to try.

Finally, teachers felt that there was a lack of suitable materials for pronunciation teaching. Teachers sometimes tried to produce their own custom-made materials, or adapt existing ones, but often lacked the technical expertise to do so effectively. What teachers often want are off-the-shelf materials that can be used straightaway in the classroom. *Pronunciation Games* (Hancock, 1995) is an often-quoted favorite.

A ranking of pronunciation features

English language teachers do not have unlimited time to spend on pronunciation (or indeed on any other aspect of language). It is therefore important that they should prioritize, and devote precious classroom time to those aspects that are considered important for intelligible speech, or those aspects that will give the maximum returns for the time spent, in terms of the intelligibility of their learners. Surprisingly few writers have committed themselves in writing to a ranking of aspects according to importance (Bradford, 1990; Gilbert, 1995; Jenner, 1987). There is little overlap between their rankings.

I shall quote Gilbert's (1995) here, as hers is the most discriminating, simplifying things to a five-point (in fact, perhaps four-point) ranking:

1. The distinction between plosives and continuants, especially as this is important for grammatical distinctions, such as *He'd/He's gone, I'd/I'll cut it.*
2. The number of syllables in speech. This is considered important because, as a result of avoidance of consonant clusters, failure to hear schwa, overgeneralization of rules, etc., learners often add or omit syllables, as in *Yestday I rent car* for *Yesterday I rented a car.*
3. Vowel length on stressed syllables, especially where there is contrast.
4. Schwa. In fact, the 3rd and 4th points may be combined into one (word stress versus unstress).
5. The signaling of new versus old/given information by the placement of the tonic.

The Lingua Franca Core outlined by Jenkins (2000; see chapter 24) is also an attempt to specify the important aspects of pronunciation on the basis of observed breakdowns in communication between nonnative speakers.

There are clearly a number of differences between these various statements of priorities. However, we can make out certain similarities that they share:

- Vowel length is mentioned by all writers.
- Consonants are also generally considered important, although writers may differ as to which particular consonants, or whether it is the consonant inventory as a whole.
- The distinction between strong and weak syllables in words is deemed important.
- The identification of tone groups, and the placement of prominence and the tonic syllable within them is remarked on.

So far, all the rankings have been by native speaker-applied linguist judges. However, this may not correspond to what nonnative speakers and non-applied linguists believe. I carried out a survey of opinions about importance by two groups: 33 members of an internet discussion group on pronunciation matters, and 115 Singaporean trainee English language teachers (reported in greater detail in Brown 2000). Table 30.1 gives the order of the 29 features used, ranked according to the internet group.

There is evidently a great difference in ranking for some items. Conclusions were:

- Consonants and spelling (and to a lesser extent, phonemic vowel length) are ranked much higher by the Singaporeans than by the internet group. This suggests that segments are far more prominent an aspect of learning the pronunciation of the language for Singaporeans (and probably others), while suprasegmentals are considered more important by the internet group.

- Weak forms and linking are the two most unimportant features for the Singaporeans. Rhythm is also rated much lower by them. These three contribute to the staccato effect Singapore speech is often said to have. All three are rated much higher by the internet group.
- Stress in multisyllable words is rated very low by the Singaporeans, but very high by the internet group. However, all other aspects of stress are ranked highly (in the top ten for both groups).
- Intonation is not thought important by either group.

Table 30.1 Ranking of 29 features by 33 international internet, and 115 Singaporean respondents

Pronunciation feature	*Internet ranking*	*Singaporean ranking*
Unmarked sentence stress, on nouns, verbs, adjectives and adverbs	1	4
Contrastive stress	2	6
Stress placement in multisyllable words	3	21
Pausing	4	1
Rhythm	5	18
Correcting stress	6	10
Stress in noun/verb pairs, eg *subject*	7	9
Linking	8	28
Morphologically determined stress, eg *photograph, photography*	9	7
Speed	10	11
Pronouncing all Cs in initial CC clusters	11	14
Weak forms	12	29
Phonemic vowel length, eg /iː/ versus /ɪ/	13	2
Pronouncing all Cs in final CC clusters	14	8
Allophonic vowel length, eg *bead* versus *beat*	15	12
Proclaiming & referring tone	16	23
Pronouncing all Cs in initial CCC clusters	17	15
Aspiration of initial plosives	18	5
Key	19	20
Loudness	20	16
All the 20 contrasting vowels of SSBE	21	27
Pronouncing all Cs in final CCC clusters	22	22
Relating pronunciation features to spelling	23	13
Non-verbal features, eg gestures	24	19
Elision	25	26
The *th* sounds /θ, ð/	26	3
Assimilation	27	25
Voice quality	28	17
Pronouncing all Cs in final CCCC clusters	29	24

Source of data: Brown, 2000

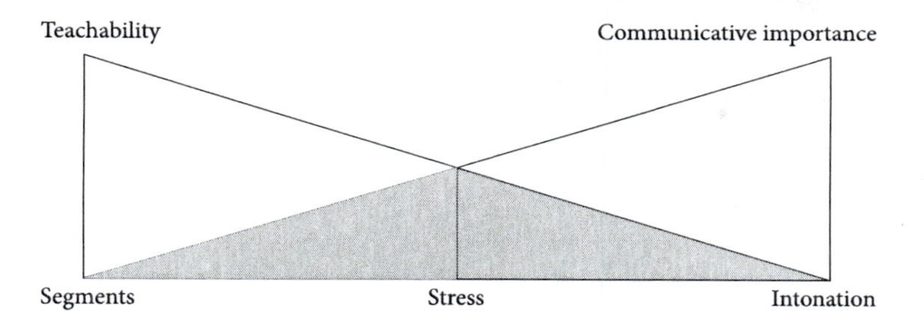

Figure 30.1 Teachability and communicative importance.
Source: Dalton & Seidlhofer, 1994

Dalton and Seidlhofer (1994) identify stress as the most important aspect for teaching purposes, by the following argument. Some elements of pronunciation, such as consonant and vowel segments, are eminently teachable. However, they are not necessarily those elements that are of communicative importance, others, such as intonation, being more important in this respect. The diagram (Figure 30.1) plots teachability against communicative importance. Stress, in the centre of the diagram, represents a maximum overlap of communicative importance and teachability. Stress is thus the most convenient focal point for any course in pronunciation.

So, what are we to make of all these, often contradictory, opinions? Clearly, more work needs to be done to produce a ranking of pronunciation features that most will agree with, including learners themselves. Following Jenkins (2000), we should maintain that such rankings should be on the basis of observation, although many would argue that it should not be exclusively on the basis of nonnative speaker considerations.

The relative importance of consonants and vowels

Introductory books on phonetics and pronunciation teaching often give a systematic account of the consonant and vowel sounds of English. This gives the impression that the consonants and vowels are as equal as the teeth of a comb. However, certain segments are much more frequent and more important than others. Here, we will briefly mention four ways in which certain consonant and vowel contrasts may be considered more important than others. This area, known as functional load, is examined in greater detail by Brown (1988, 1991).

Frequency of occurrence

Certain segments occur more frequently in connected English speech than others. Tables 30.2 and 30.3 show the relative text frequency of all the 24 consonant and 20 vowel phonemes of SSBE (figures from Fry, 1947, quoted in Cruttenden, 2001, pp. 148, 216).

Table 30.2 Text frequencies (%) of consonants

Sound	*Frequency*	*Sound*	*Frequency*
/n/	7.58	/b/	1.97
/t/	6.42	/f/	1.79
/d/	5.14	/p/	1.78
/s/	4.81	/h/	1.46
/l/	3.66	/ŋ/	1.15
/ð/	3.56	/g/	1.05
/r/	3.51	/ʃ/	0.96
/m/	3.22	/j/	0.88
/k/	3.09	/dʒ/	0.60
/w/	2.81	/tʃ/	0.41
/z/	2.46	/θ/	0.37
/v/	2.00	/ʒ/	0.10

Consonants make up 60.79% of all sounds in connected speech.
Source of data: Fry, 1947

Table 30.3 Text frequencies (%) of vowels

Sound	*Frequency*	*Sound*	*Frequency*
/ə/	10.74	/ɔː/	1.24
/ɪ/	8.33	/uː/	1.13
/e/	2.97	/ʊ/	0.86
/aɪ/	1.83	/ɑː/	0.79
/ʌ/	1.75	/aʊ/	0.61
/eɪ/	1.71	/ɜː/	0.52
/iː/	1.65	/eə/	0.34
/əʊ/	1.51	/ɪə/	0.21
/æ/	1.45	/ɔɪ/	0.14
/ɒ/	1.37	/ʊə/	0.06

Vowels make up 39.21% of all sounds in connected speech.
Source of data: Fry, 1947

Minimal pairs

We are talking about individual consonant and vowel sounds. However, we must not lose sight of the fact that these sounds combine to produce the vocabulary of the language.

As explained in chapter 12, minimal pairs are pairs of words such as *bat* and *pat* whose pronunciations are different in only one position. Contrasts for which there are relatively few minimal pairs may thus be considered less important than contrasts for which there are many minimal pairs. Tables 30.4 and 30.5 give the number of minimal pairs for SSBE vowel and consonant contrasts (from Higgins, n.d.).

Table 30.4 Number of minimal pairs for SSBE vowel contrasts

	/ɪ/	/e/	/æ/	/ɑː/	/ɒ/	/ɔː/	/ʊ/	/uː/	/ʌ/	/ɜː/	/ə/	/eɪ/	/aɪ/	/ɔɪ/	/əʊ/	/aʊ/	/ɪə/	/eə/	/ʊə/
/iː/	471	338	394	316	362	489	82	381	301	309	66	561	532	98	527	157	133	144	38
/ɪ/		446	635	228	438	271	61	222	456	178	362	334	257	59	358	88	48	28	7
/e/			302	142	227	212	43	130	233	147	36	250	222	57	213	118	32	30	11
/æ/				179	409	179	56	159	425	160	11	256	237	29	240	103	23	31	9
/ɑː/					172	156	34	75	172	127	11	184	125	37	169	51	46	48	22
/ɒ/						157	73	141	300	153	1	218	172	22	203	96	26	19	8
/ɔː/							56	142	168	180	21	251	207	71	243	106	82	92	23
/ʊ/								18	19	41	1	61	52	3	28	15	6	8	3
/uː/									119	74	9	234	200	45	208	97	26	33	11
/ʌ/										126	4	211	148	29	181	85	18	20	7
/ɜː/											8	182	141	33	149	63	35	41	14
/ə/												82	20	3	48	3	0	7	0
/eɪ/													353	90	336	154	41	47	15
/aɪ/														56	269	166	43	33	13
/ɔɪ/															75	33	14	7	6
/əʊ/																115	42	44	13
/aʊ/																	22	18	6
/ɪə/																		67	22
/eə/																			19

Source: Higgins, n. d.

Table 30.5 Number of minimal pairs for SSBE consonant contrasts

	/b/	/t/	/d/	/k/	/g/	/f/	/v/	/θ/	/ð/	/s/	/z/	/ʃ/	/ʒ/	/h/	/m/	/n/	/ŋ/	/l/	/r/	/j/	/w/	/tʃ/	/dʒ/
/p/	612	882	524	1009	401	570	227	129	66	613	222	216	3	377	620	561	84	683	374	87	433	296	197
/b/		431	400	458	350	411	129	63	34	342	79	186	2	228	385	270	37	346	289	64	196	225	179
/t/			682	731	319	405	232	117	57	1258	379	247	8	231	453	517	109	575	318	46	216	238	248
/d/				466	250	332	285	126	58	481	2660	242	7	185	414	484	1619	507	440	39	142	206	208
/k/					341	464	176	112	42	472	214	213	4	272	413	460	87	470	229	50	193	211	155
/g/						196	79	52	18	201	54	145	1	125	239	240	61	207	155	26	109	97	108
/f/							130	50	35	371	73	137	2	185	312	236	22	272	218	49	178	156	171
/v/								25	30	204	148	49	2	66	187	222	83	233	112	7	52	63	93
/θ/									9	91	59	41	2	36	60	67	10	65	37	10	42	42	36
/ð/										28	34	18	2	15	63	53	7	45	18	3	19	22	16
/s/											232	220	9	217	361	384	51	467	299	42	169	182	184
/z/												65	11	24	159	317	1135	253	50	8	17	102	94
/ʃ/													5	129	179	148	83	180	155	34	105	115	103
/ʒ/														0	9	6	0	6	0	0	1	3	1
/h/															226	139	0	216	225	70	191	95	101
/m/																359	59	513	259	52	150	172	175
/n/																	78	681	239	35	142	151	147
/ŋ/																		58	2	0	0	21	76
/l/																			589	68	204	182	202
/r/																				58	213	120	151
/j/																					48	28	45
/w/																						61	93
/tʃ/																							92

Source: Higgins, n. d.

Lexical sets

There are some phonemes that simply do not occur in many words of the language. For example, Wells (1982, p. 133) notes that the set of lexical items with the vowel [ʊ] as the stressed vowel is only around 40 words. The text frequency of this phoneme is only 1.95%, and would be lower if not for several high-frequency words, such as *put, good, look* and *would.*

Spelling

The sound-spelling correspondences of SSBE sounds have been introduced in the earlier chapters of this book. If a learner does not distinguish two sounds, and if those two sounds are represented fairly regularly by spellings that do not overlap (that is, one spelling cannot represent both sounds), then we can expect the learner to make spelling mistakes. By virtue of this, we can say that the distinction between those two sounds is relatively important. The topic of spelling, including misspelling, is studied in greater detail in the next two chapters.

Conclusion

To draw together the various threads that have been mentioned briefly in this section, it can be claimed that certain distinctions between sounds are more important than others on the basis of various criteria. Sometimes these criteria may work against each other, that is, a distinction may be considered relatively important by one criterion, but relatively unimportant by another. Table 30.6 (from Brown, 1988, 1991) shows the relative importance, on a ten-point scale, of various distinctions often conflated by learners.

Thus, for instance, if a learner does not distinguish /e, æ/, nor /ʊ, uː/, should the teacher spend time on both of them, one of them, or neither? The table shows that /e, æ/ is very important (10) and should be mastered: both vowels are relatively frequent, there are plenty of minimal pairs, and their spellings are distinct (/e/ is usually *e* or *ea*, while /æ/ is always *a*). The /ʊ, uː/ distinction, however, is relatively unimportant (3): both vowels are relatively infrequent, there are very few minimal pairs, and their spellings overlap to an extent (for example, both vowels are frequently represented by the letters *oo*, as in *good food* /gʊd fuːd/). This distinction may therefore be ignored (i) until other higher-ranking distinctions have been mastered, and (ii) provided the learner is aiming for a high level of pronunciation.

Summary

- Learners often rank pronunciation as the skill that they need to improve most.
- Teachers often neglect pronunciation teaching, for a number of possible reasons.
- Not all pronunciation features are equally important. Therefore, not everything needs to be covered in class.

Table 30.6 Rank ordering of sound distinctions according to overall importance

	Vowels		Consonants
10	/e, æ/	10	/p, b/
	/æ, ʌ/		/p, f/
	/æ, ɒ/		/m, n/
	/ʌ, ɒ/		/n, l/
	/ɔː. əʊ/		/l, r/
9	/e, ɪ/	9	/f, h/
	/e, eɪ/		/t, d/
	/ɑː aɪ/		/k, g/
	/ɪː, əʊ/		
		8	/w, v/
8	/iː, ɪ/		/s, z/
7		7	/b, v/
			/f, v/
6	/ɔː, ɜː/		/ð, z/
	/ɒ, əʊ/		/s, ʃ/
5	/ɑː, ʌ/	6	/v, ð/
	/ɔː, ɒ/		/s, ʒ/
	/ɜː, ʌ/		
		5	/θ, ð/
4	/e, eə/		/θ, s/
	/æ, ɑː/		/ð, d/
	/ɑː, ɒ/		/z, dʒ/
	/ɔː, ʊ/		/n, ŋ/
	/ɜː, e/		
		4	/θ, t/
3	/iː, ɪə/		
	/ɑː, aʊ/	3	/tʃ, dʒ/
	/uː, ʊ/		
		2	/tʃ, ʃ/
2	/ɪə, eə/		/ʃ, ʒ/
			/j, ʒ/
1	/ɔː, ɔɪ/		
	/uː, ʊə/	1	/f, θ/
			/dʒ, j/

Source: Brown, 1988, 1991

Exercises

1. Do you agree with the consensus four points of importance for pronunciation teaching (vowel length, consonants, strong/weak syllables, tone units)? Are there any others that you feel should be in that list?
2. Table 30.1 shows some sizeable differences between the viewpoints of native speaker teachers, and of learners. Can you think of other points of difference between the opinions of these two groups on matters of pronunciation?

Further reading

Jenkins (2000) argues in depth for the importance of nonnative speakers, intelligibility and observed data. Brown (1988) describes many functional load factors by which vowel and consonant contrasts can be considered important; also see Catford (1987).

31 Spelling: History

> Our alphabet is pure insanity. It can hardly spell any large word in the English language with any degree of certainty. Its sillinesses are quite beyond enumeration. English orthography may need reforming and simplifying, but the English alphabet needs it a good many times as much.
>
> Mark Twain (1835–1910), US author

Learning objectives

At the end of this chapter, you will be able to:

- explain the alphabetic principle underlying English spelling
- describe some of the main events in the history of English spelling
- give examples of magic *e*, consonant doubling and silent letters.

The alphabetic principle

We have already mentioned spelling a number of times in this book. For instance, in chapters 5, 7, 8 and 9, we listed the main sound-spelling correspondences of SSBE vowel and consonant sounds. We can do this because the spelling system (the technical term is orthography) of English, like most languages of the world, is based on the alphabetic principle. In an alphabetic spelling system, the letters in the spelling represent the individual consonant and vowel sounds in the pronunciation. This is in contrast to systems such as the logographic system for Chinese, where symbols (characters) in the writing represent whole linguistic units (words) and often constituent parts of words (morphemes), or the Japanese *kana* system, where symbols in the spelling represent whole syllables.

However, the English spelling system, while undoubtedly being based on this underlying alphabetic principle, is probably the worst example of it. That is, the correspondence between letters and sounds is far from one-to-one. The correspondence is almost perfect in languages such as Finnish. The following section explains briefly the main historical reasons for the irregularities of English spelling.

Historical sources of irregularity in English spelling

English as a language is usually deemed to begin with the 5th century invasion into Britain of Germanic tribes known as the Anglo-Saxons from present-day northern Germany and parts of Denmark and the Netherlands.

The Roman alphabet came to Britain in the 6th century with Christian missionaries. At that time, the alphabet consisted of 23 letters, which were sufficient for representing Latin, but needed to be added to in order to cope with the 35 or so phonemes of Old English.

The Vikings invaded Britain in the 9th and 10th centuries, and brought with them the spelling conventions of their language, known as Old Norse. Characteristic Scandinavian vocabulary includes /sk-/ words such as *scab, scalp, scant, scar, scoff, scoot, score, scuff, skill, skin, skirt* and *sky*.

Duke William of Normandy (France) invaded England and defeated King Harold the Second at the Battle of Hastings, in the Norman Conquest of 1066. He thus became King William I, also known as William the Conqueror. William spoke French, as did subsequent monarchs. The next English-speaking king was Henry IV in 1399. Many words of French origin were introduced into English, as well as French spelling patterns. Examples include the *qu* for /kw/ of *quick* (formerly *cwic*), the *ch* for /tʃ/ of *church* (formerly *cyrice*) and the *ou* of *house* (formerly *hus*, pronounced /huːs/ at that time).

In the 15th century, the printing press was invented by Johannes Gutenberg in Germany. It was brought to England by William Caxton, who learnt his trade in Europe and brought European printers to work for him. Before the advent of the printing press, spellings were quite flexible. However, after its arrival, spellings became more standardized, often conforming to European spelling patterns.

It is ironic that, after the standardization of spelling because of the printing press, the pronunciation of the influential London speech underwent a huge transformation known as the Great Vowel Shift. Over the course of a couple of centuries, the whole vowel system (as it were, the placement of vowels on the vowel trapezium in chapter 5) shifted. For instance, the pronunciation /huːs/ changed into modern /haʊs/. However, since spelling had recently been fixed because of printing, the spellings did not change. As a result, modern English spelling is often a better indication of how the word was pronounced before the Great Vowel Shift, in the 14th or 15th century, than of modern pronunciation.

Consonantal changes took place over the same period as the Great Vowel Shift too. This is the source of many of the 'silent' consonant letters in modern English spelling, that is, letters that do not represent any sound in the pronunciation, such as the *k* of *knight*, the *g* of *gnaw*, and the *b* of *dumb*. These letters originally represented pronounced /k, ɡ, b/ sounds.

In the 16th century, scholars felt that the historical origins of words ought to be reflected in their spelling. Thus, modern *debt, doubt, reign* have 'silent' *b* and *g* letters, even though these words have never contained /b, ɡ/ sounds in English pronunciation, nor in the pronunciation of French, from which they were borrowed into English. In the ultimate source of these words, Latin, they do have these sounds.

Since the 16th century, many words have been borrowed into English from a variety of languages. However, they have not usually been respelled or repronounced in order to conform to native English spelling and pronunciation patterns. As a result, a number of loanwords still look and/or sound foreign, e.g. *bizarre, cocoa, epitome, genre, intrigue, pneumonia*.

To sum up, there are several factors accounting for the irregular state of present-day English spelling:

- The English language has a long history of over 1,500 years, and it has been written down for that long. In contrast, the first book in Finnish was printed in 1488, and little subsequent literature appeared before the 19th century. The history of Finnish spelling has only had one third of the length of time of English spelling to develop irregularities.
- Right at the beginning of English spelling, it contained irregularities, because Christian missionaries attempted to use the Roman alphabet, which was suitable for Latin, to write English, for which it was not suitable.
- Foreign, especially European, spelling conventions have influenced English spelling at various times.
- The relative timing of the advent of the printing press with its standardization of spelling, followed by the Great Vowel Shift with its wholesale change in vowel pronunciations, means that modern spelling is not a good representation of modern pronunciation.
- Foreign loanwords have not generally been integrated into English by having their spelling and/or pronunciation changed to conform to English patterns.
- Perhaps most importantly, English spelling has never been systematically managed. No body ensures that English spelling is updated to be consistent with modern English pronunciation. In contrast, Finnish spelling was regularized at the end of the 19th century and has not needed maintenance since. The Kielitoimisto (Language Planning Department of the Research Institute for the Languages of Finland) is recognized as the regulatory authority on Finnish language matters.

As a result of all the above factors contributing to the irregularity, modern English spelling is variously labeled deep (versus shallow), irregular (versus regular), inconsistent (versus consistent) and opaque (versus transparent).

Three spelling phenomena

Following the upheaval caused by the Great Vowel Shift, and the standardization produced by printing, three spelling phenomena came about (magic *e*, consonant doubling, and silent letters), the first two of them being related.

Magic e

The phenomenon known in teaching circles as 'magic *e*' is a 'rule' that all English users know, but perhaps may not be able to explain consciously. Since it does not relate to sound-spelling correspondences in a one-to-one fashion, even native speakers have problems with it, as evidenced by schoolboy howlers such as 'In olden days, people lived in small huts and there was rough mating on the floor.' We can use the word *mating*, and the intended word *matting*, to explain magic *e*.

What is the difference between the words *mat* and *mate*? In spelling, the answer is simple: *mate* has an extra *e* at the end. In pronunciation, the difference lies in the vowel: in *mat*, the vowel is short /æ/, while in *mate*, it is the (long) diphthong /eɪ/. The same is true of all vowel letters, as in pairs such as *pet/Pete; kit/kite; cut/cute* and SSBE *rob/robe*. The words without the final *e* have short vowels (/æ, e, ɪ, ɒ, ʌ/, or perhaps /ʊ/ as in *put*), while those with the final *e* have long monophthongs or (long) diphthongs (/eɪ, iː, aɪ, əʊ, juː/). Perceptive readers will have noticed that these long vowels correspond to the names of those letters of the alphabet; that is, we call the letter A /eɪ/, etc. For this reason, the rule is remembered in English teaching circles as 'Magic *e* makes the vowel say its name.'

While that is the underlying principle, like so many other spelling rules of English there are many exceptions. For instance, the words *have* and *shave* have the same spellings, and look like examples of magic *e*. However, while *shave* has the long diphthong /eɪ/ and is therefore an example of magic *e, have* has the short vowel /æ/ and is not an example of magic *e*. The *e* letter in *have* seems to result from the avoidance in English spelling of words that end in a *v* letter; the only common counterexamples are *spiv*, foreign words like *Slav*, and abbreviations like *rev, improv*.

Consonant doubling

What happens when you add a suffix beginning with a vowel sound (such as *-ing*) to words with and without the final *e*? Taking *mat* > *matting* and *mate* > *mating* as examples, we can see that (i) the word without magic *e* doubles the consonant letter, and (ii) the word with magic *e* loses the e letter before adding the ending. Again, this is true of other vowel letters: *forget* > *forgetting; complete* > *completing; hit* > *hitting; bite* > *biting; cut* > *cutting; dispute* > *disputing* and SSBE *rob* > *robbing; probe* > *probing*. This holds for other endings starting in a vowel sound: *catty, hated, redden, eking, recital, dimmer, runny, brutish*, and SSBE *robbing, disrobing*.

It is important to separate sounds from spellings here. This phenomenon of consonant doubling relates to consonant letters in the spelling. The doubled consonant letter represents only one consonant sound in each of the above words. This is different from the doubling of consonant sounds (geminate consonants) explained in chapter 15.

Again, this is the underlying rule, but there are exceptions. The words *radish, melon, limit* and *manor* (and SSBE *robin, profit*) all break the rule by having a short vowel not followed by a doubled consonant letter; that is, they are not spelled *raddish, mellon, limmit* and *mannor* (*robbin, proffit*) but perhaps they ought to be.

Silent letters

The concept of silent letters is a simple one: the letter does not represent any sound in the pronunciation. However, many people would argue that this does not mean that English spelling would be better or simpler without the silent letters. Carney (1994) explains by distinguishing three types of silent letter.

Empty letters are those that have no function at all. That is, they do not have a sound, and they perform no function. They could be left out, leaving a plausible spelling for the word. An example of this is the letter *i* in *friend*. The spelling *frend* would still be pronounced /frend/, showing that it is superfluous. Words that rhyme with *friend* (*trend, blend*, etc.) do not contain *ie*, and people would consider you crazy if you suggested that they ought to be spelled *triend, bliend*. Indeed, in older forms of English, the word was spelled *frend*. *Frend* is also an English surname, e.g. Charles Frend (1909–1977), English film director; Ted Frend (1916–2006), British motorcycle sports competitor. The Vanish cleaner company of New Zealand produce a stain remover named Frend, without public outcry that there should be an *i* letter in the name. It is not surprising that learners sometimes misspell *friend* by putting the *i* letter in the wrong place (*freind*).

Auxiliary letters do not have a sound, but do have a function, and therefore cannot be left out. Magic *e*, as in *hat* ~ *hate*, is therefore an auxiliary letter. The letter *h* is often an auxiliary, as in *sh* (*shave* ~ *save*), *ch* (*choke* ~ *coke*), *th* (*thin* ~ *tin*).

Inert letters have no sound in the word, but do have a sound in morphologically related words. For example, *sign* has no /g/ sound, but *signal, signature, signatory* do. Some writers argue that this is reason enough to keep the *g* letter in *sign*. Certainly, the word *sign* could not be written *sin* without the *g*, because that would imply a short /ɪ/ vowel, and is the existing word *sin*. Other writers therefore suggest new spellings such as *syn* or *sine*.

Summary

- English spelling is based on the alphabetic principle of letters representing sounds.
- The English spelling system is a poor example of this, for historical reasons.
- Everyone, whether a native or nonnative speaker of English, finds English spelling difficult.

Exercises

1. In the following sentences, decide whether the underlined parts refer to letters or to sounds.

    a. There are five vowels in English: *a, e, i, o, u*.
    b. You pronounce an *r* by curling your tongue back.
    c. *sch* is found at the beginning of words like *school, schedule.*
    d. *i* before *e* (e.g. *field*) except after *c* (e.g. *receipt*).
    e. For an *l*, the tongue tip touches the roof of the mouth.
    f. *y* is sometimes a consonant (e.g. *yes*) and sometimes a vowel (e.g. *rhythm*).
    g. There are three consonants at the end of the word *pitch.*
    h. The vowel in *greed* is long, and that in *grid* is short.
    i. The *u* is silent in the word *build.*
    j. English words never end in *h*.

2. We have seen that there are many silent letters in English. Try to think of an alphabet of silent letters, that is, a word where *a* is silent, one where *b* is silent, etc. For instance, the *a* is silent in *bread*; if we leave it out, we still pronounce it [bred], the same as *bred*. The only reason for not omitting the *a* letter might be in order to maintain a visual difference between the two words.
3. The underlined letter in each of the following words is silent, in that it does not represent a sound in the pronunciation. Decide whether they are empty, auxiliary or inert.

bomb *give* *listen*
chameleon *hasten* *live*
debt *height* *receipt*
doubt *hive* *Thomas*
dumb *knife* *two*

Further reading

Crystal (2012) gives a readable account of the history of English spelling. Upward and Davidson (2011) is a more thorough, technical description. Carney (1994) is a comprehensive analysis of English spelling patterns. Carney (1997) is a more user-friendly workbook on English spelling.

32 Spelling: Literacy

You write a swell letter. Glad somebody spells worse than I do.

Ernest Hemingway (1899–1961), in a letter to
F. Scott Fitzgerald (1896–1940), both poor spellers

Learning objectives

At the end of this chapter, you will be able to:

- list some of the main problems of English spelling
- list strategies that spelling learners can exploit.

Why English spelling poses a barrier for foreign learners

The relevance of the discussion in chapter 31 of spelling in this book about English pronunciation teaching should be obvious. We have said that the English spelling system is perhaps the worst example of an alphabetic system. That is, it departs more than other languages from the principle of having one letter in the spelling represent one phoneme in the pronunciation and, vice versa, of one phoneme being consistently represented by the same one letter. We have already noted that Finnish is an example of a language with a regular, one-to-one correspondence between letters and sounds. Other languages that could be added to this list of 'good' alphabetic systems include Dutch, Icelandic, Italian, Malay, Portuguese, Spanish, Serbo-Croatian, as well as many languages for which (usually Roman alphabet-based) spelling systems have been devised in the relatively recent past.

It follows from this that most learners of English will come to the classroom speaking a native language whose spelling system is far more regular than that of English. These learners are therefore likely to find English spelling unnecessarily difficult, for several reasons:

- The correspondence between letters and sounds is far from one-to-one. Note the tables given in chapters 5, 7, 8 and 9. The only letter in English that has a one-to-one correspondence with sound, and vice versa, is *v*, which always represents /v/.

The only possible exception is *vv* for /v/, as in rare examples such as *revved* and *savvy*.

- There are many 'silent' letters in English, a phenomenon unknown in many other spelling systems.
- Consonant letters are often doubled, frequently for no apparent reason, e.g. *abridge* versus *abbreviate, adrenalin* versus *address, afraid* versus *affray, harass* versus *embarrass, inoculate* versus *innocuous*.
- Initial letters are capitalized for reasons that are not connected with pronunciation. That is, *march* and *March, welsh* ('break a promise') and *Welsh*, and *bill* and *Bill*, are spelled differently in terms of capitalization, but pronounced the same. The contexts for such initial capitals have to be learned (see chapter 12). This may prove difficult for learners from languages such as French, where the capitalization contexts are different, e.g. the French words for *March* (like all months) and *Welsh* (like all nationalities) do not start with capitals: *mars* and *gallois*. The whole concept of capital letters has to be appreciated by learners whose native language's spelling system does not have capital letters, such as Arabic, Tamil and Thai.
- Since the correspondence between letters and sounds in English is not one-to-one, but many-to-one and one-to-many, there exist homophones and homographs. Homophones are words that are pronounced the same (and therefore have the same transcription) but are spelled differently, e.g. *grown* and *groan* (both /grəʊn, groʊn/). There may be more than two words involved, as in *sight, site* and *cite* (all /saɪt/) —a measure of the extent of the problem. Homographs are words that are spelled the same but pronounced differently, e.g. *lead* (1 /liːd/ 'show the way,' 2 /led/ 'metal'). In languages with regular spelling systems, homophones and homographs are simply impossible.

To complete the picture, mention should be made of full homonyms. These are both pronounced and spelled the same, but they are different words with unrelated meanings, such as *left* /left/, which may be (i) the past tense of the verb *leave*, or (ii) the opposite of *right*. They have unrelated meanings, and unrelated historical origins. Homonymy is different from polysemy, which involves one word having related literal and extended metaphorical meanings, such as *head* /hed/ (i) of the body, (ii) of a department.

Homophones, homonyms and polysemes feature in jokes:

> A deer, a skunk and a duck went for a meal in a restaurant and started arguing who was going to pay. Not the deer: she didn't have a buck. Not the skunk: he didn't have a /sent/. So they put it on the duck's bill.

Strategies

Learners of English, whether native children or foreign learners, should be helped to decide which strategy to use, so that a particular word is most easily mastered. Because English is a poor example of an alphabetic writing system, several strategies can be used.

The first is the **phonological strategy**, by which learners pay attention to the syllables of words and the sounds within the syllables. This involves several sub-strategies:

- First, multisyllable words must be divided into their constituent syllables. For example, the noun segment /segmənt/ is made up of two syllables /seg + mənt/.
- These syllables must then be divided into their constituent sounds. So, the first syllable /seg/ has three sounds /s + e + g/.
- These constituent sounds must then be associated with their (probable) spellings. The /s/ consonant is normally spelled *s* (occasionally *c*), /e/ is regularly *e*, and /g/is *g*.
- In the second syllable of the noun *segment*, it is not so easy to associate a letter with the vowel, because it is an unstressed syllable and has the schwa vowel /ə/. However, the related verb *segment* /segment/ (where the stress is on the second syllable, which therefore has a full vowel) and the adjective *segmental* /segmentəl/ clearly show that the vowel letter in the second syllable must be *e*, and not for example *a* as in *informant*.
- A knowledge of how words are pronounced in other accents of English may also help. For instance, a British English speaker may not be sure whether /təmɑːtəʊ/ is spelled *tomato* or *tomarto*. Knowing that American English pronounces this word /təmeɪtoʊ/ shows that it cannot be *tomarto*.

The phonological strategy is the only one that is needed for languages that have good sound-spelling correspondences, such as Finnish. However, learners of English also need to consider the following strategies.

There are some words of English that are simply so irregular that it is impossible to learn them by any other strategy than **visual imagery**, that is, learning them by heart. For example, in the word *choir*, while we may relate the initial *ch-* as /k/ to words like *character*, there is no other word in English where *-oir* represents /waɪə/waɪr/. The number *one* does not pattern like any other *-one* word, such as *bone, gone, minestrone*. The only other word in which *one* represents /ʌn/ is *done*, but that still leaves the question of what represents the /w/ sound in *one*.

The **morphemic strategy** is what was referred to in the previous chapter as inert silent letters. So, there is an *n* letter at the end of *autumn*, because the adjective is *autumnal* /ɔːtʌmnəl/.

A common strategy with unfamiliar words is to think of other known words that seem similar. If a learner meets the unfamiliar word *gout*, **spelling by analogy** will allow them to relate it to known words such as *about, scout, shout*, and assume that *gout* is pronounced /gaʊt/.

However, this will not always guarantee the correct guessing of the pronunciation of English words. The word *slough* is far less common than *cough, through, enough* and *though* (and British English *plough*), but these words will not allow a learner to know which pronunciation it patterns after.

Carney (1994, p. 468) gives an example of an **etymological strategy**, that is, thinking of the (probable) historical origin of the word.

> Suppose you are writing about life at sea and find that a favorite dish of working seamen was called /bɜː'guː/. If you think that this word is just nautical slang, you will spell it <burgoo>. But if you think, perhaps because of the final stress, that it

may have something to do with French cooking, you will look for possible French elements and spell it <burgout>, presumably on analogy with *ragout*.

Conclusion

A number of final points should be made.

Phonemic transcription is a common feature of English dictionaries, English language courses and books, and books on English phonetics such as this one. However, it is not a common or important feature of dictionaries and courses in other languages. For example, Malay dictionaries do not contain phonemic transcriptions. The spelling system, being regular, is tantamount to a phonemic transcription.

There are many books on English spelling. However, such books are rare for other languages with more regular spelling systems, simply because there is little to say.

When writers discuss the difficulty of spelling, what they often mean is the difficulty of English spelling. Many of the difficulties of English spelling do not exist in other languages.

Spelling bees are common events in English-speaking countries, especially the USA. Contestants, usually schoolchildren, have to spell words of increasing rarity and irregularity. The concept of the spelling bee simply does not exist in languages with regular spelling systems.

The English spelling system is based on the alphabetic principle, but is a very poor example of it. As a result, many learners, especially those whose native language does not use the alphabetic principle in its spelling, learn to spell English by rote (referred to as visual imagery above). That is, they remember the spelling of each word visually by heart, bypassing the pronunciation. They may not be aware of the alphabetic principle, or the significant, but poor, sound-spelling correspondences that do exist.

Learners whose language has good sound-spelling correspondence, may try to apply this to English. However, since English does not have a good correspondence, they may end up producing spelling pronunciations, that is, pronunciations that are logical, given the spelling. These include pronouncing a /b/ in *debt* and *doubt*, an /l/ in *salmon*, an /s/ at the end of *chassis*, and a /t/ in *fasten*. Again, spelling pronunciations are impossible in a language with a good sound-spelling correspondence.

Teachers of English, whether to native children or to foreign learners, spend a lot of classroom time on spelling—time that could be more profitably spent on other aspects of language learning. However, this is not the case with languages with regular spelling systems. Seymour, Aro and Erskine (2003) have shown that children of most European languages achieve mastery of the spelling system after one year of school instruction. However, the level of English-speaking children (in Scotland) was far lower (see Figure 32.1). The poor sound-spelling correspondence of English is a—if not *the*—major cause of this much slower acquisition of literacy.

The majority of research into reading has been from Anglo-Saxon countries. It is necessary to carry out more research in other countries in order to gain a fuller picture of how writing is decoded. This is especially important as English is taught all over the

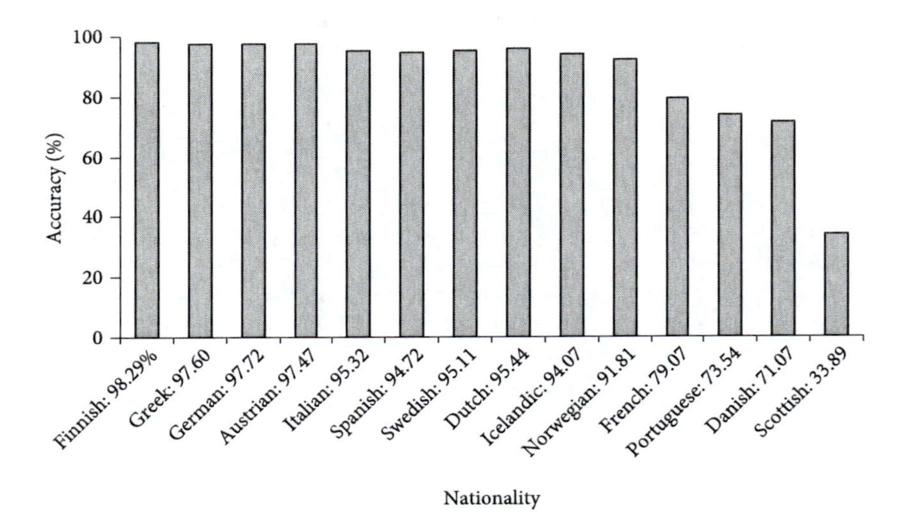

Figure 32.1 Word reading level for various nationalities after one year of instruction (Primary 1).

Source: Seymour et al., 2003

world, and the particular problems of learners from non-Anglo-Saxon countries need to be addressed.

Nevertheless, it seems clear that one major obstacle to accurate spelling and pronunciation in English is its deep, irregular spelling system. The report of a high-level conference of spelling specialists concluded as follows:

> The studies so far undertaken in individual countries are building evidence for the hypothesis that shallow orthographies are a real advantage in terms of acquiring reading proficiency for both normal and dyslexic children. Countries with deep orthographies might possibly begin to consider the political and societal feasibility of implementing orthographic reforms.
>
> (Davis, 2005, p. 14)

Considerations of spelling reform, while probably the long-term solution to this problem, are however beyond the scope of this book on pronunciation teaching.

Summary

- Learners whose native languages have more regular spelling systems may resent the difficulty of English spelling, and the need to learn phonemic symbols.

Exercises

1. For each of the following words, find another word that is pronounced the same, but spelled differently, that is, is a homophone of it.

no	*bold*	*size*	*discreet*
wait	*fair*	*toe*	*heel*
idol	*piece*	*weather*	*or*
finish	*male*	*profit*	*wrapped*
break	*serial*	*ceiling*	*cord*

2. For each of the following spellings, find two words with different pronunciations (that is, homographs) and transcribe them.

read	*tear*	*live*	*minute*
bass	*bow*	*wound*	*entrance*

3. Decide whether the following jokes involve homophones, homonyms or polysemes.

What drink do boxers like?
Fruit punch.

Why did the window see the doctor?
It was having /peɪnz/.

Why couldn't the butterfly go to the dance?
Because it was a moth ball.

What did the lion say to the others before they went out hunting?
Let us /preɪ/.

What did the hamburgers name their daughter?
Patty.

For Christmas, I got three socks from Grandma.
Why three socks?
Because I wrote to tell her I had grown another foot.

Where do you learn to make ice-cream?
/sʌndeɪ/ school.

Why isn't it safe to tell a secret on a farm?
Because the corn has ears and the potatoes have eyes.

What did the fish say when he hit a concrete wall?
/dæm/.

Two aerials got married. The ceremony wasn't much good, but the reception was amazing.

4. The following passage is in a reformed spelling system known as Cut Spelling (but respelled, according to its rules, as Cut Spelng) (Upward, 1996). Read through it and decide:

- if it is easy to read
- what changes have been made from traditional spelling
- whether it is shorter than traditional spelling.

> Wen readrs first se Cut Spelng, as in this sentnce, they ofn hesitate slytly, but then quikly becom acustmd to th shortnd words and soon find text in Cut Spelng as esy to read as traditionl orthografy, but it is th riter ho realy apreciates th advantajs of Cut Spelng, as many of th most trublsm uncertntis hav been elimnated.

Further reading

On the literacy problems caused by English spelling, see Cook (2004b) and Yule (2013). Stirling (2011) is better than most books on spelling in ELT, in that it gives strategies for coping with English spelling, rather than tedious lists of words and exceptions. Also see Stirling's (n.d.) Spelling Blog. For further details of spelling bees, see Scripps (n.d.). On homophones and homographs, see Higgins (n.d.). On spelling reform, see English Spelling Society (n.d.) and Yule (2011). For a psycholinguistic discussion of the relationship between spelling and phonology, see the 2010 (volume 53 issue 3) special issue of the journal *Language and Speech.*

33 Nonverbal communication

> I come from a place that likes grandeur; it likes large gestures; it is not inhibited by flourish; it is a rhetorical society; it is a society of physical performance; it is a society of style.
>
> Derek Walcott (b. 1930), West Indian poet, playwright

Learning objectives

At the end of this chapter, you will be able to:

- give reasons why nonverbal communication is important
- list several types of nonverbal features
- use nonverbal communication in teaching pronunciation.

The importance of nonverbal communication

It may seem incongruous, in a book on pronunciation teaching, to include a chapter on nonverbal communication. That is, pronunciation deals with uttering words, while nonverbal communication by definition does not involve words. However, nonverbal features are important for three main reasons:

- Nonverbal communication conveys a large part of a speaker's overall message. Often-quoted research by Mehrabian (1971) involved two experiments. In the first, subjects listened to a recording of a female speaker saying the word *maybe* in three different tones of voice to express liking, neutrality and disliking. They were also shown photographs of female faces expressing the same three emotions, and were asked to guess the emotions from (i) the recorded voices, (ii) the photographs and (iii) both in combination. By a ratio of 3:2, subjects' responses were more accurate when based on the photographs than on the voices. In the second experiment, subjects listened to nine recorded words, three expressing liking (*honey, dear* and *thanks*), three expressing neutrality (*maybe, really* and *oh*) and three expressing disliking (*don't, brute* and *terrible)*. The words were spoken with different tones of voice, and subjects were required to guess the emotions behind the words. Subjects' responses depended on the tones of voice rather than the words used. Mehrabian's conclusion is expressed as the formula:

Total liking = 7% Verbal liking + 38% Vocal liking + 55% Facial liking

Verbal features are the actual words spoken, while vocal features refer to tone of voice. In inconsistent messages, that is, ones where the nonverbal features contradict the verbal message contained in the words, it is the nonverbal information that is likely to determine the perceived message.

> When any nonverbal behavior contradicts speech, it is more likely to determine the total impact of the message. In other words, touching, positions (distance, forward lean, or eye contact), postures, gestures, as well as facial and vocal expressions, can all outweigh words and determine the feelings conveyed by a message.
>
> (Mehrabian, 1971, p. 45)

This is precisely what happens in sarcasm, where words (such as *That's wonderful*) may be totally overshadowed by opposite nonverbal messages (that is, facial expressions, gestures, intonation, etc., that convey the message 'That's lousy').

This research has often been misquoted to imply that these percentages apply in any communication situation. However, as Mehrabian himself warns:

> Please note that this and other equations regarding relative importance of verbal and nonverbal messages were derived from experiments dealing with communications of feelings and attitudes (i.e. like-dislike). Unless a communicator is talking about their feelings or attitudes, these equations are not applicable.
>
> Mehrabian (n.d.)

Similarly, we cannot say that spoken communication over the telephone (where there are no nonverbal features) is 55% less effective than face-to-face. Nevertheless, Mehrabian's results give an indication of the importance of nonverbal features in general. For instance, their importance in interviews is obvious, where the interviewee is trying to impress and appear likeable to the interviewers.

- Nonverbal features often accompany and work together with verbal features. Indeed, this is such a natural and subconscious process that we are often unaware of it. For example, when talking on the telephone, speakers often make the same facial expressions and gestures that they would if they were talking face-to-face, even though the listener on the phone cannot see them.

  Nonverbal features may even become a substitute for speech. For instance, many people, when travelling on holiday to a country whose language they do not speak with any proficiency, resort to gestures and facial expressions to convey meaning.

- Nonverbal communication is another channel that can be exploited in the teaching of pronunciation. This is especially true in the area of voice quality and suprasegmentals (intonation, stress, etc.). These are areas that many learners find difficult. Any method that helps to make such features more conscious, and helps to improve learners' pronunciation, should therefore not be overlooked.

Some writers (e.g. Gilbert, 1978) relate this to the distinction between the left and right hemispheres of the brain. The left hemisphere is concerned with the phonological, syntactic, lexical and morphological aspects of language. The right hemisphere handles the production and recognition of facial expressions and gestures, affective prosody and pragmatic information. Teachers that use exercises that activate both hemispheres may be more successful than those using exercises that only activate the left.

The components of nonverbal communication

Nonverbal communication is normally divided into three main aspects: proxemics, facial expressions and gestures.

Proxemics

Proxemics is the term used for the distance maintained between people as they interact. Hall (1966) found that this physical distance relates, among other things, to the social distance between the speakers. The following figures hold for American society:

- **intimate** distance for embracing, touching or whispering (15–45 cm)
- **personal** distance for interactions among good friends (45–120 cm)
- **social** distance for interactions among acquaintances (1.2–3.5 m)
- **public** distance for public speaking (over 3.5 m).

There is a cultural dimension to these distances. For instance, Latin cultures use smaller distances than those quoted above, while Nordic cultures use larger ones. One can imagine a conversation involving a Mexican and a Norwegian, with the Mexican always trying to move closer, and the Norwegian constantly backing off.

Facial expressions

In contrast, the use and interpretation of facial expressions is largely universal. Pioneering work in this field was carried out by Ekman and Friesen (1969). Ekman traveled to developed countries including Japan, Brazil and Argentina, as well as remote villages in Papua New Guinea, to investigate the interpretation of particular facial expressions. He found that certain expressions were common in all these cultures and concluded that they were the universal products of evolution, as first suggested by Charles Darwin. Ekman and Friesen then studied the physiology of facial muscles, finding that there were 43 different muscular movements, which they called *action units*. They described the combinations of these action units to produce universal expressions of six basic emotions:

- ***Happiness:*** raising the cheeks and the corners of the lips, and tightening the muscles around the eyes.
- ***Sadness:*** raising the inner eyebrows, raising the cheeks and lowering the corners of the lips.

- ***Surprise:*** raising the eyebrows, widening the eyelids and dropping the jaw.
- ***Fear:*** raising the inner and outer eyebrows, raising the upper eyelid, stretching and parting the lips and dropping the jaw.
- ***Disgust:*** mostly wrinkling the nose, with baring the teeth and lowering the eyebrows.
- ***Anger:*** narrowing the red margin of the lips, lowering the eyebrows, raising the upper eyelids and narrowing both eyelids.

Gestures

Gestures means movements of the hands and/or arms (and perhaps shoulders). Similar nonverbal communication may be achieved by movements of the head, and overall posture or stance. However, only gestures of the hands and arms will be considered here.

The following categories are based on the classificatory systems of Ekman and Friesen (1969) and McNeill (1992):

- ***Deictic*** (or pointing, or indicator) gestures have a pointing function. This may be literal (e.g. pointing to an object) or metaphorical (e.g. pointing behind you to represent past time).
- ***Counting*** gestures use the fingers to count the items in a list.
- ***Beats*** (or batonic, or emphatic gestures) use the hands to align with the stress of speech. This may be simple flapping of the hands in time with the stressed syllables of speech. They may also be used to add emphasis to the important parts of messages.
- ***Iconic*** gestures represent the meaning of the message in a direct way. They may be kinetographic (e.g. miming sweeping the floor) or pictographic, representing spatial aspects of the meaning such as size, shape and movement (e.g. outlining the shape of a circle).
- ***Affect displays*** use gestures as part of the nonverbal expression of feelings such as happiness, surprise and fear.
- ***Metaphoric*** gestures are like iconic ones, but represent an abstract idea rather than a concrete one (e.g. moving a finger in circles above the ear to represent thinking).
- ***Emblems*** are conventional representations of visual or logical meanings, e.g. the palm-forward V sign for victory, the palm-backward V sign as an obscene gesture.
- ***Regulators*** are used to control the turn-taking of speakers in a conversation, e.g. suggesting to a speaker that they should continue, or hurry up and finish.
- ***Adaptors*** are unconscious movements related to the satisfaction of bodily needs, such as moving to a more comfortable position, scratching, and smoothing the hair.

There is clearly a cultural dimension to some of the above categories. Emblems, by virtue of being conventional, are particularly susceptible to misinterpretation. For example, the gesture of forming a circle with the thumb and index finger, while holding the other three fingers erect, has several meanings around the world:

- in much of Europe and North America, it means 'OK, good.'
- in many countries including Belgium, France and Tunisia, it means 'zero.'
- in Singapore, it means 'three,' the focus being on the three erect fingers rather than the circle.

- in Japan, it means 'money,' the circle formed by the thumb and index finger representing a coin.
- in many countries around the world, it is a sexual insult relating to the female orifice or to masturbation.

Even deictic gestures may vary. For instance, in English-speaking cultures, it is acceptable to point to a person with the index finger. However, this is not acceptable in many other cultures, where the index finger would seem like a dagger. While objects can be indicated with the index finger, persons have to be pointed to with the whole hand, palm upwards. Malays point with the thumb held close to the other four fingers, which are bent back, the palm facing upwards.

While beat gestures are probably found in all cultures, the volume and extent of the gestures may vary widely. Arabs use large gestures for emphasis, while Mediterraneans typically use more gestures than other cultures. An old joke tells of a boatload of Italians whose boat sank; until they were rescued, they kept afloat by talking to each other.

The pedagogical importance of nonverbal features

Language teachers can use nonverbal features (especially gestures, but also facial expressions, and perhaps proxemics) as a resource. The categories of gestures are probably useful in the order given above, that is, deictic gestures are very useful while adaptors have no use. The first five categories (deictic, counting, beat, iconic and metaphoric gestures) usually accompany speech, while emblems and adaptors usually do not. Deictic gestures, for example, are an important component of the language teaching approach known as Total Physical Response (see chapter 25), which links language to the physical environment by requiring learners to perform actions in response to language stimuli. Deictic gestures are also often used when teaching children their native language, e.g. 'Where's your nose?'

Nonverbal features can be used in teaching vocabulary. For example, the difference between several pairs of English words depends on the distinction between (i) at or towards the speaker, versus (ii) away from the speaker: *here/there, this/that, come/go, bring/take*. This two-way distinction can be easily reinforced by obvious deictic gestures. When I learnt Thai, I remember the teacher explaining the three-way distinction between [ni:] 'this,' [nan] 'that, but not too far from the speaker' and [no:n] 'that, a long way away.' Deictic gestures made the distinction clear.

Nonverbal features can clearly be used profitably to reinforce at least three aspects of pronunciation:

- ***Rhythm:*** The rhythm of stressed syllables within an utterance can be emphasized by the use of beat gestures. A common exercise is to show learners that the rhythm of the following two utterances is the same, despite the intervening unstressed syllables in the second:

  <u>ONE</u>, <u>TWO</u>, <u>THREE</u>, <u>FOUR</u>
  a <u>ONE</u>, and a <u>TWO</u>, and a <u>THREE</u>, and a <u>FOUR</u>

  Beat gestures on the content words (the numbers) makes this clear.

- ***Tonic syllables:*** The placement of the tonic in a tone group can be emphasized by the use of appropriate beat gestures and facial expressions.

  DAVID drove to London on Friday night (It wasn't Mary)
  David DROVE to London on Friday night (He didn't fly)
  David drove to LONdon on Friday night (He drove to London, not Birmingham)
  David drove to London on FRIday night (It wasn't Thursday night)
  David drove to London on Friday NIGHT (It wasn't Friday afternoon)

- ***Word stress***: The placement of stress on different syllables in multi-syllable words can be reinforced by appropriate gestures and facial expressions. Thus, the difference between *insight* /ˈɪnsaɪt/ and *incite* /ɪnˈsaɪt/ can be shown by a beat gesture, widening the eyes and raising the eyebrows, and nodding the head on the first and second syllable respectively.

Indeed, the connection between these pronunciation features and these nonverbal features is so strong that it is very difficult for native speakers to make emphatic gestures and facial expressions coincide with non-prominent aspects of the pronunciation.

It has been shown that good teachers use nonverbal communication a lot when teaching (including teaching pronunciation). In contrast, many language learners have been found to use little or no nonverbal features in class, even those learners who seem to use nonverbal features expressively when speaking in their native language. This is especially true of those learners who are still at the stage of translating from their native language into English, rather than trying to think and plan utterances in English.

It has also been found (Lakin, Jefferis, Cheng and Chartrand, 2003) that the use of gestures improves the atmosphere within the classroom. Not only does behavioral mimicry (including the use of gestures that harmonize with those of your partner) increase liking between partners, but also, vice versa, rapport between partners can increase mimicry. This may partly explain the lack of social cohesion witnessed in classes containing learners from freely gesturing cultures, such as Latins, and those from gesturally more inhibited cultures, such as many Asians.

Mention also ought to be made of the use of nonverbal features in oral presentations. The bottom line here is that it is difficult for a speaker to engage an audience and make them feel interested and enthusiastic about the subject, if the speaker does not also exude enthusiasm. And nonverbal features are a major part of conveying your own interest. In short, a speaker who has few or no nonverbal features looks boring. This is precisely why teachers should use nonverbal features a lot.

Eye contact with the audience, with appropriate facial expressions, is an important factor. Each member of the audience should feel that the speaker is talking to them. This may be difficult with large audiences, but it is still the underlying principle.

Some people feel that gestures are an innate ability that cannot be taught: either it is part of your personality to use gestures a lot, or it is not. While there may be some interpersonal differences in this respect, the cultural differences noted above show that everyone has the potential to gesture effectively. However, gestures that look forced or unnatural may distract the audience from what the speaker is saying.

In a presentation to a large audience in a large venue, gestures must obviously be made more definite and larger to be effective.

Adaptor gestures are unconscious, and therefore cannot be used to convey any intended meaning. Mannerisms such as pushing the glasses back up on the nose, or ladies curling their hair behind their ears, may become distractions which annoy the audience. The audience may not concentrate on what the speaker is saying, but instead turn their attention to their mannerisms.

Summary

- Nonverbal communication includes proxemics, facial expressions and gestures.
- These features are important because they help to carry a large part of a speaker's overall message.
- They can therefore be exploited by pronunciation teachers for rhythm, tonic syllables and word-stress.
- There are cultural differences in the interpretation of many nonverbal features.

Exercises

1. The next time you are alone in a noisy cafe, watch people talking to each other. You probably won't be able to hear what they are saying. But you should get a good idea of how much people use nonverbal features in normal conversation. You should aim to get your learners using a similar amount.
2. Ask people of different nationalities for the meaning they attach to the following gestures:

    a thumbs up
    b crossing the index and middle fingers
    c stroking down each cheek with the thumb and index finger
    d flicking the chin with the back of the hand.

3. Vice versa, ask people of different nationalities what gestures they might use to convey the following meanings:

    a 'That person is crazy'
    b the number eleven
    c 'Come here'
    d pointing at a person.

4. Imagine you had to convey the following messages in an oral presentation. How might a gesture or some other nonverbal feature help to get the message across with clarity or impact?

    - The parts join at a right-angle, although in some models the angle is slighter greater than this.
    - 3D diagrams stand out better than 2D ones.
    - You need lubrication because, when two surfaces come into contact, you get friction and that means heat.
    - The two rods are parallel for about 3 cm and then they diverge.
    - The Pacific is a truly vast ocean.

- The flask is spun round and the centrifugal force separates out the particles from the liquid.
- The main factors affecting the safety of our roads are the drivers and the vehicles, as well as the roads themselves.
- English writing goes from left to right, while Arabic goes from right to left.
- Once an invoice has been issued, there is no way that you can delete it, or pretend that it hasn't been issued.
- The laser beam is very fine and travels in a direct line unaffected by wind or heat.

Further reading

Apart from the primary sources listed in this chapter, work by Morris on gestures is of interest: see Morris (1994) and Morris, Collett, Marsh and O'Shaughnessy (1979).

34 Listening

No man ever listened himself out of a job.

Calvin Coolidge (1872–1933), US president

Learning objectives

At the end of this chapter, you will be able to:

- use different ways of increasing learners' exposure to spoken English
- use recorded speech in class for tracking and mirroring.

Introduction

In chapter 1, it was pointed out that listening is the receptive counterpart of speaking, in the same way that reading is for writing. In other words, speaking and listening are two sides of the same coin. Writers (e.g. MacCarthy, 1976) have argued whether a learner needs to be able to hear a sound distinction in order to be able to pronounce it. However, listening, as the receptive aspect of the spoken medium, clearly has connections with speech, as its productive aspect. Wise teachers will therefore not divorce the two skills, but use them to complement each other. Indeed, many writers have noted the connection between the two, and emphasized the importance of listening. Within business circles, managers and other leaders are reminded of the importance of listening, a sentiment that dates back at least to the Greek philosopher Diogenes of Sinope (412–323 BC): 'We have two ears and one tongue so that we would listen more and talk less.'

Exposure to spoken English

Dalton and Seidlhofer (1994) (see chapter 30) make a distinction between teachability and communicative importance. Teachability refers to whether pronunciation features can be easily formulated in rules, and whether materials to introduce and practice those features can be easily produced. Typically, consonant and vowel segments are easy to describe and practice, while there is substantial disagreement over the precise nature of some suprasegmental features such as rhythm and intonation. Communicative importance relates to whether features contribute significantly to the conveying of an overall message in speech. While segments are important, there is a widespread feeling nowadays that suprasegmentals are of greater overall importance in this respect.

It is in situations such as these that exposure seems important. That is, while it may be difficult to describe and teach intonation, it is nonetheless important for communication, and may be 'picked up' by learners, who 'get a feel for it' through extensive exposure to natural instances of the spoken language.

This exposure may be of three kinds. First, it may be exposure to the language in general. This may be useful in countries where access to native speakers, or good non-native speakers, of English is scarce. Second, learners may need to be exposed to different accents of English. As was described in chapter 2, English is spoken in many countries around the world. Learners familiar, from their teaching materials, with an SSBE or GenAm accent may find it difficult to adjust to accents from elsewhere in Britain or the USA, or from other countries. Third, the language of the classroom may be a slow, deliberate style. This may be appropriate in teaching situations at lower levels, but learners at higher levels will need to be able to cope with natural input from speakers whose pronunciation contains all the features of connected speech, such as weak forms, assimilation and elision, and a relatively fast colloquial speed.

Courses have been produced using authentic native-speaker recordings as the basic materials. Protea Textware's (n.d.) *Connected Speech* CD-ROM uses video recordings of native speakers speaking on a range of topics, with accompanying exercises on aspects of pronunciation including pause groups, pitch change, word and sentence stress, linking, syllables and the IPA. The CD-ROM is available in British, American and Australian English versions. Speech recognition software allows users to record themselves and receive feedback on their performance.

Speech in Action's (n.d.) *Cool Speech* contains listening and pronunciation materials based on recordings of everyday spontaneous speech with a variety of accents.

Other easy ways of increasing learners' exposure to English include starting a film club. Rather than playing the DVD straight through, worksheets on particular language points of interest, including pronunciation points, can be used at stages during the film. Even if the learners do not understand everything that is said, they should still be absorbing the suprasegmental feel of English.

There is also an enormous amount of free spontaneous English speech on YouTube. This can be used for work on understanding fast speech and different accents of English, using nonverbal features to help decode speech, etc.

Learners can also be encouraged to set up the modern equivalent of penpals, known as e-twinning. Freely downloadable software, such as Skype (n.d.), allows learners with internet-connected computers and microphone headsets to talk to anyone else with similar equipment. Schools could thus establish 'penpal' links with native-speaker schools in other countries, allowing the English learners to improve their proficiency (including pronunciation and listening skills), and the native-speaker learners to learn about other cultures, etc.

We ought not to overlook the importance of exposure to spoken English, even if it is the spoken English of classmates. The traditional ELT activities of dictation, and pair and group work, all require learners to listen to others speaking in English.

Tracking and mirroring

The technique of tracking was mentioned in chapter 28, where its use for fossilized learners was emphasized. It has been described in detail by Rosse (1999), developing a technique promoted by Acton (1984), who acknowledges Morley (personal communication) for devising it. Rosse proposes three stages:

- ***Analysis:*** This is a listening stage, during which learners hear a recording of a native speaker. They concentrate on identifying pauses, patterns of stressed syllables, and pitch, and mark these on a word-for-word transcript of the recording using a simple notation system.
- ***Imitation:*** Having listened to the recording several times, the learners are now very familiar with it. Using their marked-up transcript, they attempt to repeat manageable stretches of speech, roughly the length of tone groups, immediately after the recorded speaker.
- ***Reproduction:*** Using the marked-up transcript, the learners try to reproduce it out loud, this time without the benefit of the recording. In other words, the learners should have internalized an auditory model.

In mirroring, learners try to imitate all the nonverbal features of the model speaker, from a video recording. That is, without paying much attention to the verbal aspect (what the speaker is actually saying), the learners mimic the gestures, facial expressions, posture, etc.

As Acton (1984, p. 77) summarizes, 'in both techniques . . . there is an important "locking in" to the total expressive system of the "other." For fossilized learners, enhancing this ability is often the breakthrough in developing more acceptable rhythm and sentence stress patterns.'

Further enhancements to the techniques include mimicking (repeating what the teacher or model speaker says, as he/she says it, without waiting for understanding) and echoing (careful listening while reproducing the sounds mentally) (Sue Sullivan, personal communication).

It can be seen that all these techniques emphasize the importance of listening. Indeed, many of them can be performed even if the learners do not understand every word being uttered. They also all involve mimicry, which was claimed by Strevens (see chapter 28) to be an important aspect of pronunciation acquisition.

Once learners have mastered the technique of tracking, they may be encouraged to continue on their own, using recordings of any person they regard as model speakers (see chapter 24).

Although tracking and other techniques can help learners to internalize suprasegmental and nonverbal aspects of English production, they are nevertheless largely receptive techniques. Learners still have to make the transition from mimicking speakers, to being able to produce their own unrehearsed speech with accurate suprasegmental pronunciation.

Recording speech

Many learners are unaware that they are doing anything wrong, until they hear themselves and it is pointed out to them. The process of having learners record themselves speaking in English has been used in English language teaching for a long time. Language laboratories and cassette recorders may seem like old technology nowadays. However, they are a cheap and easy-to-use technology, and in many countries more sophisticated technology is simply not available or affordable.

Language laboratories may nowadays be the same thing as computer laboratories, in that modern computers can easily record and play back speech as soundfiles. *Sound Recorder* is software designed for recording and playing back sounds, including speech, and is a feature of Microsoft Windows (Start > All Programs > Accessories > Entertainment > Sound Recorder). To do this, a computer must have a microphone headset. In chapter 18, instructions were given for playing recordings back at a slower speed in Windows Media Player.

More sophisticated software is available for teachers willing to learn the basics of the acoustics of speech. KayPENTAX (n.d.) make various dedicated hardware and software products, some originally intended for speech therapy purposes, including the Computerized Speech Lab, Multi-Speech, and Real-Time Spectrogram.

Summary

- Listening and pronunciation are two sides of the same coin. Pronunciation teachers should therefore not ignore the importance of listening activities.
- Exposure to English, by listening to recordings of model speakers, is an important way of helping learners get a feel for the suprasegmental features of English.
- Tracking and similar activities are an intense but worthwhile method of developing an internal auditory model of the language.

Exercises

1. Using a tape recorder or computer, record yourself spontaneously speaking English, for instance describing your favorite style of music and why you like it. Now listen to your recording. What is your reaction to the sound of your voice? Do you think you have a good voice and pronunciation for a teacher of English?
2. Again, record yourself talking for 30 seconds on a spontaneous topic, such as your favorite method of travel. Listen to the recording. Now, re-record yourself giving the same 30-second talk. What differences can you hear in your pronunciation?

Further reading

Instructions for using Sound Recorder can be found at Microsoft (n.d.). Cauldwell (2013) teaches listening with particular emphasis on connected speech processes. General introductions to listening comprehension in ELT include Anderson and Lynch (1988), Mendelsohn and Rubin (Eds.) (1995), Rubin (1994), Ur (1984) and Vandergrift and Goh (2011).

35 Testing

> The measurement of pronunciation accuracy is in the dark ages when compared to measurement of other areas of competence.
>
> Roy Major (1987, p. 155)

Learning objectives

At the end of this chapter, you will be able to:

- define types of test: proficiency, diagnostic, placement, achievement
- write tests that are valid, interactive, authentic, reliable, practical and fair.

Introduction

If, as we proposed in chapter 30, pronunciation is the Cinderella of the English language teaching world, then pronunciation testing is the Cinderella of the pronunciation teaching world. That is, it is a very, very neglected area. It is important to remember that what we are discussing here is pronunciation testing, not the testing of wider speaking skills, including oral fluency and confidence. As an indication of this, there is a journal entitled *Language Testing*. In the two decades 1993–2012, it contained 48 articles on the topic of the testing of speaking skills, oral proficiency, etc. (and many others dealing with tests such as IELTS (International English Language Testing System) and TOEFL (Test of English as a Foreign Language), that contain speaking sections). In contrast, it contained only five articles on pronunciation testing, and two of them (Holm, Dodd, Stow and Pert, 1999; Theodoros, Murdoch and Horton, 1999) were on the topic of clinical speaking disorders and thus of little relevance here. The other three (Bosker, Pinget, Quené, Sanders and de Jong, 2013; Tan and Mak, 2013; Xi, Higgins, Zechner and Williamson, 2012) were peripherally relevant to pronunciation. Indeed, the 1997 issue of *Speak Out!* on pronunciation testing contained as many articles on the topic as all other academic journals for 20 years.

Given that applied linguists sweep pronunciation testing under the carpet, it is not surprising that very few teachers of English consider testing pronunciation in any systematic way. This chapter therefore does not contain accepted good practice on pronunciation teaching, but instead introduces the main dimensions of language testing in general, with thoughts as to how these relate specifically to pronunciation, and finally some pointers to the future.

Types of tests

Applied linguists typically classify language tests into several categories, including the following:

- ***Proficiency*** tests are the broadest type of tests, measuring general language ability.
- ***Diagnostic*** language tests give more specific information about the learner's strengths and weaknesses in particular areas.
- ***Placement*** tests are designed to allow the tester to place learners in classes at the appropriate levels (beginner, elementary, lower intermediate, etc.).
- ***Achievement*** tests are closely related to a preceding course of study, and only test what was covered in that course. This often leads to the washback effect, that is, the fact that the content of the course is determined to a large extent by the content of the test at the end of the course. Since few courses treat pronunciation content in such a systematic way, this seems the least relevant for pronunciation testing.

While these may be explained as separate categories, tests often contain elements of more than one type. For instance, the IELTS test is often seen as a proficiency test, as it assesses general language proficiency. However, it contains sections relating to the four skills (reading, writing, listening and speaking) and gives separate scores for these, and thus could be considered to be a diagnostic test. For instance, a learner's reading and writing ability might be much higher than their speaking or listening ability. IELTS test scores are widely used for the purposes of immigration to English-speaking countries, entry to English-medium educational institutions, etc., and thus the test could be considered to play a gatekeeping role, in the same way as a placement test. While the IELTS test does not follow a specific course of study, there are many preparatory courses available for prospective IELTS candidates.

Characteristics of good tests

Good language tests are said to have the following characteristics.

Validity

Language tests are valid if they test what they say they are going to test. This may seem self-evident. However, teachers have, for example, given learners tests where they have to discriminate phoneme pairs on tape, and have claimed that this is a pronunciation test, when it is clearly a listening test. Many writers have claimed that the ability to hear a difference is a prerequisite for being able to produce that difference, and that listening tests are therefore relevant to pronunciation tests. Nevertheless, a pronunciation test, almost by definition, requires the candidates to pronounce. Listening tests cannot totally replace them.

The problem of validity is important for diagnostic pronunciation tests, since these presuppose that there is a list of pronunciation items that are necessary for good language learners, and that therefore need to be mastered. This is thus an analytic approach to testing, rather than a holistic one. As we saw in chapter 30, there is disagreement as to whether such a list exists, and which items should be on the list. For instance, many teachers would consider the *th* sounds /θ, ð/ suitable items for such a list, as they stick out like a sore thumb if mispronounced. However, Jenkins (2000), on the basis of observed breakdowns of communication, argues that they are unimportant, as they do not lead to such breakdowns.

Interactiveness

Since the advent of the communicative approach in the 1980s, language teaching has concentrated on communicative fluency rather than accuracy (see chapter 25). Classroom activities thus involve learners in meaningful interaction in settings that are realistic. Writers have therefore pointed out that tests should also be activities of the same kind. Communicative tests might involve learners in pairs or groups performing tasks and being assessed on their performance. Such tasks might entail a degree of unpredictability as to what the other person will say. In this way, the learner will have no opportunity to prepare in detail, and the speech (and pronunciation) will be unrehearsed and a more accurate representation of the learner's ability.

Authenticity

Similarly, the situations used in communicative tests should be realistic. There is little point, for example, in requiring learners to act out a role play where one of them is a boss criticizing a cleaner for laziness, if the learners are unlikely ever to rise to the rank of bosses, but would probably command posts higher than cleaners.

Reliability

The reliability of a language test relates to the consistency and accuracy of the measurement. For example, candidates on reliable tests should receive the same score if the test is retaken, or if it is graded by different markers.

A proficiency test of pronunciation would give an overall grade without specifying particular strengths or weaknesses in the learner's speech. Such holistic marking depends on band descriptors, that is, descriptions of the characteristics of a learner at each level. For example, the pronunciation section of the IELTS test was revised in 2008, expanding from the previous four bands (2, 4, 6 and 8) to nine bands (1 to 9). This increased the options available to examiners, who previously had tended to gravitate towards the central 6 in their judgments. The nine bands depended on pronunciation features including sounds, rhythm, stress (word level), stress (sentence level), intonation, chunking, speech rate, intelligibility, listener strain (listener effort) and accent. However, research into the ease of use of the new system (Yates, Zielinski and Pryor, 2008) showed that it brought new, different problems:

- Examiner subjects felt the criteria of intelligibility and listener effort were the most important, and also the ones they felt most confident about. However, they felt it difficult to distinguish these elements in the Pronunciation scale from similar ones in the separate Fluency and Coherence scale.

- As discussed in chapter 24, the concept of intelligibility entails the question 'intelligibility to whom?' Several examiner subjects responded that they found it difficult to ignore whether they were familiar with the testees' accents, e.g. 'Some accents that I am not used to hearing are more difficult to decipher than others. My ears are not as attuned to these sounds.'
- While accent is one of the factors, examiners rely more heavily on overall intelligibility, although this may lead to biases, e.g. 'To some extent I am hesitant to give a higher band score [than 6] to candidates if there is still a noticeable accent even if they are actually quite easy to understand.'
- Different individual examiners relied more heavily on different factors in their scoring.
- There was sometimes large variation (of more than one band) between examiners' scores and those assigned by IELTS.

In short, there is still a large amount of subjectivity, as opposed to objectivity, in examiners' ratings.

Subjectivity and intelligibility are thus major problems for pronunciation testing. The reliability of the test depends on the reliability of the marker, that is, their status and level of expertise. As we saw in chapter 30, many English language teachers neglect pronunciation teaching because they feel they do not have sufficient background understanding of the area or, if they are nonnative speaker-teachers, because they are unsure of the quality of their own pronunciation. As pronunciation testers, they would therefore make poor, subjective judgments.

The issue of intelligibility in pronunciation/speaking tests has often been questioned. Nowadays, many speaking tests are conducted by having candidates talk to each other in pairs, while the tester observes. The uncertainty over this lies in whether, by intelligibility, we mean that a candidate is understood by the tester, or by the fellow candidate. We might hark back to Yule and Macdonald's (1995) reminder (see chapter 26) that the real proof of the pudding in pronunciation teaching is whether the learner is understood after the course in the real world. The real world involves people who (i) are not applied linguists or teachers, and (ii) are interacting with the person, rather than testing them.

If learners are tested like this in pairs, it is important that the members of the pairs should be of different nationalities and/or native languages. Learners from the same nationality and/or native language may be able to speak intelligibly to each other in English, but using a pronunciation that is unintelligible to others, because of L1 interference factors.

There are two commonly used solutions to the problem of reliability. The first, employed by large-scale testing organizations such as IELTS, is to make available recordings of model candidates, that is, for instance, candidates whose pronunciation is considered good typical examples of certain bands. The second solution, often adopted in smaller-scale operations such as language schools, is for markers to have pre-marking moderation sessions, at which consensus is achieved about the scores to be given to certain learners, chosen to be a cross-section.

Practicality

Language tests should be practical. That is, they should not be difficult to administer, should not be expensive to run, and marks should be easy to interpret. This is an especial problem with pronunciation testing. A typical format is for candidates to be asked to speak for between five and 15 minutes on a given topic, or to describe what they see in a picture. The problem arises when a group of, say, 500 learners need to be tested in this way. This will inevitably take over 80 hours to administer (500 learners × 10 minutes) and, if markers are working from recordings of the candidates' speech, over 80 hours to mark. It is not surprising if testers cut corners for reasons of practicality.

Fairness

There has been much discussion recently of ethical issues related to language teaching. While these seem to have little relevance to testing specifically of pronunciation, it should nevertheless be borne in mind that tests should be fair. It does not seem fair, for instance, to test something that has not been explicitly taught. As was mentioned above, communicative tests should not involve learners in tasks in situations that they are unlikely ever to find themselves in.

The future of pronunciation testing

Testing and teaching

An observation about language work in general is that the difference between teaching and testing is often one of purpose and method, rather than type. That is, many materials that are used for teaching purposes could equally be used for testing purposes. The difference lies first in the purpose: the purpose of tests is to sample and measure learners' linguistic behavior, for one of the purposes outlined earlier in this chapter, while the purpose of teaching is to introduce new material in an explanatory way. A second difference is the method: tests are conducted under strict examination conditions, whereas in teaching, new material is presented, often with pre- and post-tasks, and practice.

Many of the exercises contained in the last section of this book, and in many other books on pronunciation, can be used either for teaching purposes, or, with little adaptation, for testing.

Testing and learning

Tomlinson (2005) makes a case for what he calls learning validity (as another kind of test validity). His view is that 'the main purpose of language testing is to provide opportunities for learning, both for the learners who are being tested, and for the professionals who are administering the test' (p. 39). This learning-while-testing is more applicable for formative tests (that measure progress during a course) rather than summative ones (that give a final measure at the end of the course). He laments the fact that 'a common complaint of teachers preparing learners for end of course summative examinations (whether they be global, national, or institution specific) is that the examinations might be valid and reliable, but the learners learn very little of communicative value during their preparation for them and while taking the examinations' (p. 40).

Major high-stakes tests, such as IELTS and TOEFL, that may determine life-changing events, such as admission to university, emigration, etc., are so powerful that they may produce undesirable washback. That is, courses are designed to prepare learners for these tests, in a narrow sense, without necessarily improving their overall proficiency.

Testing activities proposed by Tomlinson, and seemingly appropriate to pronunciation, include the following:

- For informal tests, learners may not know when they are going to be tested. Pronunciation proficiency in a foreign language should not be something that can be 'turned on' specifically for tests.
- Learners can take tests in pairs or groups, so that they learn from each other while doing the test. The caveats outlined above about such testing should be borne in mind, though.
- Learners can be given a monitoring and reflection activity after the test, requiring them to consider what they think they did well or poorly in the test, what they have learnt by doing the test, what they can do in the future as a result of the test, etc.

Portfolios

Portfolios are a popular method of assessing learners. For pronunciation, learners could be asked to submit recordings from various stages of the course. These recordings may be of the same material or passage, or of different work. In order to add a communicative and unpredictable element to the process, learners could, for example, be asked to record themselves interviewing native-speaker members of the public on topics such as what the interviewees know about the learner's country.

Computerized pronunciation testing

Computerized speech recognition programs are now available for pronunciation testing purposes. The best-known of these is *Versant for English* (Pearson Education, 2008), formerly known as Ordinate PhonePass. The test can be taken over the telephone or by internet-linked computer. It consists of six parts:

- ***Reading:*** Test-takers read aloud sentences given on a printed test paper (for telephone candidates) or on screen (for internet candidates). Example sentences are *Traffic is a huge problem in Southern California; The endless city has no coherent mass transit system.*
- ***Repeat:*** Test-takers repeat verbatim sentences between three and fifteen words in length. The sentences are not made available in printed form. Example sentences are *Biology requires study; There are three basic ways in which a story might be told to someone.*

- ***Short answer questions:*** Test-takers listen to spoken questions (not available in print) and answer with a single word or short phrase. Examples are *What season comes before spring?* (Expected answer: *Winter.*) *What is frozen water called?* (Expected answer: *Ice.*)
- ***Sentence builds:*** Test-takers are presented with three short phrases (not available in print), and have to rearrange them into a sentence. Examples are *in / bed / stay.* (Expected answer: *Stay in bed.*); *we wondered / would fit in here / whether the new piano.* (Expected answer: *We wondered whether the new piano would fit in here.*)
- ***Story retelling:*** Test-takers listen to a story of between 30 and 90 words, and have to retell as much of the story as they can in their own words. An example is *Three girls were walking along the edge of a stream when they saw a small bird with its feet buried in the mud. One of the girls approached to help it, but the small bird flew away, and the girl ended up with her feet covered with mud.*
- ***Open questions:*** Test-takers listen to a spoken question asking for an opinion, and respond with an explanation. An example is *Do you think television has had a positive or negative effect on family life? Please explain.*

The expected answers in the first four parts are verbatim words, phrases and sentences, with no variation. They are therefore scored automatically by computer using speech recognition software. The final two, open parts are scored by a human listener. Within minutes, the test-taker receives an overall score, and four subscores, for sentence mastery, vocabulary, fluency and pronunciation. The last two relate to pronunciation.

> Fluency is measured from the rhythm, phrasing and timing evident in constructing, reading and repeating sentences . . . . Pronunciation reflects the ability to produce consonants, vowels, and stress in a native-like manner in sentence context. Performance depends on knowledge of the phonological structure of everyday words as they occur in phrasal context.
>
> (Pearson Education, 2008, p. 11)

Versant claim that their mostly automatic scoring corresponds well to scores given by human raters, with a correlation of over 0.89. What is undeniable is that Versant is a faster and more efficient way of testing large numbers of test-takers for pronunciation than time-consuming scoring by human markers. For instance, it was used in the 2002 football World Cup in Korea and Japan to test the English pronunciation skills of over 15,000 volunteers.

Conclusion

As was forewarned at the outset, this chapter has consisted merely of an overview of basic language testing principles, with thoughts about how they relate to pronunciation testing. The chapter really raises questions rather than gives answers. Most English language teachers simply do not test pronunciation. It is hoped that much more work will be done on this aspect of the field.

Summary

- Language tests are of four types: proficiency, diagnostic, placement and achievement.
- Language tests should be valid, reliable and practical.
- Currently, many tests do little other than test pronunciation in terms of overall intelligibility to the tester.

Exercises

1. Think of your own experience of learning other languages. Have you ever taken a test specifically for pronunciation? Or was it always combined with speaking skills, and other aspects of the language?
2. If you have experience of the IELTS or TOEFL tests, do you think they are valid, reliable and practical tests of pronunciation? If not, in what ways could they be improved?

Further reading

General introductions to testing in language learning are Brown, H. D. (2004) and Brown, J. D. (2005), Douglas (2010), Fox, Wesche, Bayliss, Cheng, Turner and Doe (Eds.) (2007), Fulcher (2010), Hughes (2002), McNamara (2000) and McNamara and Roever (2006). Problems for testing caused by modern thinking about pronunciation targets are debated by Jenkins (2006) and Taylor (2006).

Section 3

Sample exercises

Sample exercises

The following pages contain exercises that can be used in the classroom. Each exercise consists of notes to the teacher, including explanation of the pronunciation point being presented and practiced, guidelines for conducting the exercise in class, answers, and tips for creating your own exercises along the same lines. Several of the exercises include worksheets, which are printed separately, so that class copies can be photocopied and used in class.

Many of the earlier chapters of this book have exercises at the end intended to help you the reader-teacher to understand the concepts introduced. Several of these exercises can be converted into classroom exercises, but you will need to adapt them to the level of your learners.

1 Who are we?

Pronunciation point

This exercise is intended to convince learners that there is much more to pronunciation, and to overall expressiveness, than pronouncing the vowels and consonants accurately, and putting stress in the right place. Its focus is suprasegmentals.

Conducting the exercise

- Arrange the learners into pairs, and allocate a dialogue to each pair. Have two copies of each of the dialogues (pp. 256–8), one for each member of each pair. Make one copy of the answer table (p. 255) for each learner.
- Tell the learners in each pair to choose one of the alternative sets of characters and contexts below for their dialogue, but not to tell anyone else in the class. For example, the pair with dialogue 1 can choose that 'B really wants to go to the cinema' or that 'B doesn't really want to go to the cinema, and dislikes Sylvester Stallone'. The dialogue works, whichever set they choose.
- Give the learners five minutes to rehearse pronouncing their dialogue in an appropriate way for the characters and context they have chosen.

- Ask the first pair to read the dialogue out to the rest of the class in an appropriate way for the characters and context they have chosen. They cannot use gestures or props—only their voices.
- The rest of the learners act as the audience and try to guess which set of characters and context they chose. They mark their guesses with a tick in the answer table. They should also note down in the final column any aspects of the pair's performance that helped them make up their mind. These are important, and should be comments about the pronunciation (not vocabulary, grammar, etc.).
- Repeat this with all the other pairs.
- After all the pairs have acted, ask the learners whether they thought the first pair had chosen the first or second set of characters and contexts. The number of correct answers is an indication of how well the pair acted. Also ask the learners for the pronunciation clues that helped them make up their mind.
- Make a checklist on the board of these clues. They will probably cover supra-segmentals such as speed (e.g. slow for more serious matters), loudness (e.g. louder for urgency), intonation (e.g. wider ranges with higher pitches for more animated speech) and voice quality (e.g. whisperiness for secrecy).

Create your own

Two-way dialogues like this are not difficult to create. However, you need some ingenuity in thinking of the two scenarios in which the dialogue works. This may involve rather vague expressions in the dialogue, that can be interpreted in different ways in the two situations.

2 Nonsense word role plays

Pronunciation point

A similar task involves learners acting out a scenario, but without using real words. In certain respects, this task is more difficult—but also more rewarding—than the previous one, because learners are creating the role plays themselves, and there is no distraction in the choice of words or pronunciation of difficult words.

Conducting the exercise

- Divide the learners into pairs.
- Tell each learner to think of any word of English. It should not be one, like the archetypical *rhubarb*, which may start to sound funny when repeated. It could be a number.
- Tell each pair to act out a two-minute scenario, using only the words that they have chosen for themselves. Sample scenarios are given below. Notice that, as in the last

task, they involve a range of emotions. Again, they may need to be adapted for the level of the learners.

- A role play could therefore go like this:

  A: Paper paper paper!
  B: Five five!
  A: Paper paper paper. Paper paper paper?
  B: Five five five.
  A: Paper?
  B: Five!
  etc.

- After the role play, discuss the pronunciation features that they manipulated to achieve the right effect. Again, suprasegmentals will figure prominently.

Sample scenarios

- A customer enters a shop with a faulty kettle. She is angry because she only bought it at the shop last week. The shop assistant apologizes, placates the customer, takes the kettle, writes down the customer's details, and promises to contact her the next day.
- Two friends meet in a coffee bar. One starts to tell the other a very funny story, which he claims is true. The other one doesn't really believe that it is true.
- Two work colleagues share an office. One asks the other to open the window because he/she is feeling hot and would like some fresh air. The other one says that he/she doesn't feel hot at all, and opening the window would make him/her start to feel chilly.
- Two friends meet by accident at the airport. One has just returned from a summer holiday and tells the other how great it was. However, while he/she was on holiday, he/she heard that his/her uncle had died at the age of 45.

Create your own

It is quite easy to create your own scenarios, because you do not have to write any dialogue. All you have to do is to think of a situation, preferably one involving emotions such as surprise, anger, irritation, embarrassment, happiness, sadness, etc.

3 The adverb game

Pronunciation point

In Noel Coward's (1925) play *Hay Fever*, weekend guests at the English country house of the Bliss family play a game of 'Adverbs'. It is an excellent and fun way to explore the suprasegmentals of English, as well as nonverbal aspects (gestures, facial expressions, etc.).

Conducting the exercise

- One member of the class leaves the room.
- The other members collectively choose an adverb.
- The member who left the room comes back in. By asking members of the group to do things using words, he/she tries to work out what adverb had been chosen.
- The adverb may range from simple (*quickly, loudly, excitedly*) to more difficult (*flatly, confusingly, long-windedly*). The tasks must be verbal, such as telling the time, giving your name, reciting a nursery rhyme, describing your house, etc. In Coward's play, the Bliss family use verbal as well as nonverbal tasks, such as lighting a cigarette or doing a dance. After the person has guessed correctly, the teacher can ask how, for instance, excitement is conveyed in terms of pronunciation. In the following extract from Coward's play, the adverb chosen was *winsomely*.

SOREL: Now, Myra, get up and say goodbye to everyone in the manner of the word.
MYRA: (Rises and starts with David) Goodbye. It really has been most delightful—
JUDITH: No, no, no!
MYRA: Why—what do you mean?
JUDITH: You haven't got the right intonation a bit.
SIMON: Oh, Mother darling, do shut up!
MYRA: (Acidly) Remember what an advantage you have over we poor amateurs, Judith, having been a professional for so long.

Create your own

All you need for this exercise is an inventory of adverbs. These should be chosen according to the level of the learners, and can be adverbs that have already been introduced in class, in textbooks, etc.

4 Focus on pauses

Pronunciation point

Pauses are a vital element in pronunciation. Their main functions are:

- to show the listener what belongs together in terms of meaning and grammar, in the same way as punctuation in writing
- in dialogue, to show who is speaking
- to allow the speaker to take breath
- to prevent the speaker from speaking too fast.

Conducting the exercise

- This game can be played individually or in pairs. Make one copy of the worksheet (p. 259) for each learner. Point out that the passage looks strange because it has been printed without any punctuation.
- Instruct the learners to read through it until they understand it, and then put in the punctuation: commas, full-stops (question marks, exclamation marks), quotation marks and paragraph breaks. A version of this passage with the punctuation is the worksheet for the next exercise (p. 260).
- Once the punctuation has been agreed, ask the learners to read the passage out loud, paying particular attention to pauses. A good rule-of-thumb is that a comma corresponds to a short pause, a period (full stop) to a medium one, and a paragraph break to a long one.

Create your own

Almost any passage can be used, provided:

- it is long enough
- it is at an appropriate level for your learners
- it contains dialogue
- it has several paragraphs.

Print the passage without any punctuation, apart from (i) capital letters that are always capitals (e.g. *Bertie, Dr, I*) and (ii) apostrophes (e.g. *aren't, I'm, we're*). Allow large spaces between words for learners to insert punctuation marks.

5 Reading playscripts

Pronunciation point

As the previous tasks showed, dialogues are a good way of emphasizing to learners that there is a lot more to pronunciation than simply the vowel and consonant segments. Suprasegmentals such as speed, loudness, intonation and voice quality are also important.

Conducting the exercise

- Allocate the roles to learners. Assume the role as narrator yourself, as teacher.
- Make sure that the learners understand that they have not only to read out the words, but also to convey the appropriate emotions as indicated.
- Point out textual clues. For instance, in the passage, words like *raised an eyebrow, frowning down, quickly, agitated, exclaimed, gazing down at the floor, snapped* and *pointedly* are clear indications of the speakers' moods and of how the words should be read out. Also, it must be remembered that Bertie is a rebellious five-year-old.

- Discuss any possible differences between cultures in how emotions are conveyed in speech.

The passage on p. 260 is abridged from Alexander McCall-Smith's (2005) *44 Scotland Street*. In it, Domenica, a widow with a large Mercedes, meets her neighbor Irene and her five-year-old son Bertie leaving their flat. Irene thinks her son is a genius, and has pushed him to learn Italian and the saxophone.

Create your own

Dialogues can easily be found, either in playscripts (which are, of course, virtually all dialogue) or in novels.

- Choose a dialogue at the right level for your learners.
- Try to choose a dialogue where various emotions are being conveyed.

6 Given and new information

Pronunciation point

The placement of the tonic within a tone group is often determined by whether information is given (has been mentioned before, or is known to both people) or new.

Conducting the exercise

- Divide the class into pairs. Give one learner in each pair worksheet A (pp. 261–2), and the other worksheet B. They must not look at each other's worksheet.
- The learner with worksheet A reads out either sentence 1a or 1b. The learner with worksheet B replies with the response sentence. However, the placement of the tonic within the response sentence depends on whether the first learner chose 1a (for which the reply will be *No, my brother's graduated from CAMbridge*, with the tonic on *Cambridge* as the corrected information) or 1b (*No, my BROther's graduated from Cambridge*, with the tonic on *brother* as the corrected information).

Create your own

This exercise is very easy to create. Take any sentence with more than one piece of information in it. Then write the two alternative preceding sentences, making them relate to different pieces of information.

7 Correcting and contrastive stress

Pronunciation point

When elements are being contrasted, as happens in corrections, there is a strong tendency for them to receive the tonic in their tone group, regardless of the other items in the tone group. In each of the examples in the materials, an incorrect statement is followed by alternative ways of correcting it.

Conducting the exercise

- Divide the class into pairs. Give one learner in each pair worksheet A (pp. 263–4), and the other worksheet B.
- The learner with worksheet A reads the first incorrect statement (*Yuri Gagarin was the first man on the moon*). The other learner in the pair chooses one of the alternative responses (*No, Neil ARMstrong was the first man on the moon* or *No, Yuri Gagarin was the first man in SPACE*), and reads it back to the first learner, taking care to place the tonic on (the stressed syllable of) the part that represents the correction (in capitals above).
- The first learner checks that the tonic was correctly placed for the response chosen. If so, they go on to the next statement (#2), which the learner with worksheet B reads, and the learner with worksheet A responds.

Create your own

All you need to do here is to write an incorrect statement containing more than one piece of information. Then write the alternative responses, correcting one or the other of the pieces of information.

8 Where is Julia?

Pronunciation point

Learners cannot claim to know a word unless they know its spelling, grammar, meaning, and pronunciation. For pronunciation, this involves not only knowing the vowels and consonants it has, but also where the stress placement goes.

Conducting the exercise

- This game can be played individually or in pairs.
- Distribute a copy of the worksheet (pp. 265) to each learner.
- Learners must move from the bottom of the page to the top, only going through those places whose stress pattern is oOo. (All the places on the worksheet have three syllables.)

Answer

Colombo – Karachi – Nairobi – Gibraltar – Calcutta – Toronto – Jakarta – Damascus – Chicago.

Create your own

The idea of using a maze type of puzzle has many benefits. It is fun for the learners, and can be made motivating by conducting it as a race to see who finishes first. The format is also very versatile. You can use it not only for recognition of stress placement (e.g. in three-syllable place-names, as here), but also particular vowel or consonant sounds, consonant clusters, voiced and voiceless sounds, suffixes (e.g. plural /s/ versus /z/), numbers of syllables, spelling patterns, and many more. For these reasons, they are widely used in Brown (2005) and Hancock (1995).

9 Limericks

Pronunciation point

Limericks are a fun way to practice the rhythm and word stress of English. Being a kind of poetry, the regular stress-based rhythm is emphasized, forcing learners to consider the stress placement within words. Limericks are also good for practicing connected speech processes, which are necessary in order to fit the words into the rhythm.

Conducting the exercise

- Make one copy of the worksheet (p. 266) for each learner. They can, however, work individually, in pairs or groups.
- Explain the limerick format: five written lines, *aabba* rhyming scheme, an extra silent beat (stress) at the end of the 1st, 2nd and 5th lines, giving 4, 4, 2, 2 and 4 stresses per line.

Answers

There was a young lady named Rose
Who had a large wart on her nose.
When she had it removed
Her appearance improved,
But her glasses slipped down to her toes.

Archimedes, the well known truth-seeker,
Jumping out of his bath, cried 'Eureka!'
He ran half a mile,
Wearing only a smile,
Becoming the very first streaker.

The incredible Wizard of Oz
Retired from his business because
Due to up-to-date science,
To most of his clients,
He wasn't the Wiz he once was.

An exceedingly fat friend of mine,
When asked at what hour he would dine,
Replied, 'At eleven,
At three, five, and seven,
And eight and a quarter past nine.'

There once was an old man from Esser,
Whose knowledge grew lesser and lesser.
It at last grew so small,
He knew nothing at all,
And now he's a college professor.

A diner while dining at Crewe
Found a very large mouse in his stew.
Said the waiter, 'Don't shout
And wave it about,
Or the rest will be wanting one too.'

Create your own

There are plenty of books and internet sites containing limericks. But beware: some of the limericks do not rhyme well, nor scan well (i.e. the rhythm is not perfect). Simply blank out the last word of the 2nd, 4th and 5th lines.

10 Searching for /ɪ/ words

Pronunciation point

It is important that learners should know which sounds they are aiming at; that is, which words contain which sounds. They can, of course, get this information from a dictionary. This exercise also helps learners to appreciate sound-spelling correspondences in English.

Conducting the exercise

- Present the English vowel sound /ɪ/, as in *fifth, rich, sit, with*. Make sure the learners can pronounce it accurately, distinct, for example, from long /iː/ and short /e/. Pairs of words with only one difference, such as *rich* and *reach*, and *bit* and *bet*, are known as minimal pairs.
- Make one photocopy of the worksheet for each learner (p. 267).
- The exercise may be completed in class individually, in pairs or groups, or as homework.
- Many learners will be familiar with the moves of chess. For those who are not, explain the movement of the knight chesspiece. Knights move in an L-shape, e.g. two spaces forwards/backwards and one space sideways, or two spaces sideways and one space forwards/backwards. In the following picture, the knight can move to any of the shaded spaces.

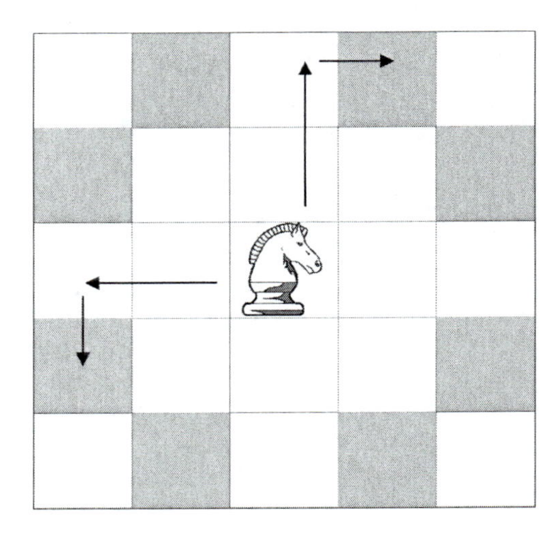

- In the game, the learners are the knight. They must move from the starting square to the top row, only landing on those squares that contain a word whose pronunciation contains the /ɪ/ vowel sound.
- The correct answer is *fill, scissors, middle, Chris, sit, list, disk, litter, women, pick.*
- Elicit from the learners the typical spellings of this vowel: usually *i* (as in the above words), sometimes *y* (e.g. *rhythm, symbol*), and occasionally *e* (e.g. *English, pretty*). There are a handful of very irregular spellings, e.g. *business, women.* Note also that this vowel is possible in many types of unstressed syllable, e.g. *happy, needed, wicket, except, careless, houses, village.*
- As a follow-up activity, get the learners to list minimal pairs and minimal sets occurring on the chessboard, and practice distinguishing them in pronunciation, e.g. *priest, pressed; sit, seat, set.*

Create your own

The format of this activity can be used to make the practice of almost any pronunciation teaching point more interesting. This is true of many of the games in Brown (2005) and Hancock (1995).

Decide on the particular pronunciation teaching point, e.g. the /θ/ consonant sound. Identify sounds confusable with /θ/ by your learners, e.g. /ð, t, s, f/. Mark the squares that represent the correct path, making sure there are no alternative paths. Fill these squares with /θ/ words, e.g. *thank, mouth, death.* Fill all the other squares with /ð, t, s, f/ words, perhaps including some minimal pair words, e.g. *tank, mouse, deaf.*

11 Wordsearches and crossword

Pronunciation point

It is important that learners of English should become familiar with the phonemic symbols, so that they can understand the pronunciation information given in dictionaries. There are many familiar classroom games and activities that involve letters of the alphabet (spelling). All of these can easily be adapted to relate to sounds, using phonetic symbols rather than letters: Scrabble, hangman, snap, Boggle, anagrams, crosswords, bingo, wordsearches, word chains (*lose, lone, line, fine, find*), jokes, rhymes, limericks, acrostics, identifying spelling errors, etc.

This exercise is a wordsearch and a crossword; Boggle is given on p. 252. Other similar exercises can be found in Brown (2005).

Conducting the exercise

- Make one copy of a wordsearch (pp. 268–9) or crossword (p. 270-1) for each learner.
- The exercise may be completed in class individually, in pairs or groups, or as homework.

Answers

US state capitals wordsearch (GenAm transcription)

Alaska	Juneau	dʒuːnoʊ
Colorado	Denver	denvər
Delaware	Dover	doʊvər
Idaho	Boise	bɔɪzi
Iowa	Des Moines	dəmɔɪn
Kansas	Topeka	təpiːkə
Maryland	Annapolis	ənæpəlɪs
Michigan	Lansing	lænsɪŋ
Mississippi	Jackson	dʒæksən
Montana	Helena	helənə
Nebraska	Lincoln	lɪŋkən
North Carolina	Raleigh	rɑːli
North Dakota	Bismarck	bɪzmɑːrk
Ohio	Columbus	kəlʌmbəs
Tennessee	Nashville	næʃvɪl
Wyoming	Cheyenne	ʃaɪæn

European capitals wordsearch (SSBE transcription)

Belgium	Brussels	brʌsəlz
Czech Republic	Prague	prɒːg
Denmark	Copenhagen	kəʊpənheɪgən

England	London	lʌndən
Estonia	Tallinn	tælɪn
Finland	Helsinki	helsɪŋki
France	Paris	pærɪs
Germany	Berlin	bɜːlɪn
Greece	Athens	æθənz
Hungary	Budapest	bjuːdəpest
Ireland	Dublin	dʌblɪn
Italy	Rome	rəʊm
Latvia	Riga	riːgə
Malta	Valletta	vəletə
Netherlands	Amsterdam	æmstədæm
Poland	Warsaw	wɔːsɔː
Portugal	Lisbon	lɪzbən
Slovakia	Bratislava	brætɪslɑːvə
Spain	Madrid	mədrɪd

Crossword (SSBE transcription)

Across: 1 *receipt* /rɪsiːt/, 4 *wicked* /wɪkɪd/, 7 *scenic* /siːnɪk/, 8 *knowledge* /nɒlɪdʒ/, 9 *sad* /sæd/, 10 *split* /splɪt/, 12 *admit* /ədmɪt/, 14 *focus* /fəʊkəs/, 17 *Europe* /jʊərəp/, 20 *idea* /aɪdɪə/, 21 *rhinos* /raɪnəʊz/, 22 *backup* /bækʌp/, 23 *miners* /maɪnəz/, 24 *colours* /kʌləz/.

Down: 1 *wrists* /rɪsts/, 2 *senile* /siːnaɪl/, 3 *text* /tekst/, 4 *wonder* /wʌndə/, 5 *column* /kɒləm/, 6 *digit* /dɪdʒɪt/, 11 *pro* /prəʊ/, 13 *inner* /ɪnə/, 14 *forearm* /fɔːrɒːm/, 15 *cannon* /kænən/, 16 *sizes* /saɪzɪz/, 17 *yearbook* /jɪəbʊk/, 18 *recall* /rɪkɔːl/, 19 *papers* /peɪpəz/.

Create your own

It is in fact rather difficult to create a wordsearch or crossword using phonemic symbols, unless you are very familiar with them and have a flair for such word puzzles.

12 Phonetic Boggle

Pronunciation point

The wordsearch gave practice in recognizing words in phonetic symbols. In the crossword, learners had to write words in phonetic symbols. This exercise using Boggle is also one in which learners have to use symbols productively.

Conducting the exercise

- Create a Boggle set with phonetic symbols, either by using a standard Boggle set and sticking symbols in place of the letters, or by using larger-sized cubes such as those sold by Teachers' Discovery*.
- Shake the dice, giving 16 randomly-chosen symbols to work with.

- Learners have to think of as many words as they can with the 16 symbols in a time limit. Whoever produces the most words wins.

*www.amazon.com/Teachers-Discovery-Erasable-Cool-Cubes/dp/B0050I4DKA

13 Cluster fun

Pronunciation point

Consonant clusters are difficult for many learners, often because their native language has a simpler syllable structure than English. This exercise gives practice in recognizing clusters, and their importance in distinguishing words.

Conducting the exercise

- This exercise can be conducted individually, in pairs or groups. Give each learner a copy of the worksheet (p. 272).
- Each word is a one-syllable word containing initial and/or final consonant clusters. On the worksheet, they are presented in phonemic symbols, as building blocks.
- To complete the exercise, learners have to remove one building block at a time either from the beginning of the word or from the end, each time leaving an existing word, until they can remove no more. The number in brackets is the number of symbols (blocks) that can be removed.
- You may need to allow learners to use a dictionary, to check possible words.

Answers

1 /spiːks/ *speaks*, /spiːk/ *speak*, /piːk/ *peak*, /piː/ *pea*
2 /klæmpt/ *clamped*, /klæmp/ *clamp*, /læmp/ *lamp*, /læm/ *lamb*, /æm/ *am**
3 /ʃrɪŋks/ *shrinks*, /ʃrɪŋk/ *shrink*, /rɪŋk/ *rink*, /rɪŋ/ *ring*
4 /straɪdz/ *strides*, /straɪd/ *stride*, /traɪd/ *tried*, /raɪd/ *ride*, /raɪ/ *rye/wry*, /aɪ/ *eye/I*
5 /flɪntʃt/ *flinched*, /flɪntʃ/ *flinch*, /lɪntʃ/ *lynch*, /ɪntʃ/ *inch*, /ɪn/ *in*
6 /præŋks/ *pranks*, /præŋk/ *prank*, /ræŋk/ *rank*, /ræŋ/ *rang*
7 /skrɪpts/ *scripts*, /skrɪpt/ *script*, /krɪpt/ *crypt*, /rɪpt/ *ripped*, /rɪp/ *rip*
8 /skjuːd/ *skewed*, /skjuː/ *skew*, /kjuː/ *cue/queue*, /juː/ *you/ewe*

*Strong form (see chapter 15)

Create your own

There are not many words of English that can be treated in this way. And many words are rare or technical. They may therefore only be suitable for learners at advanced levels. Here are some more words that can be reduced one symbol at a time.

/blæŋks/ *blanks* (3), /blendz/ *blends* (3), /klaɪmz/ *climbs* (3), /kræmpt/ *cramped* (4), /fiːldz/ *fields* (3), /glɪmpst/ *glimpsed* (4), /greɪndʒ/ *grange* (3), /kwɪlts/ *quilts* (4),

/skrʌmz/ *scrums* (3), /sɪksθs/ *sixths* (3), /səʊlvd, soʊlvd/ *solved* (4), /streɪnz/ *strains* (4), /streɪts/ *straits* (4), /stræpt/ *strapped* (3)

14 Homophones

Pronunciation point

Jokes in English very often rely on homophones. Homophones help learners to realize that the correspondence between letters in spelling and sounds in pronunciation is poor in English. This is precisely why phonetic symbols are needed for English.

Conducting the exercise

- This game must be played in pairs or in groups. Copy and cut out a set of cards (p. 273) for each pair or group of learners in the class. Demonstrate how the cards should be shuffled, and laid face down on the desk, in eight rows of four cards. The cards use SSBE transcription, but you can easily adapt them for GenAm.
- Tell learners that they should turn over two cards at a time. The cards represent two halves of a joke involving homophones. The homophone is written in phonetic symbols on the cards. The second part of each joke is shaded.
- If learners pick up two corresponding halves, they keep them. They continue their turn until they turn over two non-corresponding cards. If learners do not pick up two corresponding halves, they must turn both cards face down again.
- The person or team with most cards at the end of the game, is the winner.

Who are we?

	Alternative characters and contexts	Guess	Notes
1	B really wants to go to the cinema.		
	B doesn't really want to go to the cinema, and dislikes Sylvester Stallone.		
2	B has discovered what he/she thinks is a valuable painting in her attic.		
	B has discovered a large rash on his/her arm.		
3	Two family members are looking at a photo album.		
	Two police officers are watching a suspect at the airport.		
4	B is listening to the announcer on the television.		
	A is reading the television programs from the newspaper to his/her spouse		
5	A neighbor, Mrs Williams, has poisoned her husband.		
	A neighbor, Mrs Williams, has had her hair dyed yellow.		
6	B doesn't remember Johnny Roberts.		
	B used to be friends with Johnny Roberts at school.		
7	Two builders plan a job building an extension garage.		
	Two robbers plan a burglary.		
8	B phones for the ambulance, because A has broken his leg.		
	A married couple invite friends to a retirement party.		

Dialogue 1

A: Are you free this evening?
B: Er, yes, I'm not doing anything. Why?
A: Would you like to go to the cinema?
B: What's the film?
A: *Escape Plan*, with Sylvester Stallone.
B: Oh, good.
A: Do you like him?
B: He was quite good in the Rocky films.
A: And then he was in the Rambo films too.
B: Yes.
A: So, shall I pick you up at 6.30?
B: OK.

Dialogue 2

A: So, what do you think?
B: Well . . . I'm not really sure.
A: Do you know what I think it could be?
B: Of course. But I think it would be best to have it looked at by a specialist.
A: I suppose so.
B: When did you find it?
A: Yesterday afternoon, while I was doing some work tidying up the house.
B: Well, if I were you, I would get expert advice from a professional.
A: Yes, I'd rather know one way or the other. I'll go along tomorrow morning before work.
B: Right. I hope you get good news.

Dialogue 3

A: That's her, isn't it?
B: Which one?
A: The one with the big smile on her face.
B: What, behind the man in the red jacket?
A: That's her. Look, she's got that mole on her nose.
B: Oh yes. You're right.
A: Did you know her father spent some time in prison?
B: Really? When was that?
A: Oh, years ago. For burglary.
B: I wonder what she's doing nowadays.

Dialogue 4

A: On Channel 3 tonight, there's two hours of children's programs, starting at 6 o'clock with *Conquerors of the Wasteland*.

B: Oh, these children's cartoons nowadays! They're full of people shouting and explosions going off.

A: And that's followed at 7 by *Top of the Pops*.

B: More noise! It's no wonder our children are growing up making so much noise and damaging their hearing, with rubbish like that.

A: Then, at 8, it's the final episode of *Survivor*, where the winner is announced, who takes away $1 million in prize money.

B: More people shouting! Why can't they just get along with each other?

A: And at 9, there is a special screening of the opera *Figaro*, recorded live at the Rome Music Festival.

B: At last! Something worth listening to.

Dialogue 5

A: You're joking, surely?

B: No. Mrs Smith told me this morning.

A: When did it happen?

B: On Tuesday.

A: I had heard Mrs Williams talking about it often enough, but I never thought she was serious.

B: I wonder why she did it?

A: Maybe she was feeling very depressed.

B: I suppose so. Well, she's done it, and she'll just have to live with it.

A: Yes. Poor Mr Williams. Such a nice man.

Dialogue 6

A: Have a guess who I met at the supermarket today.

B: I don't know.

A: Johnny Roberts.

B: Who?

A: Johnny Roberts. You remember . . . the guy your sister used to go out with.

B: Oh, him.

A: Do you know what he's been doing for the last couple of years?

B: No, what?

A: Well, first he did very well in that dancing competition on TV.

B: Aha.

A: And then he got a job hosting a breakfast radio program. You can hear him every morning.

B: Really?

A: Yes. But I don't think he remembered me.

Dialogue 7

A: There are four of us. We really need a fifth.
B: What about Mike again?
A: What do you mean 'again'?
B: He was with us last year on that job at that big house in Norman Avenue.
A: Can we rely on him?
B: Yeah, he knows what this sort of job involves.
A: Does he have his own tools?
B: Yeah. Don't worry, he's a real professional. When is the job planned for?
A: The week after next.
B: So you'll ask him?
A: OK.

Dialogue 8

A: Did you manage to contact them?
B: Yes.
A: And . . . ?
B: And they said they would come.
A: Are you sure. You told them how important it was?
B: Of course. I'm sure we can rely on them. Don't worry.
A: And you gave them the address clearly?
B: Yes, I'm sure they'll have no trouble finding the address. I told them it's right next door to the post office.
A: Well, I hope you're right.
B: It's all been taken care of. Don't worry.

Focus on pauses

Domenica turned to Bertie and why aren't we in nursery school today Bertie is it a holiday I'm suspended said Bertie I'm not allowed to go back Domenica raised an eyebrow she looked at Irene who was frowning down on Bertie and about to say something suspended said Domenica quickly before Irene had the time to speak this was delicious for doing something naughty yes said Bertie I wrote on the walls oh dear said Domenica I'm sorry to hear that but I'm sure that you're sorry for what you did Irene who now looked agitated was again about to say something but Bertie spoke before she had the chance to start and now I'm going to psychotherapy that's where we're going right now we're going to see Dr Fairbairn again he makes me talk about my dreams he asks me all sorts of questions therapy exclaimed Domenica that's enough Bertie snapped Irene then turning to Domenica she said it's nothing really there was a bit of difficulty with a rather limited teacher at the nursery school unimaginative really and now we're giving Bertie a bit of self-enhancement time psychotherapy said Bertie gazing down at the floor I set fire to Daddy's *Guardian* he paused and looked up at Domenica while he was reading it *The Guardian* exclaimed Domenica how many times have I wanted to do that myself do you think I need psycho-therapy too we really must get on said Irene pushing Bertie through the door you must excuse us Domenica we have to walk to Bertie's appointment she paused before adding pointedly we don't use our car in town you see I think our car's been lost said Bertie Daddy parked it somewhere when he was drunk and forgot where he put it Bertie said Irene reaching out to seize his arm you must not say things like that you naughty naughty boy she turned to face Domenica I'm sorry I don't know what's got into him Stuart would never drive under the influence Bertie's imagining things

From McCall-Smith, A. (2005) *44 Scotland Street* . London : Abacus.

Reading playscripts

Domenica turned to Bertie. 'And why aren't we in nursery school today, Bertie? Is it a holiday?'

'I'm suspended,' said Bertie. 'I'm not allowed to go back.'

Domenica raised an eyebrow. She looked at Irene, who was frowning down on Bertie and about to say something. 'Suspended?' said Domenica quickly, before Irene had the time to speak. This was delicious. 'For doing something naughty?'

'Yes,' said Bertie. 'I wrote on the walls.'

'Oh dear,' said Domenica. 'I'm sorry to hear that. But I'm sure that you're sorry for what you did.'

Irene, who now looked agitated, was again about to say something, but Bertie spoke before she had the chance to start. 'And now I'm going to psychotherapy. That's where we're going right now. We're going to see Dr Fairbairn again. He makes me talk about my dreams. He asks me all sorts of questions.'

'Therapy!' exclaimed Domenica.

'That's enough, Bertie,' snapped Irene. Then turning to Domenica, she said: 'It's nothing really. There was a bit of difficulty with a rather limited teacher at the nursery school. Unimaginative really. And now we're giving Bertie a bit of self-enhancement time.'

'Psychotherapy,' said Bertie, gazing down at the floor. 'I set fire to Daddy's *Guardian*.' He paused, and looked up at Domenica. 'While he was reading it.'

'*The Guardian*!' exclaimed Domenica. 'How many times have I wanted to do that myself? Do you think I need psychotherapy too?'

'We really must get on,' said Irene, pushing Bertie through the door. 'You must excuse us, Domenica. We have to walk to Bertie's appointment.' She paused, before adding pointedly: 'We don't use our car in town, you see.'

'I think our car's been lost,' said Bertie. 'Daddy parked it somewhere when he was drunk and forgot where he put it.'

'Bertie!' said Irene, reaching out to seize his arm. 'You must not say things like that! You naughty, naughty boy!' She turned to face Domenica. 'I'm sorry. I don't know what's got into him. Stuart would never drive under the influence. Bertie's imagining things.'

From McCall-Smith, A. (2005) *44 Scotland Street* . London : Abacus.

Given and new information

Worksheet A

1	a	I hear your brother's graduated from Oxford.
	b	I hear your sister's graduated from Cambridge.
2		I finished the assignment last night.
3	a	Why did Jeff receive an F grade?
	b	Do you think Jeff will pass?
4		No, that's Queen Street.
5	a	When is your English lesson?
	b	Why didn't you attend the meeting at 10?
6		I don't like math.
7	a	Is he ever late for school?
	b	Why does Andrew annoy you so much?
8		I love you.
9	a	When will you start revising for the exams?
	b	What's next, after this assignment?
10		It is important.

Worksheet B

1		No, my brother's graduated from Cambridge.
2	a	Have you finished your assignment?
	b	Why weren't you at the club last night?
3		He deserves an F.
4	a	Is this Queen Street?
	b	Is that King Street?
5		I've got English at 10.
6	a	When did you realize you liked math?
	b	Why don't you want to become an accountant?
7		He's always late.
8	a	Do you like me?
	b	Why do you love Sharon?
9		I'll start revising once I've finished this assignment.
10	a	Why do you spend so long studying English?
	b	English isn't important.

Correcting and contrastive stress

Worksheet A

1	(Statement)	Yuri Gagarin was the first man on the moon.
2	(Response a)	No, Spain won the 2010 football world cup.
	(Response b)	No, Italy won the 2006 football world cup.
3	(Statement)	Oranges provide you with vitamin D.
4	(Response a)	No, Singapore is south of Malaysia.
	(Response b)	No, Thailand is north of Malaysia.
5	(Statement)	Purple is a combination of yellow and red.
6	(Response a)	No, kiwis are native to New Zealand.
	(Response b)	No, koalas are native to Australia.
7	(Statement)	Microsoft Word is a spreadsheet program.
8	(Response a)	No, polar bears live in the Arctic.
	(Response b)	No, penguins live in the Antarctic.
9	(Statement)	$24 \div 4 = 8$
10	(Response a)	No, $18 \div 9 = 2$.
	(Response b)	No, $12 \div 6 = 2$.
	(Response c)	No, $18 \div 6 = 3$

Worksheet B

1	(Response a)	No, Neil Armstrong was the first man on the moon.
	(Response b)	No, Yuri Gagarin was the first man in space.
2	(Statement)	Italy won the 2010 football world cup.
3	(Response a)	No, oranges provide you with vitamin C.
	(Response b)	No, carrots provide you with vitamin D.
4	(Statement)	Thailand is south of Malaysia.
5	(Response a)	No, purple is a combination of blue and red.
	(Response b)	No, orange is a combination of yellow and red.
6	(Statement)	Koalas are native to New Zealand.
7	(Response a)	No, Microsoft Excel is a spreadsheet program.
	(Response b)	No, Microsoft Word is a word-processing program.
8	(Statement)	Polar bears live in the Antarctic.
9	(Response a)	No, $32 \div 4 = 8$
	(Response b)	No, $24 \div 3 = 8$
	(Response c)	No, $24 \div 4 = 6$
10	(Statement)	$18 \div 6 = 2$

Where is Julia?

Julia loves traveling. However, she only wants to go to cities that have stress on the middle syllable (oOo). Starting at the bottom of the page, and only traveling to places that have the oOo stress pattern, where does she travel?

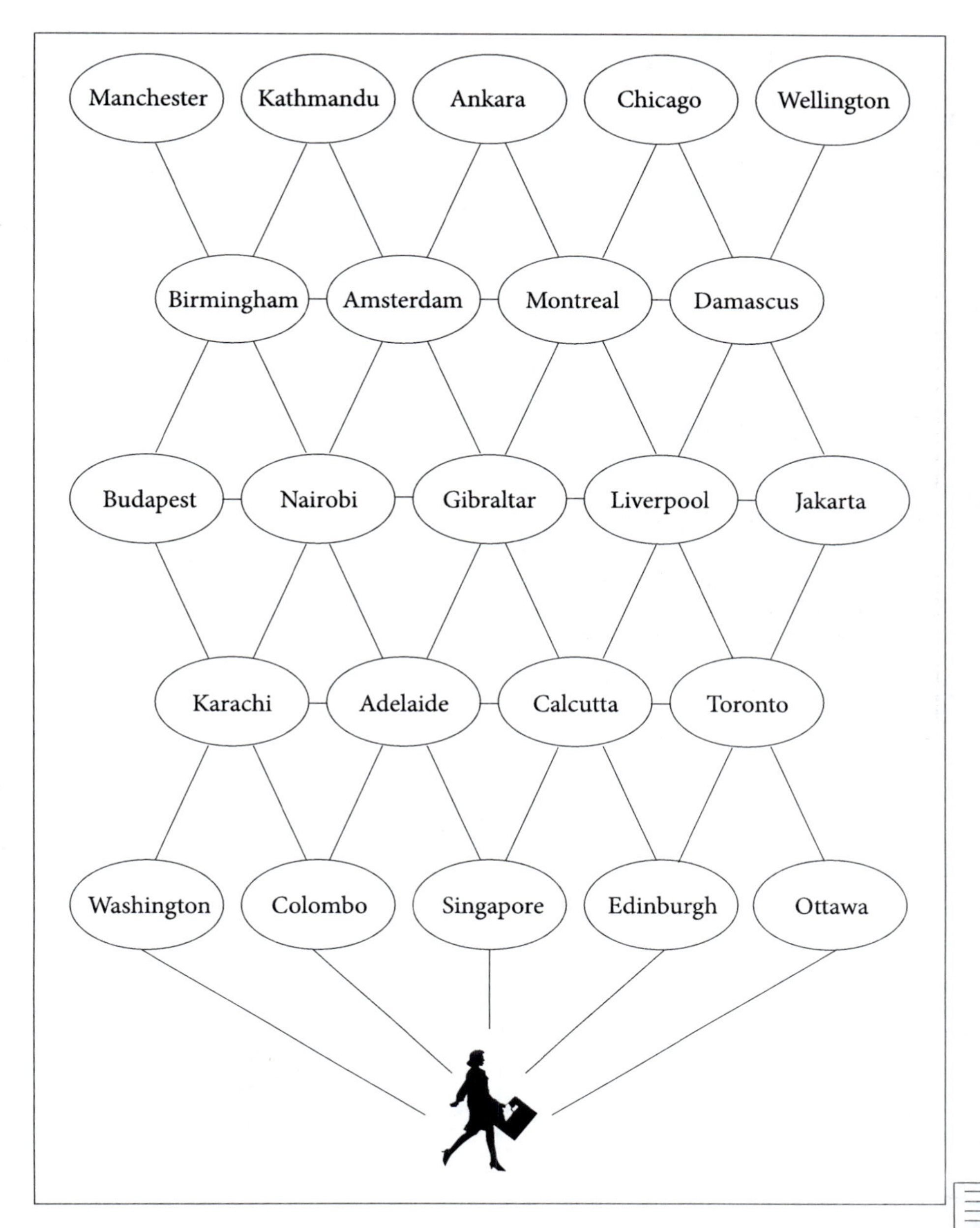

Limericks

Fill in the blanks in the following limericks.

There was a young lady named Rose
Who had a large wart on her . . . .
When she had it removed
Her appearance . . . .,
But her glasses slipped down to her . . . .

Archimedes, the well known truth-seeker,
Jumping out of his bath, cried '. . . . .!'
He ran half a mile,
Wearing only a . . . .,
Becoming the very first . . . .

The incredible Wizard of Oz
Retired from his business . . . .
Due to up-to-date science,
To most of his . . . .,
He wasn't the Wiz he once . . . .

An exceedingly fat friend of mine,
When asked at what hour he would . . . .,
Replied, 'At eleven,
At three, five, and . . . .,
And eight and a quarter past . . . .'

There once was an old man from Esser,
Whose knowledge grew lesser and . . . .
It at last grew so small,
He knew nothing at . . . .,
And now he's a college . . . .

A diner while dining at Crewe
Found a very large mouse in his . . . .
Said the waiter, 'Don't shout
And wave it . . . .,
Or the rest will be wanting one . . . .'

Searching for /ɪ/ words

fist	*league*	*geese*	*peck*	*pick*	*peak*	*she'd*	*pressed*
neat	*liter*	*desk*	*letter*	*sweet*	*beach*	*women*	*Leeds*
list	*check*	*least*	*heap*	*litter*	*selling*	*crease*	*chip*
will	*meal*	*disk*	*lest*	*seat*	*shed*	*wheel*	*sweat*
Phil	*sit*	*priest*	*guess*	*Caesar's*	*middle*	*steal*	*cheek*
risen	*bitch*	*medal*	*Chris*	*fell*	*feast*	*chick*	*scissors*
hip	*feel*	*lids*	*ceiling*	*seek*	*fill*	*leg*	*mill*
sheet	*knit*	*set*		*cheap*	*sick*	*risen*	*still*

Wordsearches and crossword

US state capitals wordsearch

The following wordsearch contains the names of the capital cities of 16 US states. The names have been written in phonemic symbols (GenAm pronunciation). They may be horizontal, vertical or diagonal in any direction. To start you off, Denver, the capital of Colorado, has been highlighted in the first row. If you are really stuck, the states are given underneath the puzzle as a clue.

d	**e**	**n**	**v**	**ə**	**r**	ɑː	l	i
ə	oʊ	k	ə	ʃ	aɪ	æ	n	z
m	ə	v	l	s	n	tʃ	ə	ɔɪ
ɔɪ	n	ɑː	ə	s	k	r	eɪ	b
n	æ	h	ɪ	r	n	æ	t	ɪ
æ	p	ŋ	e	ə	z	ə	dʒ	z
ʃ	ə	iː	k	l	p	w	uː	m
v	l	ŋ	oʊ	iː	ə	ɪ	n	ɑː
ɪ	ɪ	f	k	ʃ	b	n	oʊ	r
l	s	ə	b	m	ʌ	l	ə	k

Alaska
Colorado
Delaware
Idaho
Iowa
Kansas
Maryland
Michigan
Mississippi
Montana
Nebraska
North Carolina
North Dakota
Ohio
Tennessee
Wyoming

European capitals wordsearch

The following wordsearch contains the names of 19 European capital cities. The names have been written in phonemic symbols (SSBE pronunciation). They may be horizontal, vertical or diagonal in any direction. To start you off, *Berlin*, the capital of Germany, has been highlighted in the first row. If you are really stuck, the countries are given underneath the puzzle as a clue.

b	ɜː	l	ɪ	n	tʃ	ɒ	d	ə
r	d	ɔː	k	ə	l	b	ʌ	n
uː	ɪ	s	ə	g	iː	r	b	z
t	r	ɔː	l	eɪ	s	æ	l	n
ɪ	d	w	ʌ	h	ɔɪ	t	ɪ	ə
f	ə	dʒ	n	n	g	ɪ	n	θ
z	m	æ	d	ə	t	s	m	æ
l	p	r	ə	p	m	l	ɔː	m
ə	e	æ	n	əʊ	g	ɑː	r	p
s	t	ɜː	r	k	ʊ	v	ʌ	ɪ
ʌ	r	n	f	ɪ	ŋ	ə	tʃ	s
r	i	k	ŋ	ɪ	s	l	e	h
b	j	uː	d	ə	p	e	s	t
ʌ	z	n	ɪ	l	æ	t	k	θ
v	ɑː	l	ɪ	z	b	ə	n	ə

Countries

Belgium	Finland	Ireland	Poland
Czech Republic	France	Italy	Portugal
Denmark	Germany	Latvia	Slovakia
England	Greece	Malta	Spain
Estonia	Hungary	Netherlands	

Crossword

This crossword follows the regular rules for crosswords, except that the answers have to be entered in phonetic symbols.

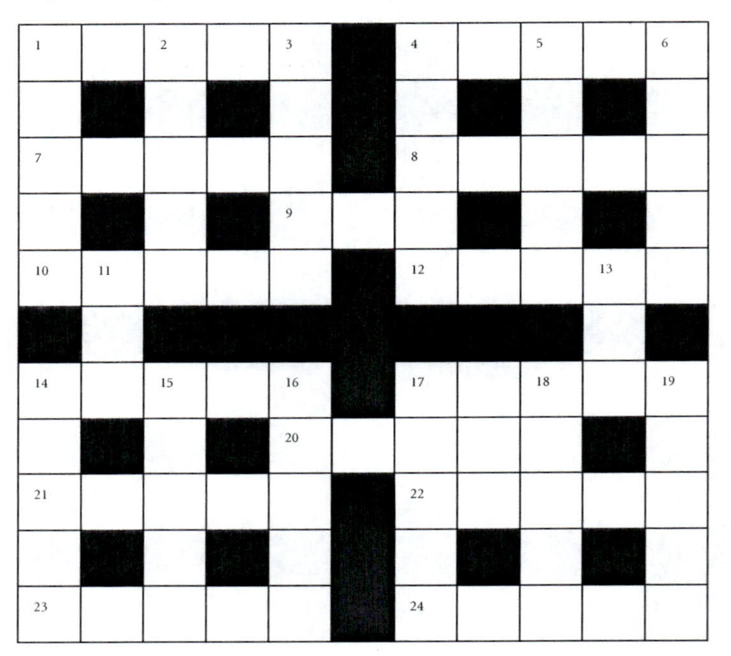

Across

1 A piece of paper that you are given which shows that you have paid for something
4 Behaving in a way that is morally wrong
7 Surrounded by views of beautiful countryside
8 *The teacher gave us a general _____ quiz.*
9 Unhappy
10 Divide something into different parts
12 Agree unwillingly that something is true
14 Thing, person or situation that people pay special attention to
17 Continent containing Britain, Germany and France
20 *I've no _____ where they've gone.*
21 Large heavy African or Asian animals with one or two horns on their noses
22 *Make a _____ copy of any work you do on computer.*
23 People who work underground to remove coal or gold
24 Red, blue, yellow and green are _____.

Down

1 The parts of your body where your hands join your arms
2 Mentally confused or behaving strangely, because of old age
3 Send someone a written message on a mobile phone
4 *I _____ how David is getting on.*
5 Tall solid upright stone post used to support a building
6 A thousand is a four-_____ number
11 Abbreviation of *professional*
13 Opposite of *outer*
14 Lower part of the arm, between the hand and the elbow
15 Large heavy powerful gun that was used in the past to fire heavy metal balls
16 *The shirts come in three _____: small, medium, and large.*
17 Book printed annually, with information about a particular subject or activity
18 Remember
19 *The Times, The Guardian* and *The Sun* are British _____.

Cluster fun

1	s	p	iː	k	s			(*speaks*) (3)
2	k	l	æ	m	p	t		(*clamped*) (4)
3	ʃ	r	ɪ	ŋ	k	s		(*shrinks*) (3)
4	s	t	r	aɪ	d	z		(*strides*) (5)
5	f	l	ɪ	n	tʃ	t		(*flinched*) (4)
6	p	r	æ	ŋ	k	s		(*pranks*) (3)
7	s	k	r	ɪ	p	t	s	(*scripts*) (4)
8	s	k	j	uː	d			(*skewed*) (3)

Homophones

What do you call a piece of wood with nothing to do?	/bɔːd/bɔːrd/.	Why did the sheepdog fail his driving test?	Because he couldn't make a /juː/ turn.
What happens when a frog's car breaks down?	It gets /təʊd/toʊd/ away.	Where do you learn to greet people?	/haɪ/ school.
Why are Saturday and Sunday the strongest days of the week?	Because all the others are /wiːk/ days.	What happens if you sit on a grape?	It gives a little /waɪn/.
Why was the boy's school report card wet?	Because his grades were all below /siː/ level.	Why did the chicken cross the football pitch?	Because the referee shouted '/faʊl/!'
What fruit do socks prefer to eat?	/peəz/perz/.	Did you hear about the vegetarian cannibal?	He only ate /swiːdz/.
Why should you not tell secrets to peacocks?	Because they are always spreading /teɪlz/.	Why did the girl run away from the dark castle?	She was afraid of the /naɪt/.
Waiter: /jɔː(r)/ sweet, sir.	Customer: Thank you. You're cute, too.	Waiter: It's /biːn/ soup, sir.	Customer: What is it now?
The magician didn't pull a rabbit out of his hat.	It was a /heə, her/.	Why are libraries so tall?	Because they have lots of /stɔːrɪz/.

Answers to exercises

1 Introduction

1 Phonetics, 2 Phonology, 3 Phonology, 4 Phonetics, 5 Phonology, 6 Phonetics, 7 Phonology, 8 Phonetics, 9 Phonology

2 Accents of English worldwide

1 Surprisingly, neither the UK nor the USA as a whole has any official language. Twenty-seven individual US states have adopted English as their official language, and three (Hawaii, Louisiana, and New Mexico) have also adopted Hawaiian, French and Spanish respectively as second official languages. All the other countries in the list have English as one of their official languages:

The UK: no official language
The USA: no official language
Canada: English and French
New Zealand: English, Maori and New Zealand sign language
India: 23 official languages, including English, Hindi and Tamil
The Philippines: Filipino and English
Barbados: only English
South Africa: 11 official languages, including English
Cameroon: English and French
Fiji: English, Bau Fijian, Hindustani
Kenya: English and Swahili
Pakistan: Urdu and English

2

1 The USA (316m, almost all of whom speak English)
2 England (53m, almost all of whom speak English)
3 South Africa (53m, of whom 5.1m (9.6%) speak English at home)
4 Canada (33m, of whom about 25.2m (75.2%) speak English)
5 Australia (23m, almost all of whom speak English)
6 Ireland (6.3m (4.5m in the Republic of Ireland, and 1.8m in Northern Ireland), almost all of whom speak English)

7 Scotland (5m, almost all of whom speak English)
8 New Zealand (4.5m, almost all of whom speak English)
9 Wales (3m, almost all of whom speak English)

The country with by far the largest number of English speakers is the USA.

3 Airstreams and the vocal cords

1

- [m] voiced
- [uː] voiced
- [f] voiceless
- [r] voiced
- [aʊ] voiced
- [h] voiceless
- [l] voiced

2 The following words contain an [h] sound:

behave	[bɪheɪv]
hate	[heɪt]
hotel	[həʊtel/hoʊtel]
rehearse	[rɪhɜː(r)s]
who	[huː]

The following words do not contain an [h] sound:

cheetah	[tʃiːtə]
cloth	[klɒθ/klɔːθ]
cough	[kɒf/kɔːf]
fish	[fɪʃ]
Fulham	[fʊləm] *
graph	[grɑːf/græf]
H	[eɪtʃ] **
honest	[ɒnɪst/ɑːnəst]
hour	[aʊə/aʊr]
when	[wen]

Notes

* And all other British place names ending in *-ham*, e.g. *Birmingham* (West Midlands). On the other hand, American place names ending in *-ham* have a pronounced [h], e.g. *Birmingham* (Alabama).

** Note that the names of letters of the alphabet do not necessarily contain the sound they usually represent. Thus, *H* does not contain [h] in British or American English. However, it does in Irish English.

5 Vowels

1

	[ɪ]		[e]		[æ]
English	[ɪŋglɪʃ]	*any*	[eni]	*cat*	[kæt]
miss	[mɪs]	*deaf*	[def]	*mash*	[mæʃ]
women	[wɪmɪn]	*friend*	[frend]	*meringue*	[məræŋ]
		test	[test]	*sank*	[sæŋk]

	[ʌ]		[ʊ]
blood	[blʌd]	*pull*	[pʊl]
lump	[lʌmp]	*stood*	[stʊd]
skull	[skʌl]	*would*	[wʊd]
touch	[tʌtʃ]		

2

	[iː]		[ɑː]		[ɔː]
feel	[fiːl]	*car*	[kɑː(r)]	*court*	[kɔː(r)t]
piece	[piːs]	*father*	[fɑːðə(r)]	*door*	[dɔː(r)]
police	[pəliːs]	*heart*	[hɑː(r)t]	*more*	[mɔː(r)]
steal	[stiːl]	*park*	[pɑː(r)k]		

	[uː]		[ɜː]
June	[dʒuːn]	*burp*	[bɜː(r)p]
moon	[muːn]	*courtesy*	[kɜː(r)təsi]
new	[n(j)uː]	*shirt*	[ʃɜː(r)t]
		term	[tɜː(r)m]

3

	[eɪ]		[aɪ]		[ɔɪ]
brain	[breɪn]	*fight*	[faɪt]	*boil*	[bɔɪl]
break	[breɪk]	*kite*	[kaɪt]	*choice*	[tʃɔɪs]
hate	[heɪt]	*my*	[maɪ]	*toy*	[tɔɪ]
stay	[steɪ]	*sigh*	[saɪ]		

	[aʊ]		[əʊ/oʊ]
brown	[braʊn]	*blown*	[bləʊn/bloʊn]
ground	[graʊnd]	*go*	[gəʊ/goʊ]
now	[naʊ]	*note*	[nəʊt/noʊt]
		show	[ʃəʊ/ʃoʊ]

4 The rounded vowels [ɔː, ɒ, ʊ, uː] are problems for ventriloquists, because lip-rounding can be easily seen.

6 The vocal organs and consonant classification

1 Ventriloquists have problems with sounds that involve the lips, because they can be seen: bilabials ([p, b, m, w]) and labio-dentals ([f, v]).

2 All the manners involve escaping air, apart from plosives.

7 Plosives and nasals

1 The following start with a plosive or nasal:

build [bɪld]
chaos [keɪɒs/keɪɑːs]
court [kɔː(r)t]
done [dʌn]
gas [gæs]
gnaw [nɔː]
ketchup [ketʃʌp]
khaki [kɑːki/kæki]
knife [naɪf]
part [pɑː(r)t]
PM [piː em]
pneumatic [n(j)uːmætɪk]
pterodactyl [terədæktɪl]
quiche [kiːʃ]
quick [kwɪk]
term [tɜː(r)m]
Thomas [tɒməs/tɑːməs]

The following do not start with a plosive or nasal:

chef [ʃef]
chest [tʃest]
germ [dʒɜː(r)m]
GP [dʒiː piː]
MP [em piː]
NB [en biː]
physics [fɪzɪks]
think [θɪŋk]

2 The following end with a plosive or nasal:

bag [bæg]
blurred [blɜː(r)d]
bring [brɪŋ]
bullet [bʊlɪt]
climb [klaɪm]
herb [(h)ɜː(r)b]
herd [hɜː(r)d]
liked [laɪkt]
monarch [mɒnək/mɑːnərk]
panic [pænɪk]
ripe [raɪp]
rode [rəʊd/roʊd]
sick [sɪk]
start [stɑː(r)t]
wrong [rɒŋ, rɔːŋ]

The following do not end with a plosive or nasal:

ballet [bæleɪ]
barge [bɑː(r)dʒ]
GP [dʒiː piː]
OK [əʊ/oʊ keɪ]
sponge [spʌndʒ]

3 *Bix* is [bɪks]. The (unaspirated) [b] at the beginning of *Beiderbecke* can therefore be misheard as an (unaspirated) [p] following an [s] (thus *spider*). Similarly, the (unaspirated) [k] following an [s] in *sky* can be misheard as an (unaspirated) [g] at the beginning of *guy*.

8 Fricatives and affricates

1 The following have [ʃ] and are of French origin: *chalet, champagne, panache, quiche*. The rest (*chair, choose, rich, such*) have [tʃ] and are native English words.

2

[θ]: *Arthur, bath, breath, thick, thought*
[ð]: *breathe, brother, then, this, those*
[t]: *Lesotho, Thailand, Thames, Thomas, thyme*
[th]: *carthorse, coathanger, lighthouse, prophethood, sweetheart*

9 Approximants

1

[l]: *like*
[r]: *red, rhyme, wrinkle*
[w]: *once, water, Y*
[j]: *Europe, ewe, U, union, yes*

2

The sounds [p, b, m, w, f, v] must involve some movement of the lips.
The sounds [ʃ, ʒ, tʃ, dʒ, r] are typically accompanied by lip-rounding.

11 Syllable structure

1

boing! is the only English word with a long vowel + [ŋ] sequence.
depth is the only English word with a [pθ] final cluster.
fifth is the only English word with a [fθ] final cluster.
kiln is the only English word with a [ln] final cluster.
sclerosis is the only English word with a [skl] initial cluster.
smew is the only English word with a [smj] initial cluster.
sphragid is the only English word with a [sfr] initial cluster.
thwart is the only English word with a [θw] initial cluster.
view is the only English word with a [vj] initial cluster.
warmth is the only English word with a [mθ] final cluster.

2

[sp] *spell* [spel]
[st] *stand* [stænd]
[sk] *score* [skɔː(r)]
[sf] *sphere* [sfɪə/sfɪr] (but [sf] is considered irregular: see the discussion in chapter 11)
[sv] *svelte* [svelt] (a Swedish loanword, and the only example)
[sm] *smell* [smel]
[sn] *snap* [snæp]
[sr] *Sri Lanka* [sriː læŋkə/lɑːŋkə] (the only example; many people pronounce this as [ʃriː], cf *shrug*)
[sl] *slide* [slaɪd]
[sw] *swing* [swɪŋ]
[sj] *sue* [sjuː] possible in SSBE (but many speakers omit the [j] here)

3

[stwæm]: irregular ([stw] is an impermissible initial cluster) and non-occurring
[naʊn]: regular and occurring (*noun*)
[ɔɪŋk]: irregular ([ŋ] cannot follow long vowels) but occurring, as the onomatopoeic word *oink!*
[snɑːm]: regular, but non-occurring; therefore a potential syllable
[fjel]: irregular (the vowel after [j] in a two-consonant initial cluster must be [ʊː, ʊə]) and non-occurring
[smɑːh]: irregular ([h] cannot be a final consonant) and non-occurring
[tʃɪks]: regular and occurring (*chicks*)
[sleɪp]: regular, but non-occurring; therefore a potential syllable
[ʃliːzd]: irregular ([ʃl] is an impermissible initial cluster) and non-occurring
[rɑːʒ]: irregular as a word-final syllable (because of the [ʒ]) but occurring, as a possible pronunciation of the word *raj*, and in *garage, mirage, barrage.*

4

risk	*supermarket*
flask	*blanket*
stress	*limousine*
handkerchief	*thermostat*
elevator	*Australia*
ice-cream	*McDonald's*
cosmetic	*love story*
correspondent	*wireless microphone*

5

beer	[pia]
sheep	[hipi]
bus	[pahi]
John	[hoːne]
plough/plow	[parau]
school	[kura]
Bible	[paipera]
snake	[neke]
biscuit	[pihikete]
blackberry	[parakipere]
football	[futupoːro]
bacon	[peːkana]
cricket	[kirikiti]
doughnut	[tounati]
elephant	[arefana]

12 Phonemes

1 Sample minimal pairs

[iː, ɪ]: *seat, sit* [siːt, sɪt]

[n, ŋ]: *ran, rang* [ræn, ræŋ]
[æ, aɪ]: *fat, fight* [fæt, faɪt]
[k, g]: *pick, pig* [pɪk, pɪg]
[ɔː, əʊ/oʊ]: *law, low* [lɔː, ləʊ/loʊ]
[f, θ]: *deaf, death* [def, deθ]

2

/l/ →	(i) [l̥] before a vowel
	(ii) [ɫ] elsewhere
/p/ →	(i) [pᵐ] before [m]
	(ii) [p] elsewhere
/d/ →	(i) [dˡ] before [l]
	(ii) [d] elsewhere

13 Accent differences

1

a phonemic system
b allophonic realization
c lexical distribution
d phonemic system
e phonotactic distribution
f phonemic system
g lexical distribution
h phonotactic distribution (before voiced/voiceless consonants)
i phonemic system
j phonotactic distribution

2
Grass and *farce* rhyme in SSBE. However, in rhotic accents, only *farce* will contain an /r/. Additionally, many American and northern England accents have /æ/ in *grass* but /ɑː/ in *farce*.
Laugh and *caugh* (*caff*, i.e. *café*) rhyme in northern England accents (and GenAm), but not in SSBE. *Study* and *wudy* (*would he*) also rhyme in northern England accents with an [ʊ] in both words, but not in SSBE or GenAm.

14 Phonology

1 Sample items

- *child > children, foot > feet, man > men, sheep > sheep, cactus > cacti.*
- *break > broke, broken, catch > caught, caught, grow > grew, grown, put > put, put, sing > sang, sung.*

2 In all these words, the *-ed* is pronounced /ɪd/. They are not examples of the regular *-ed* rule, because:

- in the regular rule, /ɪd/ occurs after /t, d/, which is not true of any of these examples.
- these are not the past tenses or participles of verbs. If you take off the *-ed*, you are not left with a verb, that is, there is no verb *nake, beard, rug, jag, wick, crook, sacre* or *rag*.

Instead, these are all simply adjectives.

3 The sounds /s, z, ʃ, ʒ, tʃ, dʒ/ are the six [+ sibilant] sounds of English.

4 The sounds /t, d/ are the only two sounds that are [+ coronal, + anterior, – continuant, – nasal].

15 Weakening and linking

2 Sample words/phrases

1	/n/	*penny*	13	/s/	*missing*
2	/nn/	*penknife*	14	/ss/	*bus stop, misspell*
3	/l/	*silly*	15	/z/	*busy*
4	/ll/	*real life, table lamp*	16	/zz/	*Brussels Zoo*
5	/d/	*ladder*	17	/ʃ/	*wishing*
6	/dd/	*midday*	18	/ʃʃ/	*fish shop*
7	/m/	*summer*	19	/ŋ/	*singing*
8	/mm/	*homemade, roommate*	20	/ŋŋ/	*
9	/v/	*revving*	21	/h/	*rehearse*
10	/vv/	*five verses*	22	/hh/	*
11	/θ/	*nothing*	23	/ʒ/	*pleasure*
12	/θθ/	*death threat*	24	/ʒʒ/	*

* Geminate /ŋ, h, ʒ/ are not possible in English because (i) /ŋ/ does not occur syllable-initially, (ii) /h/ does not occur syllable-finally, and (iii) /ʒ/ only occurs as a single consonant word-medially (see chapter 11).

16 Assimilation and elision

1

Expression	*Explanation*
art gallery	/t/ > /k/ before velar
broad beans	/d/ > /b/ before bilabial
Citizen Kane	/n/ > /ŋ/ before velar
disused	/s/ > /ʃ/ before /j/ /dɪʃjuːzd/; or coalescent assimilation /dɪʃuːzd/
goodbye	/d/ > /b/ before bilabial
Great Britain	/t/ > /p/ before bilabial

headmaster	/d/ > /b/ before bilabial
input	/n/ > /m/ before bilabial
John Major	/n/ > /m/ before bilabial
Mrs Young	/z/ > /ʒ/ before /j/ /mɪsɪʒ jʌŋ/; or coalescent assimilation /mɪsɪʒʌŋ/
please yourself	/z/ > /ʒ/ before /j/ /pliːʒ jə(r)self/; or coalescent assimilation /pliːʒə(r) self/
SUV	/s/ > /ʃ/ before /j/ /eʃ juː viː/; or coalescent assimilation /eʃuː viː/
salad cream	/d/ > /g/ before velar
tennis shoes	/s/ > /ʃ/ before /ʃ/
tenpin bowling	/n> /m/ before bilabial (twice)
United Kingdom	/d/ > /g/ before velar

2

Expression	*Explanation*
backhand	elision of /h/ in unstressed syllable
family	elision of /ə/
handshake	elision of /d/ between consonants
left luggage	elision of /t/ between consonants
loved ones	elision of /d/ between consonants
penthouse	elision of /h/ in unstressed syllable
temperature	elision of /ə/
West Side Story	elision of /t/ between consonants

17 Connected speech processes

1

- *spose, triffic:* informal spellings of *suppose, terrific,* after elision of /ə/.
- *a cuppa:* elision of /v/ and linking (from *a cup of tea*).
- *a wannabe, a whatchamacallit:* spellings (to be found in dictionaries) of *want to be* (with elision of /t/), and *what you may call it* (with weakening of the vowels in *you* and *may,* and coalescent assimilation of /tj/).
- *Godzone:* a respelling of *God's own* (country), showing linking of the /z/.
- *Pokemon—gotta catch 'em all: gotta* (weakening of the vowel in *to,* and linking), *'em* (elision of /ð/ in *them*).
- *Pikachu:* linking, and coalescent assimilation of /tj/ (*peek at you*).
- *Juthinkesaurus: do you* (elision of the vowel in *do,* coalescent assimilation of /dj/), elision of /h/ in *he,* intrusive /r/ in *saurus* (*saw us*).
- *fang club:* assimilation of /n/ > /ŋ/ before velar.
- *eclipse:* elision of /h/, and linking (*he clips*).
- *sects:* elision of /t/ between consonants, thus identical with *sex.*
- *seen a mall:* from *seen them all* (elision of /ð/ in *them,* and linking of /m/).

2

Expression	*Explanation*
bat and ball	elision of /d/, assimilation /n/ > /m/
concertgoer	assimilation /t/ > /k/
every second counts	elision of /d/, assimilation /n/ > /ŋ/
factory	elision of /ə/
king and queen	elision of /d/, assimilation /n/ > /ŋ/
last year	elision of /t/ (then /lɑːʃ jɪə, læʃ jɪr/ or /lɑːʃɪə, læʃɪr/ by assimilation or coalescent assimilation)
sandcastle	elision of /d/, assimilation /n/ > /ŋ/
Soviet Union	coalescent assimilation /tj/ > /tʃ/
Tottenham	elision of /ə/, elision of /h/
vegetable	elision of /ə/
Westminster	elision of /t/
windpower	elision of /d/, assimilation /n/ > /m/

3

Name	*Explanation*
Arizona Diamondbacks	elision of /d/, assimilation /n/ > /m/
Boston Bruins	/n/ > /m/ before bilabial
Charlotte Bobcats	/t/ > /p/ before bilabial
Cleveland Browns	elision of /d/, assimilation /n/ > /m/
Cleveland Cavaliers	elision of /d/, assimilation /n/ > /ŋ/
Detroit Pistons	/t/ > /p/ before bilabial
Green Bay Packers	/n/ > /m/ before bilabial
New England Patriots	elision of /d/, assimilation /n/ > /m/
Oakland Raiders	elision of /d/ between consonants
Washington Capitals	/n/ > /ŋ/ before velar

4

In *car 4 sale, house 2 let,* the function words *for* and *to* are normally unstressed and pronounced with their weak forms /fə(r), tə/. They are therefore not identical to *four* and *two* /fɔː(r), tuː/.

5

Weak forms: the representation of the vowels (presumably /ə/) in *ter (to), shoulda (should have), fer (for), he'd've (he would have),* and /ɪ/ for /iː/ in *bin (been)*. Note that the actor Robbie Coltrane plays Hagrid in the films with a rhotic West of England accent. This is fine for the spelling *fer* (for *for*), but not for *ter* (for *to*), which would not have an /r/ in either rhotic or non-rhotic accents.

Linking: *shoulda* (*should have*).

Elision: /t/ in *wasn'* (*wasn't*), *wouldn'* (*wouldn't*), and *bes'* (*best*); /d/ in *an'* (*and*); /h/ and /v/ in *shoulda* (*should have*); /v/ in *o'* (*of*); /h/ in *he'd've* (*he would have*); /ð/ in *'em* (*them*).

There are also contractions (*wasn't, I'm, I'll, I'd, won't, wouldn't, he'd, there's*).

6

a Many processes are taking place in these examples. Note in particular:

- coalescent assimilation in *don't chew* (*don't you*); *round John* (*round yon*)
- linking [w] in *chew on* (*you want*)
- linking in *wear cologne* (*walk alone*); *monk swimming* (*amongst women*)
- epenthesis of /k/ in *a monk* (*amongst*)
- elision of /t/ in *monk swimming* (*amongst women*)

b In terms of distinctive features:

- *horse* /hɔː(r)s/ and *whores* /hɔː(r)z/ differ in [±voice] (for /s/ and /z/)
- *clowns* /klaʊnz/ and *clouds* /klaʊdz/ differ in [±sonorant, nasal] (for /n/ and /d/)
- *Reagan* /reɪgən/ and *breaking* /breɪkɪŋ/ differ in [±voice] (for /g/ and /k/) and [±coronal, anterior, high, back] (for /n/ and /ŋ/)
- *rots* /rɒts, rɑːts/ and *rocks* /rɒks, rɑːks/ differ in [±coronal, anterior, high, back] (for /t/ and /k/)

18 Pausing and speed

1

a

Shirley said, 'The teacher is stupid.': A pause after *said*
'Shirley,' said the teacher, 'is stupid.': A pause after *Shirley*, and another after *teacher*

Cheese sandwich, apple pie, a drink?: A pause after *sandwich*, and another after *pie*
Cheese, sandwich, apple, pie, a drink?: A pause after *cheese, sandwich, apple,* and *pie*

b

4 + 6 ÷ 2 = 5: A pause after *six*, and another after *two*
4 + 6 ÷ 2 = 7: A pause after *four*, and another after *two*

2

Eats shoots and leaves (meaning 'it eats shoots and it eats leaves'): A pause after *shoots*.

Eats shoots and leaves (meaning 'it eats, it shoots and it leaves'): A pause after *eats*, and another after *shoots*. This meaning would normally have a comma after *eats*.

3

Here is the passage as it appears in the book, with punctuation. A long pause will correspond to a paragraph break (that is, a change of topic or speaker); a medium pause to a sentence break (a period (full-stop), question mark or exclamation mark, showing the end of a grammatically complete sentence); and a short pause to a comma, showing that we are at the end of a stretch that belongs together but is not grammatically complete, or (. . .), showing hesitation.

'Good morning,' said Deep Thought at last.

'Er . . . Good morning, O Deep Thought,' said Loonqwall nervously, 'do you have . . . er, that is . . .'

'An answer for you?' interrupted Deep Thought majestically. 'Yes. I have.'

The two men shivered with expectancy. Their waiting had not been in vain.

'There really is one?' breathed Phouchg.

'There really is one,' confirmed Deep Thought.

'To Everything? To the great Question of Life, the Universe and Everything?'

'Yes.'

Both of the men had been trained for this moment, their lives had been a preparation for it, they had been selected at birth as those who would witness the answer, but even so they found themselves gasping and squirming like excited children.

'And you're ready to give it to us?' urged Loonqwall.

'I am.'

'Now?'

'Now,' said Deep Thought.

They both licked their dry lips.

'Though I don't think,' added Deep Thought, 'that you're going to like it.'

'Doesn't matter!' said Phouchg. 'We must know it! Now!'

'Now?' inquired Deep Thought.

'Yes! Now . . .'

'Alright,' said the computer and settled into silence again. The two men fidgeted. The tension was unbearable.

'You're really not going to like it,' observed Deep Thought.

'Tell us!'

'Alright,' said Deep Thought. 'The answer to the Great Question . . .'

'Yes . . . !'

'Of Life, the Universe and Everything . . .' said Deep Thought.

'Yes . . . !'

'Is . . .' said Deep Thought, and paused.

'Yes . . . !'

'Is . . .'

'Yes . . . !!! . . . ?'

'Forty-two,' said Deep Thought, with infinite majesty and calm.

19 Word stress

1

All the names have stress on the first syllable, apart from *Southampton*, where it is on the second.

2

Stress on the first syllable: Douglas /ˈdʌgləs/, Helen /ˈhelən/, Jonathan /ˈdʒɒnəθən, ˈdʒɒːnəθən /, Raymond /ˈreɪmənd/, Sandra /ˈsɒːndrə, ˈsæːndrə/
Stress on the second syllable: Denise /dəˈniːz/, Elizabeth /ɪˈlɪzəbəθ/, Melissa /məˈlɪsə/, Yvonne /ɪˈvɒn, ɪˈvɑːn/

3

a not a compound
b a compound
c a compound
d not a compound
e not a compound
f a compound
g a compound
h not a compound
i not a compound
j a compound
k not a compound
l a compound

20 Tone groups

- *If you understand the instructions clearly, there's no problem. Clearly* modifies understand, and the tone group boundary is after *clearly.*
- *If you understand the instructions, clearly there's no problem. Clearly* modifies the second clause, and the tone group boundary is after *instructions.*
- *The boy and the girl in jeans were late.* Both the boy and the girl were wearing jeans. There is no tone group boundary after *boy.*
- *The boy, and the girl in jeans were late.* Only the girl was wearing jeans. There is a tone group boundary after *boy.*

21 Tones

1 The most likely tones are given below.

A: That's not the right answer.
B: (Disbelieving) No? (Echo question, therefore a rise: | / NO |)

A: Is Istanbul the capital of Turkey?
B: (Factually) No. (Matter-of-fact statement, therefore a fall: | \ NO |)

A: Is that the right answer?
B: No, but you're warm. (Reservation, with continuation, therefore a fall-rise: | ∨ NO |)

A: Have you ever been convicted of a crime?
B: No.
A: Have you ever been refused a visa?
B: No. (Routine answers, therefore level tones: | ¯ NO |)

A: You'll drive me home, won't you?
B: (Indignantly) No. (Indignation, therefore rise-fall: | ∧ NO |)

2 Here is the passage, with paragraph breaks shown.

To end the news, here are the main points again.

The prime minister has set off on an official visit to Pakistan. Before he left, he said that he would be covering many topics with his counterpart, Mr Rahman. In particular, he hoped to bring the controversy over the recent cricket tour to a satisfactory conclusion. He now continues to India, the next stop on his South Asian tour.

Official statistics just released show a sharp increase in the number of deaths on the road over the recent Christmas period. As a result, the traffic police state they are carrying out an investigation into the causes of the rise, and will be stepping up breathalyzer testing over the coming Easter holiday.

In the latest round of league matches, West Ham edged out Newcastle 2–1, to ease their relegation worries. Fellow relegation-battlers Stoke drew 1–1 with Aston Villa, and are now three points behind West Ham. The two teams meet in a bottom-of-the-table six-pointer on Saturday.

The Scottish film *Edinburgh Tales* has been nominated for four Oscars, including Best Picture, and Best Actor for George McQueen. The winners will be announced at the ceremony on Tuesday evening.

And that's the end of the news.

24 Targets

5

- Josh Groban: A 'perfect' (quasi-native) pronunciation of only the lyrics of the songs.
- Jessica Lange: As close an imitation as possible of the pronunciation of Patsy Cline.

- Mr Zhang: A pronunciation that is easily understood by Canadians. Maybe a Canadian target pronunciation (unless he has strong identity concerns).
- Mr Patel: A pronunciation that is understood by other Indians. It may contain many features of the pronunciation of Indian languages.
- Mr Schmidt: A pronunciation that is easily and clearly understood by a wide range of nationalities (of air transport controllers).

31 Spelling: History

1

a Letters (these five letters represent far more than five vowel sounds)
b Sound
c Letters (note that *sch* does not represent the same sounds in SSBE pronunciation of these two words)
d Letters
e Sound
f Letter
g Letters (they represent one sound in this word)
h Sounds
i Letter (there is no such thing as a silent sound!)
j Sound (many English words end in a letter *h*, e.g. *cheetah, English, pitch, graph,* but they do not represent an /h/ sound)

2 *bread, limb, science, handsome, bye, halfpenny, gnaw, chasm, friend, marijuana, knew, salmon, mnemonic, autumn, young, psychology, racquet, iron, island, mortgage, build, wring, grand prix, key, rendezvous.* The only letter that cannot be silent is *v*.

3 Empty: *chameleon, dumb, give, height, knife, listen, Thomas*
Auxiliary: *hive*
Inert: *bomb (*cf *bombard), debt (debit), doubt (indubitably), hasten (haste), receipt (reception, receptacle), two (twice, twenty, twelve, twin)*
The *e* in *live* is empty when it is the verb /lɪv/, but auxiliary (magic *e*) when it is the adjective /laɪv/.

32 Spelling: Literacy

1

know	*bowled*	*sighs*	*discrete*
weight	*fare*	*tow*	*heal*
idle	*peace*	*whether*	*oar* (SSBE *awe*)
Finnish	*mail*	*prophet*	*rapped, rapt*
brake	*cereal*	*sealing*	*chord, cored* (SSBE *cawed*)

2

read /riːd, red/	*live* /lɪv, laɪv/
bass /beɪs, bæs/	*wound* /waʊnd, wuːnd/
tear /tɪə/tir, teə/ter/	*minute* /mɪnɪt, mainjuːt/
bow /bəʊ/boʊ, baʊ/	*entrance* /entrəns, ɪntrɑːns/ɪntræns/

3 The examples using phonemic symbols must be homophones. Of the rest, *punch, ball, Patty* and *ears* are homonyms, and *grow, foot, eye* and *reception* are polysemes. That is, the polysemes have related historical origins, while the homonyms do not. However, as a modern user of English, you may think there is a relationship where there is none historically, and not see one where historical dictionaries give one.

4 I doubt that it is necessary to give a version of the passage in traditional orthography, as the changes are so small and logical that it is easy to understand. The changes made in Cut Spelng include:

- omitting 'silent' letters, that is, letters irrelevant to the pronunciation, as in the *h* of *wen* (*when*), the *w* of *riter* (*writer*), the *w* of *ho* (*who*) and the first *o* of *trublsm* (*troublesome*)
- omitting any spelling for unstressed post-stress vowels, as in the *e* of *sentnce* (*sentence*), the *o* of *acustmd* (*accustomed*) and the *a* of *traditionl* (*traditional*)
- simplifying doubled consonant letters, as in the *c* of *acustmd* (*accustomed*) and the *p* of *apreciates* (*appreciates*)

In addition, three substitutions are made:

- /dʒ/ is always written as *j*, as in *advantajs*
- /f/ is always written as *f*, as in *orthografy*
- /aɪ/ is always written as *y*, as in *slytly*

Since all the above changes involve shortening and omitting (which is why this is called Cut Spelng), the passage is now 13.6% shorter than a version in traditional orthography (267 letters as against 309).

33 Nonverbal communication

2 In different countries and cultures, the gestures can mean:

a 'OK,' 'one,' a sexual insult, hitch-hiking, and pointing the direction
b protection, 'OK,' breaking a friendship, swearing an oath, and copulation
c 'thin and ill, gaunt,' 'attractive,' thinking, success, sadness, a threat, 'crafty,' and 'effeminate'
d 'no,' aggressive disinterest, disbelief, and 'I don't know'

3

a Most gestures involve pointing to the head, usually around the temple. However, different movements of the pointing finger are then used. In Germany, a gesture as if screwing the index finger into the cheek is used.

b In some cultures, raising both index fingers is enough. In others, a two-part gesture, showing all ten fingers on both hands (for 'ten'), and then one finger (for 'one') is used.

c In western cultures, waggling the index finger towards you, palm up, is used. However, this is considered rude in many other cultures, where four fingers, palm up, are used for the same gesture. In many Asian cultures, the same gesture is used, but palm down.

d In western cultures, it is acceptable to point with the index finger. However, in other cultures, this is considered rude, and the whole hand, palm up, is used for pointing at a person (although the index finger can be used for pointing at things). In some Asian cultures, the extended thumb is used to point, palm up.

Resources

As was pointed out in the preface, this book looks at phonetics and the teaching of pronunciation in the same way that you have to look at icebergs: you can see the 10% that is above the surface of the water, but you know that there is still 90% below the water. This book has therefore described as much as can be fitted into a publication of this length. Also, it has been selective in presenting only those aspects of the subject that are felt to be of importance to language teachers. However, there is clearly much more depth to the fields of phonetics, phonology and pronunciation teaching than can be presented here.

This chapter therefore lists a number of resources for the reader who wants to go into the subjects in greater detail. I have been selective in choosing only those resources that I think are suitable for teachers, and that go significantly beyond the coverage of this book. On the principle that the longer this list, the less likely readers are to follow up any of the references, I have kept the list short. I have also annotated the entries so that readers can see immediately which ones are relevant to their particular interests.

Websites are not permanent. All the websites listed below were accessible on 1 June 2013.

Online resources

Phonetics

AEASP (American English as a Second Pronunciation) (n.d.) aeasp.com. *3D animations of the vowel and consonant sounds of American English.*

CompleteSpeech (2011). *SmartPalate (EPG) system demo.* www.youtube.com/watch?v=UXM3gNxGO2M. *A commercial 14-minute video introduction (by www.completespeech.com) to electropalatography, which shows contact between the tongue and the roof of the mouth during speech.*

'f@nEtIks: the sounds of spoken language' (n.d.) www.uiowa.edu/~acadtech/phonetics. *Animated head diagrams (sagittal sections) of the segments of American English, German and Spanish.*

Hall, D. C. (n.d.). *Interactive sagittal section.* www.chass.utoronto.ca/~danhall/phonetics/sammy.html. *Moveable sagittal section, with accompanying (English and non-English) IPA symbols, but without sound.*

Kelly, C. I. (n.d.). *American English pronunciation practice.* www.manythings.org/pp. *Listening practice in American minimal pairs.*

Ladefoged, P. (n.d.). www.phonetics.ucla.edu. *Websites created by the late Peter Ladefoged to accompany his books Vowels and consonants, and A course in phonetics.*

Maidment, J. (n.d.). *SIPhTrA* (System for Interactive Phonetics Training and Assessment). www.phon.ucl.ac.uk/home/johnm/siphtra/webtut.htm. *Internet tutorials on various aspects of phonetics.*

Maidment, J. (n.d.). *The vowel machine.* blogjam.name/vowel%20machine. *Exercises in recognizing British English vowel sounds.*

Maidment, J. (n.d.). *Phonetic flash.* www.phon.ucl.ac.uk/home/johnm/flash/flashin.htm. *Various exercises to practice British English vowels and consonants.*

Smith, J. (n.d.). *Online phonetics resources.* www.unc.edu/~jlsmith/pht-url.html. *A maintained listing of resources of various kinds to be found on the internet.*

Accents of English

Audio Archive (n.d.). www.alt-usage-english.org/audio_archive.shtml. *Sound files of American and other accents, with transcripts.*

Azzaro, G. (n.d.). *Worldwide accents of English.* www.gazzaro.it/accents/files/accents2.html. *Sound files of worldwide English accents, with transcripts.*

British Library (n.d.). *Sounds familiar?* www.bl.uk/learning/langlit/sounds/index.html. *Sound files of British accents.*

British Library (n.d.). *British Library sounds.* sounds.bl.uk. *Sound files of British accents.*

George Mason University (n.d.). *The speech accent archive.* accent.gmu.edu. *Recordings of English from various native and non-native accents.*

Meier, P. & Muller, S. M. (n.d.). *International dialects of English archive* (IDEA). web.ku.edu/idea. *Sound files of worldwide English accents.*

Text-to-speech (n.d.). www.oddcast.com/home/demos/tts/tts_example.php?sitepal. *A text-to-speech device that uses computer speech synthesis technology to produce acceptable pronunciations of English words using 29 voices from different countries (UK, USA, Australia, South Africa, etc.). It chooses only one word of homograph pairs, but can handle nonsense words. It also works in 29 other languages.*

YouTube (n.d.). www.youtube.com. *A rich source of material with a variety of genres and accents.*

Pronunciation teaching

Fraser, H. (2001). *Teaching pronunciation: A handbook for teachers and trainers.* Melbourne: DETYA. helenfraser.com.au/downloads/HF%20Handbook.pdf. *A research-based volume aimed at teachers of migrants in Australia, with many FAQs.*

Pronunciation teaching materials

Pronunciation Power (n.d.). (CD-ROM or downloadable materials) www.englishlearning.com. *For Canadian English.*

Speech in Action (n.d.). (books, e-books, apps and online materials) www.speechinaction.com. *Listening and pronunciation materials based on recordings of everyday spontaneous speech, from a variety of accents.*

Dictionaries, transcription and spelling

American Literacy Council (n.d.). americanliteracy.com. *Founded in 1876, the council conducts research and disseminates strategies for the improvement of literacy.*

Simplified Spelling Society (n.d.). www.spellingsociety.org. *A 100-year-old British society dedicated to discussion of spelling irregularities that hinder literacy for native speaker children and foreign learners.*

Stirling, J. (n.d.). *The spelling blog*. thespellingblog.blogspot.co.nz. *A blog about all things to do with English spelling and literacy.*

Print resources

Phonetics

Ball, M. and Rahilly, J. (1999). *Phonetics: The science of speech*. London: Arnold. *A good introduction for anyone wanting to explore the physical aspects of articulatory, acoustic and auditory phonetics.*

Catford, J. C. (2001). *A practical introduction to phonetics* (2nd edition). Oxford: Clarendon Press. *With plenty of practical exercises, an introduction to segments, but surprisingly quiet on suprasegmentals.*

Collins, B. and Mees, I. (2008). *Practical phonetics and phonology. A resource book for students* (2nd edition). London: Routledge. *Deals with various accents, with accompanying audio CD.*

Cruttenden, A. (2008). *Gimson's pronunciation of English* (7th edition). London: Edward Arnold. *An essential reference work.*

International Phonetic Association (1999). *Handbook of the International Phonetic Association: A guide to the use of the International Phonetic Alphabet*. Cambridge: Cambridge University Press. *An introduction to phonetic symbols, written by the authority, with example transcriptions of 29 languages.*

Knowles, G. (1987). *Patterns of spoken English: An introduction to English phonetics*. London & New York: Longman. *A good, non-technical account, especially useful for the reader interested in the literary significance of phonetic phenomena.*

Ladefoged, P. (2004). *Vowels and consonants: An introduction to the sounds of languages* (2nd edition). Oxford: Blackwell. *A comprehensive introduction to segments in languages.*

Ladefoged, P. & Johnson, K. (2011). *A course in phonetics* (6th edition). Boston: Wadsworth/ Cengage Learning. *A thorough coursebook in general phonetics. As it covers many non-English sounds that ELT teachers will not need, it may be too comprehensive for their purposes. It includes exercises, but no answers, so may be best used with a qualified phonetics teacher.*

Laver, J. (1994). *Principles of phonetics*. Cambridge: CUP. *A very comprehensive reference book to the subject.*

Roach, P. (2009). *English phonetics and phonology: A practical course* (4th edition). Cambridge: Cambridge University Press. *Probably the most readable and balanced introduction to the topic.*

Wells, J. C. & Colson, G. (1971). *Practical phonetics*. London: Pitman. *A personal favorite, despite being over 40 years old. Divided into 24 short, digestible chapters, with plenty of examples and exercises (but no answers).*

Phonology

Clark, J. and Yallop, C. (1995). *An introduction to phonetics and phonology* (2nd edition). Oxford: Blackwell. *A comprehensive work, covering articulatory and acoustic phonetics, and phonological analysis.*

Couper-Kuhlen, E. (1986). *An introduction to English prosody*. London: Edward Arnold. *Covers the forms and functions of stress, rhythm and intonation.*

Cruttenden, A. (1997). *Intonation* (2nd edition). Cambridge: Cambridge University Press. *A comprehensive treatment of the form and function of intonation, in both British and American analyses, with historical and sociolinguistic discussion.*

Davenport, M. and Hannahs, S. J. (2010). *Introducing phonetics and phonology* (3rd edition). London: Hodder Education. *A clear and easy book for the beginner, but without any treatment of intonation.*

Katamba, F. (1989). *An introduction to phonology*. Longman. *Although called an introduction, this work goes into this technical subject in a fair degree of detail.*

McMahon, A. (2002). *An introduction to English phonology*. Oxford: Oxford University Press. *Good further reading for anyone interested in distinctive features.*

Pennington, M. (1996). *Phonology in English language teaching*. Harlow: Addison Wesley Longman. *An introduction to English phonology, with educational, international and socio-linguistic viewpoints.*

Tench, P. (1996). *The intonation systems of English*. London: Cassell. *A simple introduction to tone groups, tonics and tones, illustrated with many examples.*

Trask, R. (1998). A dictionary of phonetics and phonology. London: Routledge.

Accents of English

Foulkes, P. and Docherty, G. (Eds. 1999). *Urban voices: Accent studies in the British Isles*. London: Edward Arnold. *Fourteen studies reporting research, with audio CD.*

Hughes, A., Trudgill, P. & Watt, D. (2005). *English accents and dialects* (5th edition). London: Edward Arnold. *An introduction to British accents.*

Jenkins, J. (2000). *The phonology of English as an international language*. Oxford: Oxford University Press. *A thought-provoking perspective on international English (see chapter 24 of this book).*

Jenkins, J. (2009). *World Englishes: A resource book for students* (2nd edition). London: Routledge. *A workbook, with many examples and materials.*

Wells, J. C. (1982). *Accents of English*. Cambridge: Cambridge University Press. *Three-volume in-depth treatment of the history and current pronunciation of British, American and other worldwide accents.*

Pronunciation teaching

Brown, A. (1991). *Teaching English pronunciation: A book of readings*. London: Routledge. *A collection of 29 previously published writings.*

Brown, A. (1992). *Approaches to pronunciation teaching*. London: Macmillan. *A collection of 12 papers, with plenty of practical materials.*

Celce-Murcia, M., Brinton, D., Goodwin, J. & Griner, B. (2010). *Teaching pronunciation* (2nd edition). Cambridge: Cambridge University Press. *A comprehensive treatment of the teaching of (American) English pronunciation, with two audio CDs.*

Dalton, C. & Seidlhofer, B. (1994). *Pronunciation*. Oxford: Oxford University Press. *A thorough examination of the subject, with reprints of exercises from other workbooks.*

Kenworthy, J. (1987). *Teaching English pronunciation*. Harlow: Longman. *Contains important sections on intelligibility, concern for pronunciation, spelling, and common pronunciation problems for learners from nine major languages.*

Morley, J. (1987). *Current perspectives on pronunciation*. Washington, DC: TESOL. *Seven papers by famous names in the field.*

Morley, J. (1994). *Pronunciation pedagogy and theory: New views, new directions*. Alexandria, VA: TESOL. *Another collection of seven papers by famous names in the field.*

Pronunciation teaching materials

Bowen, T. & Marks, J. (1992). *The pronunciation book: Student-centred activities for pronunciation work*. Harlow, Longman. *Over 70 exercises for all levels, immediately usable in the classroom.*

Bradford, B. (1988). *Intonation in context: Intonation practice for upper-intermediate and advanced learners of English*. Cambridge: Cambridge University Press. *An intonation workbook based on the discourse intonation model, with audio cassette.*

Brazil, D. (1994). *Pronunciation for advanced learners of English*. Cambridge: Cambridge University Press. *A discourse-based approach to English pronunciation and intonation.*

Connected Speech (n.d.). (CD-ROM) www.proteatextware.com.au. *Listening and pronunciation practice, with British, American and Australian versions, and at different levels/speeds.*

Gilbert, J. B. (2012). *Clear speech: Pronunciation and listening comprehension in American English* (4th edition). Cambridge: Cambridge University Press. *The latest edition of this best-selling coursebook for intermediate to high-intermediate students.*

Gilbert, J. B. (2012). *Clear speech from the start: Basic pronunciation and listening comprehension in North American English* (2nd edition). Cambridge: Cambridge University Press. *A version of Clear Speech for elementary learners.*

Hancock, M. (1995). *Pronunciation games*. Cambridge: Cambridge University Press. *Very popular with teachers, as it contains 36 photocopiable activity sheets of fun activities.*

Hancock, M. (2003). *English pronunciation in use: Intermediate*. Cambridge: Cambridge University Press. *Sixty two-page units for intermediate level and above, with audio CD.*

Hewings, M. (1993). *Pronunciation tasks: A course for pre-intermediate learners*. Cambridge: Cambridge University Press. *Sixty-six units, with two audio cassettes.*

Laroy, C. (1995). *Pronunciation*. Oxford: Oxford University Press. *A less technical holistic approach for all levels, concentrating on rhythm, stress and articulatory settings. It aims to build students' confidence and overcome cultural aversion to sounding English.*

Marks, J. (2007). *English pronunciation in use: Elementary*. Cambridge: Cambridge University Press. *Fifty units for elementary learners, with audio CD.*

Pronunciation Power (n.d.). (CD-ROM or downloadable materials) www.englishlearning.com. *For Canadian English.*

Rogerson, P. & Gilbert, J. B. (1990). *Speaking clearly: Pronunciation and listening comprehension for learners of English*. Cambridge: Cambridge University Press. *A version of Clear Speech for intermediate and advanced learners of British English.*

Speech in Action (n.d.). (books, e-books, apps and online materials) www.speechinaction.com. *Listening and pronunciation materials based on recordings of everyday spontaneous speech, from a variety of accents.*

Dictionaries, transcription and spelling

Brown, A. (2005). *Sounds, symbols and spellings*. Singapore: McGraw-Hill. An introduction to the symbols for British sounds, with exercises designed for language teachers.

Jones, D. (2011). *Cambridge English pronouncing dictionary* (18th edition, edited by P. Roach, J. Setter & J. Esling). Cambridge: Cambridge University Press. *The latest edition of Daniel Jones's English Pronouncing Dictionary, first published in 1917.*

Wells, J. C. (2008). *Longman pronunciation dictionary* (3rd edition). London: Longman. *An invaluable reference for anyone seriously interested in English phonetics. It includes British and American pronunciations, and notes on many phonetic phenomena.*

Journals

Phonetics

Journal of the International Phonetic Association
journals.cambridge.org/action/displayJournal?jid=IPA
Journal of Phonetics www.journals.elsevier.com/journal-of-phonetics
Language and Speech las.sagepub.com

Pronunciation

As We Speak (TESOL Speech, Pronunciation and Listening Interest Section (SPLIS)) www.tesol-splis.org
Speak Out! (IATEFL Pronunciation Special Interest Group) www.reading.ac.uk/epu/pronsig_new.htm

ELT (with a fair number of articles on pronunciation)

ELT Journal eltj.oxfordjournals.org
English Teaching Forum americanenglish.state.gov/english-teaching-forum
English Teaching Professional www.etprofessional.com
International Review of Applied Linguistics in Language Teaching www.degruyter.com/view/j/iral
Modern English Teacher www.onlinemet.com
TESOL Journal www.tesol.org/read-and-publish/journals/tesol-journal
TESOL Quarterly www.tesol.org/read-and-publish/journals/tesol-quarterly

Organizations

IATEFL (International Association of Teachers of English as a Foreign Language)
www.iatefl.org
The International Phonetic Association
www.langsci.ucl.ac.uk/ipa
TESOL (Teachers of English to Speakers of Other Languages)
www.tesol.org

Glossary

Absorbed /l/: an /l/ that is absorbed (i.e. disappears) into a preceding /ɔː/ vowel, as in *fault*.
Accent: the way a person pronounces a language, which may depend on their geographical origin, social status, profession or idiosyncratic factors, etc.
Affricate: the English sounds /tʃ, dʒ/, that being with complete closure, that is released into a fricative stage.
Airstream: the movement of air through the vocal organs, necessary for making speech sounds. All English speech sounds are made on a pulmonic egressive airstream.
Alliteration: words alliterate if they have the same consonants in their onsets.
Allophones: the sounds that belong to a phoneme and realize the phoneme in particular contexts.
Allophonic realization: accent differences of allophonic realization involve corresponding phonemes in the two accents. However, the articulations used to realize the phoneme(s) are different.
Alphabetic writing system: a writing system that uses letters, such as the *a, b, c,* etc. of the Roman alphabet, to represent the individual consonant and vowel sounds in the pronunciation.
Alveolar: a sound such as /n/, produced by the tongue tip and/or blade and the alveolar ridge.
Alveolar ridge: the ridged part of the roof of the mouth, just behind the upper teeth.
Approximant: a sound such as /w/ where the active articulator comes towards the passive, without touching it or causing frication.
Aspiration: the burst of voiceless air when a voiceless plosive is released, as in the /p/ of *pit*.
Assimilation: the process in which sounds change under the influence of surrounding sounds, e.g. white mouse /waɪt maʊs/ > /waɪp maʊs/.
Back of the tongue: the part of the tongue that lies opposite the velum, and is used in velar sounds such as /k/.
Bilabial: a sound such as /m/, produced by the two lips.
Blade of the tongue: the part of the tongue that is just behind the tip, and is used in alveolar sounds such as /t/.
Cardinal vowels: a set of language-independent reference vowels representing the range of humanly possible vowel sounds.
Central approximant: a consonant sound such as /j/, where the air escapes without frication in the centre of the oral cavity.
Central vowel: a vowel produced with the tongue neither front nor back in the horizontal dimension.
Clear /l/: an /l/ articulated with the body of the tongue raised towards the hard palate.
Closed syllable: a syllable with a final consonant(s).
Cluster: two or more consonants, within either the onset or coda of a syllable.
Coalescent assimilation: when /s, z, t, d/ followed by /j/ become /ʃ, ʒ, tʃ, dʃ/ respectively, as in *got you* > *gotcha*.

Coda: the last position in a syllable, occupied by nothing or up to four consonants in English.
Complementary distribution: two sounds are in complementary distribution if one sound only occurs in a particular environment(s) and the other sound never occurs in that environment(s).
Connected speech processes: processes including weak forms, linking, assimilation and elision, which commonly occur in connected speech.
Consonant sound: a sound in whose production there is an obstruction in the oral cavity.
Content word: a noun, main verb, adjective or adverb.
Contraction: the conflation of two words, such as *I am* > *I'm*.
Contrast: see minimal pair.
Coronal section: a cross-section view of the head, from the back to the front.
Dark /l/: an /l/ articulated with the body of the tongue raised towards the velum.
Dental: a sound such as /θ/, produced by the tip of the tongue and the upper teeth.
Diphthong: a vowel sound such as /aʊ/, during which the sound changes, because of movement of the tongue and/or lips.
Distinctive feature: a feature (such as [± voiced]) that helps to distinguish segments (such as /f, v/).
Egressive airstream: outward movement of air for speech.
Elision: the process in which certain sounds are lost in certain circumstances, e.g. *best friend* /best frend/ > /bes frend/.
Epenthesis: the insertion of a sound in particular contexts, e.g. *ham(p)ster*.
Foot: in Abercrombie's analysis of speech rhythm, the stretch of speech extending from one stress up to, but not including, the next.
Frication: the hissing noise produced during a fricative such as /s/.
Fricative: a sound such as /f/, during which air escapes from the mouth with a hissing noise (frication).
Front of the tongue: a misleading term for the part of the tongue that lies opposite the hard palate. It is used in front vowels such as /iː/, and for palatal consonants such as /j/.
Function word: the opposite of content words, i.e. articles, prepositions, conjunctions, pronouns, auxiliary verbs, etc.
Geminate consonants: two identical consonants, one at the end of one syllable, and the other at the beginning of the next, as in *penknife*.
Glottal: a sound such as /h/, produced by the two vocal cords.
Glottal stop: a complete closure produced by the vocal cords.
Grammatical word: = function word.
Hard palate: the hard part of the roof of the mouth, between the alveolar ridge and the soft palate.
High vowel: a vowel such as /iː/, produced with the tongue high in the vertical dimension (tongue height). Also called a close vowel.
Homographs: two words with unrelated meanings, such as *wind* /wɪnd/ 'breeze' and *wind* /waɪnd/ 'turn,' that are spelled the same but pronounced differently.
Homonyms: two words with unrelated meanings, such as *bark* /bɑːk/ 'noise of a dog' and *bark* /bɑːk/ 'covering of a tree,' that are both spelled and pronounced the same.
Homophones: two or more words with unrelated meanings, such as *pray* and *prey*, that are pronounced the same (/preɪ/) but spelled differently.
Homorganic: articulations made at the same place of articulation.
Inaudible release: the release of a plosive with insufficient air pressure for it to be audible.
Intervocalic: between two vowel sounds.
Intonation: the use of pitch (range and movement) to convey various types of meaning. This works with other features such as pauses, loudness, and stress.
Key: the use of an expanded or restricted pitch range.
Labio-dental: a sound such as /f/, produced by the lower lip and upper teeth.
Larynx: the voice box behind the Adam's apple, containing the vocal cords.

Lateral approximant: the manner of articulation of the /l/ sound, where air escapes over the sides of the tongue (lateral) without frication (approximant).

Lexical distribution: accent differences of lexical distribution represent the differing use of particular phonemes in particular words or groups of words, such as the use of /ɑː, æ/ in *grass*.

Lexical word: = content word.

Linking: the joining of words, so that the speech sounds fluent and connected. The phenomenon includes linking [j, w, r].

Long vowel: a vowel such as /ɑː/, that is longer than a vowel such as /ʌ/. Long monophthongs have a colon as part of their symbol. Diphthongs are also long.

Loudness: the volume (loud ~ quiet) of speech.

Low vowel: a vowel such as /æ/, produced with the tongue low in the vertical dimension (tongue height). Also called an open vowel.

Mid vowel: a vowel such as /e/, produced with the tongue neither high nor low in the vertical dimension (tongue height).

Minimal pair: a pair of words with a contrast, that is, with identical pronunciation except that one word has one sound where the other word has a different sound, as in *pit, bit*.

Mondegreen: the mishearing of a phrase.

Monophthong: a vowel sound such as /ɑː/, during which the sound remains relatively constant, because the tongue and lips do not move.

Morphophonology: the way that morphemes are regularly manifested in pronunciation.

Nasal stop: a sound such as /m/, during which air escapes through the nose, but not through the mouth.

Onset: the first position in a syllable, occupied by nothing or up to three consonants in English.

Open syllable: a syllable without any final consonant.

Oral stop: a sound such as /b/, during which air does not escape through the nose or mouth.

Orthography: = spelling.

Palatal: the place of articulation of the /j/ sound, produced by the front of the tongue and the hard palate.

Palate: = hard palate.

Palato-alveolar: a sound such as /tʃ/, produced between the blade/front of the tongue and the alveolar/palatal region.

Pause: a silence in speech.

Peak: the central position in a syllable, occupied by a vowel sound.

Pharynx: the cavity above the vocal cords, up to the velum.

Phoneme: an abstract unit of (vowel or consonant) sound. There are 44 phonemes in the SSBE accent, and 40 in GenAm. Phonemes distinguish words, e.g. /pɪt, bɪt/, /pɪt, pæt/.

Phonemic system: accent differences of phonemic system involve differing numbers of phonemic units. That is, one accent makes a contrast that another accent does not.

Phonetic similarity: two sounds are articulated in very similar ways, for example, they have the same, or very similar, three-term labels.

Phonetics: the study of the way sounds are produced.

Phonology: the study of how sounds function in particular languages.

Phonotactic distribution: accent differences of phonotactic distribution describe the positions, in terms of syllable structure, in which phonemes may occur in differing accents. The commonest example of this in English is the rhotic versus non-rhotic use of /r/.

Phonotactics: = syllable structure.

Pitch: the note (high ~ low) at which the vocal cords vibrate during speech.

Plosive: = oral stop.

Post-alveolar: the place of articulation of the SSBE /r/ sound, produced by the curled tip of the tongue and the alveolar/palatal region.

Progressive assimilation: where one sound affects the following sound.
Pulmonic airstream: air moved through the vocal organs by the action of the lungs.
Regressive assimilation: where one sound affects the preceding sound.
Retroflex: the place of articulation of the GenAm /r/ sound, produced by the tongue bent backwards.
Rhotic: the use of /r/ in coda position, as in *murder*. While SSBE is non-rhotic, GenAm and the majority of native English speakers in the world are rhotic.
Rhyme: the peak + coda of a syllable. Words rhyme if they have the same sounds from the vowel of the stressed syllable onwards.
Rhythm: a concept over which there is disagreement. Some writers take it to be the regularity of occurrence of stresses and syllables, others the length of vowels in syllables (see chapter 22).
Sagittal section: a cross-section view of the head, from the side.
Schwa: the neutral, indistinct, unstressed vowel, as in *about, cheetah*.
Segmental: to do with vowels and consonants.
Short vowel: a vowel such as /ʌ/, that is shorter than a vowel such as /ɑː/.
Soft palate: = velum.
Speed: the rate (fast ~ slow) of speech.
Stop: a sound such as /p, m/ involving complete closure between the articulators.
Stress: the way in which one syllable in a multi-syllable word stands out by being louder, longer, and/or at a different pitch than the others.
Suprasegmental: to do with features including voice quality, rhythm, intonation and stress. Suprasegmentals extend over stretches longer than a segment.
Syllable: a unit of speech comprising a vowel, perhaps with preceding and following consonants.
Tail: the part of a tone group after the tonic syllable.
Tap: the /ɾ/ sound, found as a realization of the /r/ phoneme in some accents of English, and also as a realization of the /t/ phoneme intervocalically, as in *phonetics*. The tongue tip makes a quick aerodynamic movement to the alveolar ridge.
Tip of the tongue: the point at the front of the tongue.
Tone: the pitch (rise, fall, etc.) on the tonic syllable.
Tone group: the stretch of speech over which a pitch contour extends.
Tonic syllable/word: the syllable/word that is the intonational focus of the tone group.
Trill: an articulation where one articulator vibrates aerodynamically against another.
Uvula: the hanging appendage at the back of the velum. It is not used in English speech sounds.
Velar: a sound such as /k/, produced by the back of the tongue and the velum.
Velum: the soft palate, at the back of the roof of the mouth.
Vocal cords: flaps of muscle and skin in the larynx behind the Adam's apple.
Vocalic /l/: an /l/ articulated without alveolar tongue contact.
Voice quality: long-term settings of the vocal organs, such as lip protrusion, nasalization and whisperiness.
Voiced: a sound such as /m/, during which the vocal cords are vibrating.
Voiceless: a sound such as /f/, during which the vocal cords are not vibrating.
Vowel sound: a sound in whose production there is little or no obstruction in the oral cavity.
Weak form: the unstressed pronunciation of many function words, often involving the schwa vowel, e.g. *at* /ət/.
Word stress: see stress.

References

Abercrombie, D. (1956). *Problems and principles: Studies in the teaching of English as a second language*. London: Longmans, Green.

Abercrombie, D. (1964). *English phonetic texts*. London: Faber and Faber.

Abercrombie, D. (1965). Pseudo-procedures in linguistics. In D. Abercrombie (Ed.) *Studies in phonetics and linguistics*. London: Oxford University Press.

Abercrombie, D. (1967). *Elements of general phonetics*. Edinburgh: Edinburgh University Press.

Abercrombie, D. (1983). Daniel Jones's teaching. *Work in Progress*, Department of Linguistics, University of Edinburgh, 16, 1–8.

Acton, W. (1984). Changing fossilized pronunciation. *TESOL Quarterly*, *18*(1), 71–85. Also in A. Brown (Ed.) (1991) *Teaching English pronunciation: A book of readings* (pp. 120–135). London: Routledge.

Adams, D. (1979). *The hitchhiker's guide to the galaxy*. London: Pan Books.

Aitken, J. (1984). Scottish accents and dialects. In P. Trudgill (Ed.) (1984) *Language in the British isles* (pp. 94–114). Cambridge: Cambridge University Press.

Anderson, A. & Lynch, T. (1988). *Listening*. Oxford: Oxford University Press.

Arnfield, S., Roach, P., Setter, J., Greasley, P. & Horton, D. (1995). Emotional stress and speech tempo variation. *Proceedings of the ESCA/NATO workshop on speech under stress* (pp. 13–15), Lisbon.

Avery, P. & Ehrlich, S. (1992). *Teaching American English pronunciation*. Oxford: Oxford University Press.

Bada, E. (2006). Pausing, preceding and following 'that' in English. *ELT Journal*, *60*(2), 125–132.

Baron, N. S. (2000). *Alphabet to email: How written English evolved and where it's heading*. London: Routledge.

Bialystok, E. & Hakuta, K. (1994). *In other words: The science and psychology of second language acquisition*. New York: Basic Books.

Bloom, B. S. (1956). *Taxonomy of educational objectives*. New York: David McKay Co Inc.

Bolinger, D. (1961). *Forms of English: Accent, Morpheme, Order*. (Ed. I. Abe & T. Kanekiyo). Cambridge, MA: Harvard University Press.

Bolinger, D. (1981). *Two kinds of vowels, two kinds of rhythm*. Bloomington, IN: Indiana University Linguistics Club.

Bosker, H. R., Pinget, A.-F., Quené, H., Sanders, T. & de Jong, N. H. (2013). What makes speech sound fluent? The contributions of pauses, speed and repairs. *Language Testing*, *30*(2), 159–175.

Bowler, B., Cunningham, S., Moor, P. & Parminter, S. (1999). *New Headway pronunciation course*. Oxford: Oxford University Press.

Bradford, B. (1988). *Intonation in context*. Cambridge: Cambridge University Press.

Bradford, B. (1990). The essential ingredients of a pronunciation programme. *Speak Out!* (Newsletter of the IATEFL Phonology Special Interest Group), 6, 8–11.

Brazil, D. (1997). *The communicative value of intonation in English*. Cambridge: Cambridge University Press.

Brazil, D., Couthard, M. & Johns, C. (1980) *Discourse intonation and language teaching*. London: Longman.

Brown, A. (1988). Functional load and the teaching of pronunciation. *TESOL Quarterly, 22*, 593–606. Also in A. Brown (Ed.) (1991) *Teaching English pronunciation: A book of readings* (pp. 211–224). London: Routledge.

Brown, A. (1989). Models, standards, targets/goals and norms in pronunciation teaching. *World Englishes, 8*, 193–200.

Brown, A. (1991). *Pronunciation models*. Singapore: Singapore University Press.

Brown, A. (2000). Priorities in pronunciation teaching: responses from Singaporean trainee teachers and international experts. In A. Brown, D. Deterding & E. L. Low (Eds.) (2000) *The English language in Singapore: Research on pronunciation* (pp. 121–132). Singapore: Singapore Association for Applied Linguistics.

Brown, A. (2005). *Sounds, symbols and spellings*. Singapore: McGraw-Hill.

Brown, A. (2006). Misspellings as indicators of writers' phonological systems: Analysis of a corpus by Singaporean secondary students. In A. Hashim & N. Hassan (Eds.) *Varieties of English in SouthEast Asia and Beyond* (pp. 119–132). Kuala Lumpur: University of Malaya Press.

Brown, H. D. (2004). *Language assessment: Principles and classroom practices*. White Plains NY: Pearson Education.

Brown, J. D. (2005). *Testing in language programs: A comprehensive guide to English language assessment*. New York: McGraw-Hill.

Cambridge Advanced Learner's Dictionary (2005, 2nd edition). Cambridge: Cambridge University Press.

Carney, E. (1994). *A survey of English spelling*. London and New York: Routledge.

Carney, E. (1997). *English spelling*. London: Routledge.

Carr, P. (1993). *Phonology*. Basingstoke: Macmillan.

Carroll, L. (1865). *Alice's adventures in Wonderland*. London: Macmillan.

Carroll, L. (1872). *Through the looking-glass, and what Alice found there*. London: Macmillan.

Catford, J. C. (1987). Phonetics and the teaching of pronunciation: A systemic description of English phonology. In J. Morley (Ed.) *Current perspectives on pronunciation* (pp. 87–100). Washington DC: TESOL.

Catford, J. C. (2001). *A practical introduction to phonetics* (2nd edition). Oxford: Oxford University Press.

Cauldwell, R. (2013). *Phonology for listening: Teaching the stream of speech*. Birmingham UK: Speech in Action.

Cauldwell, R. & Hewings, M. (1996). Intonation rules in ELT textbooks. *ELT Journal, 50*(4), 327–334.

Celce-Murcia, M. (1987). Teaching pronunciation as communication. In J. Morley (Ed.) (1987) *Current perspectives on pronunciation* (pp. 1–12). Washington, DC: TESOL.

Chomsky, N. & Halle, M. (1968). *The sound pattern of English*. New York: Harper & Row.

Cobuild Advanced Learner's Dictionary (2003, 4th edition). London: HarperCollins.

Cook, V .(2004a). *Accomodating brocolli in the cemetary: or why can't anybody spell?* London: Profile.

Cook, V. (2004b). *The English writing system*. London: Hodder Education.

Coward, N. (2002). *Hay Fever*. London: Methuen (original 1925).

Crookes, G. & Schmidt, R. W. (1991). Motivation: Reopening the research agenda. *Language Learning, 41*(4), 469–512.

Cruttenden, A. (1994). *Gimson's Pronunciation of English* (5th edition). London: Edward Arnold.

Cruttenden, A. (2001). *Gimson's Pronunciation of English* (6th edition). London: Edward Arnold.

Cruttenden, A. (2008). *Gimson's Pronunciation of English* (7th edition). London: Edward Arnold.

Crystal, D. (1997). *English as a global language*. Cambridge: Cambridge University Press.

Crystal, D. (2012). *Spell it out: The singular story of English spelling*. London: Profile Books.

Dalton, C. & Seidlhofer, B. (1994). *Pronunciation*. Oxford: Oxford University Press.

Dancovicova, J. (1994). Variability in articulation rate in spontaneous Czech speech. Unpublished M. Phil. thesis, University of Oxford.

Dauer, R. (1983). Stress-timing and syllable-timing reanalyzed. *Journal of Phonetics, 11*, 51–62.

Davies, A. (2003). *The native speaker: Myth and reality*. Clevedon: Multilingual Matters.

Davis, C. (2005). A report of the OECD-CERI Learning Sciences and Brain Research *Shallow vs non-shallow orthographies and learning to read* workshop 28–29 September 2005. Retrieved 1 June 2013 from www.oecd.org/dataoecd/54/39/35562310.pdf.

Delattre P. (1968). *The general phonetic characteristics of languages*. Santa Barbara, CA: US Office of Education and the University of California, Santa Barbara.

Deterding, D. H. (2001). The measurement of rhythm: a comparison of Singapore English and British English. *Journal of Phonetics, 29*, 217–230.

Dörnyei, Z. (Ed.) (2003). *Attitudes, orientations, and motivations in language learning*. Oxford: Blackwell Publishing.

Douglas, D. (2010). *Understanding language testing*. London: Routledge.

Edwards, G. (1995). *'Scuse me while I kiss this guy and other misheard lyrics*. New York: Fireside.

Edwards, H. T. (2003). *Applied phonetics: The sounds of American English* (3rd edition). Clifton Park NY: Delmar Learning.

Ekman, P. & Friesen, W. V. (1969). The repertoire of nonverbal behavior: Categories, origins, usage, and coding. *Semiotica, 1*, 49–98.

Ellis, G. & Sinclair, B. (1989). *Learning to learn English: A course in learner training*. Cambridge: Cambridge University Press.

English Raven (n.d.). *English language teaching methodology*. Retrieved 1 June 2013 from www.englishraven.com/methodology.html.

English Spelling Society (n.d.). The English Spelling Society. Retrieved 1 June 2013 from www.spellingsociety.org.

Esling, J. H. & Wong, R. F. (1983). Voice quality settings and the teaching of pronunciation. *TESOL Quarterly, 17*, 89–95. Also in A. Brown (Ed.) (1991) *Teaching English pronunciation: A book of readings* (pp. 288–295). London: Routledge.

Faber, D. (1986). Teaching the rhythms of English: a new theoretical base. *International Review Of Applied Linguistics, 24*, 207–216. Also in A. Brown (Ed.) (1991) *Teaching English pronunciation: A book of readings* (pp. 245–258). London: Routledge.

Fanon, F. (1952). *Black Skin, White Masks*. (Translated by C. L. Markmann, 1967, New York: Grove Press).

Fonagy, I. & Magdics, K. (1960). Speed of utterance in phrases of different lengths. *Language and Speech, 4*, 179–192.

Forster, E. M. (1924). *A passage to India*. London: Dent.

Fox, J., Wesche, M., Bayliss, D., Cheng, L., Turner, C. E. & Doe, C. (Eds.) (2007). *Language testing reconsidered*. Ottawa, University of Ottawa Press.

Franken, A. (2003). *Lies and the lying liars who tell them: A fair and balanced look at the right*. London: Penguin.

Fry, D. B. (1947). The frequency of occurrence of speech sounds in southern English. *Archives Néerlandaises de Phonétique Expérimentale* 20.

Fudge, E. C. (1984). *English word stress*. London: George Allen and Unwin.

Fulcher, G. (2010). *Practical language testing*. London: Hodder Education.

Gardner, R. C. (1982). Language attitudes and language learning. In E. B. Ryan & H. Giles (Eds.) *Attitudes towards language variation* (pp. 132–147). London: Edward Arnold.

Gardner, R. C. & Lambert, W. E. (1972). *Attitudes and motivation in second language learning*, Rowley, MA: Newbury House.

Giegerich, H. J. (1992). *English phonology: an introduction*. Cambridge: Cambridge University Press.

Gilbert, J. B. (1978). Gadgets: Non-verbal tools for teaching pronunciation. *CATESOL Occasional papers, 4*, 68–78. Also in A. Brown (Ed.) (1991) *Teaching English pronunciation: A book of readings* (pp. 308–322). London: Routledge.

Gilbert, J. B. (1995). Priorities, if there is no separate pronunciation class. *Speak Out!* (Newsletter of the IATEFL Phonology Special Interest Group), *16*, 26–30.

Goldman-Eisler, F. (1968). *Psycholinguistics: experiments in spontaneous speech*. London: Academic Press.

Gósy, M. (1991). The perception of tempo. In M. Gósy (Ed.) *Temporal factors in speech: a collection of papers* (pp. 63–106). Budapest: Research Institute for Linguistics, Hungarian Academy of Sciences.

Grabe, E. & Low, E. L. (2002). Durational variability in speech and the rhythm class hypothesis. In C. Gussenhoven & N. Warner (Eds.) (2002), *Laboratory Phonology 7* (pp. 515–546). Berlin: Mouton de Gruyter.

Graham, J. G. (1994). Four strategies to improve the speech of adult learners. *TESOL Journal, Spring 1994*, 26–28.

Hall, E. T. (1966). *The hidden dimension*. New York: Doubleday.

Halliday, M. A. K. (1970). *A course in spoken English: intonation*. Oxford: Oxford University Press.

Hammerly, H. (1973). Teaching pronunciation and generative phonology. *Foreign Language Annals, 6*, 487–489. Also in A. Brown (Ed.) (1991) *Teaching English pronunciation: A book of readings* (pp. 173–177). London: Routledge.

Hancock, M. (1995). *Pronunciation Games*. Cambridge: Cambridge University Press.

Higgins, J. (n.d.). Minimal pairs for English RP. Retrieved 1 June 2013 from myweb.tiscali.co.uk/wordscape/wordlist.

Holm, A., Dodd, B., Stow, C. & Pert, S. (1999). Identification and differential diagnosis of phonological disorder in bilingual children. *Language Testing, 16(3)*, 271–292.

Honikman, B. (1964). Articulatory settings. In D. Abercrombie, D. B. Fry, P. A. D. MacCarthy, N. C. Scott & J. L. M. Trim (Eds.) *In honour of Daniel Jones* (pp. 73–84). London: Longman. Also in A. Brown (Ed.) (1991) *Teaching English pronunciation: A book of readings* (pp. 276–287). London: Routledge.

Hughes, A. (2002). *Testing for language teachers* (2nd edition). Cambridge: Cambridge University Press.

Ibrahim, M. (1980). *The marriage of the rocks and other poems*. Singapore: Chopmen Press.

IELTS (n.d.). IELTS: English for international opportunity. Retrieved 1 June 2013 from www.ielts.org.

International Phonetic Association (1999). *Handbook of the International Phonetic Association: A guide to the use of the International Phonetic Alphabet*. Cambridge: Cambridge University Press.

Jakobson, R. C., Fant, G. M. & Halle, M. (1952). *Preliminaries to speech analysis: The distinctive features and their correlates*. Technical Report 13. Massachusetts: Acoustics Laboratory, Massachusetts Institute of Technology.

James, C. (1980). *Contrastive analysis*. London: Longman.

Jenkins, J. (2000). *The phonology of English as an international language*. Oxford: Oxford University Press.

Jenkins, J. (2006). The spread of EIL: A testing time for testers. *ELT Journal, 60*(1), 42–50.

Jenkins, J. (2009). *World Englishes: A resource book for students* (2nd edition). London: Routledge.

Jenner, B. (1987). The wood instead of the trees. *Speak Out!* (Newsletter of the IATEFL Phonology Special Interest Group), *2*, 2–5.

Jerome, J. K. (1983). *Three men on the Bummel*. Harmondsworth: Penguin. (Originally published 1900).

Jones, D. (1950). *The phoneme: Its nature and use*. Cambridge: Heffer.

Jones, D. (2006). *Cambridge English pronouncing dictionary* (17th edition, edited by P. Roach, J. Hartman, & J. Setter). Cambridge: Cambridge University Press.

Katamba, F. (1989). *An introduction to phonology*. London: Longman.

Kaye, A. S. (2005). Gemination in English. *English Today*, *82*, 43–55.

KayPentax (n.d.). Retrieved 1 June 2013 from www.kayelemetrics.com.

Kent, R. D. & Read, C. (2002). *The acoustic analysis of speech* (2nd edition). Albany NY: Singular Thomson Learning.

Kenworthy, J. (1987). *Teaching English pronunciation*. Harlow: Longman.

Kerr, J. (2000). Articulatory setting and voice production: Issues in accent modification. *Prospect*, *15*(2), 4–15.

Keys, K. & Walker, R. (2002). Ten questions on the phonology of English as an international language. *ELT Journal*, *56*(3), 298–302.

Krashen, S. D. (1981) *Second language acquisition and second language learning*. Oxford: Pergamon.

Krashen, S. D. (1982). *Principles and practice in second language acquisition*. Oxford: Pergamon.

Ladefoged, P. & Johnson, K. (2010). *A course in phonetics* (6th edition). Boston: Wadsworth/ Cengage Learning.

Ladefoged, P. & Maddieson, I. (1995). *The sounds of the world's languages*. Oxford: Blackwell.

Lado, R. (1957). *Linguistics across cultures*. Ann Arbor, MI: University of Michigan Press.

Lakin, J. L., Jefferis, V. E., Cheng, C. M. & Chartrand, T. L. (2003). The Chameleon Effect as social glue: Evidence for the evolutionary significance of nonconscious mimicry. *Journal of Nonverbal Behavior*, *27*, 145–162.

Larsen- Freeman, D. and Anderson, M. (2011). *Techniques and principles in language teaching* (3rd edition). Oxford: Oxford University Press.

Lass, R. (1984). *Phonology: An introduction to basic concepts*. Cambridge: Cambridge University Press.

Laver, J. (1980). *The phonetic description of voice quality*. Cambridge: Cambridge University Press.

Laver, J. (1994). *Principles of phonetics*. Cambridge: Cambridge University Press.

Le Page, R. B. & Tabouret-Keller, A. (1985). *Acts of identity: Creole-based approaches to language and ethnicity*. Cambridge: Cambridge University Press.

Lenneberg, E. H. (1964). The capacity of language acquisition. In J. A. Fodor and J. J. Katz (Eds.) (1964) *The Structure of Language: Readings in the philosophy of language* (pp. 579–603). Englewood Cliffs, NJ: Prentice Hall.

Levelt, W. J. M. (1989). *Speaking: From intention to articulation*. Cambridge, MA: MIT Press.

Levis, J. (1999). The intonation and meaning of normal yes/no questions. *World Englishes*, *18*(3), 373–380.

Levis, J. (2001). Teaching focus for conversational use. *ELT Journal*, *55*(1), 47–54.

Longman Dictionary of Contemporary English (2003, 4th edition). London: Longman.

Low, E. L., Grabe, E. & Nolan, F. (2000). Quantitative characterizations of speech rhythm: syllable-timing in Singapore English. *Language and Speech*, *43*, *4*, 377–401.

MacCarthy, P. (1976). Auditory and articulatory training for the language teacher and learner. *English Language Teaching Journal*, *30*, 212–219. Also in A. Brown (Ed.) (1991) *Teaching English pronunciation: A book of readings* (pp. 299–307). London: Routledge.

Macdonald, D., Yule, G. & Powers, M. (1994). Attempts to improve English L2 pronunciation: The variable effects of different types of instruction. *Language Learning*, *44*, 75–100.

Macdonald, S. (2002). Pronunciation views and practices of reluctant teachers. *Prospect, 17*(3), 3–18.
Major, R. (1987). Measuring pronunciation accuracy using computerized techniques. *Language Testing, 4*, 155–169.
Marks, J. (1999). Is stress-timing real? *ELT Journal, 53*(3), 191–199.
McArthur, T. (1998). *The English languages*. Cambridge: Cambridge University Press.
McArthur, T. (2002). *Oxford guide to world English*. Oxford: Oxford University Press.
McCall-Smith, A. (2005). *44 Scotland Street*. London: Abacus.
McLaughlin, B. (1990). Restructuring. *Applied Linguistics, 11*, 113–128.
McNamara, T. F. (2000). *Language testing*. Oxford: Oxford University Press.
McNamara, T. & Roever, C. (2006). *Language testing: The social dimension*. Malden, MA: Blackwell.
McNeill, D. (1992). *Hand and mind: What gestures reveal about thought*. Chicago: University of Chicago Press.
Mehrabian, A. (1971). *Silent messages*, Wadsworth, CA: Belmont.
Mehrabian, A. (n.d.). Silent messages. Retrieved 1 June 2013 from www.kaaj.com/psych/smorder.html.
Mendelsohn, D. J. & Rubin, J. (Eds.) (1995). A guide for the teaching of second language listening. San Diego, CA: Dominie Press.
Microsoft (n.d.). Sound Recorder. Retrieved 1 June 2013 from www.microsoft.com/resources/documentation/windows/xp/all/proddocs/en-us/app_soundrecorder.mspx?mfr=true.
Molan Network Project (2010). *Handbook on good practice that serves to motivate language learners*. Retrieved 1 June 2013 from www.molan-network.org/docs/molan_handbook_0_0.pdf.
Morris, D. (1994). *Bodytalk: A world guide to gestures*. London: Jonathan Cape.
Morris, D., Collett, P., Marsh, P. & O'Shaughnessy, M. (1979). *Gestures: Their origins and distribution*. London: Jonathan Cape.
Munro, M. & Derwing, T. M. (2011). The foundations of accent and intelligibility in pronunciation research. *Language Teaching, 44*(3), 316–327.
Nakamura, M. (2005). Parametric phonetics: An exercise in the dynamic characterization of sound patterns. Paper presented at the Phonetics Teaching and Learning Conference, University College London, 2005. Retrieved 1 June 2013 from www.phon.ucl.ac.uk/home/johnm/ptlc2005/pdf/ptlcp11.pdf.
Nietzsche, F. (1878). *Human, All Too Human*. (Translated by R. J. Hollingdale, 1996. Cambridge: Cambridge University Press.)
O'Connor, J. D. (1973). *Phonetics*. Harmondsworth: Penguin.
O'Connor, J. D. & Arnold, G. F. (1961). *Intonation of colloquial English*. London: Longman (2nd edition 1973).
Odden, D. A. (2005). *Introducing phonology*. Cambridge: Cambridge University Press.
Oxford Advanced Learner's Dictionary (2005, 7th edition). Oxford: Oxford University Press.
Pearson Education (2008). *Versant English test: Test description and validation summary*. Retrieved 1 June 2013 from www.versanttest.co.uk/pdf/ValidationReport.pdf.
Pennington, M. (1996) *Phonology in English language teaching*. Harlow: Addison Wesley Longman.
Pennington, M. C. & Richards, J. C. (1986). Pronunciation revisited. *TESOL Quarterly, 20*(2), 207–225.
Pisoni, D. B. & Remez, R. E. (Eds.) (2004). *The handbook of speech perception*. Oxford: Blackwell.
Protea Textware (n.d.). Connected speech. Retrieved 1 June 2013 from www.proteatextware.com.
Purcell, E. T. & Suter, R. W. (1980). Predictors of pronunciation accuracy: a reexamination. *Language Learning, 30(2)*, 271–287.
Quirk, R. (1962). *The use of English*. London: Longmans.
Ranalli, J. M. (2002). Discourse intonation: To teach or not to teach. Retrieved 1 June 2013 from www.birmingham.ac.uk/Documents/college-artslaw/cels/essays/csdp/Rannali4.pdf.

Renandya, W. & Farrell, T. S. C. (2010). 'Teacher, the tape is too fast!' Extensive listening in ELT. *ELT Journal, 65*(1), 52–59.

Richards, J. C. & Rogers, T. (2001). *Approaches and methods in language teaching* (2nd Edition). Cambridge: Cambridge University Press.

Roach, P. (1998). Some languages are spoken more quickly than others. In L. Bauer & P. Trudgill (Eds.) (1998). *Language myths* (pp. 150–158). London: Penguin.

Roach, P. (2009). *English phonetics and phonology: A practical course* (4th edition). Cambridge: Cambridge University Press.

Rogerson, P. & Gilbert, J. B. (1990). *Speaking clearly*. Cambridge: Cambridge University Press.

Rosse, M. (1999). Tracking–a method for teaching prosody to ESL learners. *Prospect, 14, 1*, 53–61.

Rowling, J. K. (1999). *Harry Potter and the prisoner of Azkaban*. London: Bloomsbury.

Rubin, J. (1994). A review of second language listening comprehension research. *The Modern Language Journal, 78*, 199–221.

Saito, K. (2012). Effects of instruction on L2 pronunciation development: A synthesis of 15 quasi-experimental intervention studies. *TESOL Quarterly, 46*(4), 842–854.

Scobbie, J. M. & Wrench, A. A. (2003). An articulatory investigation of word final /[ph]l[/ph]/ and /[ph]l[/ph]/-sandhi in three dialects of English. In M. J. Solé, D. Recasens, & J. Romer (Eds.) *Proceedings of the 15th International Congress of Phonetic Sciences*, (Barcelona). Rundle Mall: Causal Productions. Retrieved 1 June 2013 from eresearch.qmu.ac.uk/2248.

Scripps (n.d.). Scripps national spelling bee. Retrieved 1 June 2013 from www.spellingbee.com.

Seymour, P. H. K., Aro, M. & Erskine, J. (2003). Foundation literacy acquisition in European orthographies. *British Journal of Psychology, 94*, 143–174.

Shaw, W. D. (1981). Asian student attitudes towards English. In L. E. Smith (Ed.) *English for cross-cultural communication* (pp. 108–122). New York: St. Martin's Press.

Skype (n.d.). Skype. Retrieved 1 June 2013 from www.skype.com.

Smith, G. P. (2003). Music and mondegreens: Extracting meaning from noise. *ELT Journal, 57*(2), 113–121.

Speech in Action (n.d.). Cool speech: Hot listening, cool pronunciation. Retrieved 1 June 2013 from www.speechinaction.com.

Spolsky, B. (2000). Language motivation revisited. *Applied Linguistics, 21*(2), 157–169.

Stevens, K. N. (1998). *Acoustic phonetics*. Current studies in linguistics (No. 30). Cambridge, MA: MIT.

Stirling, J. (2011). *Teaching spelling to English language learners*. Raleigh, NC: Lulu.

Stirling, J. (n.d.). *The spelling blog*. thespellingblog.blogspot.co.uk.

Strevens, P. (1974). A rationale for teaching pronunciation: The rival virtues of innocence and sophistication. *English Language Teaching Journal, 28*, 182–189. Also in A. Brown (Ed.) (1991) *Teaching English pronunciation: A book of readings* (pp. 96–103). London: Routledge.

Suter, R. W. (1976). Predictors of pronunciation accuracy in second language learning. *Language Learning, 26*, 233–253.

Swan, M. & Smith, B. (2001). *Learner English: a teacher's guide to interference and other problems* (2nd edition). Cambridge: Cambridge University Press.

Tan, A. (1989). *The teenage workbook*. Singapore: Hotspot Books.

Tan, J. & Mak, B. (2013). Distinguishing features in scoring L2 Chinese speaking performance: How do they work? *Language Testing, 30*(1), 23–47.

Taylor, D. (1993). Intonation and accent in English: what teachers need to know. *International Review of Applied Linguistics, 30*, 1–21.

Taylor, L. (2006). The changing landscape of English: Implications for language assessment. *ELT Journal, 60*(1), 51–60.

Tench, P. (1978). On introducing parametric phonetics. *Journal of the International Phonetic Association, 8*, 34–43.

Tench, P. (1996). *The intonation systems of English*. London: Cassell.

Theodoros, D., Murdoch, B. E. & Horton, S. (1999). Assessment of dysarthric speech: a case for a combined perceptual and physiological approach. *Language Testing, 16(3)*, 315–351.

Thompson, S. (1995). Teaching intonation on questions. *ELT Journal, 49*(3), 235–243.

Tomlinson, B. (2005). Testing to learn: A personal view of language testing. *ELT Journal, 59*(1), 39–46.

Truss, L. (2003). *Eats, shoots and leaves: The zero tolerance approach to punctuation*. London: Profile Books.

Upward, C. (1996). *Cut spelling: A handbook to the simplification of written English by omission of redundant letters*. Birmingham UK: Simplified Spelling Society.

Upward, C. & Davidson, G. (2011). *The history of English spelling*. Chichester & Malden: Wiley-Blackwell.

Ur, P. (1984). *Teaching listening comprehension*. Cambridge: Cambridge University Press.

Vandergrift, L. & Goh, C. M. C. (2011). *Teaching and learning second language listening: Metacognition in action*. London: Routledge (Taylor and Francis).

Vaughan-Rees, M. (2010). *Rhymes and rhythms: A poem-based course for English pronunciation* (2nd edition). Reading: Garnet.

Voice of America (n.d.). The roots of Special English. Retrieved 1 June 2013 from learningenglish.voanews.com.

Walker, R. (2010). *Teaching the pronunciation of English as a Lingua Franca*. Oxford: Oxford University Press.

Wardhaugh, R. (1974). The contrastive analysis hypothesis. In J. Schumann & N. Stenson (Eds) *New frontiers in second language learning* (pp. 10–19). Rowley, MA: Newbury House.

Wells, J. C. & Colson, G. (1971). *Practical phonetics*. London: Pitman.

Wells, J. C. (1982). *Accents of English*. Cambridge: Cambridge University Press.

Wells, J. C. (2000). *Longman pronunciation dictionary* (2nd edition). London: Longman.

Wells, J. C. (2007). *English intonation: An introduction*. Cambridge: Cambridge University Press.

Wells, J. C. (2008). *Longman pronunciation dictionary* (3rd edition). London: Longman.

Wells, J. C. (n.d.). Estuary English. Retrieved 1 June 2013 from www.phon.ucl.ac.uk/home/estuary.

Willing, K. (1988). *Learning styles in adult migrant education*. Adelaide: National Curriculum Resource Centre.

Wong, R. (1987). *Teaching pronunciation: Focus on English rhythm and intonation*. Englewood Cliffs, NJ: Prentice Hall/Regents.

Xi, X., Higgins, D., Zechner, K. & Williamson, D. (2012). A comparison of two scoring methods for an automated speech scoring system. *Language Testing, 29*(3), 371–394.

Yates, L. & Zielinski, B. (2009). *Give it a go: Teaching pronunciation to adults*. Sydney: Macquarie University. Retrieved 1 June 2013 from www.ameprc.mq.edu.au/__data/assets/pdf_file/0011/157664/interactive_sm.pdf.

Yates, L., Zielinski, B. & Pryor, E. (2008). *The assessment of pronunciation and the new IELTS Pronunciation scale*. IELTS Research Reports volume 12. Retrieved 1 June 2013 from www.ielts.org/pdf/Vol12_Report1.pdf.

Yavaş, M. (2011). *Applied English phonology* (2nd edition). Chichester: Wiley-Blackwell.

Yuan, J., Liberman, M. & Cieri, C. (2006). Towards an integrated understanding of speaking rate in conversation. Paper given at the Ninth International Conference on Spoken Language Processing (Interspeech 2006—ICSLP), Pittsburgh, Pennsylvania. Retrieved 1 June 2013 from papers.ldc.upenn.edu/Interspeech2006/Interspeech_2006_Speech_Rate_Paper.pdf.

Yule, G. & Macdonald, D. (1995). The different effects of pronunciation teaching. *International Review of Applied Linguistics, 33*(4), 345–350. Also in J. Morley (Ed.) (1994) *Pronunciation pedagogy and theory: New views, new directions* (pp. 111–118). Alexandria, VA: TESOL.

Yule, V. (2011). Recent developments which affect spelling. *English Today, 27*(3), 62–67.

Yule, V. (2013). *Writing systems: How they change and the future of spelling*. Brisbane: Bookpal.

Index

absorbed [l] 54–5
accent differences 74–80
affect 170, 181
affricate 47
airstream 15
alliteration 62–3
allophonic realization (accent difference) 75
approach 166–70
approximant 34, 50–5
aspiration 5, 38
assimilation 100–2

cardinal vowels 20–2
clear [l] 54
coalescent assimilation 103–4
coda 6, 62
complementary distribution 70–1
connected speech processes 8, 91–8, 100–4, 105–10
consonant 6, 55–6
consonant cluster 62
content word 91–2
contraction 103
contractive analysis 192–4

dark [l] 54
diphthong 6, 24, 26–7
distinctive features 84–9

[ə] 122–3
effectiveness of teaching 174–8
egressive 15
elision 102–3
English as a foreign language 12
English as a native language 12, 191
English as a second language 12, 191–2
English as a world language 11
epenthesis 108

feature 9
first language influence 191–4
foot 9
fossilization 186–9
frequency 199–200
fricative 17–18, 34, 45–7
function word 91–2

geminate consonants 96–8
General American 13, 24–9, 76, 161
glottal 18
glottal stop 18, 40–1

[h] 17–18
homograph 213
homonym 213
homophone 213

[i] 27–9
identity 159
image 159
importance 195–203
importance: functional load 199–203
importance: ranking 196–9
inaudible release of plosives 39–40
integration of loanwords 66–7
intelligibility 40–1, 77–8, 158–9, 162
intonation 6, 132–6, 137–43

key 141

lateral 34, 53–5
lateral approach/release 55
lexical distribution (accent difference) 75–6
Lingua Franca Core 162–3
linking 94–6

lisping 48–9
listening 227–30

magic e 208–9
manner of articulation 33–4
meter 6
method 166–70
minimal pair 71, 200–2
mondegreen 109–10
monophthong 6, 24–6
morphophonology 82–4
motivation 180–4

nasal 34, 41–3
nasal approach/release 41–2
nasal cavity 32
nasalization, anticipatory 42–3
native speaker/language 12
nonverbal communication 219–25

official language 13
onset 6, 61
oral cavity 32

paratone 9, 141
pause 6, 114–16
peak 6, 61
pharynx 32
phone 9
phoneme 9, 69–73
phonemic system (accent difference) 74–5
phonetic similarity 71–2
phonetics 3–4
phonics 5–6
phonology 4–5, 82–9
phonotactic distribution (accent difference) 75
place of articulation 33
plosive 34, 36–41
pronunciation 5, 6
prosody 6
pulmonic 15

Received Pronunciation 13, 161
reluctance of teachers 196
rhoticity 63, 75
rhyme 6, 63, 79
rhythm 6, 145–9
rounded 23

segmentals 6
semi-vowel 50–1
silent letters 209–10
skills 4
speed 6, 116–18
spelling 20, 25, 26, 28, 37, 41, 46, 47, 51, 52, 53, 78, 106–7, 123, 203, 206–10, 212–16
spelling: consonant doubling 209
Standard Southern British English 13, 24–9, 76, 161
stop 33
suprasegmentals 6
syllable 9, 61–7
syllable structure 6, 61–7
symbols x, 72

tail 140–1
target 157–64
testing 231–7
timing 6
tone 137–43
tone group 9, 132–6
tongue division 31–2
tonic 134–6

[u] 27–9
unrounded 23

vocal cords 16, 32
vocal organs 30–2
vocalic [l] 54–5
voice quality 6, 151–3
voiced 16
voiceless 16
vowel 6, 23–29
vowel length 6, 23, 39, 64

weakening/weak forms 92–4
word stress 6, 121–30
word stress and nouns/verbs 127–8
word stress and suffixes 126–8
word stress: compound stress 128–9
word stress: stress shift 129–30